BEHIND THE BALLOTS

The Personal History of a Politician

JAMES A. FARLEY

GREENWOOD PRESS, PUBLISHERS
WESTPORT, CONNECTICUT

The Library of Congress has catalogued this publication as follows:

Library of Congress Cataloging in Publication Data

Farley, James Aloysius, 1888-
   Behind the ballots.

   Reprint of the 1938 ed.
   1. United States--Politics and government--1933-1945.
2. Politics, Practical. I. Title.
E748.F24A3 1972   320.9'73'0917 [B]   78-114521
ISBN 0-8371-4738-7

Originally published in 1938
by Harcourt, Brace and Company, New York

First Greenwood Reprinting 1972

Library of Congress Catalogue Card Number 78-114521

ISBN 0-8371-4738-7

Printed in the United States of America

To my wife, Elizabeth A. Farley

CONTENTS

BEHIND THE BALLOTS

I. My Early Life

PERHAPS half the youngsters of America had a childhood similar to my own. My parents, of course, were poor but honest. The place of my birth was Grassy Point on the shores of the Hudson River about thirty-five miles above New York City, a village small enough to make everyone feel comfortably acquainted and large enough to provide the companionships, the interests, and the excitements which figure so largely in the career of a growing boy.

I received my education in the public schools where I did enough studying to get by, excelling in those studies which appealed to me and doing indifferently in those which failed to strike my fancy. After all, school was secondary to most of us; our main delight was in the hours after class when we ran, jumped, tussled, swam, played baseball, and otherwise worked ourselves into a state of healthy exhaustion. The youngsters in the neighborhood were pretty good lads. The games we played were those indulged in by youngsters everywhere, especially by children brought up in humble circumstances and compelled to provide their own methods of amusement. A few childish incidents that were a bit mischievous cling in my memory, but on the whole there was nothing about "our gang" that marked it as being any better or any worse than the average group of normal children.

Perhaps the one thing which impressed itself on my early years more than anything else was the Hudson River itself. As it flows by Grassy Point and near-by cities and towns, the river named after the ancient explorer is truly a majestic stream, with a channel both wide and deep, a current already influenced by the tides sweeping in from the Atlantic Ocean, and a jagged riverbank

3

flanked on either side by smoky-blue mountains extending almost to the water's edge. In the early morning, especially in summer, the river valley is often obscured by a misty fog while the near-by mountains glisten and shine in the reflected splendor of the rising sun. We unconsciously enjoyed the beauty of the valley country.

But the Hudson River was far more than a mere thing of beauty to Grassy Point and its neighboring communities. It was the hub around which revolved almost every activity in the village whether social or economic. We swam in the Hudson during the warm summer months, attended picnics on the river islands, enjoyed a sail on rare occasions, and skated over its surface whenever the winter was severe enough to provide, as it often did, a thick coating of ice from shore to shore. And, in the meanwhile, the river helped provide a means of livelihood for the family breadwinners. There were numerous brickyards in the vicinity all because bricks could be shipped by water at a minimum of expense to New York City. Like the Hudson River itself, that awesome metropolis was a constant magnet towards which everything and everyone in the valley seemed to be drawn.

Because Grassy Point was ideally located for brick-making, I happened to be born there. I was born on May 30, 1888, the son of James Farley and Ellen Goldrick Farley, the latter's parents being John and Rose Goldrick, both of whom came to America from Ireland either in 1847 or 1848. Grandfather Goldrick worked as a laborer in the brickyards of near-by Haverstraw until his death. My father was the son of John and Margaret Farley who migrated from Castletown, County Meath, Ireland, in 1847. Thus, on both the masculine and the distaff sides, my ancestry dates to the flood of homesick and heartsick immigrants who were driven to seek refuge in America by the dreadful and devastating potato famine which struck "Ould Ireland" about the middle of the last century.

Every family has its little stories and anecdotes, originating half in truth and half in fancy, which are handed down by word of mouth and develop into a kind of family folklore. I heard a great many of those simple tales about the "Old Folks" from my mother, and from numerous aunts and uncles, and being under the spell of their influence, I cherished after growing up a desire to visit the place where the family came from across the water. After the exciting presidential election of 1936, I found an opportunity to gratify that wish. So I set out for Ireland accompanied by Ambrose O'Connell, my personal assistant in the Post Office Department, and Edward L. Roddan, of the Democratic National Committee.

After a glimpse of Dublin and other historic points, we motored out to Castletown in County Meath where I enjoyed a visit with Peter McDonnell, a man of middle age who made a modest living as a truck farmer. When my grandfather left Ireland, he had left behind him two brothers James and Patrick; and Peter McDonnell was the grandson of one of these. I could recognize a distinct family resemblance in his features. With Peter acting as a guide, we drove out along the countryside until we came to a place where houses were scarce and vegetation was thick despite the raw cold of late November. We entered a field, and several rods back from the road he pointed out a depression which he identified as the site of the Farley homestead. On this plot of ground, Grandfather and Grandmother Farley had bade a tearful good-by to the members of their family, most of whom they never saw again, and set out on a long tramp to Dublin—the first lap of their journey to an unknown land. Sturdy people! No wonder that subsequent hardships in America seemed easy to endure.

But to get back to America and especially to the Hudson River Valley. My Grandfather Farley located in Verplanck's Point in Westchester County where my father was born. Mother was born across the river in Haverstraw, located in Rockland County. Throughout most of his adult life, Father was associated with the brick-making business, first as a laborer and later as part owner of three small schooners engaged in the brick-carrying trade; also as a manufacturer of common bricks, operating two small yards. As a youngster, I was proud of the fact that he was captain and part owner of a brick schooner which voyaged twice a week, and sometimes oftener for long hours meant nothing in those days, from Grassy Point to New York City and back. This was the period before the scows came into general use. There were dozens of similar schooners on the river, all of them following more or less the same pattern in their round of duties. Early in the morning loading would commence, the average load running from 70,000 to 90,000 bricks. If wind and tide were right, the little vessels were able to make the thirty-five-mile run and pull up at some point in Manhattan, Queens, or Brooklyn the following morning.

One of my fondest recollections is the thrilling memory of a voyage to New York City on one of these brick schooners, an event looked forward to with great eagerness for many weeks. It was shortly after Father's death when I was ten years old. The exciting adventure was made possible by the invitation of my Uncle Tom Farley, who captained the good ship, *William H. Barnes*. The trip was actually eventless but it gave me a feeling of happiness which no ocean voyage on the most sumptuous of liners has since been able to equal. I roved about the tiny deck for hours fascinated by the simple maneuvers required for steering the vessel, watching the twinkling lights of villages and towns along the riverbank. It was another treat to go below for a hearty dinner with the few crew members, then turning in for a night's sleep in a sailorman's bunk. The schooner *Barnes* dropped anchor the next morning at the foot of Jane Street in New York City, and to this day, the recollection of that first sail comes back when I pass there. The brick schooners were later driven off the river by the uglier but more economical scows while the brick business itself dwindled away to only a fraction of what it formerly was.

School Days

I started to school when I was five years old, attending the grade school at Grassy Point. The principal's name was J. Martin Case. He was a graduate of Amherst College where he made a name for himself as a football player and for that reason he was an early hero of mine. For the most part we got along fairly well. One incident, however, has always remained in my memory. After my father's death, Mr. Case took added interest in my welfare and apparently wanted to provide the kind of personal guidance and supervision that a fatherless lad is apt to lack. He must have arrived at the conclusion that a little more concentration on my part would be desirable because for one whole term he refused to let me go out for play with the other boys and he also kept me after school each night for fifteen minutes. Throughout these periods of forced internment, I was compelled to spend the entire time writing the single word "carelessly." In response to numerous and vigorous protests, Mr. Case merely responded that he was doing it for my own good and to make me more proficient in my studies. The form of punishment is still a bit puzzling because I was never wanting in application or persistence. However, maybe the early lessons taught me by Principal Case were a spur to my later diligent application as a letter-writer.

After completing the seventh grade at Grassy Point, I entered the eighth grade at near-by Stony Point, which belongs to the same township, and continued on there through the high-school course. Stony Point is familiar to every American schoolboy as the scene of "Mad Anthony" Wayne's stirring victory over a superior British force during the crucial period of the Revolutionary War. This historical incident made a vivid impression upon the youthful minds of most youngsters in the school, so much so that we felt a personal pride in Mad Anthony's accomplishment, much as though he had been one of the earlier graduates.

The entire Hudson River Valley is reminiscent of early American history of the liveliest sort, going back not only to Revolutionary and Colonial days but to the time of the early Dutch settlers who were the first inhabitants after the Indians. During the Revolution, iron was dragged over the mountains by horse, and sometimes by hand, to be forged at points in the vicinity into guns for use against the Redcoats. We were given a great deal of this history to absorb in our school days, and as it always had a fascination for me, I did better in that subject than in any other branch of study.

Another place of national fame which became familiar to me at an early age was West Point, a little further up the river, the imposing site of the United States Military Academy. But, although I was a frequent visitor there in my school days and later on as a young man, it would be a bit dishonest to intimate that I was attracted by the history and traditions of the famous old academy or the military achievements of its mighty men. The attraction was the West Point football team. In those days—and perhaps now too—football was almost exclusively a college game, and my only opportunity to see the headliners in that sport was to watch the Army team perform. On Saturday after Saturday, I was in the stands along with a few cronies. In fact, my first visit was with Mr. Case, the school principal. The cadets enjoyed a reputation for their feats upon the gridiron, and some of the dramatic incidents of those early games are just as clear in my mind as if I had been a participant instead of an onlooker. The much-publicized squads of Harvard and Yale were frequent visitors to the "Point" in those days, and the glamour which surrounded them seems almost incredible. For days and weeks before the players trotted onto the turf for the annual clash, the newspapers in near-by cities and villages carried long and detailed stories about the merits of the respective teams, their strong points and weak points, and these accounts had the fans on edge with the feeling that nothing on earth was as important as the winning of that game. No wonder that memories are still keen! I recall Charlie Daly, who first made his reputation as a "gridiron great" at Harvard, playing his first game in a West Point uniform against his old team mates. He missed a tackle near the goal line which enabled Bob Kernan of Harvard to score a touchdown and thus defeat the cadets. Other gridiron names of those days run through my mind: Rockwell, Hogan, Glass, Bloomer, Shevlin, and Rafferty—most of whom saw action at the Point at one time or another.

During the years spent in grade school my existence was carefree, as it usually is for youngsters of about that age. There was nothing to worry about and little to do except a few chores and the customary homework in studies which wasn't particularly exacting. My father was a conscientious, hard-working man who was attaining a moderate success in manufacturing brick so that he was always able to provide for the family in simple yet substantial manner. I have only a few recollections of my father because of his early death, but some of them are still vivid and may be worth recounting.

One incident recalls my first visit to a United States Post Office. Father sent me down to the Grassy Point office on March 18, 1897, to get a copy of the New York *Evening World* which carried an account of the stirring ring battle between Corbett and Fitzsimmons. The opportunity to do such an errand made me feel important, and I hurried to the post office and back as fast as my legs would carry me. Father was in the yard waiting, and I handed him the newspaper over the fence. The front page carried a screaming headline telling how Fitzsimmons had knocked out his opponent; Father took the paper eagerly, but his face soon took on a look of profound disappointment. He could not conceal his sorrow over the fact that the "Englishman," as he called Fitz, had trounced the "Irishman."

My youngest brother Bill was born on election day of 1896. He was brought into the world by the family physician, Dr. Sengstacken, a kindly neighborhood doctor of Dutch ancestry. Dr. Sengstacken was a Republican and he suggested in a jocular way that the new arrival be christened William McKinley Farley. Although only eight years of age, I was already an ardent Democrat—no doubt because my father was one—and I protested with all the vigor at my command against the doctor's suggestion. The name William was all right, but I felt that the newest of the Farleys should be christened William Bryan instead of William McKinley. He was actually named William after my father's business partner, William H. Barnes.

As a rule my behavior was pretty good and it seldom went beyond the usual childish pranks that pass almost unnoticed in a family of five boys. But on one occasion I took it upon myself to do something that brought more than a passing reprimand. Father had gone to New York City to discuss business affairs with his partner, Mr. Barnes, as he frequently did, and I knew on what train he was returning. I went over to the barn and informed the "stable boss," Peter Sullivan, that he was to hitch up a horse for me to meet the train. Peter refused to believe that my father had left such instructions, but after persistent teasing and coaxing, he did as requested and hitched up a horse to a buckboard wagon. Being about nine years old, I was pretty proud and happy to be seen driving over to the station where I waited for some time for the train to arrive. When Father got off, he was the most surprised man in all the world, and his angry scolding soon took all the joy out of the childish venture. He left word with Peter Sullivan never to trust me with a horse again, no matter what plea was put up.

Father's Death

The death of my father was the result of an unusual accident which happened in January, 1898, a few months before my tenth birthday. A neighbor's child had died, and as the two families were on intimate terms, we were preparing to attend the funeral services. There were quite a number of Irish Catholic families in Grassy Point and near-by communities, and they followed the traditional custom of turning out almost in a body for wakes and funerals. In fact, Grassy Point was noted for the size and character of its funerals. The somber-looking black motor cars now provided by "morticians" for such occasions were unknown in those days, and each family rode in its own conveyance. Early in the morning, Father had gone out to hitch up John, the family carriage horse, a great favorite of the five Farley boys. He was a large black animal that looked well in harness and could travel at a lively gait. The horse had been confined to the stable for about a week without exercise and was feeling pretty frisky. When Father took him outside the stable to water and hitch him up, he jumped around in high spirits. He was on a long halter. Suddenly, without the slightest warning, the horse reared up his heels and gave Father a vicious kick in the ribs. He secured the horse, walked one hundred and fifty yards to the house, entering through the front door, and threw himself down on a couch in the living-room. His face was drawn and pale as he whispered what had happened. Mother sent one of the boys flying for a doctor while she attempted to ease his pain. Trembling and awe-struck, I stood by, realizing that my father was a very sick man. He lived only a few days and died in the middle of the night. We were not awakened, and my first knowledge of what happened came in the morning when I looked out the window and saw the undertaker's wagon in front of the house.

The only pictures Father ever had taken were a few tintypes, which were quite fashionable in those days, and they were always a trifle indistinct. My chief recollection is that he was about six feet tall, wore a heavy black mustache, and smoked cigars almost continuously. I had an aunt, Mrs. Mary Gogarty, who died a few years ago, and she told me that I resembled my father in many ways, particularly in my manner of walking at a fast gait in short, quick steps. Years later in Washington, I was dining in a restaurant when a man walked up and asked if my name wasn't "Jimmy Farley." It developed that he was Dan Campbell, a former resident of Grassy Point who had moved away many years before; we hadn't seen each other in thirty years. He said that all I needed was a mustache to make me the living image of my father.

Things had taken a serious turn in the Farley household. The business of making a living shaped itself on the family horizon and obscured everything else. Before that everything had been taken more or less for granted. Father was a comparatively young man and he had always been able to do the providing without any difficulty. We had plenty of good wholesome food, warm clothing, a comfortable house, and some things classed as luxuries. We had been spared the grinding poverty which had visited other and less fortunate families in the neighborhood. But Father was dead, and his weekly earnings had been virtually his only source of income. Mother was left with five small children. My oldest brother John was eleven years old; I was just under my tenth birthday; Phil was just under nine; Tom was a year or two younger; and Bill was less than two years old.

Mother had never paid the slightest attention to Father's business affairs. She had busied herself entirely with bringing up the family, and as a result she knew absolutely nothing about his property when he passed away. Her lawyer, Judge William McCauley, who settled the estate, discovered that my father owned one-quarter interest in the brick schooner *Barnes,* which Uncle Tom captained, and a half interest in the brick schooner *Shamrock* which was reputed to be one of the fastest on the Hudson River. The *Shamrock* was afterwards wrecked on Long Island Sound during a storm, and nothing was salvaged for the estate. In addition there was a $3,000 life insurance policy, the full amount of which was paid upon Father's death. These were rather slender resources with which to face the future with a growing family of five boys, all of school age and too young to step out as the family breadwinners.

Perhaps the outlook faced by my mother has been duplicated

in untold millions of humble homes under similar circumstances, or under circumstances far more trying. Yet the story of courage, faith, and sacrifice which it involved will never lose its freshness or its appeal. She had absolutely no training or experience that fitted her to earn a livelihood for the family. She was in middle age and had lived the customary sheltered life of a woman of moderate means, occupied solely with the work of bringing up her children and doing all her own washing, cooking, cleaning, and household work. The money from Father's estate could be stretched to last for some time—but not until the boys were old enough to go to work if they were to receive a proper education. There were no wealthy relatives who could assume the burden until the boys matured. The burden was hers alone.

While we were too young to understand fully the trial which my mother faced, I think we older boys did appreciate in a general way the problem which confronted her. We tried to augment the family income by selling newspapers, running errands, and doing whatever odd jobs promised to yield a few nickels and dimes. Starting at about twelve or thirteen years of age, I worked each summer in the brickyards as a "machine-boy," since that was the only place open for an unskilled youngster who was not sufficiently developed to do the hard round of duties required of full-time employees.

The duties of the "machine-boys" were quite simple and fairly easy for a lad with a rugged constitution. The principal job was to wheel molding sand from the kiln shed to the machines where it was used to keep the molds sanded so that the bricks would slip out more easily. Another duty was to keep the yard free of dust so that when the bricks were dumped on the flat to be edged later in the day, the dust would not cling to the bottom of the bricks. The yards opened about four o'clock in the morning. The bricks, of course, were dried by the sun, and if Old Sol was strong enough—as it generally was in summer—we could complete the day's work about noontime. That gave us plenty of time for a swim in the Hudson in the afternoon.

The pay for a machine-boy was ninety-two cents a day. On one occasion, several other boys and myself banded together and struck for a flat wage of one dollar a day. As I look back, I can't be certain whether we were really interested in getting the eight-cent pay raise or in getting a vacation. In any event, we lost the strike and went back to work at the old rate of ninety-two cents.

Tending Bar

The meager aid of the few dollars we were able to earn was not enough; the family purse was running low. A couple of years after Father's death, my mother adopted about the only course that promised to yield enough funds to keep us going. With her last $1,500, she purchased from a neighbor, a Mrs. Allison, a small grocery store and saloon located in a house about one hundred yards from where we lived. For herself, it meant an almost unbelievable amount of added labor. In addition to performing her household duties, which included preparing the food and keeping the boys neat and clean, she had to spend long hours tending store and keeping the accounts straight.

I was pressed into service to help with the new Farley establishment both before and after school hours. The grocery store occupied a large room on the ground floor, and the saloon was in an adjoining room with a connecting door. I have heard similar establishments described by the pleasanter sounding term of "beer-parlor," but the fact remains that it was a saloon in every sense of the word. While more beer was dispensed than any other beverage, hard liquor was sold and consumed on the premises. The restrictive laws were far more lax then than they are today, and at times my duties included practically all those of a full-time bartender. I tapped beer kegs, served out drinks of all kinds, and did my best to keep the customers satisfied and in good humor.

Most of the trade consisted of laboring men from the neighborhood who dropped in for a glass of beer on their way home from work or in the evening. While a saloon is hardly an ideal place for a youthful upbringing, as I look back now I am unable to recall any incidents of an unpleasant nature. That was, no doubt, because most of the patrons were known to us and known to each other and early closing was the usual rule. Most men are inclined to be talkative and confidential under the loosening influence of a couple of drinks, and the fellow behind the bar has to listen in the course of a week to more tales of personal and family woes than almost any individual on earth. I learned a great many secrets about the inhabitants of Grassy Point from my brief experience as a bartender, all of which I had sense enough to keep to myself.

We were making a living out of the green goods and wet goods establishment, but the saloon was a constant source of worry to my mother. She hated to think that her children were being brought up in an atmosphere where the consumption of liquor was a common sight and where its unwholesome aspects were only too frequently apparent. Like all women who came from poor or moderate circumstances, she had seen a great deal of poverty and wretchedness caused by men's addiction to strong drink and she dreaded its possible influence upon members of her own growing family.

The early experience in the liquor traffic had one salutary effect. Because she was so deeply worried over the brief venture into the saloon business and the participation of her sons in carrying it on, Mother never lost an opportunity to advise me against the use of liquor in any way. She also had a strong dislike for smoking. Recognizing her strong feeling on the subject, I respected her wishes. When I was confirmed at the age of twelve years, I took a pledge to abstain from the use of alcoholic beverages until I was twenty-one, the usual pledge given to Catholic youths. It was easy to observe the pledge, and at its expiration I was already deep in local politics. Using that as a reason, although there was usually some liquor in the house, Mother never offered it to me and she always emphasized the point that while engaged in political affairs it was better not to drink at all. As a result of her continued warnings and pleadings and out of regard for her feelings, I have never started smoking or drinking, and never felt the lack of either. My brothers Tom and Phil never smoked, and John and Bill did not commence until they went to war.

Some years later, just after the presidential election of 1932, I received a letter of congratulations from a former schoolteacher, Mrs. Jessie M. Rodermond, which I cherished because of its kindly reference to my mother. The letter said:

"Please allow me to add my congratulations to the many you have received. I have known you from birth, and have watched you choose the hard upward path which leads to success. You are a reflection of a fine, good, noble mother whom I was proud to call my friend. God bless her! If she were alive today, I know how proud she would be of her 'Big Jim.' "

As the younger boys came along in age, I was gradually relieved of duty in the store and sought other occupations during the summer months when school was not in session. Several summers I worked in the Bannon & Sutherland Shipyard, driving a horse which hoisted lumber from the barges to the boats under construction. I also became a painter in the shipyard and general handyman. The pay was small but it was highly acceptable at the time.

I finished high school at Stony Point, graduating in June, 1905. There were only three graduates and one of them, Miss Norma Bowers, is now principal of the high school. In 1935, at her request, I went there to deliver an address to the graduating class. Due to the system of grading students then in vogue in New York State, it had been possible for me to finish the eighth grade and the high-school course in three years. The winning of the coveted diploma was very pleasing, but the pleasure was short-lived. The state school authorities at Albany, reviewing the examination papers, rejected the second year English paper, changing the passing mark of 75 to one of 72 or 73. Consequently the State Board of Regents did not issue me a high-school certificate. I deeply regret that I never went to the trouble of taking the examination over again. English was always a bugaboo. I liked history and mathematics and did rather well in those subjects; in fact, I recall passing the final examination in algebra with a mark of 98 per cent.

Hunting a Job

After my graduation from high school, it was up to me to find a job and make a living. I was giving every spare moment available to the one topic which even then occupied my attention nearly to the exclusion of everything else. Almost from the time that I could first decipher newsprint, the news of election contests had outranked even the sports pages in juvenile interest, and I was uncompromising in my devotion to Democratic candidates for state office, most of whom were defeated by wide margins. New

York went Republican with disappointing regularity in those days. Politics, however, had to take a back seat for a while. In the fall of 1905, I enrolled in the Packard Commercial School of New York City to study bookkeeping, commuting each day by train from Grassy Point, which consumed about an hour's time each way.

After the bookkeeping course was completed late in the following spring, the business of looking for a permanent job began in earnest. After two or three days of pavement pounding, during which I walked untold miles, the Merlin Keiholtz Paper Company, 192 W. Broadway, hired a new and industrious bookkeeper by the name of James A. Farley. The salary was eight dollars per week, out of which, of course, had to be paid the daily train fare from Grassy Point and other incidentals such as lunch money. The net return was hardly great enough to suggest riotous living on the part of a young man seventeen years of age, but I was glad enough to get it. It was some time before the firm saw its way clear to increasing the weekly stipend to ten dollars. Even then I left because the chances for advancement seemed too slight and not primarily because the pay was too low. The pay envelope was always turned over to Mother to help the family budget.

My next job was with the United States Gypsum Company, a position obtained through the good offices of the Packard Commercial School. Advised in advance that an opening was available, I practiced long and carefully on a brief talk, outlining my qualifications, to the new boss. It must have been duly impressive because he decided to try me. When he mentioned that the salary would be eighteen dollars a week, the sum seemed almost unbelievably large. The United States Gypsum Company was my employer for fourteen or fifteen years during which I went up the lower rungs of the ladder, acting successively as bookkeeper, company correspondent, and finally as salesman. The last-named job suited me best because it provided an opportunity for me to travel about the state and meet people—an invaluable asset to a young gentleman who had his heart set on a political career.

Playing Baseball

Baseball was practically the only form of recreation which interested me after leaving school. Like so many American youngsters, I had started playing at an early age when my fingers were barely able to grasp the ball. There was the usual succession of neighborhood and schoolboy nines. Later, after I was grown, a local team at Grassy Point called the "Alphas" gave me a job as regular first baseman. The ball players got a lot of attention, and it was considered quite a distinction to play on the team. The spirit of rivalry between Haverstraw, Stony Point, Tompkins Cove, and other near-by communities was very keen, and the crowds turned out in large numbers for the Saturday and Sunday afternoon games. At various times, I played with Haverstraw, Verplanck's Point, and on a few occasions with the Peekskill team, for which the managements rewarded me with sums ranging from two or three up to five dollars a game. The last was considered rather a fancy figure to fork over, and the fellow who got it was supposed to be good. The local newspapers covered the games in ample fashion, and for a long time after baseball had become a thing of the past for me, I preserved a newspaper which carried the banner sports headline, "Farley's double clears the bases."

In those days, I considered myself quite a performer on the diamond but looking back now I'm not so sure. The truth is I was about the average player found in amateur and semiprofessional ranks. Being long and lank, I could reach for thrown balls and do a fairly good job otherwise of covering the bag. I was also a fair hitter and, because of my size, sometimes connected in lusty fashion and gave the ball quite a ride. But I wasn't very fast and I hated to slide. Because of my height, the fans nicknamed me "Stretch," and even to this day, if I happen to be visiting the neighborhood, some old-time fan will come along and greet me by that nickname.

Entering Politics

The decade between the ages of twenty years and thirty years was swallowed up, except for the time given to business, by a constant study of the art of practical politics in local affairs. At the age of twenty, the Democratic leaders had enlisted me for electioneering work, especially for the role of hauling straight-voting but lazy citizens to the polling booths, an important factor in minor contests. In my twenty-first year, before I had cast my first ballot, the neighboring Democrats elected me as a member of the county committee. Frankly, I was burning with ambition for political preferment although in retrospect the extent of that ambition seems curiously modest. The highest office to which I then looked forward was to be a member of the New York State Senate. Dancing and other forms of social activity were thrust aside while I devoted the daylight hours to business and commuting and the nights to studying whatever paths might be open to political success.

Confiding my hopes to a very limited circle of relatives and acquaintances, I met with discouragement at every hand. My mother especially was disturbed over the possibility of seeing me immersed in politics, believing that it would lead to nothing but disappointment and failure. Time and again in her own quiet way, she advised me to forget about public life, to enjoy myself like other young men, and to concentrate on the chances for advancement in business.

There was one friend, whose advice I sought, who was far more disturbed than my mother in advising me against a political career and far more emphatic in expressing his views. He was Pat Morrissey, whose cousins ran a grocery store in Grassy Point. Like many others of its kind, the Morrissey store had developed into a combined loafing place and village forum for the men of the community who liked to sit around and expound their views on public questions. In summer, the informal meetings took place on the spacious front porch, or "front stoop" as we called it; in winter they were adjourned to the back of the store where a full-bellied stove of old-fashioned design made things comfortable.

One night I called at the store and asked to see Pat in private. He went out to the porch where I revealed my intention to run for the job of Town Clerk—in a Republican community—and asked his opinion. Pat gave it to me. He said that of all the men he had ever known personally in Rockland County who had

entered politics, not one had made a success of it. He said the only
Republican he had ever known in Rockland County who was
really successful was a Republican Supreme Court Judge, who
had dominated the affairs of the G.O.P. locally for almost thirty
years, and even he had been disappointed in his great ambition
to be nominated for Governor. Morrissey gave me a truthful
warning: that men are inclined to neglect other interests and
duties after becoming mixed up in politics and then, when success
has passed them by, to become disappointed and embittered. Then
he concluded:

"However, no matter what advice I am giving you, if you have
made up your mind that you want to run, then run you will and
nothing can be done about it. So run and get it out of your system.
If you win, good luck to you."

The fact is that my mind was made up, and while I appreciated
the viewpoint of those who disagreed, nothing in the world could
have induced me to abandon the urge to take a fling at politics.
The possibility of defeat, and the means that could be used to
ensure a victory, had been carefully weighed in my own mind.
Stony Point was a Republican Township, and the gentleman
who held the job of Town Clerk was a man of substance who
wielded a wide degree of influence and commanded a great deal
of respect in the community. On the surface, it hardly seemed
probable that an "upstart of twenty-two years" belonging to the
Democratic Party could take the job away from him.

But it seemed to me that some of the old-timers were taking
things too much for granted, that they were overlooking a good
many opportunities for making friends and thus making votes.
I got the Democratic nomination without any trouble and then
started about the task of winning the election, something made
considerably easier by the fact that my distinguished opponent
wasn't inclined to take me seriously and did very little campaigning on his own account.

Playing first base on the Alpha baseball team had given me the
chance to become known pretty generally, and, with that as a
foundation, I started out to become personally acquainted with
every voter in the town or at least with as many as I could. A
great many of the young people, even though they were normally

Republicans, were red-hot baseball fans and they came to my support in large numbers. The result was that on election day the town political seers almost fell over backwards when they learned that young James A. Farley, Democrat, had taken over the eminent position of Town Clerk. Baseball had given me a modest start. I had made a good beginning, and it whetted my appetite for more.

Having won out unexpectedly, I set to work in deadly earnest to make good and to build a place for myself in the Democratic Party. The town was still Republican, and the change of a few votes would have been sufficient to swing control back to that party at the next election. But that never happened. The voters of Stony Point re-elected me on three successive occasions; and during those eight years in the Town Clerkship, I discovered a great many invaluable facts about public officeholding and what makes for success in running for office.

The daily commuting back and forth to New York City was a wearisome grind. I left home every morning about seven o'clock and failed to arrive home until after seven in the evening. After having dinner with the family, it was my usual routine to walk from Grassy Point to the Town Hall at Stony Point, where the Town Clerk's office was located, a distance of about one mile. This was done at least four or five nights a week, although such faithful attendance was not required by law. Even if there was nothing to be done, I went there anyway because the job overshadowed all other interests. Frequently a few cronies would drop in and we would chew over politics for hours on end. Always in winter the place would be stone cold upon my arrival because there was no janitor, and I would have to build a fire myself. It was usually a wood fire scraped together from whatever was available because the town furnished only a limited supply of coal.

The Town Clerk was not a salaried official; he got his pay in the form of fees for services rendered. For example, he got a fixed amount for serving as secretary to the Board of Health, another sum for serving as clerk to the Board of Assessors, and four dollars a day for attending the Town Board meetings. The Town Board frequently concluded its business in fifteen or twenty minutes and then "reconvened," with exactly the same members, as the Board of Health. The fact that they got paid separately for each service may have had something to do with this strange procedure.

There were other fees also. A license for fishing or hunting cost $1.10 of which amount $1.00 was forwarded to the State Treasury at Albany and the other ten cents was for the Town Clerk. A dog license brought twenty-five cents to the Town Clerk, and for issuing a marriage license the fee was $1.00. The aggregate amounted in the course of a year to a pretty sizeable sum.

This fee business offered just the right opportunity to build up a little "good-will." Although my job in New York paid me barely enough to get along, and the added funds would have been most welcome, I was far more concerned about building a political future than I was about cash on hand. Bearing that fact in mind, I never accepted the ten-cent fee from the hunters and fishermen of the community, who numbered more than two hundred, and as a result they remembered me on election day. The dog owners also got off without paying the twenty-five-cent fee and they were likewise kindly disposed towards the new Town Clerk.

And of course it would be unthinkable to take a dollar from a young man and his bride-to-be who were about to set up housekeeping. I learned also that young ladies about to enter the married state were as a rule very bashful about coming to the Town Hall to apply for the necessary license. In that case, it was a good idea to bring the license to the bride's home or to the home of the bridegroom. I performed that service on occasions without number, sometimes delivering a couple of licenses on the same night. It did me no harm on election day.

The years in the Town Clerkship also marked my beginning as a letter-writer, a form of electioneering which came to occupy an extremely important place in my later career. I never overlooked an opportunity to send a letter to the voters of the town, informing them about the state of the public business or giving other information which they were entitled to have. Individuals who wanted information or help also got it in the quickest time possible with a note from me explaining what was being done and why. The result was that every voter in the community got a letter from me at some time or other, and it was clearly apparent that this had created a very favorable impression. I never forgot the lesson.

The first contest for the Town Clerkship was won by a margin of twenty-odd votes. I was re-elected by a plurality of 288 votes out of 680 cast, or better than two to one. Commenting upon the election results and the unprecedented vote, a local newspaper said:

"This is unquestionably the result of Mr. Farley's courteous treatment of all the citizens of the town whose business takes them to the Town Clerk's office. Farley can be found morning, noon and night always ready to oblige a citizen of the town no matter what the inconvenience and it would seem that his activities in this direction are gladly appreciated."

After serving as Town Clerk, I was also elected as Town Supervisor for a couple of terms. I recall sitting with a few friends in a Haverstraw Restaurant the night before the balloting was to take place the first time. It was a three-cornered race. We started arguing about the outcome and during the course of the discussion, I marked down the total vote each candidate would probably receive. When the returns were in the next day, it was shown that my estimates were only fifteen or twenty votes out of the way. Even in those early days, I had learned the value of careful checking in figuring results.

During this period, a few friends induced me to branch out and to seek the office of County Superintendent of the Poor, a position that paid $1,500 annually and put the holder in a position to be known all over the county. I agreed to enter only after a careful check-up of the leaders disclosed the fact that my chances of getting the party nomination were excellent. The meeting was held in the firehouse at West Nyack, New York. Shortly after the meeting opened, someone proposed that the nomination should be voted on by ballot, instead of by a show of hands as was formerly done. I became suspicious. Those present voted fifteen to ten in favor of paper ballots, and later I lost the nomination by the same vote—because a certain leader who had pledged me his support went back on his word. It was the first time that I had been the victim of the "double-cross" in politics, and the thing hurt for a long time. However, I learned afterwards that men who do those things never get anywhere because no one trusts them. They dig their own political graves by deception and treachery. If there is one type of man who can't succeed in politics, it's the man who habitually lies.

The first really important political position I ever filled was the office of Democratic County Chairman for Rockland County to which I was elected early in 1918. This fulfilled a secret ambition of many years' standing because the county chairmanship was a handy steppingstone for an individual who wished to become active in state political affairs. It offered an opportunity to mingle with the leaders who picked the party candidates for office, and to attend the state conventions with a good deal of authority.

Booming Al Smith

I entered upon the duties of the chairmanship with a rush of zeal because it was my intention to build the county organization into a stronger force than it ever had been before and to make it a real factor in New York State politics. Having had a good deal of experience in local politics by that time, I had acquired a few ideas on what could be done to improve the county organization. And being duly impressed with the importance of the new post, I did something in the spring of 1918 which to a more experienced person might have seemed a bit presumptuous on the part of a mere county chairman serving his first time.

I paid a visit to the offices of the New York City Board of Aldermen to urge the President of the Board, Alfred E. Smith, to become a candidate for the Democratic nomination for Governor. Being admitted to his presence, I told Smith that he would get an unprecedented vote in New York City, that he would get an unusually large vote upstate because his long years of service in the legislature had made him popular with Republicans and Democrats alike, and that no other candidate could hope to run as well in the fall election. I added that my private business and my activity in the Benevolent and Protective Order of Elks caused me to travel about the state constantly and afforded me a good chance to judge political sentiment.

Smith said little or nothing but sat there looking me over in quizzical fashion while the speech was in progress. He was apparently trying to decide in his mind how much this newcomer from upstate knew about politics and how much of what he said could be relied upon. Finally, he got up from his chair, thanked me for calling, and said:

"You go over and give that information to Commissioner Murphy and then come back and tell me what he said."

The pleasant manner in which Smith received me on my first entry into "big-time" affairs was exceptionally pleasing, but his instructions to see "Commissioner Murphy" made me nervous and ill at ease. He was referring, of course, to Charles F. Murphy, leader of Tammany Hall, who was always given the title of commissioner by his fellow leaders in Democratic politics. Calling on Al Smith didn't faze me for a moment, but the idea of actually telling the great Murphy whom he should nominate for Governor left me almost breathless.

It took me some little time to get up the necessary courage, but I went to see Mr. Murphy and urged the case for Smith to the best of my ability. At the time, there was a well-defined belief that no Tammany Hall Democrat could hope to be elected chief executive of New York State and that it was only wasting time and money to try it. Inasmuch as Murphy was a realist who always endeavored to see things as they were, and seldom bothered about making useless gestures, it was generally assumed that he was cold, or at best lukewarm, on the proposition of nominating Smith for the Governorship. However, the latter had made an excellent record during his years in the State Assembly and a number of leaders were of the opinion that he could break the old prejudice against a Tammany man. I pleaded with Murphy to give Smith a chance, insisting that he would run well upstate despite opinions to the contrary. He listened in courteous fashion and, without committing himself one way or another, asked me to call again whenever I was in a position to give him more information about probable sentiment upstate. A few days later I went back and related the entire conversation to Smith.

At the state convention, held in the early fall, I was in attendance as a delegate and got a thrill out of voting to nominate Al Smith who was subsequently elected—the first boy from the "Sidewalks of New York" to make the grade. We came together in party meetings several times that year, and like a great many others I fell under the spell of his powerful personality. He had a knowledge of the business of New York State that gave him an advantage over all opponents in debate and he had an ability to explain campaign issues in simple homely phrases unrivaled by any stump orator of the day. He was at his best in hostile surroundings, and whenever anyone tried to heckle him or place him at disadvantage, he always came out on top. It was only natural that his fame should gradually become nationwide.

When Smith went to Albany as Governor, I thought there was a pretty good chance of getting appointed to a position which had appealed to me for a long time. It was the post of Secretary to the State Industrial Commission. While not one of the better-known state offices, or one sought after generally, the position was important because the commission had a great deal to do with the enforcement of laws and regulations relating to labor. At that time, and earlier, the Democratic Party was making an enviable record in New York State because of its efforts to put on the statute books humane legislation for the benefit and protection of working men and women. Having come from a family of laboring people, and having earned a living that way myself on occasions, I was extremely anxious to know more about the subject, to become acquainted with what had been done to promote better working and sanitary conditions, and to learn what more could be done by government action along the same lines.

When I revealed what was in my mind to a few friends, they suggested that I pay a visit to Charles F. Murphy for the dual purpose of getting his opinion and finding out what were the probable chances of getting such an appointment. I called on Murphy in the office at Tammany Hall where all his callers were received. I put the proposition before him and asked for some advice. Murphy was a very courteous man but slow-spoken and noted for always saying what was on his mind in the fewest possible words. He said that the man who was appointed Secretary to the State Industrial Commission should be acquainted with the details of the labor laws already on the statute books and also have a broad knowledge of New York City itself and its complicated problems. While he was impressed with my earnestness and ability, he felt that I was too inexperienced for the place and that it should go to someone else. He added that Governor Smith had given a great deal of thought to the matter and they were casting about for a man qualified to do the job and do it well.

My talk with Murphy was about as pleasant as a wetting in a cold rainstorm. It dampened all my enthusiasm for politics for the time being and left me a bit embittered. Murphy's attitude seemed unreasonable. I had worked very hard for the success of the party and if given the place on the Industrial Commission would have made the whole business thoroughly familiar by long hours of study and work. But the more I thought it over, after the first disappointment had died down, the more reasonable Murphy's attitude seemed to be. He could very easily have put me off by saying that the post was already promised to someone else or he could have promised to help and then done nothing about it or secretly recommended someone else. Instead of that he had chosen the forthright course by plainly saying that I was unqualified and that he intended to back someone else. It gave me a new respect for Murphy and once again taught me the all-important fact that to be successful in party politics a man must keep his word. No matter how unpleasant it may be, the only course is to give the facts straight from the shoulder. There is an old saying that truth-telling saves a lot of embarrassing situations later on. That is especially true in public life. I have had literally thousands of men come to me asking for support for this place or that, and in every case, it has been my policy to relate the situation exactly as it was. Very often the truth was distasteful, but the individuals always appreciated the fact that they were not being deceived. There is nothing baser than to promise help to a man looking for an appointment, knowing that you have no intention of giving it.

A few months later, a friend of Governor Smith's advised me that the Governor wanted to appoint me as one of the port wardens of New York City. There were several port wardens in those days, and their principal duty was to survey the cargoes on boats coming into the harbor to see if damage had been done by water or shifting cargo. The place paid approximately $5,000, but the wardens for the most part employed assistants who did the actual work and were paid out of additional fees received from the ship-owners. The place was a sinecure, and Governor Smith had urged its abolition, but the legislature up to that time had failed to act. As the work could be done without interfering with my private business, I agreed to take it and Governor Smith made the nomination. The place was always a political football, and the Republican members of the State Legislature held up confirmation until the closing day of the session, when Smith forced the nomination through. I performed the duties of port warden for about a year, during which time it was evident to me that there was no real necessity for the place. When Nathan Miller, a Republican Governor, came into office, I was legislated out of office by a bill reducing the number of port wardens. Only the Republicans were allowed to remain in. As a matter of fact, the number should have been reduced even further.

My energies were devoted mostly to business during this period although politics was still a favorite hobby and got perhaps a lot of attention that should have been directed to private affairs. I was re-elected county chairman with gratifying regularity and through that office was able to keep in close touch and to get better acquainted with the state Democratic leaders.

Meeting Roosevelt

I was married in the spring of 1920 to Elizabeth A. Finnegan who lived in Haverstraw, a neighboring town to Grassy Point. She had graduated from the Plattsburg Normal School but later gave up the idea of teaching school and accepted a secretarial position in New York City. We became acquainted during her high-school days and later we commuted together back and forth to the Big City. A few months after we were married, I took Bess to a reception in New York at the headquarters of the National Democratic Club on Fifth Avenue to meet the Honorable James M. Cox and the Honorable Franklin D. Roosevelt, candidates respectively for the Presidency and the Vice-Presidency of the United States.

An invitation had been extended to me as a county chairman and the opportunity to shake hands personally with the national standard-bearers of the party impressed me as quite an honor.

Apparently, however, several thousand other faithful party workers had been similarly honored because the place was overflowing
with people. In addition to that, it was about as hot a midsummer
day as could possibly be imagined and we had to stand in line
literally for hours for a chance to meet Governor Cox and his
running-mate. Then we were whisked by in a couple of seconds
to make room for hundreds of others still waiting in line. After
being jostled about in the crowd for a few minutes, Bess had suggested that we leave without entering the reception line, but I
insisted upon staying. Later she told me that if she had ever
realized that politicians spent their time going through nonsensical
performances like that she never would have married me.

It was the first time that Franklin D. Roosevelt and I had ever
shaken hands, but the chances are that in such a mob he wouldn't
even have remembered the fact a few minutes afterwards if someone had asked him. Certainly neither of us ever imagined that we
would be closely associated in later years.

Roosevelt was only fairly well known to the general public in
New York State at that time. About ten years earlier he had
gotten off to a whirlwind start as a fledgling member of the State
Senate in Albany. Smashing all precedents, he had defied the
party leaders of the day, and particularly the Tammany chieftains,
by opposing the election of William (Blue-Eye Billie) Sheehan,
of Buffalo, to the Senate of the United States. It was during the
period before popular elections of United States Senators and the
State Legislature did the electing. Roosevelt gathered around him a
few other rebels against the rule of the "bosses," and together they
held the balance of power. The result was a spectacular deadlock,
broken only when the "bosses" gave in, agreed to abandon Sheehan,
and accepted a compromise candidate agreeable to Roosevelt. That
incident quickly focused the national spotlight on the brilliant
young state senator from Hyde Park, and a few years later President Woodrow Wilson offered him the position of Assistant Secretary of the Navy which he accepted. Roosevelt did excellent work
during his eight years in the Navy Department, but his duties kept
him in Washington most of the time so that he lost personal contact with many of the party leaders in his home state.

In 1914, still a rebel, F.D. had entered the Democratic primaries to oppose the Honorable James W. Gerard, then Ambassador to Germany, for the nomination for United States Senator. Both were connected with the Wilson administration at the time, but Gerard was the choice of the organization leaders. It was the first time that Roosevelt's name had ever appeared on a state-wide ballot, and consequently it was the first opportunity ever given to me as a voter to approve or disapprove his candidacy. As a firm believer in organization politics, I entered the polling booth and cast one vote for Gerard, who won the nomination by a large plurality. There was no disposition on my part to give aid and comfort to the fellows who believed in kicking over the traces and disrupting party harmony.

The ticket of Cox and Roosevelt was buried in the fall of 1920 under the avalanche of votes that carried Warren G. Harding into the Presidency—and also carried thousands of other Republican candidates into office, including members of the Senate and House of Representatives, governors, mayors and sheriffs, and all varieties of county and local officeholders. It was a crushing defeat for the Democratic Party, and among those who went down in the slide was Governor Smith of New York. He had made a fine record during his two years in office and was very popular, but although he ran ahead of the national ticket, the handicap was too great. It looked as though the party was in for a lean period and that little short of a political earthquake could dislodge the grip of the G.O.P., which had taken control of things almost from the Atlantic to the Pacific. The country was getting "back to normalcy" with Harding.

It was a good time for a Democrat to pay attention to business and mind his own affairs. I was still employed as a salesman in the building-supply business although afterwards I decided to branch out for myself. With Harry B. Finnegan, a brother-in-law, as a partner, I formed a small company of my own to handle builders' supplies. Later we merged with another small firm owned by the brothers Sam and Harry Schiff. This firm was afterwards merged with five others into the General Builders Supply Corporation.

Smith versus Hearst

The year 1922 saw the Republicans already on the defensive, due to the blunderings of the Harding administration, and the Democratic leaders were in a bustle of excitement over the chance to snatch back a little of the power that had gone aglimmering two years earlier. The prospects were especially good in New York, and because the Empire State is looked upon as one of the most significant political barometers in the nation, both sides started girding early for a fray which everyone realized would have an effect all over the United States.

In the summer of 1922 I made a call upon Al Smith in the office he occupied as President of the United States Trucking Corporation, to discuss the expected battle over the Governorship. His friend and former secretary, George R. Van Namee, was there and also a political writer for a New York morning newspaper. I suggested that it might be good strategy for me to start the ball rolling by calling a meeting of the Rockland Democratic County Committee and then have the committee adopt a resolution urging Smith to make the race. The suggestion was agreed upon and later it was carried out.

Earlier in the morning I had received a telephone call from John Maher who was secretary to W. J. Connors of Buffalo, popularly known as "Fingy" Connors, a picturesque character who had made himself a fortune in the contracting and stevedoring business in Buffalo and who also wielded considerable power in state politics. Maher said his boss would like to see me that afternoon in the Hotel McAlpin, and I agreed to go over.

We knew at the time that a knock-down and drag-out fight was in prospect over the composition of a state ticket, and the probable line-up of candidates was pretty well known. William Randolph Hearst, the publisher, after many years of virtual retirement from active politics, was anxious to get back into the picture, and his agents were already going about the state endeavoring to line up support for him for the gubernatorial nomination. Years before that, Hearst had been the party nominee for Governor, and it was an open secret that his real ambition was to be President of the United States. He conducted a furious campaign on the earlier occasion that whipped up public feeling to a white heat but he lost the election to Charles Evans Hughes, a defeat that stung him bitterly. He soured on the thought of officeholding for a long time but the old ambition had returned and he was back looking for a chance to get into the arena.

I dropped into the McAlpin, and Maher was very friendly, although before going there I didn't have the slightest idea of what he wanted. He made known what he wanted without wasting words. He explained that Hearst was certain to be the next Democratic candidate for Governor because he had the support of Charles F. Murphy and the New York City organization, that it was an excellent chance to become associated with a winning ticket, that I could be extremely helpful in the drive to line up delegates, and that for that reason they wanted me on their side. Thanking him for the compliment, I explained the fact that my support had already been pledged to Al Smith and that I had no intention of deserting him. Maher said that was too bad and asked if there was any objection to Mr. Connors himself discussing the situation with me. I said none at all, and he went inside to inform his boss.

A few minutes later Fingy came bursting out from the inner room, and there was no doubt at all from his whirlwind approach that he intended to dazzle me by his splendor and magnificence. He had on a flashy gray checkered suit and a gaudy silk shirt; a gleaming diamond pin was set in a brightly colored necktie; and when he waved his hands in conversation, it seemed as if each finger was adorned by at least one diamond ring. Fingy was an aggressive fellow who had made his way up through the hard-boiled ranks of the stevedores, and he was accustomed to drive his way straight through to anything he wanted. On this occasion, he was out to impress a young, inexperienced fellow from upstate, and his methods were simple and direct.

Coming to the point at once, Connors said he had everything in life that he wanted for himself but that his one ambition was to play a part in nominating a man for Governor of New York State and possibly for President. He felt that Hearst was the right man to nominate because of the powerful support he could muster through his many newspapers and that, if elected, the publisher would be the next logical candidate for President on the Democratic ticket. "You can be helpful," said Connors, "in lining up delegates from upstate and we can give you whatever money you need in doing the work." Fingy then reached into his pocket and pulled out a fat roll of bills, bigger than anything of its kind I had ever seen. On the outside was a bill, evidently of large denomination. I told Connors that the money didn't interest me, that Smith was my personal choice and the choice of the people in my county, and that he would get my support. Fingy took the refusal to go along good-naturedly and suggested that we might have another meeting if I changed my mind.

A sharp struggle for delegates continued all that summer and early fall. By the time the convention was at hand, it was apparent that a close contest was bound to occur between the Hearst and Smith factions with no effort being made to conceal the ill feeling between the two camps. I boarded the train for Syracuse where the convention was to be held and immediately bumped into Connors and Maher and several other delegates bound for the same destination. They had engaged a drawing-room in which to play cards, and I was invited to join them. Although they were all for Hearst, no direct mention was made of the approaching contest. Every so often, however, Fingy would throw out a remark in a casual, off-hand manner evidently intended for my benefit. "Did you know, John, we succeeded in getting the delegates from Wayne County?" His remarks were always addressed to someone else in the party, but he was hoping that his comments would lead me to open up the conversation. "It looks as if with Tammany's support, Hearst will have the nomination hands down." I was young in the business and well aware of the fact. Despite Fingy's wily efforts, I refused to fall for his blandishments and kept my mouth closed. We reached Syracuse, a ride of several hours from New York, without a word passing between us about candidates or politics.

Big-Time Politics

The convention at Syracuse has always remained in my memory as one of the outstanding occasions of a busy lifetime. It was actually the first time I had been privileged to play an important role in "big-time" politics and, far more appealing, it was the first time that the men who ran things allowed me to sit in on those "behind-the-scenes" conferences which provide the thrill of politics. The desire to watch the inner wheels go around had a strange fascination for me—as it has for most people; I was like a duck who had been searching for water all his life and had finally found it. The leaders couldn't hold enough secret powwows to satisfy me.

Governor Smith had been formulating his plans in the most careful manner and he proceeded with caution, all the more so because he knew that Murphy and a few of the other leaders were far more interested in Hearst than they were in him. Upon reaching Syracuse, I went to call upon Smith at his apartment to wish him luck and to renew my pledge of support. He seemed highly pleased, told me candidly that he wasn't sure just what Murphy had in mind, and then directed me to open Smith headquarters in the Onondaga Hotel and to proceed with the all-important job of lining up the delegates from the rural sections and the other districts outside of New York City. It was pleasant music to my ears, and I hopped to the task fairly brimming over with energy and enthusiasm. Throughout the convention, I remained practically in charge of headquarters, at Smith's orders, and this gave me an unequaled opportunity to try out my own notions of how to conduct a campaign of that kind. There were over a thousand delegates to the convention eligible to vote on candidates, and a few of us went over the entire list in the most thorough manner imaginable. We split up the work and started buttonholing every single one that could be found. The result was that long before the balloting was scheduled to get under way we were able to present a detailed list of delegates to Smith, showing conclusively that he could be nominated over Hearst, no matter what strength the publisher thought he had. And what is more important, the Smith leaders were able to show this same poll to Murphy and the other Tammany leaders who were backing Hearst, thus convincing them that it would be useless to open up a partisan fight on the convention floor.

I happened to be present at one very interesting conference between Smith and W. H. Fitzpatrick, the leader from Buffalo, who had been a close friend and political ally of Murphy for many years. The blunt old fellow told Smith that he thought a great deal more of Murphy than he did of him. But he added that Murphy was making a mistake in supporting Hearst, due to wrong advice given him by people in New York City, and that he was going to support Smith merely to save his friend Murphy from the folly of his own judgment. He repeated again that he would rather have Murphy's "little finger" than Smith's whole body and he wanted the latter to know that fact. Then he walked out. The refreshing frankness with which Fitzpatrick told his story was a revelation to me. Yet before the convention was over, I learned that the plain-spoken individuals were usually the men who came out on top. The business of pretense and shamming is tossed overboard when strong and realistic politicians meet together behind closed doors and get down to cases. They know how to give and take and they dislike to waste words in the process.

Just to keep the record straight, I paid a call upon leader Murphy to explain that Rockland County was going to cast its ballots for Smith. He was sitting in his hotel room with his coat and vest off, and we had a friendly chat for several minutes. He said he appreciated being told in direct fashion that I was against him and that, no matter what happened, there would be no ill feelings afterwards. "Whatever you do is all right with me," he added. Later he told other delegates about the incident and expressed a very friendly feeling towards me. Before the convention was over, I went to see him again with a couple of friends to urge that George K. Shuler be given a place on the ticket as candidate for State Treasurer. Murphy agreed to help him and kept his word, much to the surprise of a great many people who never even heard of Shuler before that time.

Having failed in their efforts to put over Hearst as gubernatorial candidate, a movement was started by the backers of the publisher to have him named as the party candidate for United States Senator. There was little opposition to that proposition among the delegates, and the nomination would have been put across with a bang except for one thing—the courageous and persistent refusal of Alfred E. Smith to go along under any such arrangement. His own political life was at stake, and he knew it;

but the matter involved a question of deep personal conviction. Against the long and angry protests of the Tammany leaders and others, Smith stood his ground and in the end he won out.

The incidents connected with this effort to find a place on the ticket for Hearst were highly dramatic, and there is no doubt that the outcome ultimately found an echo in future campaigns for the Presidency. When he decided to try a come-back in politics, the first thing necessary in Hearst's mind was to remove his most feared rival from the path to success. With that in mind, the publisher proceeded in his customary ruthless manner to destroy Smith in the public eye by cruel assaults on his record and character. The Hearst papers in New York State carried a series of stories, accompanied by screaming headlines and vicious cartoons, to the effect that because of some action Smith had taken as Governor, he had been responsible for the children of New York City receiving low grade milk and that as a result their health had been affected. The exact details escape me now, but the charges were brutal and absolutely without a shred of evidence to give them justification. The situation was aggravated by the fact that Smith's aged mother had read the stories and that they had upset her terribly. Angered and resentful, Smith was determined that, if he didn't run himself or was defeated because of a party split, he would never consent to run on the same ticket with Hearst.

The news of Smith's attitude soon leaked out, and the convention and the various headquarters were in a hubbub of excitement. Having been outmaneuvered in the Governorship fight, the Wigwam chiefs were in a sullen mood and they decided to bring pressure upon the one individual who stood in the way of the compromise they wanted. There was a constant stream of visitors to the Smith apartment as different leaders took over the job of convincing him that he was wrong and that his stand was endangering the chances of party success. I was present when John H. McCooey, the rotund leader from Brooklyn with the pink-skinned face of a cherub, came in to urge that Smith give way and agree to the nomination of Hearst for Senator. John was a very mild man and he spoke only a few sentences in an earnest tone of voice. His talk was mostly a plea for party harmony, but pretty soon they were engaged in a heated altercation. Flushed with anger,

Smith lashed out at McCooey in a blistering reply, telling the latter that he should have known better than to have approached him with such a suggestion. I don't recall the exact words used by Smith, but they were hot enough to burn. McCooey went out flustered and upset, having failed to accomplish his mission or to get even a hint that the matter could be ironed out in a way satisfactory to the leaders.

By that time it was apparent that Smith was certain to be nominated for Governor, regardless of whether Murphy and his allies agreed to go along or took the opposite course of putting up a last-ditch fight for the publisher. Later on in the same day as the McCooey incident, I called again at Smith's apartment to report on the situation and found him in bed, nursing a sore foot that was too painful to walk on. We were there with others discussing the party slate when the door opened and in came the portly figure of Bourke Cochran, a Congressman from New York City who had been high in the party councils for untold years. Bourke had the gift of the golden tongue. His eloquence was a match for that of any man in the public affairs of his time, and many people considered him the equal as an orator of the great William Jennings Bryan. Short and rather stout, he had a heavy thatch of gray hair that gave him an impressive appearance and helped to hold the eye of his listeners. This was the last gun of the opposition. Bourke had come to break down Smith's resistance to the nomination of Hearst for Senator. He immediately launched into a stirring appeal to his small audience for party harmony, painting a glowing picture of the prospects for Democratic success in the fall election if grudges were forgotten and ill feelings were thrust aside for the common cause. He spoke with fire and fervor, emphasizing his remarks with graceful gestures, and for a newcomer like myself it was a positive delight to hear the cleverly-turned phrases in which he expressed his thoughts. Bourke was an artist with words. He went on for several minutes while Smith sat on the bed, arms folded and a black scowl on his face, listening intently to every word and yet unmoved. Finally it was the latter's turn.

Still sitting on the bed, making no effort to conceal his wrath and indignation, Smith fairly exploded in a scorching denunciation of the attacks made against him in the Hearst newspapers. He declared that the articles on the milk situation were grossly in error and that the insinuations they contained went far beyond the limits of fair and decent criticism. He told of the intense suffering they had caused his mother and he wound up by serving notice that no matter what political support it cost him, no matter what the consequences, he would never consent to run on the same ticket with William Randolph Hearst. Once or twice, Cochran made an effort to interrupt, but Smith shut him off by saying, "I listened to what you had to say, and now you listen to me." His short, harsh sentences were unlike the polished utterances of Cochran's, but it was a magnificent performance; and the incident gave me a fresh view of Smith's force and courage.

Finding that he was unable to move his antagonist, Cochran shook hands amiably and then bowed himself out of the room. The door closed behind him, then opened again, and Bourke stood in the doorway long enough to say, "Al, I wish you to understand distinctly that I did not come here of my own volition." It was his way of explaining that Murphy sent him there and that secretly he admired and approved of Smith's stand. In view of that, his eloquence seemed all the more amazing.

The bold and forthright stand of Al Smith prevailed. A compromise Senate candidate was chosen in Dr. Royal S. Copeland and thus the viciousness of Hearst's attacks proved his own political undoing, something that frequently happens in such cases.

The New York State Assembly

For many, many years Rockland County was a G.O.P. stronghold, and the voters continued their allegiance to the Republican cause with monotonous regularity even when the Democratic Party was making gains in adjacent counties through the appeal mainly of its program for social welfare legislation. The prospects of defeat often made it difficult for the Democratic Party to complete a slate of candidates for local offices. The strength of a political organization consists to a large degree in the ability to get voters to the polls, and when interest is slack in local affairs, the candidates for state office usually suffer a corresponding slump in their total vote.

In 1922 I asked a number of persons to run for the State Assembly on the Democratic ticket and received a polite refusal in each instance. No one wanted the nomination. As it was my task as county chairman to complete the ticket, I finally decided to run for the assembly myself, although the thought of going to Albany for the legislative session instead of tending to business in New York City was distasteful. The Democratic Party has remarkable recuperative powers, a fact demonstrated many times during the past century by a series of strong "comebacks" following in the wake of shattering defeats. A reaction against the Harding administration was under way all over the country, and I was carried to victory along with the tide.

The assembly term was for one year only. Like everything connected with politics, the new job proved exceptionally interesting to me, and I hung up something of a record for a first-termer by introducing a total of nineteen or twenty bills which were enacted into law. They were not of major importance and were directed mostly to curing the evils of the "fee system" in local government, the reform of which had seemed necessary ever since, many years before, I had served as Town Clerk for the Village of Stony Point. A number of petty abuses had crept into the fee business, accompanied by subterfuge in numerous instances, and the resentment of the public brought about an embarrassing situation for many officials who were strictly honorable in rendering their accounts. By placing a number of positions on a small-salary basis, the state legislature was able to do away with the abuses, improving the morale of the officials without injuring the public service.

The fashioning of legislative measures is a complicated process requiring a great deal of intense study, especially for a man without legal training. Living in Albany for the duration of the session, I frequently returned to the Assembly Chamber at night to go over the bills on the calendar and to draft the bills in which I was interested. One night I was there particularly late when Speaker Machold, the Republican leader, entered the chamber. He came over to the desk, saw what I was doing, and said, "Farley, you're all right. The only trouble with you is you're a Democrat."

The routine character of the work done by a state legislature under normal circumstances seldom borders on the spectacular or the sensational. Even when far-reaching legislation is under consideration, touching upon social or economic matters, the bulk of the labor is generally performed by a few veterans who hold key committee chairmanships and who are equipped by long years of service to carry the battle against the opposition. A novice is supposed to tread softly and to exhibit the proper degree of deference towards the more experienced party leaders. I observed the rule of precedence, and the solitary year of service would have passed on without significance save for an episode that projected the action of the legislature into a national political issue with a sharp bearing upon the Presidency.

It was the era of national Prohibition, and a controversy over the merits or evils of Volsteadism was beginning to sweep the land, in many areas, especially in the industrial states, cutting sharply across the established party lines. The old party labels were being displaced by the new tags of "wet" and "dry," and a number of men high in public life were known to the general public for their attitude towards Prohibition and for no other reason. The volume of interest swelled like a storm cloud, and the discussion, carried on everywhere, became not only heated and emotional but on occasions somewhat irrational as well. The "drys" had a tremendous advantage, despite the support given the "wet" cause by the daily press, because the Prohibition amendment was already in the Constitution and little short of a national upheaval could displace it.

When the ban against alcoholic stimulants was first written into the Constitution, the dry leaders had very shrewdly capitalized on their strength by pushing to enactment a number of state enforcement acts, under the theory of "concurrent enforcement" by the Federal and state governments. This plan, in general, contemplated the joint enforcement of the severe provisions of the Volstead Act by state police officials as well as by the agents of the Prohibition bureau. The New York legislature had enacted such a state enforcement act, known as the Mullen-Gage law. Having rallied from the shock of their first great defeat, the leaders in the wet movement had decided to concentrate on the Empire State and were pushing for repeal of the Mullen-Gage act. Both sides

were well represented at Albany when I got there, preparing for
the fray.

The struggle to erase the "Baby Volstead Act" from the New
York statute books was far from an ideal test of strength on the
deeper issue of national Prohibition, and the public had little idea
of the extent to which it worried and harassed the leaders of
both parties in the legislature. A number of individuals who were
sincerely and unalterably opposed to the Eighteenth Amendment
were afraid that, if the Mullen-Gage law was wiped out, the dry
forces would gain popular support by denouncing it as a lawless
act and a blow at the majesty of the Constitution. There was one
person with a firm grasp of all the implications whose political
future depended almost entirely upon the settlement finally arrived at for this delicate problem. This person was Alfred E.
Smith, beginning his second term as Governor, and already being
talked about as a likely candidate for the Presidency on the Democratic ticket in 1924.

Behind Smith, and also behind the movement for repeal, was a
determined band of able party leaders who were dead set against
evading or compromising the issue. The most insistent of the
group were Tammany Leader Charles F. Murphy, and State
Senator Jimmy Walker. They availed themselves of every opportunity to impress upon the Governor the need for decisive action.
The press was alive to the importance of the story, and, stirred
up by liberal newspaper coverage, interest in the fate of the
Mullen-Gage act soon traveled across state lines until the attention of the nation was centered upon Albany.

As he was titular leader of the party, those of us in the legislature, especially the younger members, were interested in Governor Smith's attitude and anxious to know what course he wanted
us to pursue. I called upon Smith in his office along with three
other assembly members before the bill came up for a vote. We
had a long talk about the legal and technical questions involved
in the actual measure as it had been drawn, and there was a discussion about the political effects of repeal upon the electorate.
The Governor talked freely about the bill but he did not offer
specific advice on how he wanted the legislature to vote or disclose
what course he himself intended to pursue. Just before leaving

he told us to "work it out for yourselves." It was easy to see that he was deeply concerned over the measure, and I got the impression that he would have been glad to have either the senate or the assembly turn down the repealer, thus saving him from the necessity of taking action.

After heated debate, the State Senate passed the bill repealing the Mullen-Gage act, and the fate of the measure then passed to the State Assembly. On two separate occasions, Charles Donohue, the Democratic leader, moved to discharge the bill from the committee, only to meet defeat. On the last day of the session, he entered a motion once again to discharge the committee and pass the bill. Four or five Republicans from wet districts lined up with Donohue's forces. I intended from the start of the controversy to vote for the repealer. The outcome was in doubt until the last moment when the clerk announced that the repealer had passed by the narrow margin of one vote! In other words, each member of the Assembly of New York, including myself, had held the balance of power without realizing it.

A terrific clamor went up from both camps when it was announced that Governor Smith had signed the repealer, and from that time on he became the acknowledged leader of the anti-Prohibition forces throughout the nation. There was a dramatic touch to the episode which undoubtedly went a long way to kindle interest in Smith and his chances for the Presidency.

If the Mullen-Gage act controversy hurled Smith into the limelight as the outstanding champion of repeal, it also retired me to private life without delay. When the question was before the legislature, I had received literally hundreds of letters from Rockland County constituents urging me to uphold the state enforcement act while not a single one was received urging the opposite course. Nevertheless, each letter-writer received an answer in which I disclosed my intention to vote for the repealer. My course of action was based upon the supposition that every one of the petitioners had voted against me in 1922 and would do so again whereas the Farley voters were ardent foes of the dry regime. I assumed that the vote on re-election would correspond closely to what it was the first time. It was a bad calculation as I soon discovered just after the polls closed on election night of

1923. The Republican candidate, Walter S. Gedney, was carried to victory by approximately fifteen hundred votes, and thus Rockland County reaffirmed its faith in Volsteadism.

I was sitting at home talking over the results when an Italian friend of mine from near-by Nyack called on the telephone. He was heartbroken over the outcome and wanted to know what he should do with the fireworks and drum corps he had assembled to celebrate my expected triumph. I didn't know the answer so he said, "Well, I'll let the drum corps play anyhow and I'll save the fireworks for the Fourth of July."

Believing that the oil scandals and other troubles of the Harding administration had paved the way for a certain return to power, the Democratic party leaders entered the Madison Square Garden Convention of 1924 in a cocksure mood and then came out of that Kilkenny brawl a few weeks later with hope gone and their lines smashed to pieces by the fierce factional quarreling. The wet forces had rallied behind Governor Smith for the presidential nomination and the dry forces behind William Gibbs McAdoo, precipitating a deadlock that lasted for more than a hundred ballots and setting a new convention record before a compromise candidate, John W. Davis, finally emerged with the worthless nomination.

As a district delegate, I attended the sessions day after day, performing minor services for the Smith leaders and following the proceedings with eager interest. Like everyone present, I was greatly impressed by the "Happy Warrior" nominating speech of Franklin D. Roosevelt, and for the first time I came to know him personally on friendly and intimate terms. As the weary balloting went on and on, the futility of the deadlock became apparent. I was sitting with Al Smith and a couple of other leaders in his headquarters in the Manhattan Club on Madison Avenue when he said, "Jimmy, it's about time to find out what this is all about and take steps to correct the situation." About sixty ballots had already been taken, and his words indicated that the Happy Warrior knew he had no chance for the nomination. Yet feeling was so bitter that forty-odd more ballots had to be taken before the choice was made.

We were back on the convention floor some time later when Jimmy Walker, then a state senator, came down the aisle at a rapid gait. He took a seat beside Roosevelt and, in his customary impulsive manner of speaking, asked the latter's permission to present his name as a compromise candidate for the presidential nomination. "Frank, you are the only man who can be nominated now with any hope," said Jimmy. "There has been so much feeling generated between Smith and McAdoo that if either one gets the nomination he will be badly beaten. The Smith people can't object to you, and you are the only one who will be acceptable to the McAdoo crowd." Roosevelt thanked Walker with a smile and shook his head in refusal, saying, as nearly as I can remember, "I appreciate the compliment, Jimmy, but it's impossible. In the first place, there is my physical condition to consider. And the Smith followers might misunderstand. I'm going to stay with him until the end."

Walker always had shrewd political insight and, in view of the temper of the convention and the friendly attitude of the McAdoo supporters, the compromise suggested might have been accepted with enthusiasm by the tired delegates.

Being defeated for re-election to the New York State Assembly in 1923 was not particularly disappointing as a long period of service in the legislature would have interfered seriously with my business activities in New York City. Late in the fall of that year, I received a telephone call from Governor Smith's secretary saying that the Governor wanted to appoint me as deputy to Colonel Frederick Stuart Greene who was Superintendent of Public Works. The position paid $7,500 annually and required full-time residence at Albany.

The Boxing Commission

After thinking it over for a week or so, I went to Albany for a conference with the Governor during which I thanked him for the courtesy but explained that I preferred to stay in New York City. The Governor talked about other things for a few minutes and then said, "What do you know about boxing?" In reply to this rather puzzling question, I responded that I knew nothing at all about boxing and had seen only a few bouts as a spectator. Smith explained that there was a vacancy on the State Athletic Commission, which had supervision over the ring game, and that he would like to have me accept the appointment. The post was "honorary," without salary or other compensation, and the duties could be performed on a couple of afternoons a week. I agreed to take it.

The fight business was in the flush of prosperity, an unbelievable boom-time period of million dollar gates, high pressure publicity, audiences drawn from society's "Four Hundred," and a popular following that must have raised envious feelings among the old-time ring gladiators who often fought for little more than the glory of winning. The evolution of boxing to the status of a big business enterprise was due to an unusual combination of circumstances. Sports of all kinds were doing well, the prize ring especially so because of the unrivaled appeal of the heavyweight champion, Jack Dempsey, the ingenuity of a great promoter, Tex Rickard, and the writing skill of New York sports writers like Damon Runyon, "Bill" McGeehan, Sid Mercer, Bill Corum, Paul Gallico, Jimmy Dawson, George Underwood, Wilbur Wood, Dan Parker, John Kieran, Hype Igoe, and a host of others who could make an ordinary heavyweight combat seem as thrilling and dramatic as the battle of Waterloo. Rickard was unmatched at the art of ballyhoo and in Dempsey he had a superb attraction to exploit. People who had never seen a prize fight before wanted to see the "Man-killer" in action. His prowess became a sort of legend, and his appearance in the ring meant a packed house any time.

Just by way of variety, Rickard added an international appeal to the fighting business by matching Dempsey against Georges Carpentier, the gallant French fighter, and later against Louis Firpo, the huge and ungainly Argentine heavyweight. Tex would have introduced a few foreign champs if he had found them available.

While the fighters were drawing well at the box office, the game unfortunately was always shrouded in a mist of ugly rumors concerning the tactics of the promoters and managers, and there was sharp agitation, evidenced at Albany, to outlaw the sport altogether. A few years earlier the legislature had enacted the Walker law, sponsored by Jimmy Walker, later Mayor of New York City, a measure intended to save the fighting game from extinction by placing it under the strict authority of a state commission. Governor Smith disliked the ring business entirely, was always fearful that it might explode with repercussions on the state administration, and because of that attitude, he was deeply concerned over the way in which the State Athletic Commission handled its work. He told me his views on the matter in asking me to take the appointment.

I looked forward to service on the commission as a pleasant diversion that could be handled without too much interference with business, although I took the new duties in deadly seriousness. Mrs. Jane Duffy, my secretary, tells me that I appeared for the first meeting clad in winged collar, black coat, and striped trousers, apparel that must have created consternation among the fighters and managers who appeared there for hearings. They felt more at home in the presence of less formal garb.

The other two commissioners were George F. Brower, of Brooklyn, and "Professor" William S. Muldoon, a grand old man of the sporting world who had been champion wrestler back in the days when the incomparable John L. Sullivan was in his prime. Muldoon was approaching eighty years of age, yet he was still alert mentally and physically due to a lifetime of careful living which excluded the use of alcohol or tobacco. He operated a "health farm" where he helped tired businessmen and others who had become physical wrecks to regain their normal strength and activity. The "professor" and myself promulgated a "no smoking" rule at indoor fights which the sports writers promptly denounced as a serious infringement on personal liberty, something akin to the tyranny of national Prohibition. The outcry was so general that some time later the rule was dropped, although Muldoon threatened to resign when the smoking ban was lifted. The old gentleman was very positive in his likes and dislikes, and the commission was very often in hot water because of his arbitrary and unyielding attitude.

Shortly after taking over the new duties, I went to see Walker to find out something about the commission and its work. He said that it would be wise at the first meeting for the commission to elect Brower as chairman instead of Muldoon because of the constant criticism being directed at the latter's rulings, although no one questioned his honesty of purpose. The suggestion was carried out, much to the indignation of the "professor" who sat with arms folded, refusing to participate, as the other two votes were cast for Brower. He threatened to resign but after a great deal of pleading on the part of Bernard Gimbel and other good friends, he consented to remain on the commission. We soon became fast friends, and until his death several years later, he was kindly and considerate in our personal relations, despite frequent disagreements over matters of commission policy.

It wasn't very long until my idea about the new post's being a pleasant diversion was rudely shattered. The commission had made a simple ruling in regard to a battle for the heavyweight championship and thereby touched off a storm of controversy that raged for nearly two years in the daily press, and odd as it may seem, was later puffed up into a state and national political issue. It was an unforeseen happening, and being entirely inexperienced in the touchy business of public relations, I soon landed myself without trying into the very center of the storm. I have since grown accustomed to verbal wallopings in political fights, but that first encounter with the sharp-witted gentlemen of the sporting world still stands out as the hardest pounding of all. On occasions, I took more punishment than most of the fighters.

The incident grew out of a ruling by the commission that Jack Dempsey had to defend his heavyweight title against the Negro boxer, Harry Wills, or not fight at all in New York State. This stand was taken before my term of service began, but the ruling seemed all right, and I endorsed it. Rulings along the same line had been adopted frequently by the commission, and at first no one paid it much attention. Wills had formally challenged Dempsey and posted a forfeit with the commission. The heavyweight champion and his manager, Jack Kearns, indicated a willingness to have the fight take place, and negotiations were proceeding in desultory fashion under the direction of Rickard, who dominated the promotion field. The promoter, however, didn't like the idea of staging Wills in a championship fight, perhaps because of his earlier experience with the Jeffries-Johnson encounter, and he was actually angling for a bout between Dempsey and Gene Tunney, the ex-Marine and former champion of the A.E.F., who had developed into a serious contender for the heavyweight crown.

Rickard was accustomed to having his own way in the boxing business, regardless of state authorities, and he had powerful backing because of his many successful promotions. He started a vigorous campaign to sidetrack Wills and force the commission to recognize a title bout between Dempsey and Tunney. The sports writers lined up, some for and some against, and the issue was drawn. Like all such controversies, there was merit on both sides. While the commission could make a lot of regulations, there was a question as to how far it could legally go in enforcing them. At the beginning in 1924, it was broadly hinted that Governor Smith was against permitting Wills to fight in New York, fearing that it might injure his chances for Southern support in the presidential fight, but the truth was that the Governor didn't have the slightest interest in the controversy one way or the other.

As the squabble dragged along through another winter and summer, it became evident that Rickard had no intention of letting Wills appear under any circumstances. It was simply a case of whether he had the power to make the commission reverse its ruling and permit the Dempsey-Tunney bout to take place in New York City, a desirable spot because of the accommodations available for a large crowd. The merchants and hotel men were lined up with Rickard, a reasonable position for them to take in view of the added profits at stake. The pressure on the commission got hotter and hotter, and finally Professor Muldoon took the lead in advocating a permit for the Dempsey-Tunney bout. He was secretly against Dempsey's fighting Wills, fearing that a victory for the colored man might bring on serious racial trouble in New York and elsewhere.

The question was agitated constantly, and the commission came in for a lot of ironic criticism. Bill McGeehan, a sports writer with a flare for biting ridicule, christened us the Three Dumb Dukes, and the name stuck from that time on. It was far from pleasant but there was nothing that could be done about it. Politics also came bounding in with a roar when the Negro voters of New York, numbering many thousands, got the idea that Rickard and Dempsey were actually drawing the "color line" and discriminating against Wills merely because of his race. The Negro voters were right in their surmise, and from that time the whole thing was a hot potato.

At dinner one evening, a friend of mine said he was deeply concerned over the torrent of criticism and felt that a public statement should be issued explaining why a state commission, operating under authority of law, could never be a party to a scheme for denying a man the right to its protection, simply because he happened to be a Negro. He said that if outlined in the proper way, with emphasis given to the legal and Constitutional points involved, the public would get a different slant on what was taking place. I told him to write out what he had in mind on the back of a menu card, and the next day I handed it almost verbatim to the newspapermen. When they got up to go, I asked Sid Mercer if he thought the statement was all right, and he replied, "Yes, Jim, but you should have put American flags in all four corners." Looking back now, I realize that it was a very fervent patriotic appeal.

A gentleman by the name of Herbert Bayard Swope, managing editor of the New York *World*, whom I did not know intimately at the time, had asked to see me, and an appointment was made for dinner a couple of nights later. I was there on time and received a telephone call that Mr. Swope would be late. I had met him casually on a few occasions. Shortly afterward, a handsome gentleman, imposing in manner and appearance, came up to the table with a grand flourish, introduced himself as Mr. Swope, and then proceeded to give me his candid and very uncomplimentary opinion of the way in which the Athletic Commission was conducting itself. "Farley," said Herbert, "if I didn't have a high regard for you, I wouldn't be here tonight. You have just issued the most asinine statement ever issued by a member of the commission." It was a very strong beginning, and I suggested that he keep right on. We had a long and frank talk about the probable effect of the ban against the Dempsey-Tunney fight. Swope felt that it would be an unforgettable blunder on my part to drive away from the metropolis a sporting spectacle which the public wanted to see and which would bring several million dollars of added revenue into the pockets of New York merchants and businessmen. His attitude was reasonable, and I agreed with him, explaining also why it would be fatal for me to reverse my stand. The feeling in the sporting world had been whipped up to such an extent, and rumors had spread so thick and fast, that if I agreed to license the bout, not even my own family would believe that it was done except for money. There was no choice but to stand firm and take the beating, unpleasant though it was.

Swope explained that he had first spoken to Governor Smith and that the latter said it was all right to talk to me. Smith told Swope that if there was any element of negligence or wrongdoing in my attitude, he would remove me from the commission at once. But if it was a case of honest opinion, he would never interfere. The Governor was known for his courageous views in matters of that kind, and I knew that, regardless of what pressure was brought to bear by businessmen or others, he would never yield an inch. Before leaving, Swope said that his newspaper, the *World*, might have to attack me for my stand. I told him to go right ahead, but to be sure to spell the name correctly. As a result of that meeting, Herbert and I became very fast friends.

The heat of the battle got under Gene Tunney's skin about the same time, and he issued a long blast to the newspapers, denouncing me as a "figure-head and a puppet" and adding a few other unflattering remarks. I made no answer, and later Gene sent me a very gentlemanly apology for what he called his "brain-storm." Tunney's one ambition in life was to win the heavyweight championship, towards which he had been aiming for several years, and he was naturally upset over the commission's refusal to permit him to have a crack at the title in New York, his native city. A few days later, Tex Rickard announced that the Dempsey-Tunney fight would take place in Philadelphia, where the Exposition was then in progress, something he had been threatening to do for a long time. I went over to Philadelphia to see the fight with Paul Starrett and Andrew J. Eken, but somehow the seats Mr. Rickard sold me were not very good. We were back from the ring, at a poor angle, and the rain made visibility even poorer. After it was over we were outside waiting for a cab when a couple of men sloshed by in the mud, evidently New Yorkers because one of them said, "If it wasn't for that damn fool Farley, the bout would have been held at the Polo Grounds, and we would have been almost home by now."

I enjoyed serving on the Athletic Commission and remained there for several years, yet I must confess that even politics seemed easy in contrast to some of the puzzling and irritating problems that cropped up in trying to regulate the boxing business. On the whole the experiment was fairly successful, and several other states later set up commissions modeled after the one in New York State with the idea of giving the fans greater protection for their money. We made a ruling, after several unexpected fiascos in major bouts, intended to prevent such contests from ending in the first round or so on a claim of foul. It worked fairly well. One night I was at the Polo Grounds talking to Muldoon when Bill McGeehan came along. I said, "Professor, you know Bill McGeehan." The old gentleman, who resented the title of "Dumb Duke," stared fiercely at Bill, squared his shoulders, and for a time I feared was going to challenge the newspaperman to a bout despite his eighty years. Bill regretted the incident because he had no idea the professor felt so badly.

The only alleged incident in connection with my service on the Athletic Commission which lingered on, to be repeated in print dozens of times, actually never happened. It concerned the issuance of free passes to boxing shows. Because I was supposed to have asked for so many passes for friends, Rickard was supposed to have said, "You take the Garden, and I'll take the Annie Oakleys." He never said that to me and he never said anything like it because there was no occasion for such a remark. Whether he told that tale to newspapermen, I don't know and never did. I don't recall when the story first appeared in print, and it would make no difference anyway inasmuch as I practically never bother to issue denials. Most tales of that sort die a natural death. It is being mentioned now only because I have been asked by the editors to mention it.

Rickard and I were hostile to one another from the time of our first meeting. He came down to the commission for a visit and during the course of the conversation he mentioned a number of sports writers who were, he said, on his pay roll for publicity work. Whether these remarks were thrown out as a kind of implied threat I don't know, but they made a bad impression. Certainly, if he was paying money to news writers, he should have been the last man to mention it. Later, I came to know intimately many of the individuals he mentioned and I'm still willing to bet a hat that most of them never accepted a penny from his pocket. Newspapermen are tough, hard-hitting men and severe critics, but a great majority are on the level and scrupulously honest. Rickard at the time had a national reputation, due to his picturesque background and his unquestioned ability as a promoter, and the knowledge of his power made him inclined to be overbearing and dictatorial. The fact that the Dempsey-Tunney fight had to be taken to Philadelphia sharpened his enmity, and later on, because of a disagreement over seat prices, he took the return match between the two boxers to Chicago. I tried to enforce a ruling that would have ensured a greater supply of low-priced seats for the "bleacher fans" who supported the regular boxing shows, although the power of the commission to enforce such a ruling was dubious.

However, regardless of who was right and who was wrong, I was in no position to be currying favors with Rickard. On the contrary, I actually bought hundreds of dollars' worth of seats for the big events to be distributed to business acquaintances and others. The Madison Square Garden Corporation used to send down a certain number of seats to the commission for members and employees, and this number was not changed during my period of service. If Rickard gave away too many free passes for his shows, and there is no doubt that the custom was greatly abused, he surely didn't give them to me.

Electioneering for Roosevelt

In the summer of 1928, Governor Smith called a conference of the Democratic State Committee at Albany to pave the way for a reorganization. The chairman, Edwin Corning, was in poor health and anxious to be relieved of his duties, and the same was true of Hugh Reilly, the secretary. A number of leaders from all parts of the state were present in the Governor's office as the list of available persons was thoroughly canvassed, and Smith outlined the qualifications he wanted in the men selected. M. William Bray of Oneida County, later Lieutenant Governor, was agreed upon as the best choice for chairman. Someone suggested my name, among many others, for secretary, and I got the impression that Governor Smith was against having me serve in that capacity. Inasmuch as this rather humble post later became the steppingstone which led to my appointment as presidential campaign manager for F. D. Roosevelt, perhaps his opposition was gifted with a touch of prophecy. The Governor first said he was opposed to the appointment of anyone who held a state job, although the Athletic Commissionship was not generally regarded as a political post. The conversation turned to others and each one in turn was eliminated for one reason or another. Governor Smith paused, glanced out the window for a few minutes, suddenly swung around in his chair, and said, "Jimmy, I guess you will have to be secretary of the committee."

Later on in the summer another conference was called at Albany to discuss a nominee for the Governorship. Smith had already been nominated for the Presidency, and it was highly important to choose a strong state ticket that would add strength to the Democratic cause and help swing over the Empire State's important bloc of forty-five electoral votes. A half dozen outstanding Democrats were tentatively discussed, including Senators Wagner and Copeland, either one of whom might have been drafted to make the race. George H. Lunn, Peter G. Ten Eyck and Joab H. Banton, district attorney in New York City, were considered, but nothing really definite was decided upon. Because Smith was a Catholic, it was imperative to choose a non-Catholic for the Governorship to balance the ticket. When Senator Copeland's name was mentioned, Smith growled out a hot dissent accompanied by a few frank remarks and then turned with an apology to Mrs. Caroline O'Day whose presence he had momentarily forgotten. Mrs. O'Day laughingly responded, "Governor, don't let me cramp your style." Smith still resented the fact that Copeland was an ally of publisher Hearst who had fought him so bitterly six years before and then was opposing him for the Presidency.

The decision to nominate F. D. Roosevelt for the Governorship was made at a morning conference in the suite occupied by Governor Smith in the Seneca Hotel at Rochester, just prior to the opening of the state convention. The details of the Seneca Hotel meeting will be revealed at greater length a little further on in this book.

In the 1928 campaign, I took charge of the Roosevelt headquarters at the Hotel Biltmore in New York City, working on the state campaign to the exclusion of the fight over the Presidency. It was a close contest, and the first thing that struck me was the lack of accurate information around headquarters regarding the Democratic organization in "upstate counties," meaning the vast area above New York City. In some instances, even the list of county chairmen and local workers was either missing or too old to be of much use. We whipped an organization into shape in the best way possible, and as election day drew near it became apparent that Roosevelt was going to run exceptionally well in the upstate counties. We had hoped for a margin of 100,000 votes, but it was a Republican year. The sound defeat administered to Governor Smith had its effects all over the country, including his home state which he lost. However, we saved something from the wreckage because Roosevelt was elected Governor over his Republican opponent, Albert Ottinger, by a margin of 25,564 votes. There was some talk that a recount would be demanded because of the closeness of the vote, and Democratic attorneys were hurried upstate to protect Roosevelt's interests in a few counties from which the returns were slow in coming in. I remained on the job without sleeping for nearly three days and nights before it was known definitely that there was no chance of an upset in the gubernatorial contest.

After the election, I continued the job of rebuilding the party upstate where organization had been more or less neglected, particularly in those counties which usually went Republican by a wide margin. This activity pleased Governor Roosevelt because two years later, before the state campaign got under way, he let it be known that he wished to have me promoted to the job of state chairman. At first it was suggested that William Bray continue as state chairman, leaving the job of running the campaign to me, but as that seemed like an unworkable arrangement, I demurred. Louis McHenry Howe was one of those insisting upon my election as chairman, and Bray volunteered to step aside in order to defer to the Governor's wishes.

While acting as state chairman, I had the first real opportunity to employ the method of making acquaintances by constant letter-writing and personal meetings which had proved sound election-eering tactics in my earlier days in town politics at Stony Point. Accompanied by a close friend, Daniel H. Skilling, who later became Secretary of the State Committee, I visited places where a State Chairman had never been seen before, a practice which increased our total vote in subsequent elections.

The business of political organization seems so mysterious and vague to many people that I am going to digress long enough to give an idea, in skeleton form only, of the framework upon which the Democratic Party is based. There are about 9,000 election districts in New York State, varying slightly from year to year, and experience has shown that the total number of votes in each district runs from as low as 10 up to 900. There are at least two, and often more, members of the county committee in each election district, and under the election law of the state, this member of the county committee must be elected to that position by the voters. Therefore the county committee member is looked upon as the leader of the election district. The members of the county committee, in much the same way, elected a county chairman or leader although the exact form varies in different places.

The state committee is an elected body composed of two persons from each of the 150 assembly districts in the state, and it has been the aim of the party leaders to have one man and one woman elected in each district. The state chairman is elected by the committee. The value of such a close-knit and far-reaching organization can be readily demonstrated. If the workers in the individual election districts succeed in getting ten voters, who otherwise might not have been interested, to the polls, the total would run close to 90,000 votes and many an election in New York State has been decided by a smaller margin. In fact a number of people competent to judge held the opinion that the Roosevelt victory for the Governorship in 1928 was due to the more efficient upstate organization work carried on that year. There were willing workers who got the voters to the polls in rural Republican districts where the Democratic candidates had never before had help. A good measure of the credit for that fine showing was due to Mrs. Roosevelt and the other women at headquarters who helped organize the feminine vote. I went into every county in the state during my service with the state committee and we managed to get local tickets in the field wherever possible because, as I have said, local contests stimulate interest and bring out a larger vote.

A strong organization can do more than merely assist voters to the polls on election day. The members distribute propaganda, defend the party position, hold rallies, and carry on other very necessary activities. The view that the men and women in the lower ranks only put forth activity when jobs are in sight is erroneous. The women especially will work like beavers if they believe in the cause. This was shown conclusively in the 1936 presidential campaign when women all over the country swung into action because they liked the humane policies of the Roosevelt administration.

We have urged Democratic leaders all over the country to organize along the lines of the party in New York State, especially in giving equal voice to the ladies. It has been done on a large scale, particularly in Pennsylvania, and the results have been excellent.

In much more than mere organization, the Democratic Party in New York State has been the political workshop for the United States during the past decade and a half. The emergence of virile party leaders who had strong national appeal and who were ready to step in when the Republican Party lost its sway was more than a mere coincidence. Even in the days of Coolidge and Hoover, the Empire State remained in the Democratic column, and the party grew in strength because of the liberal and progressive policies sponsored by Al Smith, Robert F. Wagner, F. D. Roosevelt, and other men associated with them in the conduct of state affairs. The first three, however, very largely gave direction to the movement which resulted in the recognition once again of the party of Jefferson and Jackson as the true guardian of liberal principles in the United States.

New York was well in the vanguard of states enacting protective laws for women and children in industry. The sweatshop was very largely eliminated by statute, and the factory inspection laws went far towards ensuring proper sanitation and other wholesome working conditions. The Workmen's Compensation Act, providing financial aid for those injured, was simplified and made to operate more to the advantage of the employees who had no funds to spend for legal counsel. A good start toward social security for the superannuated employees, something badly needed in an industrial age, was made during Roosevelt's term as Governor.

Even in the matter of conservation of natural resources, New York went ahead of most states under the wise laws put into force by Democratic governors and legislators. The park system was developed, and provisions were made to protect the vast timber lands in the Adirondack and Catskill areas. The fact that these measures were well understood and appreciated by the electorate was the chief reason why national attention was focused on New York when the country was looking for new leadership. Because of his services in the United States Senate, Robert F. Wagner will be known for many years for the liberal and humane legislation enacted into Federal statutes under his guidance. He was well fitted for the task because of his previous service in the State Senate at Albany where he pioneered in the fight to throw the protection of the law around working men and other people of small income. Neither radical nor unreasonable, Wagner inspired public confidence by the soundness of his views, and the success of the Democratic Party has been largely due to his untiring efforts.

Fortunately, I was thrown into early association with Wagner, Smith, and Roosevelt in state politics, and their views influenced my own as they did those of other men and women in public life. They were a step ahead of most men in comprehending the vital social and economic needs of the times and they were aided by the reactionary and standpat attitude of the Old Guard group which dominated the policies of the Republican Party. The preliminary battle was first fought out in New York State where the Democratic Party won contest after contest against G.O.P. leaders who refused to see the light or to heed the march of progress. When the time came to go forth onto a larger stage, Roosevelt and Wagner were ready for the fray. The issues and the principles involved were largely the same. Perhaps without realizing it, the doughty leaders who transformed the Empire State into a Democratic stronghold were preparing themselves for a heavier role in shaping the nation's destiny.

II. The Pre-Election Campaign of 1932

WHEN the history of the present era in American politics is written, it will be dominated largely by the overshadowing figure of one individual. Whether friend or foe, every reasonable man and woman is ready, I think, to concede the influence of Franklin D. Roosevelt in shaping the course of contemporary government in the United States. He stands in the panorama of public life like a mountain peak above the plain.

To those who disagree with him, he is a sinister force seeking to undermine and destroy traditional principles of government. To those of us associated with him, he is now, as he has been, the living voice of democracy and the greatest popular leader of his age. In writing this material, however, it is not my purpose to add to the controversy. Rather, I hope, to present honestly my own views—my understanding of the events and the men and women who have had a hand in making present-day history.

In this chapter an effort is made to go behind the scenes in the job of nominating a man for President of the United States, to reveal the magnitude of the task, and to bring home the mistakes, the errors, and the inevitable, unavoidable mishaps. Each reader must decide for himself whether he thinks destiny or blind luck guided our faltering footsteps over these pitfalls. For those who like to speculate on the big "IF" in human affairs, the story may be interesting because on several occasions, if the "worst" had happened, the result might have been vastly different and the New Deal, as we know it, might never have happened.

My only regret is that in telling this story, it is impossible to give credit to all the men and women who did such praiseworthy work in bringing about the first nomination of the present Chief Executive. It was a thrilling fight and a glorious victory, and there are still many unsung heroes in every state who did valiant work and whose names are not included in this record.

A political campaign is a matter of years—not weeks or months. Long before the public hears the tumult and the shouting, the preliminary "build-up" has been under way, and every step taken during this preparatory period is usually the result of long and painstaking consideration. Once in a while, a man in public life may be able to reach the top as the result of a political "accident" and without having organized effort put forth in his behalf; yet such cases are the exception and not the rule.

A good perspective on the manner in which the Roosevelt star flashed its way onward and upward through the political skies can only be had by going back to 1928, a presidential campaign year which saw the Democratic Party experience a disaster as overwhelming as anything that ever happened in its century of existence. Governor Alfred E. Smith, of New York, was the presidential standard-bearer that year, and after a whirlwind campaign, he had been buried under an avalanche of Republican votes that hurt all the more because of the fact that some of the states in the Solid South had forgotten their long traditions and gone over to the enemy.

The outcome was both disappointing and discouraging, and when it was all over, Governor Smith issued a statement to the effect that he was through forever with running for public office, that— while his interest in public affairs would always be keen—his days as an active participant were over. He was turning his back on politics, after a quarter of a century in public life, to begin the task of earning a more remunerative living for himself and his family in private business. Al Smith was one of the most colorful figures of his generation, and the announcement of his retirement was a keen disappointment to his legion of friends even though they understood and sympathized with his course. To those of us who had been closely associated with him in the councils of the party, his retirement from the active field was a matter of special regret.

The country was so thoroughly under the control of the G.O.P. that it seemed as if all the Democratic leaders might retire without creating much of a furore. People everywhere, or so it seemed, were singing the praises of Coolidge and Hoover prosperity; and the cause of the opposition party seemed hopeless. In Democratic ranks, there was actually a feeling of despondency; the party rout had been so complete. The general view was that the nomination for the Presidency in 1932 would be an empty honor and not much else. Breaking the power of the Republican Party seemed impossible. In fact, a great many newspapers and magazines were carrying learned articles to the effect that the venerable party of Jefferson, Jackson, and Wilson had outlived its usefulness and was about to vanish from the political stage. Certainly not a very cheering picture!

The Vote-Getting Governor of New York

But there never was a disaster great enough to bring about the death of the Democratic Party, and the literary pall-bearers who volunteered to perform the funeral rites found themselves with a very live corpse on their hands indeed. Even in the darkest hour of 1928 there was a ray of hope. Franklin D. Roosevelt had been elected Governor of New York despite the Hoover landslide, and modern history had demonstrated time and again that the men who occupied the Governor's Mansion at Albany had a pretty good chance of being considered for the White House—other things being equal. That had been illustrated in striking fashion by the public careers of Grover Cleveland, Theodore Roosevelt, Charles E. Hughes, and Governor Smith.

The Republican Party had been having too much luck for its

own good. The Pollyanna chorus had swelled to such proportions that the party chieftains thought life would always be like that. They neglected to heed ominous signs; they shook their heads in disagreement when Western Senators and Representatives warned them that revolt was brewing in the Farm Belt and, instead of searching for adequate remedies, replied by smugly mouthing a few moth-eaten phrases about fundamental principles of government. The G.O.P. leaders very kindly prepared the way for the rebirth of the Democratic Party when they neglected the farm problem.

Mr. Hoover's optimistic campaign prediction in 1928 that poverty was about to be abolished seemed a trifle ludicrous in view of what commenced to happen scarcely a year after he took over the extremely heavy burdens of the Presidency. The long and dreary story of the depression—of unemployment, bread lines, empty factories, dispossessed home owners, and busted banks—is too fresh in the minds of the public to need repetition here. The significant fact for the record is that the political pendulum was swinging swiftly to the opposite extremity of the arc. The Democratic nomination for the Presidency in 1932 might be worth something after all.

Like everything in politics, the roots of this story are buried back in the annals of other years. It burst into the sunlight of popular attention on the afternoon of November 5, 1930, when a group of news correspondents were lounging about in Democratic State Headquarters on the fourth floor of the Hotel Biltmore in New York City. While waiting for news, they were discussing in surprised and eager tones the sweep of the previous day's election which had seen Franklin D. Roosevelt re-elected to the Governor's chair by the unprecedented plurality of 725,001. The outcome had been anticipated, but the bulging margin by which it was accomplished had turned it from a mere state event into a political happening of nationwide importance. The men and women who make politics their business started to cast their eyes toward Albany.

The reporters, of course, were expecting the customary post-election statement from the victorious side. It was my job as state chairman to issue it. After receiving election returns at the Biltmore headquarters on election night, Governor Roosevelt had returned to his executive offices at Albany on the noonday train. With the help of Louis McHenry Howe, I labored long and hard over the statement for the press, which the two of us had determined should be something more than the usual routine patter of words in the style that press and public had been led to expect on such occasions. The final draft contained a paragraph which I am going to quote because it was intended for consumption, not only by the voters of New York State, but by the voters in every state of the Union.

"I fully expect," said the statement, "that the call will come to Governor Roosevelt when the first presidential primary is held, which will be late next year. The Democrats in the Nation naturally want as their candidate for President the man who has shown himself capable of carrying the most important state in the country by a record-breaking majority. I do not see how Mr. Roosevelt can escape becoming the next presidential nominee of his party, even if no one should raise a finger to bring it about."

In effect, the foregoing paragraph was the first battle cry of the Roosevelt forces. To borrow a phrase coined by his distant cousin, Theodore, Governor Roosevelt's hat was in the ring— tossed there by two enthusiastic and ambitious supporters who felt that the time had come to strike.

Knowing just when the Governor would arrive at Albany, I got him on the telephone at the first opportunity and warned him about the statement just issued to the press, linking his name with the Presidency. Believe it or not, that was the first time that a word about his possible candidacy for the highest office in the land had ever passed between us, and I was in doubt as to how he would take it. He laughed and replied, "Whatever you said, Jim, is all right with me." That was the actual birth of the Roosevelt presidential boom and his brief OK. started in motion an intense and far-flung campaign of action, the plans for which had been maturing in our minds for many months previous.

The actual truth of the matter is that I, and several other people who were close to the Governor, had been pondering over his chances to be the party standard-bearer in 1932 ever since his first election to the gubernatorial chair. Some of them may have been thinking about it even before that. I know that Governor Roosevelt himself would have been less than human if, upon occasion, he had not allowed his own mind to dwell upon the possibility that the honor of the Presidency might come his way. But there is an ancient and deep-seated belief in politics that it is both unwise and unlucky to start talking about such things too soon. The office-holder who lets the presidential bee start buzzing in his bonnet, when his mind should be concentrated on his own job, may get stung in a manner he doesn't like. It is equally bad to have the men and women around him thinking in the same way. For that reason, presidential talk around Governor Roosevelt was taboo by common consent and without anybody's having to say so out loud.

Now, however, we had the necessary springboard. The Republican candidate for Governor in 1930 was Charles H. Tuttle, and he put up an ineffective campaign. While the re-election of Roosevelt was a foregone conclusion, we had bent every effort possible to pile up a record-breaking majority in order to impress his vote-getting ability upon the country generally. On election eve, we were so confident that I wanted to issue a statement predicting the Governor's re-election by a plurality of more than 600,000 votes. This estimate was based upon reports received from Democratic workers in every district in the state.

Governor Roosevelt himself urged caution. He pointed out that if this estimate proved out of line, the public would never again give heed to a political prophecy coming from me. And he added the more important fact, that a landslide prediction might cause our workers to let down, thus causing defeat of State Assembly candidates in doubtful districts. The wisdom of what he said was apparent; my pre-election forecast was whittled down to 350,000 votes. When the election was over, the total plurality was found to be more than double that figure—a total so huge that its size caused seasoned politicians all over the country to blink in astonishment. A gentleman of almost unrivaled vote-getting ability was about to make his entry onto the national political scene.

Although he had given tacit consent to the use of his name in connection with the presidential nomination—after it had already been given out, Governor Roosevelt was in no position to begin an active campaign on his own behalf, or even to announce his candidacy formally. He had a big job to do in running the affairs of New York State in the midst of a business depression and he had little time for active political work. That had to be taken over by someone else.

Teaming with Louie Howe

Since he has occupied the White House, F. D. Roosevelt has become known as a smasher of precedents. He smashed one "right off the bat" at the beginning of his presidential boom by entrusting the management of his preconvention campaign to two men who were virtually unknown and inexperienced in the vast field of national politics—Louis McHenry Howe and myself. I was later given the actual title of Roosevelt manager, but the two of us labored in complete harmony, and there was never any quarrel over the division of authority. We were put in charge even though several nationally known Democrats had already espoused the Roosevelt candidacy and any one of them would have jumped at the chance to become campaign manager.

Because during the intervening ten years we have been caught up together in a whirlwind of mighty events, during which period I have seen him times without number in all manner of moods and under all kinds of circumstances, it is difficult for me to go back and describe accurately the qualities in Roosevelt which first attracted me. The first impressions are confused with the many sides of his character and nature revealed later. However, I think there were two things that set him apart in my mind and marked him as a little different from other men.

In the first place, F.D.R. had a most ingratiating manner of making other people feel at ease in his presence and of convincing them that they were filling a highly important role in the business at hand. In fact, he was, and still is, a sentimentalist in his relations with those around him with a tendency to be overindulgent at times. He was unlike Smith in that respect. As I have pointed out, the latter could be extremely harsh on occasions in private conversation, and he always said what was on his mind regardless of the effect it had on the other fellow's feelings. I recall visiting Smith during his second term as Governor to make a request which seemed perfectly reasonable to me. Perhaps I was asking too much and should have known better, but the fault was due to inexperience and poor judgment. The "dressing down" I got from Smith seemed needlessly severe and left a most disagreeable impression upon my memory. I am no good at tossing out bad-tempered words in a personal quarrel, and there was nothing to do but sit there and "take it" until—to be wholly candid—the tears almost came to my eyes. Roosevelt would never do that. Frequently I made suggestions about how to proceed in national politics that must have seemed absurd in view of his wider knowledge, but he never let me down in abrupt or rude fashion. He would give the appearance of turning it over very gravely in his mind and then he would explain very kindly and patiently why the suggested move would do more harm than good. He knew public sentiment in the South and West as well as he knew that of the Atlantic Seaboard, and the practical lessons he taught me were really invaluable.

The second thing about Roosevelt was the fact that he was one of the most alive men I had ever met. He never gave me the impression that he was tired or bored or that he was one of those inconspicuous workhorses who get ahead by tireless and methodical plugging. He was quick, alert, keen; when he talked he emphasized his points with sharp gestures and constant changes of facial expression. He would have been a great actor. Also, without sensing it in very plain terms, I had an intuition that there was a touch of destiny about the man, that he was intended to play a big role in the affairs of his fellow countrymen, and over the years since then I have heard a number of men express the same view in somewhat identical words. There was an old fellow at Albany, a Tammany man who never liked Roosevelt, who said he had a feeling like that when F.D.R. first arrived as a young fellow to take his seat in the State Senate. "I can remember him," said the old fellow, "when he strode down the aisle to take the oath. He was handsome as a Greek god, and I said, 'There's a bird who will have to be watched.' "

Throughout the preconvention campaign, Roosevelt gave me a pretty free rein and allowed me the widest latitude in determining how the job of corraling votes should be carried on, but I always tossed individual problems right back in his lap because of a genuine regard for his mature judgment on political matters.

If the two men just described were noteworthy for their forceful personalities, Louie Howe was not. He was just about the opposite in every respect. When we first became acquainted, Howe seemed about the oddest little duck I had ever known and for some time he had me completely puzzled. I like to meet people and to be friendly with them, but Louie made no effort to be friendly and quite often didn't even bother to be polite. He acted just as he pleased. However, we were drawn together by our mutual interest in the political future of the Governor.

At the time that we began our association in the preconvention campaign, Louie Howe was approaching sixty years of age. He was about five feet and five inches tall; he weighed in the neighborhood of one hundred and five pounds; his face was pallid and furrowed; and he was in such frail health that he was constantly faced with the problem of how to conserve his small stock of physical energy. It would be hard to imagine a man who cared less about his looks. He wore white, stiff collars, several sizes too large; he smoked cigarettes constantly and let the ashes fall all over him; his hair was often uncombed; and his clothes were rumpled. His trousers generally had about the same crease as an old burlap bag.

Nevertheless, what Louie lacked in personal appearance, he more than made up in other ways. I have heard numerous individuals claim the distinction, but there is little doubt that he was entitled to be known as the original "Roosevelt-for-President Man." As far back as 1910, when he was covering the Albany legislature as a political reporter, Howe had been tremendously attracted by the youthful Senator Roosevelt and decided that a brilliant career in public affairs lay ahead of him. He decided that they should make a common cause together. Before long Howe was working for Roosevelt as his secretary and assistant, and the association continued unbroken from that time on. They spent the years in Washington working together, and when in the prime of life "Franklin" was stricken by the dreadful infantile paralysis, "Louie" was by his side doing what he could to help, and constantly trying to keep alive the ambition for a career in public office. He lived in the Roosevelt homestead and was accepted almost as a member of the family.

The re-entry into public life in 1928 of his political hero was a great moment of triumph for Louie Howe, and this triumph became all the sweeter when the turn of the political wheel seemed destined to make Governor Roosevelt a logical candidate for the Presidency. Howe thought of nothing else during his waking hours. He was a man of intense loyalty and devotion, rebuffs never discouraged him, and he was grim as a little bulldog in hanging onto what he wanted.

He looked over all visitors with a coldly critical eye, wondering where they would fit into the great scheme he had in mind. I actually recall one or two occasions in which he said in substance to such visitors: "You make a good appearance and you seem to know something about politics and to have some influence. I think you can be useful to Franklin." That was all he cared about, and he had no other test for any man. I recall one visitor who came away angry and swearing because Louie looked him over, evidently wasn't impressed, and so didn't even bother to be civil. Howe realized that other people could do the glad-handing while he stayed behind the scenes and helped pull the strings.

When Louie and I and a small group of fellow conspirators settled down to the task of capturing the presidential nomination for Governor Roosevelt, we were entering on a task of staggering proportions and one that might well end in nothing but disappointment and heartbreak for all concerned. It had happened to other and more experienced men before. We were starting the job a year and a half before the nominating convention got under way, but as it turned out finally, even that early beginning was none too soon.

There is no game in the world as uncertain as politics because success depends not only upon the ability of the person engaged in it but upon the good will of thousands of well-wishers and in the last analysis upon the attitude taken by the general public. The job of judging how the public will react is almost incredibly difficult. There is no sure road to success, and there are no hard and fast rules. Every development in a political campaign must be weighed in the light of circumstances at the time it arises. What could have been done six months ago might be fatal now. It is easy to offend the public by being too cocky, by being too upstage, by talking too much, by talking too little, by failing to grasp how popular sentiment is shifting. And, of course, grand opera never has had and never will have as many prima donnas as politics. Many a promising career has been ruined because some aspirant for office forgot himself momentarily and wounded the feelings of a party patriarch.

This bit of homely philosophy is indulged in merely to illustrate the basic problem which confronted the few men who had assumed the task of conducting the Roosevelt presidential candidacy. Looking back now, the right course seems fairly easy. But it was not so apparent at the time. Two main courses, directly opposed to each other, were possible. We could sit back and conduct what might be called a passive campaign—that is, limit ourselves to making friendly contacts and the issuance of press statements extolling the Roosevelt qualities. That would avoid the risk of antagonizing "favorite-son" candidates until the time was ripe for the big push. Or we could turn on the pressure immediately, openly disclose our objective, and set about the job of rounding up enough delegates to make nomination a certainty. We chose the latter course although its hazards were self-evident. It was certain to make F.D. the outstanding candidate, and history showed plainly that the outstanding candidate very often fell by the wayside when the opposition "ganged up" to block his nomination. That danger was particularly great in a Democratic convention because of the rule requiring a two-thirds vote to nominate. There was the fact also that a candidacy started too early was apt to suffer a hurried and painful death because of public apathy. That is known as the "morning-glory" type of candidacy, and most aspirants shun it as they would the plague. We decided to go after the votes.

Having committed Governor Roosevelt's forces to an aggressive campaign, our next job was to consider practical methods and means of securing delegates throughout the forty-eight states and in those territories which are authorized to have representation in the national convention. The amount of work involved in such a program is stupendous. But national politics is big business, and we set about the task of mastering every detail that would have a bearing on the nomination of a presidential candidate. In the end this mastery of detail was a primary cause in bringing about the nomination of our candidate at Chicago.

A New Political Combination

Sometime after the election of 1930, Governor Roosevelt left on his annual visit to Warm Springs, Georgia. This tiny health resort had been the scene of his successful fight to overcome the ravages of infantile paralysis, and after that time he always made it a habit to spend Thanksgiving Day there, if possible. We had worked together in complete harmony during the gubernatorial fight and together had undertaken a number of innovations in campaigning which, while small, had been highly successful. The combination had been pleasing to him because from Warm Springs F.D. wrote me a letter which is still one of my prized possessions. In it, he said:

"This is the first chance I have had to sit down for a few minutes and write you connectedly about the campaign. You have done a wonderful piece of work, and I don't need to tell you how very appreciative and grateful I am.

"As I went through the State I got expressions everywhere showing that no man since the days of David B. Hill has such hearty backing and enthusiastic co-operation from the organizations as you have.

"It is not merely a fine record, but a great opportunity for us to consolidate the gains. The enclosed letters are fine, but they do not tell half the story, and everywhere our people are looking for just what we propose to give them—information, encouragement and practical help throughout the year and not just the two or three weeks before Election.

"When I think of the difficulties of former State Chairmen with former Governors and vice versa (!), I have an idea that you and I make a combination which has not existed since Cleveland and Lamont—and that is so long ago that neither you nor I know anything about it except from history books."

Not long after the gubernatorial election, in my capacity as New York State chairman, I had sent out a small booklet to active Democratic workers throughout the country, principally to state chairmen, vice-chairmen, national committeemen, and others holding positions of importance. This manual contained merely a roster of the New York State Committee and a few other routine facts concerning organization. It actually contained nothing of vital significance. Many persons were curious at the time and since then as to why this booklet was given nationwide distribution. Amusing as it may seem, this was actually the opening "feeler" of the Roosevelt campaign even though it said nothing about politics or candidates. With an eye to the future, Louie and I wanted to start a correspondence with the key men and women of the Democratic Party in other states. There had to be a beginning, and obviously we had to avoid anything that might seem controversial. This tiny booklet brought the desired results. Courteous replies came in from every section of the country, and in many instances, an acquaintanceship began that was of immense importance in the months to come. In fact, many of those replying voluntarily expressed their admiration for Governor Roosevelt and suggested that he would make a splendid standard-bearer for the party in 1932. Copies of these letters were sent to the Governor without comment. You may be sure the originals were carefully filed away.

The success of this sally suggested another similar venture. We had a tabulation made showing the vote-getting ability of Governor Roosevelt in upstate counties where the population was mostly rural. This tabulation showed the vote cast for the other Democratic gubernatorial candidates as far back as 1916 when Judge Samuel Seabury was a candidate. This was likewise sent broadcast to party leaders throughout the country and in addition to Democratic Senators and Representatives and to all those who had written in expressing interest in the Roosevelt movement. Nothing was said in the pamphlet to amplify the story told by the figures themselves—yet, just the same, I have always felt that the tabulation was eminently successful. To men and women skilled in the ways of practical politics, it disclosed in graphic fashion that the Chief Executive of New York State was a vote-getter in both the urban and rural areas, and candidates of that kind are always in demand. Many times after that, people mentioned that tabulation and told how they had been influenced by it. An interesting sidelight is the Governor's comment made on election night in campaign headquarters after he had made a short address to the party workers thanking them for their efforts; he expressed the belief to me privately that never again would the huge gubernatorial plurality of 1930 be duplicated. He felt that the element of luck had been a large factor in piling up the impressive totals. As a matter of fact, these figures were later eclipsed by his successor, Governor Herbert H. Lehman, and by himself as a candidate for President.

Throughout the fall and spring, we were busy as beavers compiling useful and necessary information concerning the list of state primary and convention dates for 1932, the number of delegates each state was entitled to, and the probable opposition to be faced, and above all, contacting men and women who were in a position to help direct the Roosevelt campaign in their home states. Gradually we were building up a potent organization, national in character. Most of those who enlisted did so voluntarily without being requested by us. The Governor had a host of friends around the country who had known him when he was Assistant Secretary of the Navy in the Wilson administration. They were personal admirers anxious to help, and most of them were political figures in their own right. While this work was done quietly, it was done thoroughly. And our contacts convinced us that we were first in the field and hence off to an early start over the other contestants.

Political organization work costs money, of course, no matter how frugally the funds are expended. While the actual working force was relatively small, we had a great deal of incidental expense because of the huge correspondence carried on and the constant use of the long-distance telephone in building up our field force. I think the letter-writing campaign waged by the Roosevelt preconvention campaign committee eclipsed anything of its kind ever known before or since in American politics. We went on the theory, gained from hard experience in New York State, that people love the personal touch; they delight in believing there is a close link between them and the folk who run the show and, above all, they want the knowledge that their efforts are being appreciated by the "higher-ups" in the organization. That desire for recognition is very human, and we attempted in every way possible to be obliging. In addition to that, we answered all letters from people who wanted to make campaign suggestions, no matter how silly or useless the suggestions were, because every person in the world thinks he knows more about politics than the next fellow. The telephone also was a great aid in helping us build up good will with party leaders, especially with men and women in small and distant states who were usually overlooked. I constantly sent in lists of names to Louie Howe, and he in turn had Governor Roosevelt call those people personally. It pleased their pride, and later many of those folk were among our last-ditch supporters when the balloting got under way.

We also had a few Roosevelt "scouts," or observers, who roamed about the Rocky Mountain states and the Southwestern states looking out for our interests and, while they were not on a salary basis, we paid their expenses. One of these was Lester Dillingham of Idaho, who died shortly after the campaign ended. As it was intended to enter Governor Roosevelt in primary contests throughout the country to demonstrate his popular appeal, other and heavier expenses were bound to pile up.

The first contributions which formed the nucleus of a campaign fund were contributed in March, 1931, by the following: Frank C. Walker, New York attorney, $5,000; Henry Morgenthau, Senior, former Ambassador to Turkey, $5,000; William H. Woodin, industrialist, $5,000; William A. Julian, Ohio businessman and Democratic leader, $1,000.

Other men, who should be included among the real financial fathers of the Roosevelt campaign because of their liberal contributions, were Edward J. Flynn, Democratic leader of the Bronx in New York City; Jesse I. Straus, New York merchant; Herbert H. Lehman, Lieutenant Governor of the State; Joseph P. Kennedy, financier and businessman; and Robert W. Bingham, Louisville publisher and later Ambassador to Great Britain.

The success experienced in keeping our high-powered campaign in operation was due in large measure to the fact that the committee treasurer, Frank C. Walker, was able to scrape up the cash just when it was needed most. We were operating on a hand-to-mouth basis, and on more than one occasion it actually happened that we didn't have enough money in the till to buy postage stamps from Uncle Sam or to pay off our extremely capable staff of clerks and stenographers. On those critical occasions, Frank Walker put aside his own business, put on his hat, and started on a round of visits to men of means who might be persuaded to put up some money for the presidential candidacy of his good friend, F.D.R. He always came back with enough funds to keep the show going. One of the men closely associated with Walker in the thankless task of fund-gathering was Eddie Dowling, noted actor and theatrical producer, who devoted practically his entire time to the campaign, in addition to contributing financially. Eddie also set up a stage and screen division of Roosevelt boosters which was most effective.

Two other men who rendered invaluable assistance because they were always willing not only to give financial help but to solicit contributions from others, were Henry Morgenthau, Senior, and the Honorable James W. Gerard. The latter is the same gentleman who had been opposed for the Democratic senatorial nomination many years earlier by the youthful F. D. Roosevelt. Gerard had come to have a great liking for his old rival, however, and being generous with his purse as well as in his feelings, he came to the rescue whenever we sent a call for help in his direction. I hate to think what might have happened if the men just mentioned had not been around to pull us over the financial dry spots.

By the spring of 1931, we had our organization, the headquarters for which had been set up at 331 Madison Avenue, New York City, functioning in a highly efficient manner, and the outlook was most encouraging. Louie Howe was in charge at headquarters, and I was there with him, neglecting my private business for the more fascinating work of campaigning. About this time, the Hoover administration was being overwhelmed with troubles, and more and more it began to look as though 1932 might be a good year for the Democrats. Other outstanding Democrats were beginning to cast longing eyes at the White House, and a few preliminary skirmishes disclosed that the nomination was certainly not going to the Governor of New York State by default. A challenge was coming our way.

The first indication of how battle lines were forming was furnished at a meeting of the Democratic National Committee which took place early in March, 1931, at the call of Chairman John J. Raskob. Prior to the actual meeting, Raskob set political tongues awagging by sending out a letter in which he revealed his intention to have the committee adopt a resolution recommending repeal of the Eighteenth Amendment as a plank in the 1932 party platform.

This proposal seemed innocent enough on its face, but beneath it was buried sufficient dynamite to provoke another of those interminable rows which had brought about the self-destruction of Democratic Party hopes on prior occasions. Everyone knew that sentiment against the dry regime was rising fast and that suitable action would have to be taken by the party in 1932. But the issue had nearly wrecked the party in the campaign of 1928 when Governor Alfred E. Smith was the party standard-bearer, and the factional wounds of that bitter conflict were barely healed. It was far too early to inject such a controversial matter into proceedings when the outstanding need was for harmony—particularly as we knew the move was cleverly designed to embarrass the Roosevelt cause in the Southern states, where it was generally believed that the New York Governor was wet but not as "dripping wet" as Al Smith and some of the other candidates.

Away down deep was the common knowledge that a titanic struggle was going to take place over the presidential nomination and that without publicly saying so, Chairman Raskob and his allies intended to use the all-important machinery of the national committee to stop Roosevelt if they could. It was a menace that could easily wreck everything we had in mind, and the shock troops hurried into action immediately.

The Raskob letter went out generally, and a copy was sent to Governor Roosevelt. He immediately dropped a note to Mr. Raskob asking the latter to communicate with him before anything further was done on the proposal. Raskob agreed in a courteous reply, but stories in the press indicated that he was determined to press the resolution. We decided to take action.

A meeting of the Democratic State Committee was summoned to meet at Albany where a resolution was adopted setting forth the fact that the national committee had no authority to pledge or advise the party on controversial political questions. The wording of this resolution had been agreed upon in general terms at a bedroom conference in the Executive Mansion that morning attended by the Governor, Louie Howe, Edward J. Flynn, and myself. Later in the White House, F.D. made these "bedroom" conferences quite famous.

Armed with the resolution adopted by the state committee, I hurried down to Washington and registered at a little-known hotel near the Capitol the day before the national committee was to meet. I had a two-fold purpose—to dodge the press and to talk over with friendly party leaders the best line of policy to pursue on the Raskob resolution. Among those who conferred with me were Senator Cordell Hull of Tennessee, Governor Harry Flood Byrd of Virginia, and a number of national committee members. I found Southern Senators and Representatives already deeply disturbed over the expected injection of the wet issue and determined to fight with all their power. They felt that if the Prohibition question was permitted to take precedence over the economic situation, the party was bound to suffer.

In the meantime, we started telephoning members of the national committee, both men and women, all over the country, telling them of the seriousness of the Raskob threat and asking them to hurry on to Washington to fight the proposal. It was the initial test of the nationwide organization which we had been rapidly assembling, and it stood the ordeal in magnificent fashion. I made a count of noses before the meeting got under way; it disclosed the fact that we could defeat the Raskob proposal by at least two to one, if it came to an actual showdown. We also had a number of speakers primed and ready to enter the lists.

During these early days of the fight, Governor Byrd of Virginia participated in most of the strategy meetings called by the Roosevelt side and he was looked upon as an inner member of the council. Byrd and his brother, Admiral Richard E. Byrd, the noted explorer, were personal friends of Roosevelt. Later, however, the Virginia Governor drifted over to the other side as it became apparent that a deadlock might take place at the convention, thus giving someone else a chance to get the nomination. There was little doubt that he was tempted by the hope that the nomination would come his way.

The subsequent meeting of the national committee almost made history. Mr. Raskob tossed in his wet bomb, touching off an explosion of oratory that reminded the listeners of the famous Madison Square Garden Convention of seven years before. The opponents of the resolution were led by Senator Joseph T. Robinson, Senate Democratic leader, who delivered a sizzling attack on Raskob in which he accused the chairman of attempting to steam-roller the party. Although not a member of the committee, Governor Smith was present and was given unanimous consent to speak on behalf of the Raskob proposal. Senator Cameron Morrison of North Carolina delivered an impassioned plea for national Prohibition, during the course of which he was heckled by outraged wets—and the heckling was none too courteous. The net result was a victory for us. Chairman Raskob sensed that enough votes were ready to reject his proposal, so a showdown was postponed. But in the meantime, the oratorical thunder produced screaming headlines all over the country, and the Republicans chuckled to themselves. They felt certain that the Democratic Party was headed for suicide once again.

The Smith-Roosevelt Feud

A little cloud "no bigger than a man's hand" hovered over that committee meeting in Washington, and the effect of it was not lost upon keen political observers. It was to foreshadow one of the most extraordinary estrangements in political history—an estrangement that has been of primary importance in subsequent party history. It was really the first time "Al" Smith and "Frank" Roosevelt had been arrayed on opposite sides of the same question. True enough, both of them were for repeal of the Eighteenth Amendment. Smith's position was known to everyone, and Governor Roosevelt, on at least two occasions before that meeting, had declared himself for repeal. But they fell out over the Raskob resolution because each one was a master politician and each one realized that the whole thing was just so much maneuvering for advantage in the 1932 presidential race. Nothing was said by either party, but the realization was there.

Perhaps it might be well to digress for a moment to discuss one of the most talked-of "incidents" of recent times, the so-called Smith-Roosevelt "break." Their close alliance had become one of the traditions of Democratic Party annals. Everyone recalled the dramatic occasion when Franklin D. Roosevelt, a command-ing figure of a man despite his crutches, had appeared on the platform in the Madison Square Garden Convention to nomi-nate for the Presidency, his pal, Al Smith, the boy who rose to greatness from the "Sidewalks of New York." His reference to Smith as the "Happy Warrior" had become a household phrase.

I also did my bit for Smith at the Madison Square Garden meeting, although in a far more humble role. It was my job to lug the New York State banner around and around the huge Garden during the two-hour demonstration for the Empire State's "favorite son" which took place at the end of the nominating speech. And during the rest of the time, I occupied myself car-rying messages and acting as general handy-man for F.D.R. and the other "bigwigs" who were directing the strategy in the camp of our candidate.

Again in 1928, still supported on crutches, Frank Roosevelt had nominated Smith at the Houston Convention of the party, and on that occasion he was happy to see his fond wish come true. Smith was made the standard-bearer of the Democrats, and in the campaign that followed no one worked harder for his elec-tion than his faithful friend, F.D.R.

In the light of those earlier circumstances, a myth grew up during the 1932 campaign that something very bitter and per-sonal had happened to bring about the coldness that marked their conduct during the preconvention campaign of 1932. It would be idle to deny that a few differences did crop up during the time when Roosevelt was Governor and Smith was on the sidelines as one of his advisers, especially over the fact that several of the men and women who had been closely associated with the Happy Warrior in Albany were not retained in the new ad-ministration. But those things always happen, and both men had been too long in politics to attach more than passing significance to minor disagreements of that nature.

There was no "break" between Smith and Roosevelt in the sense that one single incident was the cause of their seeking sepa-rate political paths after so many years of intimate association. On the contrary, it was a case of two extremely able and popular public men, each of whom cherished an understandable ambition to be President of the United States. This view is confirmed by the fact that on at least two and perhaps three times during the preconvention campaign the two men engaged in personal conference. Almost to the last, I felt, and so did many others, that a head-on collision would be avoided.

Naturally my sympathies were on the side of Governor Roosevelt in that estrangement and they still are. During the time when Al Smith was active in state and national politics, I always supported him to the limit of my ability and never for a moment entertained the thought that his place in the party should be disputed by anyone else. His crushing defeat for the Presidency hit me with the force of a personal blow because I felt he was far too fine and able a public servant to be humiliated in that manner. But after that disastrous campaign, when he announced that he was through forever with politics, I took him at his word. So did Governor Roosevelt and everyone else who had been closely associated with him, and this belief was strengthened by his absence from the usual party councils. Even now, I am convinced that Governor Smith was thoroughly sincere in announcing his retirement. He changed his mind later when it became evident that things were faring badly for the Hoover administration and that the Democratic candidate in 1932 would probably be elected.

In any event, Smith failed to disclose his real desire and purpose until well along in the spring of 1932, and by that time the Roosevelt candidacy had advanced to such an extent that no reasonable man could expect the New York Governor to retire from the race. He was entitled to his fair chance at the Presidency, and even had he desired to do so, his backers never would have consented to his withdrawal.

While the Smith-Roosevelt feud was highly regrettable, its occurrence was not wholly unexpected by those who had been associated with them in New York politics. For some reason, known only to himself, Smith always had a tendency to underrate the ability of his successor, even when they were working side by side in the smoke and fire of political battle. Roosevelt's genuine confidence in the Happy Warrior was not returned, and they were never as close as the public imagined. In the salty language which

he used in private conversation, Al had been known to refer to
F.D. as a visionary and to speak lightly in other ways regarding
the latter's knowledge of public questions. On the other hand,
I can honestly say that even though he was deeply hurt at the
misunderstanding that arose between them, I have never to this
day heard F. D. Roosevelt utter a single unkind or uncharitable
remark about his former colleague.

Roosevelt was not the first choice of Governor Smith for the
gubernatorial nomination in 1928. The Democratic convention
that year was held at Rochester, and I was present when the state
leaders got together in two lengthy meetings for the purpose
of naming a state ticket that would be helpful to the Happy
Warrior's presidential campaign. Smith himself was present on
both occasions and during the discussion of available candidates
he gave me the distinct impression that his preference was for
either Townsend Scudder, a Justice of the State Supreme Court,
or Herbert H. Lehman, a banker who had been very liberal in
his contributions to the party. Several other names were proposed
by the leaders present, and there was considerable disagreement as to which man would make the most likely candidate.
Throughout both meetings my choice had never wavered. Finally
I made a formal motion to the effect that Franklin D. Roosevelt
was the choice of the Democratic leaders for the gubernatorial
nomination and proposed that Governor Smith telephone him personally at Warm Springs, Ga., and plead with him to make the
race for the good of the party. That resolution was unanimously
carried, and in keeping with its provisions, the Happy Warrior
shortly after got in touch with F.D. by long-distance telephone
and asked him to make the sacrifice.

I suggested drafting Roosevelt at that meeting of Democratic
leaders even though a few hours previously Mrs. Roosevelt, who
was anxiously concerned about the state of her husband's health,
pleaded with me and others who were friendly to his candidacy,
not to propose his name because it would take him away from
Warm Springs. As a good Democrat, Mrs. Roosevelt was in
Rochester attending the state convention but she left by afternoon train before learning of the action we had taken. F.D.R.

himself really wanted to spend another year at Warm Springs but he yielded to Smith's importunities because he wanted to help carry the Empire State for the Democratic ticket, both state and national.

It was a fateful day in the history of the party and the country, although no one realized it then, when the leaders succeeded in drafting F. D. Roosevelt for the first place on the state ticket. Had Scudder, or Lehman, or some other man been nominated and elected to the Governor's chair, the chances are about a thousand to one that Roosevelt would not have been the presidential nominee in 1932. In that event, of course, the history of the New Deal might never have been written.

Perhaps it was only fitting that Roosevelt's re-entry into active public life should come about as a gesture of friendship for someone else. Because, in my judgment, Al Smith never properly appreciated the wonderful loyalty and support which had been given him by F.D.R. throughout the decade from 1918 to 1928. For Roosevelt could have been lukewarm, like a great many others, or he could have contented himself by merely announcing his support of Smith and then leaving the work for others. But he never shirked and he did not give divided loyalty. The mere fact that he had placed his stamp of approval on a member of Tammany Hall had a tremendous effect in producing good will for the Happy Warrior around the country. As a Catholic I had felt a thrill of pride when Roosevelt lashed out with wholesome indignation against the religious intolerance which was being employed to defeat the Smith candidacy. Apparently Governor Smith never saw the situation in the same light. But, however Smith felt, there is positively nothing in the record that could be construed, then or now, as an act of disloyalty on the part of Franklin Roosevelt towards Al Smith.

Selling Roosevelt to the Party

To get back to our story of the preconvention campaign, the summer of 1931 saw a number of "dark-horse" candidates and "favorite-son" candidates for the Democratic presidential nomination springing into the limelight. It was plainly apparent that competition was getting keener. Observing what was taking place,

Louie and I decided it was time to take a few observations to see how the political winds were really blowing.

For many years I had been active in the Benevolent and Protective Order of Elks, holding office in the order occasionally and generally attending the Grand Lodge Conventions wherever they were held. I usually devoted my summer vacations to that purpose, and as a result had been in attendance at Elks Conventions from Maine to California. The meeting in 1931 was scheduled for Seattle, Washington, early in July, and I had made plans many months in advance to be there, solely with the thought of attending the convention and enjoying a bit of scenery en route. But Louie had other thoughts. He saw an opportunity to mix a little politics with good comradeship. We talked it over, and at his suggestion the Governor's advice was sought. The Governor decided that we should get together about a week in advance to discuss what could be done.

Sunday morning I was up bright and early and on my way to the Roosevelt home at Hyde Park, seventy-five miles up the Hudson River from New York City. At his suggestion I was equipped with a Rand-McNally map of the United States, a flock of train schedules, and the latest available list of Democratic National Committee members and state chairmen. We ate lunch and then adjourned to his tiny office, off in a wing of the house, where we spread out the documents and went to work. Out of that huddle, which lasted more than two hours, came an intensive schedule that was to keep me busy almost every minute of the time from the moment I left New York City until I returned. The itinerary was decided upon in large measure by the Governor, who had a keen sense of selection in determining what states it was wise to visit and what states it was wise to shun.

Shortly after noon on Monday, June 29, I was off on a journey from coast to coast that was to enable me to cover eighteen states in nineteen days, a journey that was to consist mostly of "sleeper jumps" from state to state, while sandwiched in between were all kinds of meetings, conferences, confabs, and luncheon engagements with Democratic chieftains. I was a kind of roving political "listening post," whose purpose was to gather up every available scrap of information regarding conditions in the territory through which I passed. The weather on occasions was almost unbearably hot. The task of meeting people occupied practically every minute between train rides, and yet I managed to send back by special delivery either to Louis Howe or the Governor personally, a series of eighteen separate reports which gave a detailed description of individuals and conditions in as many states. The trip was not without merit.

Perhaps the role of "political drummer" had never before been attempted on such a wide scale, or in such a plain manner, and the experience gained on the Pacific Coast trip did more than anything else to give me a grip on national politics. I always look back upon it as a sort of graduation from the political minor league. My knowledge had come chiefly from the School of Hard Knocks and it was gratifying to know that most of the knowledge gained in that way was pretty useful. An ability to grasp the little human traits and homely qualities that people like had enabled me many years before to get a start by being elected Town Clerk of Stony Point, New York. Now the same qualities were helping me to sell a presidential candidate to the nation. If I got to a city and found as many as five hundred people waiting there to look me over, I shook hands with each one personally. I was extremely careful to get first and last names correctly and of course never disputed the views of others if it was at all possible to agree. It always creates a bad impression to start off with an argument. By carefully observing those simple and essential rules, I managed to strike up the kind of informal, easy-going friendships that make future understandings a great deal easier to arrive at.

After leaving New York, the first stop on the trip was at Indianapolis where I conferred, among others, with Earl Peters, the state chairman, who was an ardent Roosevelt booster and very anxious to have us capture the state delegation. The situation at the time seemed very favorable but my report was too optimistic because at a later date trouble developed in the Indiana delegation that had a large bearing on the presidential situation. The next stop after Indianapolis was Chicago. A description of each visit would be wearisome, but a few incidents happened on that trip that were significant in revealing how the political winds were blowing. Of course the main purpose of the trip was to "sell" the availability of F.D.R. as the party nominee for President; but most of the folks along the route had never seen me before, and too ardent salesmanship on my part might have created an unfavorable impression. In addition to that, politics is a complex game, and very often there are combinations taking place beneath the surface that are not visible to the naked eye. One false step might be disastrous. Since I was more or less a newcomer in national politics, it was well to be wary.

I never talked to individuals about the presidential nomination unless I was certain of the other fellow's position. Usually, I sparred around a bit by suggesting that we had three outstanding potential candidates for the Presidency in New York State —Alfred E. Smith, Owen D. Young, and Franklin D. Roosevelt—and that it was my purpose to discover what the public thought of them as possible standard-bearers. This was the line I was using on William W. (Bill) Howes, the national committeeman of South Dakota, as we sat in a lunchroom at Aberdeen on a roasting hot day. Bill was a canny politician who had been in the game for years, usually working hard for the Democratic ticket only to see it go down under a Republican landslide on election day. He knew the game backwards and forwards. We sat there for some time exchanging generalities, without disclosing what either of us really had in mind. Just before it was time to go, Bill decided to let me know what he really thought. He plumped his fat fist on the table and growled in a deep voice:

"Farley, I'm damned tired of backing losers. In my opinion, Roosevelt can sweep the country, and I'm going to support him."

Naturally, the information was pleasing. In fact, it was more than that; it showed conclusively that the Democrats of the nation were turning to the New York Governor because they felt he was the one man who was certain to win the Presidency if nominated. And the whole world loves a winner. I heard the same idea expressed over and over again on visits to other cities, but never as forcibly as it was expressed by Bill Howes in the South Dakota lunchroom.

The Fourth of July found me at a luncheon in Butte, Montana, given by such outstanding party workers as Senator Burton K.

Wheeler, James E. Murray, afterwards elected Senator, J. Bruce Kremer, the national committeeman, Thomas J. Walker, brother of Frank C. Walker, and Dr. T. J. B. Shanley. They were all such ardent Roosevelt backers that there was little for me to do except make arrangements to keep in close touch during the pre-convention period.

I went on to Seattle and the Elks Convention, but on the side I continued to make a little Democratic medicine wherever possible. Scott Bullitt, the national committeeman, was carrying on a vigorous campaign for the Roosevelt cause in the State of Washington, and during the Seattle visit we had an opportunity to go over in detail what should be done to ensure victory. Bullitt was an aggressive fellow with a quick mind and an engaging personality. Unfortunately, he passed away some months after our Seattle talk. While I never discussed the matter with F.D.R., I always felt that Scott had an excellent chance of being offered a place in the Roosevelt Cabinet.

Perhaps the best way to convey my impression of the political outlook is to quote from a lengthy report which I sent to Governor Roosevelt and to Louis Howe from Seattle under the date of July 6, 1931. This letter said in part: "Since I left New York I have visited Indiana, Wisconsin, Minnesota, North and South Dakota, Montana, and am now in Seattle. There is apparently an almost unanimous sentiment for you in every one of these states and the organization in every instance is for you wholeheartedly. Here and there, and not very frequently, is sentiment for Smith. To be frank with you, that comes mostly from ardent Catholic admirers and in some instances from strong wet advocates. On one or two occasions I have heard Baker's name mentioned but that is all.

"In my talks with the different leaders they indicated that there occasionally crops up a boost for Ritchie or Young and in nearly every instance it comes from the power group. They apparently are trying to get back of either one or the other in the hope that they may be able to tie up some votes for Young and Ritchie, to be used later on when they decide what candidate they are going to support to try to keep you from getting the nomination. In the states I have visited, it doesn't appear at the moment that they are going to get anywhere, but that is something we will have to watch very carefully. I will check on this situation in the states I am to visit after leaving Seattle. . . . I am satisfied that they are going to have considerable difficulty in obtaining delegates because the consensus of opinion among the leaders is that you are the one man who can win. The leaders are getting that from the Democrats and they are being told by the Republicans that the sentiment is so general that, to be frank with you, Governor, it is almost unbelievable. If I continue to find the same sentiment in the other states that I have found already, my statement upon reaching New York will be so enthusiastic that those who read it will think I am a fit candidate for an insane asylum. . . .

"I am satisfied, Governor, that the leaders want to be on the bandwagon. I have also discovered that there are a lot of Democratic candidates for Governor and state offices who believe there is a real chance of winning with you as the nominee, and they feel there is absolutely no hope if anyone else is named; so these potential candidates are your strongest boosters because they believe with you as the nominee, they can win. This group of men in every section will be very helpful in getting solid Roosevelt delegations."

Another report, sent to Governor Roosevelt five days later from San Francisco, disclosed one other phase of the work we were trying to do, namely, to head off the favorite-son candidacies which had proved so harmful in deadlocking previous national conventions. This letter said:

"In my travels throughout the states I have visited, I have done everything possible to further the desire on your part to have an early convention and to instruct for you.

"Have indicated that they must all get away from the 'favorite-son' idea, on the theory that it is only used for the purpose of tying up blocks of delegates to be manipulated.

"I have told the different people along the line that we do hope they will not in any case instruct for their Governors or United States Senators, in the hope that lightning might strike.

"It has been brought to my attention that the reason a number of these Senators and Governors want their names presented to the convention as presidential candidates is because they feel it is the only way that they can be considered for the Vice-Presidency, believing that if their names go before the convention in such a manner they might have some luck.

"Have tried to impress upon everyone I have met the importance of getting away from this.

"Governor, the presidential job must be a great one, judging from the way they are all anxious to have it."

Whenever it was necessary on the trip for me to talk at a luncheon or other public gathering, the name of Governor Roosevelt was always conspicuous by its absence. At Portland, Oregon, a dinner had been arranged by Carl Donaugh, the state chairman, and, quite unexpectedly, I was called upon to talk. Being somewhat at a loss for words, I delivered a short discourse on the organization methods employed by Tammany Hall!

The most amusing episode happened at Kansas City, Missouri. While I was on the Pacific Coast, Louie Howe had advised me by telephone and telegraph that it would be extremely unwise for me to visit Kansas City because of the fact that ex-Senator James A. Reed wanted the delegation pledged to him as a favorite son. I explained to Louie that friends of mine had already made arrangements, the proposed visit had been announced, and that to back out at the last minute might be misconstrued to our disadvantage. We argued over it but I was determined to go. Jim Aylward and Jerome Walsh were on hand to receive me at the station. They had arranged a luncheon in my honor for the next day, but were a bit upset over the fact that ex-Senator Reed had declined to attend. The gruff old warrior said that he never had and never would introduce a Tammany Hall Democrat to a Kansas City audience and that was that. He was going on a fishing trip.

Before the luncheon took place, friends of Senator Reed convinced him that it would show bad taste on his part if he failed to attend, and as a result of their pleadings, he changed his mind. Had the Senator really gone fishing, my mind would have been far more at ease. I was all too conscious that Jim Reed had one of the most caustic tongues ever known in the United States Senate and that few men were able to engage in verbal combat

with him and come out on the winning end. Certainly not myself
. . . but Reed was in a friendly mood. He gave me a most
gracious introduction, ribbed me a bit as a "Traveling Elk on
a tour," made only passing reference to politics, and tried in every
way possible to make me feel at home. Nevertheless, the "Traveling Elk" was still wary of the Missouri wildcat. When it came
my turn to speak the fright was beginning to wear off, but I took
no chances. Jim Reed never got as many oratorical bouquets
thrown his way as he did on that occasion. And once again, the
name of Roosevelt was carefully omitted. Before leaving, Reed
came to the hotel room to express his thanks and to wish me
luck.

The trip was very strenuous, and the end of it found me
back in New York City more in need of a vacation than when
it began. But the results were worth the effort. After one day's
rest, I hurried to Hyde Park to relate every single incident of
the trip in detail to the Governor and Louie Howe. Naturally
the report was optimistic. Beyond question, it showed that Democratic leaders in the Middle West and Far West were turning
to the New York executive because they felt he had the political
appeal which a candidate must have to be successful.

The long trip across the continent, although arduous and tiresome, was really invaluable because of the personal knowledge
it gave me of the individuals who controlled the party machinery.
Between leaving and returning to New York City, I shook hands
with thousands of men and women, and among them were over
1,100 individuals who held "key" positions in the party. That
is, they were state chairmen, county chairmen, and local leaders,
or occupied some other position that gave them authority. Many
of them were delegates at the Chicago Convention. I took careful note of each name and address, and later I sent each one of
the 1,100 a personal letter. I believe that with this excellent beginning, I have since come to know more political leaders throughout the forty-eight states than any man in the country.

The Western trip was particularly gratifying for another reason. It demonstrated that we had adopted the right strategy
in deciding to put the Governor out in front by means of an aggressive campaign. As a result of those tactics, he was not losing

friends. On the contrary, he was gaining friends and that, coupled with his natural appeal, put him far ahead of the other aspirants. From that time on, we continued to push the campaign and to speak of Roosevelt as a certain winner.

Colonel House and Other Leaders

Throughout the fall of 1931, we were busy perfecting the pre-convention organization and arranging to have Roosevelt's name on the ballot in the various state primaries which began early the following year. There was no doubt that, of all the prospective candidates, he alone had a national appeal, and we intended to demonstrate that fact.

The campaign was picking up strength constantly. The New York Governor was looked upon as the most progressive candidate in the field, and a number of Senators and Representatives who were well-known nationally had openly espoused his cause. In addition, several prominent Democrats who had been outstanding figures in the Wilson administration were anxious to be helpful. One of these was Colonel Edward M. House, who, although he never held office, had been known as perhaps the most intimate adviser of the war-time President.

We felt that Colonel House could be helpful in contacting the Wilson followers throughout the country. The Governor, Louis, and myself kept him advised of what was going on and frequently sought his counsel. On one occasion Governor Roosevelt called upon him at his home in Massachusetts at Manchester-by-the-Sea. I constantly sent him copies of letters passing between headquarters and party workers throughout the country.

For the most part, Colonel House was most helpful although at times he felt that he should have been consulted even more than he was. I have a memorandum in my possession in which he complained somewhat plaintively that Howe was trying to do too much for any one man and that he seemed unwilling to let other people know what was going on. He also suggested that a man should be kept in Washington to meet Southern and Western leaders who wanted to join the Roosevelt camp but who were liable to go away disappointed if they had no one to receive them sympathetically.

There was some merit in Colonel House's suggestion, but on the other hand, I understood Louie's position perfectly and was inclined to agree with him. The fact is that the main job of running a campaign must be done by a few individuals at most. If a large committee were formed—a thing which Colonel House favored—the result would have been too much talk and too little action. The best way is to call in individual helpers from time to time and have them work on specific jobs. Howe knew, also, that if secrets are passed around generally in politics, the information ceases to be a secret after the third person is informed and becomes public knowledge.

Late in the fall of 1931, I went to Washington for a lengthy conference with Senator Burton K. Wheeler of Montana, Senator Clarence C. Dill of Washington, and Senator Cordell Hull of Tennessee. They had announced their support of the Roosevelt candidacy at an early date, and continued to be most helpful throughout the entire preconvention period. Men who reach the United States Senate are usually very shrewd in the ways of politics, and their advice was most welcome. On this visit, Senators Wheeler and Dill thought it would be a good idea for Governor Roosevelt to stop off at Washington on his return from Warm Springs, Georgia, for a series of conferences with legislative leaders. Senator Hull thought that such a course would be extremely unwise, and after a long discussion, we decided against the proposed Washington visit by the Governor.

Knowing the purpose of my visit to Washington, political reporters representing newspapers in all parts of the country besieged me to ask about the progress of the campaign. I predicted that Governor Roosevelt would be nominated for the Presidency on the first ballot at the forthcoming Democratic convention. This prediction, made repeatedly by me during the months that followed, attracted nationwide attention and provoked more controversy than perhaps any other statement of the campaign. I was sincere in making the statement, but in the back of my mind there was the further thought of calling attention to the Governor as the outstanding candidate. So many verbal brickbats were hurled in my direction by angry opponents who disliked the "first ballot" talk that even some of the Roosevelt supporters became alarmed and suggested that this kind of confident prediction might be harmful and should therefore be soft-pedaled. But I declined. We had set our course and there was nothing to be gained by becoming fainthearted.

The Republican press became quite indignant over these "first ballot" predictions, complaining editorially that it was unjust to the other candidates in the Democratic fold. Of course, the wish was father to the thought. Even at that early date, it was evident that the G.O.P. leaders were counting upon another Democratic family row to enhance their chances. In an editorial entitled "Roosevelt's Farley," the New York *Herald Tribune* said that, while I had a faculty for making friends quickly, the old warhorses in the party would never let a political newcomer like myself select the party nominee without even consulting them. Being an uncompromisingly Republican paper, the *Herald Tribune* was beginning to dislike the formidable look of the Roosevelt candidacy.

Garner Enters the Lists

On one of these flying visits to Washington, where I went as often as possible in order to build up new acquaintances, I had a brief visit lasting about ten seconds with the individual who later held the key to everything we were trying to accomplish. There was no way of knowing it at the time, and the fleeting encounter perhaps would have been forgotten entirely except for the fact that there was something about the man that impressed itself on my memory. The gentleman was Speaker John Nance Garner of the House of Representatives.

I was standing on the Democratic side of the cloakroom in the rear of the House Chamber when a man came out, moving swiftly, and started down the stairway to the floor below. Congressman Joe Gavagan, of New York, who was talking to me, said, "Just a minute, Mr. Speaker; I want you to meet Jim Farley. You two men should know each other." Garner acknowledged the introduction in a polite but serious manner, responding, "How do you do, Mr. Farley. I hope things are going well with you." Then he stepped back and for a second or two very calmly looked me over from head to toe in about as frank an appraisal as I had ever experienced. It was apparent that he recognized the name and knew why I was there, and for a moment I was afraid that he was going to let go with a few explosive remarks about individuals who used the lobbies of Congress to promote presidential politics. He said nothing more, however, and continued on down the stairs.

With his ruddy face and piercing eyes, Garner had a sort of resemblance to Jim Reed of Missouri, although he was considerably shorter, talked in a higher voice, and moved more rapidly. His steady gaze and rather stern manner were a little too sharp for an easy-going fellow like me, and I felt as a result of this first encounter that he was hardly the kind of man with whom I could get acquainted on affable and friendly terms. It was a snap judgment and about as far wrong as any judgment could be. In the six or seven years since then, the turn of events has thrown us together in close personal and political association, and as a result of those meetings I have come to look upon him as one of the truly great public men of this generation.

Possessed of a sharp, penetrating mind, Garner has spent an entire lifetime studying government, and particularly the American system of democracy. Out of that study and of the wealth of experience acquired in nearly forty years of life in Congress, he has formed a definite and fixed code of beliefs on what he thinks are the functions and duties of government, and also on what he considers the proper kind of conduct for men in public life. House members told me afterwards that he never voluntarily mentioned his own candidacy for the presidential nomination during the preconvention period and that he never hinted that he would like support, even from the old-timers with whom he had served year after year.

In later conversations and conferences, I discovered that Garner seldom goes off on the kind of long-winded, dull, rambling discourses that some men indulge in and that spoil most conferences by setting everybody else on edge. He has the habit of waiting until the conversation lags and then expressing his view in quick, short sentences, throwing in a few homely figures of speech that appeal to people and are hard for those who disagree with him to answer. Garner is as stubborn as a Texan mustang in hanging on to his views and he never hesitates to speak up, even if everybody else at the meeting holds views exactly opposite to his own. In addition to the administration duties which bring us together frequently, I early formed a habit of calling him up on the telephone from time to time to ask his views on how things were going and to get his reaction on individual problems facing me. It has proved to be a very wise custom.

The year 1932 was at hand, and the various primaries and conventions held in the early months would tell the story. Either Governor Roosevelt had the nationwide strength we claimed, or his candidacy was due for an early demise. Having talked about popular support, we faced the time to prove its existence.

The list of opposing candidates, actual or potential, who were prepared to contest the issue with the Governor of New York State was as imposing an array of national figures as this country has seen in modern times. That may seem like an exaggeration—yet it is nevertheless true. They were strong men personally, powerful in their knowledge of politics, vigorous in their views, and fearless in advocating the policies and measures in which they believed. To defeat them, either singly or together, was a man-size task.

Early in the field was the distinguished-looking Albert C. Ritchie, the popular Governor of Maryland, who had become a national figure by his vigorous opposition to the Eighteenth Amendment—even when that position was not particularly popular. He had a host of friends around the country. Governor Harry Flood Byrd was certain to be the favorite-son candidate of Virginia, and Governor George White, the favorite-son candidate of Ohio. Ex-Senator James A. Reed was in a receptive mood and was assured of his home state of Missouri. Speaker John Nance Garner, of the House of Representatives, was entering the lists with the support of his own state of Texas, and the added backing of publisher William Randolph Hearst who was largely instrumental in entering the Garner name in other state primaries. Senator J. Hamilton Lewis was the favorite son of Illinois, and Governor William H. Murray of Oklahoma. The signs indicated that Alfred E. Smith, the titular party leader, was more and more inclined to enter the race, while, behind the scenes, a number of people were quietly seeking active support for Newton D. Baker,

Secretary of War in the Wilson Cabinet, and Owen D. Young, noted New York industrialist.

This was a formidable field, and the men sponsoring the Roosevelt candidacy never lost sight of that fact for a moment. There was not a trick in the trade which was unfamiliar to the skillful and crafty veterans who were directing the opposition. But we had one advantage—and it proved to be of compelling significance before the balloting was over. The other candidates in the field, notably Ritchie, Smith, Reed, Garner, and Murray, were strong individualists. Each one of them, quite naturally, wished to be the candidate of the Democratic Party for President of the United States. They were not primarily concerned with "stopping Roosevelt." While there were many reasons for their getting together, there were just as many reasons why too close an alliance might prove harmful. The fact was always uppermost during the subsequent meetings of the opposition in Chicago.

The Democratic National Committee held a meeting in Washington on January 8, 1932, to select a convention city and to make other arrangements for the forthcoming party conclave. This meeting saw a large delegation of Roosevelt lieutenants in attendance because another outburst over the wet and dry issue was feared. However, the matter was disposed of when the committee voted to refer Mr. Raskob's "Home Rule" liquor plan to the convention without recommendation. The post of committee secretary was vacant, and knowing the power wielded by officers of the committee, we supported Robert H. Jackson of New Hampshire for the post. Jackson was elected without opposition, and while his election was not a matter of outstanding importance, it indicated the strength of the Roosevelt forces and the thorough manner in which things were being done. Chicago was selected as the convention site.

While in Washington I had an opportunity to talk over campaign plans with leaders from all parts of the country. One of these was Homer Cummings of Connecticut. We discussed a proposal to form a large committee to handle the Governor's campaign. I pointed out that a committee of that kind might do more harm than good, because differences of opinion were certain to arise at committee meetings and because of the more important fact that a great many ardent supporters would be offended if their names were left off. It was agreed that the best course to pursue was to go ahead as then organized. In the months that followed Homer acted as liaison man between headquarters and Senators and Representatives in Washington who were friendly to the cause. This led to stories in the opposition press that he was to supplant me as chairman of the Roosevelt Committee but the Governor quickly spiked that report in a statement issued by Louie Howe.

The first public pronouncement of his candidacy for the Presidency was made by Governor Roosevelt on January 23, 1932, in a letter to F. W. McLean, Secretary of the Democratic State Committee of North Dakota. The state convention there had already endorsed his candidacy but in order to have a slate of delegates in the primary, it was necessary for the Governor himself, under the state law, to announce his candidacy in his own handwriting. Roosevelt used this letter to McLean as a vehicle to serve warning upon his opponents that he intended to wage his battle for the Presidency as a political progressive who believed that government must be made to serve the needs of the whole people.

That date of January 23 is important. On the same day, the Democratic Territorial Convention met at Fairbanks, Alaska, and drew up a resolution instructing the six delegates selected to vote for the nomination of Franklin D. Roosevelt. They were the first delegates actually pledged to his candidacy. This had been made possible as the result of the letters which had passed between our headquarters in New York and the influential party leaders in Alaska. The territories and possessions of the United States are given a total of thirty-eight votes in a Democratic National Convention, a bloc equal to the vote of a state like Michigan, and you may be certain that we did not neglect or overlook them in our drive for delegates. By getting on the job early, we were able to land over thirty of these thirty-eight convention votes.

The Happy Warrior Enters

The campaign was really getting hot; each day it became more apparent that the fortunate candidate who carried off the Democratic nomination would have an excellent chance to succeed the unhappy Mr. Hoover in the White House. There was still the great unsettled question—what did Al Smith intend to do? All through this period the Smith-Roosevelt relationship threaded its way in and out of practically every conference that was held to discuss campaign strategy. It was a puzzling situation, and even in the inner ranks of Roosevelt advisers there was a sharp conflict of opinion over the best method of meeting the problem. Frequently the suggestion was made, I think on one or two occasions by myself, that the Governor should request a conference with the Happy Warrior for the frank purpose of ascertaining the latter's position regarding the presidential nomination. But the suggestion was vetoed by the Governor himself who reasoned along the following lines. The situation was a delicate one; he appreciated the fact that as the party's nominee in 1928, Governor Smith had polled more than 15,000,000 votes and was still the titular leader of the Democratic Party. He had a right to express his own views in his own time, and the Governor felt that an effort to force the issue would be unfair. He expressed the view that the Happy Warrior would do the right thing at the right time.

In the meantime, Smith let it be known that he was feeling very much hurt over my own activities in behalf of the Roosevelt candidacy. Late in January, he had a long conference with Bob Jackson of New Hampshire, in which he complained bitterly that even though he had made me politically, I was busy promoting the Roosevelt candidacy without consulting him or deferring to his wishes. He took the attitude that my first loyalty was to him instead of to Roosevelt, and it was apparent that he wanted Jackson to convey that thought to me.

When Bob told me of the conversation, I felt disturbed even though it seemed to me that Smith's attitude was unreasonable. I immediately telephoned his office and suggested that we get together for a chat and thrash the whole thing out. The appointment was made, and we met on February 1, 1932, in his office at the Empire State Building.

At the outset, I told the ex-Governor that, whatever he might think, I was extremely grateful for the many courtesies he had extended me in politics. I pointed out that he always had my full support throughout the period when he was active in politics. But since I had become associated with Governor Roosevelt I was doing everything in my power to secure for him the presidential nomination and intended to keep on doing so. I added the sincere wish that this would not affect the personal friendship that had existed between us for years.

In his reply, the ex-Governor was extremely cordial. He indicated that he had no criticism to make of my activities, and we chatted for some time about political conditions in general. He asked, "Jimmy, what is New York going to do?" My reply was, "Governor, I don't know." Then we agreed to meet again and swap views before the slate of delegates-at-large was made up. At this time, Mr. Smith had made no public pronouncement, and I left his office, still not knowing whether he intended to become a candidate.

A few days later, early in February, the entire country knew the answer. Governor Smith made his famous pronouncement that while not actively seeking another nomination at the hands of his party, he would accept if it were offered to him. This meant that his enthusiastic supporters in Massachusetts and other states were at liberty to go ahead and enter his name in the primaries. The battle was on.

A day or so later, funeral services were held in New York City for John M. Voorhis, venerable sachem of Tammany Hall. Governor Roosevelt arrived early. Mr. Smith arrived shortly afterward, and they shook hands in friendly fashion. At the Governor's suggestion, they had a conference later that day at the Roosevelt home on Sixty-fifth Street. There was still no open break. The Governor told me later that Mr. Smith expressed the view that the Democrats of Massachusetts were very bitter over his defeat in 1928, and said that for that reason he had allowed them to enter his name in the primaries. There was no indication that they were to be used as a part of a "Stop Roosevelt" movement, and I got the impression that the Governor felt they might be found in his column eventually.

On the Political Merry-Go-Round

By this time, it was becoming more and more apparent that the race was one of Roosevelt against the field. While several candidates were seeking delegates, there was no one of them with sufficient support to conduct a national drive for delegates. Their efforts were confined to certain states where their backers considered them strong. Thus Governor Bill Murray of Oklahoma was to contest the issue in North Dakota, where it was felt his extreme views on agricultural and money problems would have an appeal. The Smith people were active in Massachusetts, New Jersey, Pennsylvania, and New York. The Garner forces were concentrating on Texas, California, and Georgia. These were scattered states but their combined vote was heavy and a coalition of opposing forces might prove dangerous.

March was a busy month, and an important one. A sharp undercover struggle was already under way for control of New York State's ninety-four votes, the largest single bloc in the convention. The delegation from the Empire State is so large that it is always important and is frequently decisive. We had hoped earlier to get a substantial plurality of the delegates, if not all of them. The upstate leaders were friendly for the most part. But the Tammany leaders were beginning to shy away, thinking mostly of their own local problems. In January, I suggested to John F. Curry, Tammany leader, that New York instruct for Roosevelt, but he refused.

I was on the political merry-go-round almost constantly during the spring months, dashing from state to state in the effort to get delegates committed to the Roosevelt candidacy. I swung up through New England, took another quick trip to Michigan, and in between times paid several visits to Washington. One Washington visit was highly significant because I had a long talk with Senator James H. Lewis, who was slated to be the favorite son of Illinois in the convention. Lewis was friendly to the New York Governor, and we were hoping that at an early moment in the convention Illinois' mighty bloc of fifty-eight delegates might be shifted over to our candidate. If that could be arranged, the nomination would be nearly "sewed up," regardless of what the opposition tried to do.

This shuttling back and forth over a long period of weeks left me somewhat exhausted and, when Louie Howe suggested during a talk at headquarters that I should attend the Iowa State Convention at Davenport on March 27, I rebelled. The leaders there had given us definite commitments of friendship, and the trip seemed to be unnecessary. The matter was allowed to drop, and I supposed it was forgotten when later in the day the telephone operator said Governor Roosevelt was trying to reach me from Albany. Right away I knew what was going on, and I was peeved enough to throw Louie out the window. He had simply called Albany, related the situation to the Governor, and then proposed that the Governor insist upon my going to Iowa. There was nothing to do but get out the traveling bag and start off once again. It was well that I did.

The Iowa delegation was not brought into camp without a struggle. Upon arriving at Davenport, I found that spokesmen for some of the rival delegates had been at work. A well-defined campaign was under way to block the instruction of delegates—the one thing we wanted most of all. It was my job to convince them that anything less than actual instruction for Roosevelt would be unwise. Meanwhile, Bob Jackson was in Maine watching the situation there and he was having plenty of trouble. The opposition was working hard to get the Pine Tree State, so much so that Governor Roosevelt was informed of what was going on and he advised Jackson by telephone against asking for an instructed delegation. He felt that it might antagonize some elements and that a friendly delegation was the best we could get. Later the same night Jackson telephoned me in Iowa and said that despite the Governor's instructions, he wanted to go ahead and try for an instructed delegation. I advised him to follow his own hunch. He did, and as a result succeeded in swinging the convention his way. According to prearranged instructions, Bob telephoned me the minute the Maine delegation was definitely pledged. Shortly afterward, I related this information in a speech to the Iowa Convention, and the Democrats in attendance seemed duly impressed.

We always looked back upon March 29 as a red-letter day for the Roosevelt candidacy, if not the turning point of the entire campaign. Iowa gave us twenty-six votes and Maine twelve. Those two states are far apart on the map—their people have little in common politically. When they took similar action on the same day, it demonstrated to us and to the country that Roosevelt had nationwide political appeal.

When the National Convention met at Chicago in June, the opposition made desperate efforts to break both the Iowa and the Maine delegations and they almost succeeded. Fortunately, their efforts were useless because of Louie Howe's hunch in sending me to Davenport and Bob Jackson's hunch in going after an instructed delegation in Maine. I'm glad the hunches didn't get mixed, or the outcome might have been very unlucky for us.

Because Louie remained at headquarters almost constantly while I was off on the circuit looking after the field forces, it was necessary for us to get together frequently to compare notes and to exchange views on how the campaign was going. We had complete confidence in one another, and in those conversations nothing was held back or left unsaid. The conversations usually took place in the Madison Avenue headquarters where Louie had a small office, well hidden from the general public, which was unlike anything I have ever seen around campaign headquarters either before or since. His desk usually looked as though the charwoman had used it to dump the accumulated waste papers of the night before. It was piled high with an untidy heap of old newspapers, pamphlets, press releases, and other printed material. Only Louie himself or his secretary knew which were valuable and which were worthless. He had a couch near the desk on which he was compelled to rest frequently because of his poor physical condition.

On returning from one of my frequent political excursions, I always told Louis every incident that had happened, described every individual encounter, and reviewed for his benefit every scrap of conversation that took place. My memory is pretty good, and frequently I went on for as much as fifteen or twenty minutes without interruption telling about visits with leaders whom we hoped to win over to the Roosevelt cause. Louie would sit in front of me in his favorite pose, his elbows resting on his knees, and his face cupped in his hands so that practically nothing was visible of his features except his eyes. He would wait patiently until I got through, turn the matter over in his mind for a moment or two, and then give me his opinion on the character and the motives of the people I was describing. In all my experience in public life, I have never met a man who had Howe's uncanny faculty for accurate judgment of individuals whom he knew only as they were described to him by others.

The primaries in the spring of 1932 taught us that the going might be a lot rougher than some of the Roosevelt advisers had anticipated. The Roosevelt delegates came off victorious in handy fashion in New Hampshire, Georgia, and one or two other states while the effective leadership of Joseph Guffey of Pittsburgh ensured us the lion's share of the huge Pennsylvania delegation, the second largest in the convention. But on the other hand we lost Massachusetts to Smith and California to Garner. When those two large delegations went over to the enemy, our dream of capturing the nomination without a real struggle at Chicago went up in smoke. Encouraged by the success of the "Stop Roosevelt" forces, Al Smith went to Washington for a Jefferson Day address in which he attacked the "Forgotten Man" talk of Governor Roosevelt delivered several weeks earlier.

Hull Presidential Timber

We continued to hold frequent meetings of the Roosevelt high command which was constantly expanding as more state leaders were drawn in. I recall one occasion early in May when Homer Cummings and myself had gone to Colonel House's New York apartment for a luncheon talk on campaign progress. After reviewing the situation and discussing what should be done, we started chatting generally about politics. Colonel House said that his idea of an ideal candidate for Vice-President was Senator Cordell Hull of Tennessee. I agreed with him. The Colonel said further that, although he could not conceive of Governor Roosevelt's being stopped, his next choice for President was also Mr. Hull. I agreed that no better choice could be made.

While always faithful to the Governor's cause, Colonel House had been somewhat disturbed when Roosevelt issued a statement early in 1932 coming out definitely against the League of Nations. He expressed the view that if Speaker Garner remained silent on that issue, the pro-League people, led by Newton D. Baker, would flock to his candidacy. But we had little to fear on that score in view of the fact that publisher Hearst, an unrelenting foe of the League, was sponsoring the Garner candidacy.

The fact that Colonel House looked upon Senator Hull as good timber for the Presidency may come as a surprise to a lot of people who knew nothing about the Tennessean until his later appointment as Secretary of State in the Roosevelt Cabinet. However, for a great many years Hull had been playing a quiet behind-the-scenes part in Democratic councils, and in that way the men associated with him had come to respect his views and to admire him personally. He had served in Congress for a number of years, first as Representative and then as Senator, and at one time he was Chairman of the Democratic National Committee.

While holding definite and well-considered views on public questions, Hull never really made himself known to the American people while in Congress because of a somewhat retiring disposition and an inclination to avoid anything that smacked of "limelight" tactics. He never adopted the course, followed by some of his colleagues, of sounding off on any current question just to see his name in print, or of issuing a statement merely because it was sensational and not because he thought it was true. He was one of the earliest members of the Senate to get aboard the Roosevelt band wagon, a position he took because of a liking for the economic views of the New York Governor, and immediately he went to work with a will to help bring about his nomination. I came to know him intimately as a result of my frequent trips to Washington during the preconvention period. He was devoted and untiring in his labors, and the advice he gave was nearly always correct. I conferred with him alone on many occasions, and he sat in on a number of general conferences. It has been my experience that when men sit up close around the table in political discussion, especially when stakes are high, a good glimpse of their real character is almost always possible. Ambition is pretty heady stuff, and it is frequently difficult for an individual to overlook his own personal interests for the sake of the cause he is serving. I don't intend that as a general criticism, or intimate that I am any different in that respect from other men. However, in a life devoted to politics, it is natural for a man to size up those with whom he is in constant contact, and with whom he must deal. I formed the opinion early that Cordell Hull was the most unselfish man I had ever met in politics, and nothing has happened since to cause me to change that opinion. Holding such an opinion, it was easy for me to agree with Colonel House that he was capable of filling any position of honor, including the Presidency, with distinction.

Fight for a Convention Chairman

When June arrived, the preliminary skirmishing was over, and the battle lines were sharply drawn. It was Roosevelt against allcomers with a sharp and perhaps unpleasant personal fight in prospect. By this time it was clearly evident that Governor Roosevelt was the overwhelming choice of the Democrats who resided beyond the Mississippi, while at the same time he had nearly all the South, the Border States, and a good part of the East. There was no section where his candidacy was "weak," something that could not be said about his opponents. As preconvention manager, I continued to claim that he would be nominated on the first ballot. I dropped around frequently to the Tammany leaders to urge them to get on the band wagon, but they were stubborn; so on June 11, I issued a statement that Governor Roosevelt could be nominated and elected even without New York State.

This prediction stirred up the wrath of the press, and the usually reserved New York *Times* suggested editorially that if Roosevelt was going to be stopped, Farley was the man to do it. The editorial writer gravely referred to me as an "architect of political disaster," which was the highest-sounding epithet I had had hurled my way up to that date.

In politics, it is well to take nothing for granted. The backers of Governor Roosevelt knew that there were two vitally important jobs remaining to be done, either one of which might spell the difference between victory and defeat. The first task, after having the delegates promised, was to "nail them fast" by having each friendly delegate definitely pledged to the cause; otherwise some of them might wish to stray off the reservation at Chicago. The other task was to control the machinery of the Chicago Convention in order to prevent a slip-up. A flare-up had occurred during the course of the spring preconvention campaigning which gave us ample warning that the opposition, acting as a unit, intended to put up a sharp fight to wrest control of the convention for themselves. To present that picture accurately, it is necessary to go back a little.

After the overwhelming Republican landslide of 1928, Chairman John J. Raskob of the Democratic National Committee had set resolutely about the task of repairing the party's political fences. To do the job, he brought in Jouett Shouse, of Kansas, to act as chairman of the Executive Committee, and Charles Michelson, well-known Washington newspaperman, to direct publicity. They had done their work well, and there was no disposition on our part to underrate Raskob's efforts in rebuilding the party or to find fault with the men associated with him.

But Raskob's entire training was in the field of Big Business and he distrusted any political move which he felt might even call into question the superior judgment of the financial and industrial giants with whom he had always been associated. He looked on a political organization as a form of personal property and thought he should be able to direct it in much the same way that he would a privately owned business corporation. It never occurred to him that the Democratic Party was a very human thing in which several millions of Americans had a vital interest. Holding such views, it was only natural that he should want to use the organization of the Democratic Party to help Al Smith, who brought him into politics, and the men allied with Smith. In addition to that he had already formed a deep distaste for the views of Governor Roosevelt who made no secret of his belief that a few curbs on unbridled financial speculation and bad industrial practices might be helpful.

Although a good organizer, Raskob really never attained a working knowledge of practical politics and he gave the job of manipulating the backstage strategy to Shouse, who saw eye-to-eye with him on the economic questions of the day. Shouse was

extremely clever at politics and he soon won the personal friendship of Democratic leaders all over the country who admired his
ability and resourcefulness.

A meeting of the Arrangements Committee which was empowered to make preliminary arrangements for the convention
was held on April 4 in Chicago, and although not a member, I
had gone out there in order to keep an eye on things and to help
put over the Roosevelt program. The Arrangements Committee
was empowered to elect a temporary chairman, or keynote speaker,
for the convention, and our choice was Senator Alben Barkley of
Kentucky. Arriving at Chicago we discovered that Mr. Shouse
had beaten us to it by carrying on a campaign to have himself
named keynoter, and, not realizing what was going on, many
members favorable to us had already promised to give him their
support. It was an awkward situation and little time remained to
do anything. When the committee met, Mr. Shouse announced
his candidacy and pressed for an early vote, but our leader managed to stall the vote off.

Hoping to effect a compromise, Governor Harry F. Byrd of
Virginia suggested during the recess a plan whereby the committee would recommend Barkley for keynoter and Shouse for
permanent chairman. The latter said it was all right with him
provided Governor Roosevelt personally would give his approval.
We went upstairs to the suite occupied by Bob Jackson and myself
and telephoned Albany. Jackson read the proposed compromise
resolution to the Governor who promptly pointed out that the
Arrangements Committee had no authority to recommend a
permanent chairman and never had done so in the party history.
He added, however, that if the Arrangements Committee wished
to reward Shouse for his efficient work, he had no objection to a
resolution recommending Barkley for "keynoter" and merely
"commending" Shouse for the position of permanent chairman.
In that way, the Governor explained that our forces were not bind-
ing themselves to any course of action when the convention actually met. This compromise, in the wording suggested by Roosevelt, was adopted and the incident was ended for the time being,
although later it was "blown up" into a major issue that caused a
lot of ugly feeling on both sides.

A short time later, the Roosevelt forces definitely decided to carry out their original intention to support another candidate besides Mr. Shouse for the all-important post of permanent chairman. This decision was arrived at for reasons that were most adequate. In the first place, Mr. Shouse was a paid employee of the national committee, and as such it was questionable whether he should be selected to preside over a meeting of delegates chosen by the people to select a presidential candidate. In the second place, the fact was beyond dispute that he was co-operating with Mr. Raskob in the latter's efforts to block the nomination of Governor Roosevelt. Several of our friends throughout the country had informed us of what Mr. Shouse was doing, and he had made speeches publicly urging Democrats to send uninstructed delegates to Chicago. In reply to one of these speeches, Governor Roosevelt had pointed out that the surest way to disenfranchise the American voters who wished to express a presidential preference was to have all the delegates go uninstructed.

The feeling in the Roosevelt camp was that Mr. Shouse had permitted his zeal in opposing the Governor's candidacy to bias his action as executive chairman of the committee. And if he allowed his feelings to influence him on one occasion, why not another? The post of permanent chairman is perhaps the most vital in a political convention because his parliamentary rulings may easily influence or determine the selection of the party nominees.

Everything is fair, or seems to be, in war or politics. The opposition later did everything in their power to impute bad faith to Governor Roosevelt in the Shouse matter. Hoping to make political capital out of it, they charged him with agreeing to the selection of Mr. Shouse as permanent chairman and then running out on the bargain. The wording of the resolution itself and the testimony of men and women who were there completely refute that charge.

The bald fact of the matter is that even if Governor Roosevelt had been maneuvered into approving the selection of Mr. Shouse, his friends never would have permitted such a deal to go through. Such a bargain would have been unfair to the candidate and unfair to the great majority of voters who were supporting his candidacy. Certainly, hard-bitten men like Reed, Smith, Ritchie, and Murray, who were using every available means to block Governor Roosevelt's candidacy, would not permit a known foe to preside over the convention if they could help it. Why should the Roosevelt forces do so?

We had decided upon Senator Thomas J. Walsh of Montana as our candidate for the delicate post of permanent chairman. He had won a place in history by his magnificent exposé of the Teapot Dome Scandal during the Harding regime and in the Madison Square Garden Convention in 1924 he had won the admiration of the country by his wise and impartial rulings as convention chairman. Under the date of May 23, Senator Walsh wrote me a letter never until now published. In that letter he modestly suggested that it might be good party strategy to nominate someone else rather than himself for permanent chairman but he added that under no circumstances should the selection of Mr. Shouse "be tolerated." That view was held by every other leader in the Roosevelt camp. I quote from the letter:

"As something has been said about my filling the place of permanent chairman of the convention, I thought I ought to write you, in view of the imminent probability that we shall be detained here, that you ought to have someone else in mind.

"In addition to the circumstances mentioned I have voted for a duty on oil and feel obliged to vote for the duty on copper and lumber. The fuss raised about Barkley's voting for a duty on coal may be renewed with emphasis should I be made permanent chairman, after voting as indicated. . . .

"Be good enough to write me about the matter and be assured I have not the slightest ambition to fill the place if you and the others in charge of the campaign think it unwise, under the circumstances, for me to be the choice. . . .

"P.S. In any case, for abundant reasons, I am sure the selection of Shouse should not be tolerated."

In line with our policy of leaving nothing to chance or circumstance, the Roosevelt forces held a Sunday meeting on June 5 at the Hyde Park home of the Governor to map out battle tactics for the Chicago Convention. As the Hyde Park home is somewhat off the beaten trail, it was possible to hold this meeting without the presence of newspapermen who were not informed that it was being held. Including the Governor, Louis Howe and myself, there were seventeen men at this meeting, and during the discussion a number of important decisions were made.

In the first place, it was definitely decided that we should back Senator Walsh for the permanent chairmanship. The Montana Senator, who was present, agreed to enter the contest, and I was authorized to make the announcement. The next order of business was to select a floor-manager for our forces. In earlier discussion, Louie had suggested J. Bruce Kremer or Daniel C. Roper of South Carolina, but I held out for Arthur Mullen of Nebraska. He was a keen student of politics, was an old hand at conventions, and was well liked by all factions in the party. I sponsored Mullen at this meeting and his name was agreed upon.

The choice of a man to nominate Governor Roosevelt was more difficult. Senator Robert F. Wagner of New York had been approached sometime earlier, but it was my impression that ex-Governor Smith had requested him not to do it. His position was difficult as he had been associated with both men intimately for many years, and had no wish to offend either. The next man tentatively agreed upon was Claude G. Bowers, author and newspaperman, who had electrified Democratic gatherings on previous occasions by his superb oratorical powers. Claude, however, was scheduled to attend the convention as a delegate from New York City, and the Tammany Hall leaders were putting pressure on him to stay with them on the balloting. Governor Roosevelt was interested in the availability of former Supreme Court Judge Thomas Dowd of Salamanca, New York, who was known as a fine public speaker. I suggested John Mack of Poughkeepsie who had nominated the Governor for his first public office twenty years before. He was the final choice.

Next came the question of whom we would support for the key post of chairman of the Resolutions Committee, the convention group that writes the party platform. We were determined to take no chances on that one. Senator Hull of Tennessee was decided on for chairman and, as a safety measure, it was decided that several other of our experienced leaders, including A. Mitchell Palmer, Attorney General in the Wilson Cabinet, and Joseph C. O'Mahoney of Wyoming, should serve on this committee. J. Bruce

Kremer of Montana was agreed on as our candidate for chairman of the Rules Committee. No action was taken on other committee chairmanships because we decided to leave them vacant for a purpose.

I was designated as the direct representative of Governor Roosevelt at the convention, and Senator Hull was made chairman of a special advisory committee. Governor Roosevelt revealed for the first time that in the event of his nomination, he intended to fly to Chicago in order to address the convention.

The schedule adopted at this Sunday meeting was in substance the program followed later in Chicago. One other subject was also discussed at that meeting which, before it was laid aside, developed into a major bone of contention between the opposing factions—the proposal to amend the two-thirds rule. The suggestion for abolishing the rule had cropped up from time to time during the preconvention period, and several state conventions urged its abandonment. The proposal had wide and respectable support. But in the meeting at Hyde Park, it was decided to hold the entire matter in abeyance until we reached Chicago. I think every man at the Hyde Park meeting felt that the time had come for the Democratic Party to get rid of the undemocratic two-thirds rule which had grown into a kind of monster, blocking the path of party success and causing bitter deadlocks that ended in disaster for everyone. Governor Roosevelt was about to enter the approaching convention with an undisputed majority of the party desiring his nomination. He had no close rival. The question was who was to control the party destiny, the majority or the minority. The decision to postpone action until we reached Chicago was not due to lack of conviction; it was simply a case of wanting to pursue the right course at the right time.

Governor Roosevelt's personal attitude on this matter is indicated by a letter which he wrote some months earlier to Justus S. Wardell, our California leader, who had written to inquire about his position. In his reply, dated December 22, 1931, the Governor said: "This is just a line to tell you how grateful I am for the fine way you are handling things. I hear from several people who have come here from California that our friend McAdoo is still hoping to get into the game in some way. I have a note from Dockweiler in which he says that he is doing everything possible. Keep me in touch with things because, as you know, I greatly value your judgment.

"By the way, about the two-thirds rule, my thought is that it is an anachronism anyway, and, as you know, particularly in our conventions. Nevertheless, I hesitate to have Jim Farley say anything about it because it might sound like a confession of weakness at this particular moment."

This letter shows that the two-thirds problem had arisen early and that the leaders wanted to do something about it. While he felt the rule should go, Governor Roosevelt was urging caution then and he continued to do so at the Hyde Park meeting and afterwards.

Putting on the Pressure

Convention time was drawing near, and Louie Howe was plugging away on arrangements for the Roosevelt headquarters which were to be located, along with others, in the Congress Hotel at Chicago. Louie was determined to make the layout the best of its kind ever devised and to my way of thinking he succeeded. Louie had a few characteristics that were invaluable in the rough and tumble of politics. For one thing, he was careful never to let confidential information get into the possession of people he did not know and trust. With that thought in mind, he arranged for a special telephone switchboard at headquarters to be manned by thoroughly competent and reliable operators brought on from New York. Thus he ensured against "leaks" and at the same time saved time and trouble because the operators knew the people we wanted and knew how to reach them quickly.

My own equipment for the Chicago Convention included a huge, brightly colored map on which different colors were used to show the states committed to the competing candidates. The purpose, naturally, was to show that Governor Roosevelt had far more support than all his opponents combined. The map was to be displayed conspicuously in a corridor of the Congress Hotel where it would be visible to all delegates, friendly and unfriendly alike. This map, which later was the target for a great many humorous sallies, was suggested by Governor Roosevelt himself to Frank Walker who relayed the suggestion to me.

The map was another of those details that did not seem especially important at the time. But after the convention many delegates told me that it impressed them in graphic fashion with the fact that the Governor was actually the majority choice. The opposition must have felt the same way about it because the leaders never overlooked an opportunity to heap derision on what they scornfully called "Field Marshal Farley's Map."

By this time we were beginning to feel the fury and force of our foes. They had gotten off to a late start; but most of the well-known leaders and veteran wheel horses, who were past masters at convention politics, were on their side, and they were preparing for a mighty drive at Chicago. Lacking a real issue, they were spreading the story that Governor Roosevelt was a nice fellow—but wishy-washy—no backbone—a rather amusing angle in view of what some of these same gentlemen had to say about him a few years later. I was still convinced that the Governor was going to be nominated on the first ballot, but, to copper-rivet the job, a few states would have to be fastened down so hard and fast that not even a political hurricane could get them away from us.

One glance at the gaudy-colored Roosevelt map was sufficient to show where the shock troops of the opposition could be smashed to smithereens even before their lines were really formed. The key to the nomination rested in the three neighboring Midwestern states of Ohio, Indiana, and Illinois. They were going to Chicago with a large bloc of delegates. If two of those states, or even one of them, could be induced to vote solidly for Roosevelt, the nomination of the New York Governor would be practically assured, no matter what tactics the opposition pursued.

By this time it was apparent that the majority of the New York delegation would be aligned with the coalition. In addition, Mayor James J. Walker was scheduled to answer removal charges before Governor Roosevelt later in the summer, and the Wigwam chiefs were already casting about for a way to save Jimmy's scalp.

On the week end of June 11-13, I hurried out to Indiana for a last-minute pep talk to the Indiana leaders who were going to hold their state convention a week later, the last one in the entire country. The Hoosier State was entitled to thirty votes in the National Convention; and how I wanted those votes! On my earlier stop at Indianapolis while en route to the Elks Convention the previous year, I had reported to Governor Roosevelt and Howe that all the leaders were friendly; but on this visit it was evident that someone was, to use a phrase common in politics, "giving us the foot" and it was well-nigh impossible to locate just who was doing it.

I visited Earl Peters at Fort Wayne and again urged upon him the necessity for a delegation definitely pledged to Roosevelt, not forgetting to mention that the leaders who gave us the votes needed to clinch the nomination would be very pleasantly remembered. As a further inducement, I promised that if Indiana instructed its delegates, I would make certain that any man named by the delegation would be made chairman of the Committee on Permanent Organization at the Chicago Convention. He suggested that Paul V. McNutt, who was expected to be the party nominee for Governor, could fill the post with distinction, and the place was left open to await the latter's decision.

From Fort Wayne, I hurried on to Chicago for a chat with Mayor Anton Cermak and Michael Igoe, the Democratic National Committeeman. Cermak professed to be friendly but he said little could be done because Senator Lewis was insisting upon a complimentary vote. Igoe was personally friendly but would go along with the Chicago organization.

Returning to New York, I found a letter there from Colonel McNutt, in reply to one of mine, in which he definitely declined to help us get an instructed delegation. His letter said:

"Upon receipt of your letter I started to make careful inquiry in all sections of the State concerning the attitude of the Democratic Leaders concerning an instructed delegation. While Governor Roosevelt has many staunch supporters in this State I find that an overwhelming majority of the Democratic Leaders feel they should not be hampered by instructions. Undoubtedly this feeling will be reflected by the delegates."

The letter was a disappointment because all along we had thought McNutt was on our side, but I wasn't yet ready to give up. I dropped a note to Governor Roosevelt at Albany, saying:

"I attach copy of a letter I have just received from Paul V. McNutt of Bloomington, Indiana. I think it would be a good plan if you were to call Mr. McNutt on the telephone and tell him the importance of an instructed delegation. I am sure it would be very helpful."

The letters sent to Indiana asking for an instructed delegation were similar to those sent to Roosevelt leaders in other states. They were exceptionally helpful because they kept us informed of what was actually going on and gave us a check on what the leaders were really thinking. Some of our most ardent friends, like Mrs. Isabella Greenway of Arizona, were opposed to instructed delegates but changed over at our request.

We also communicated with either the chairman of each delegation or the Roosevelt spokesman asking for a list of the men and women who would represent the delegation on the convention committees. This was part of the plan to control the organization of the convention. We also wired, asking each chairman to state if his delegation was bound by the unit rule. The unit rule is a device used in Democratic conventions whereby the action of the majority binds the entire delegation. The adoption of the rule was optional with each delegation. I quote one of the replies received:

"We vote as a unit on everything." The foregoing was received from the Honorable Huey P. Long, chairman of the Louisiana delegation. Huey probably meant to say, "I vote as a unit," because no boss ever had a closer grip on things than he did.

Eve of the Convention

On Sunday morning, eight days before the convention opened, I arrived in Chicago with Edward J. Flynn and Vincent Dailey, to open the Roosevelt headquarters. The show would soon be on.

The newspapers were still carrying long dispatches concerning the Republican convention, which had just ended, and the general belief was that the straddling plank adopted on repeal of the Prohibition Amendment, coupled with the prevailing economic distress, would kill off the G.O.P. chances for victory in the fall. That was encouraging. Sandwiched in with a lot of gossip about the Democratic candidates, the newspapers also carried a purported statement from Jouett Shouse saying, "We have Roosevelt licked now." We realized that it might be a misquotation but nevertheless it was disturbing.

I hung out the map and prepared to receive the press. The reporters flocked in and started firing questions on repeal. This was the burning issue because the "Stop Roosevelt" forces were hoping that many of the delegates pledged to the Governor's support from the supposedly dry South and West would oppose a wet plank. Asked about this, I replied:

"We Democrats must meet the issue fairly without any pussyfooting. The country is waiting for the Democratic Party to make the proper step. Republicans and Democrats alike will be disappointed if the convention does not meet the issue squarely, without equivocation or straddling."

The Governor had said earlier that he would stand on whatever wet plank the convention adopted, and the opposition never succeeded in making the issue an embarrassment. Of course, I repeated my first-ballot prediction in this interview with the press.

There was a period of tense excitement and eager anticipation for those who were on the scene during the long week before the convention actually got under way at the Chicago Stadium. There was a thrill in the atmosphere, the feeling that a good fight was about to take place. The old party war horses love that sort of thing; it sets the blood coursing in their veins. They delight in wandering through the hotel corridors, looking wise and whispering secretly about trades and agreements. They exchange views and swap gossip. They compare notes on what the various headquarters are giving out and take a squint at the candidates if they can. Many of the old-timers renew friendships that date back for as long as forty years. And, of course, each fellow has a weather eye cocked for the band-wagon rush. A real politician never likes to admit that he has been caught napping.

To the politicians who like action and plenty of it, there was no disappointment at Chicago. The air was soon filled with charges and countercharges; rumors that this or that was about to happen flew thick and fast. The headquarters of the contending candidates were almost side by side in the Congress Hotel, and delegates and visitors alike were cordially welcomed by each camp in turn. Behind closed doors, the strategists of the contending armies were sitting for hours on end trying to devise methods of increasing their own voting strength while weakening that of their opponents.

Al Smith was on his way to Chicago, a fighting figure thoroughly aroused and now openly allied with the "Stop Roosevelt" forces. Other candidates likewise were in Chicago or headed there, including Jim Reed, Governor Ritchie, Governor Byrd, and "Alfalfa Bill" Murray of Oklahoma. The last-named wore a bright scarf wound tightly around his neck despite the hot weather.

Smith was a dynamic personality. His ability to stir his followers in conversation or public address was almost unrivaled. There was no telling what effect his personal appearance would have upon the convention delegates, and there was no doubt that he was coming there to sway them if he could. In an interview at New York before leaving, the Happy Warrior's remarks were filled with the type of sharp and pithy comments that always made him such good newspaper copy. He had a genius for reaching the headlines with an apt phrase. On that occasion, he referred to my first-ballot predictions as "Farley's Fairy Stories" and "boxing baloney"—this last a thrust at my former service on the boxing commission.

Leaving a few hours behind Smith were the Tammany Braves, headed by Leader John F. Curry and filled with importance because the newspapers were asserting that they would hold the balance of power at Chicago.

I was genuinely convinced that Governor Roosevelt was certain to be the nominee but I was aware that the national political field was a new one for me and that one bad slip might prove my undoing. I knew that the Tammany Braves would be able to master their grief if that happened. Already, they were hinting that I had signed my political death warrant by backing Roosevelt.

A day or so after he reached Chicago, Smith had a conference with William Gibbs McAdoo, a Garner delegate from California; and the press was filled with reports that the two men, who had contested so bitterly for the presidential nomination in the Madison Square Garden Convention of 1924, had sealed a compact to stand fast against Roosevelt's nomination.

The first broadside of the battle was hurled for the opposition

forces by Frank Hague, the "Boss" of Jersey City, who had been
selected as the floor-manager for the Smith forces. On Thursday,
June 24, Hague issued a lengthy statement in which he declared
that Governor Roosevelt could not carry a single state east of
the Mississippi River, and if nominated, had "no chance of winning in the November election." The Jersey leader then mentioned each one of the other candidates by name, and said that
any one of them would make a stronger candidate than the New
York Governor.

The statement, of course, was obviously exaggerated and was
intended merely as an opening gun in the onslaught against the
Roosevelt candidacy and as a bid to bring the opposing candidates
into closer alliance. I immediately telephoned what Hague had
said to Governor Roosevelt at Albany. Later that day I made
public the following reply:

"Governor Roosevelt's friends have not come to Chicago to
criticize, cry down, or defame any Democrat from any part of the
country. This, I believe, is sufficient answer to Mr. Hague's statement."

This statement, issued in my name, was dictated to me personally by Governor Roosevelt in his telephone conversation. He
knew the Hague outburst would pass away without effect and he
was careful to avoid bitter remarks that might crop up later. The
nomination would be worthless if it was to be preceded by another
deadlock brought on by grudges and ill feeling.

There was a curious repercussion to this incident. The Hague
statement was worded in such a way that several outstanding newspaper correspondents interpreted it as an indirect offer on the part
of ex-Governor Smith to withdraw from the field in favor of another candidate, if Governor Roosevelt would do likewise. This
story became so widespread that Mayor Hague felt it necessary
to issue a denial on the following day.

The fact is that Governor Smith spoke the truth when he said
at his first press conference in Chicago that he was there to make
himself the nominee of the party. He felt that he was entitled
to another chance at the Presidency. The failure of the other
candidates to realize that essential fact was one of the major
blunders of the opposition. They believed the whispered tale that

the Happy Warrior's real objective was to block the nomination of Governor Roosevelt because he felt the latter was unfitted for the Presidency. Governor Ritchie told me personally after the convention that he never realized that ex-Governor Smith was a serious contender until he reached Chicago. These conflicting ambitions on the part of the other contenders were the cause of their failure to unite on any one individual. If someone else had been the leading candidate instead of the New York Governor, I believe Governor Smith would have fought him just the same.

During the few days remaining before the convention opened, we perfected our organization. Senator Hull, who wished to devote all his time to working on the economic planks of the platform, asked to be excused as chairman of the Resolutions Committee. We substituted former Senator Gilbert Hitchcock of Nebraska, who had been Democratic floor leader in the Senate during the Wilson administration. Knowing a sharp fight was in prospect in the Walsh-Shouse controversy, we decided upon Vincent Miles of Arkansas, to be chairman of the Committee on Permanent Organization.

The Two-Thirds Rule Again

The first big rally and organization meeting of the Roosevelt camp took place on Thursday, June 24, with approximately sixty-five leaders, representing every delegation, in attendance, and before it was over I fervently wished that we had clung to the earlier rule against big committee meetings. What started out to be a friendly get-together developed into a sort of noisy town-meeting. I was presiding.

Almost before we realized what was taking place, the meeting was stampeded into taking hasty and ill-advised action on the abolition of the two-thirds rule, a piece of strategy that plagued us for several days and very nearly split the Roosevelt following wide open. The incident came up unexpectedly. Several other matters had been disposed of when Senator Huey Long took the floor and offered a resolution setting forth that the friends of Governor Roosevelt intended to do all in their power to abolish the two-thirds nominating rule in favor of a majority rule. In keeping with our prior understanding with Governor Roosevelt and the other advisers at the Hyde Park meeting, I promptly pointed out that the meeting really had no power to take such action, that it was unfair to the candidate to do so without consulting him, and that the proper thing was to have the resolution go over. That was done, and we proceeded to talk against the manifest unfairness of the two-thirds rule. The delegates were obviously impressed. Huey saw his chance—the kind of a situation in which he always delighted. He asked permission to second his own motion and then with coat open and arms flying he delivered a stem-winding, rousing stump speech that took his listeners by storm. This was perhaps Huey's first entry onto the national scene, and he went over with a terrific bang. The upshot was that the leaders adopted a resolution pledging the Roosevelt forces to fight for the abolition of the two-thirds rule. The fat was in the fire, and, for the time being at least, Huey was Cock of the Walk.

The incident hit me like a blow on the nose. My confidence was badly shaken for the first time. Besides that, there was no disguising the fact that the blame was mine for letting the meeting get out of hand, even though there wasn't any way to prevent it. I was annoyed and uncertain what to do. We went back up to headquarters, and I telephoned Albany to inform Governor Roosevelt what had taken place. The wires were down, due to a bad storm in upper New York State, and it was some time before we succeeded in making a connection. In the meantime, the newspaper correspondents were on my trail demanding a statement. After listening to the whole story, the Governor told me not to worry, to let things drift along, that he was confident a way out of the mess would be found without doing us any damage.

Louie Howe arrived in town the next morning, and I hurried to the station to meet him. He had read an account of what happened in the newspaper. Like the Governor, he advised me not to worry, to let it ride along, and to see how it affected our forces. He added that if it became necessary, we would back off from the position taken by the meeting but that it would have to be done without being construed as a sign of weakness.

In the meantime, the proposal to abandon the rule created little short of a sensation. As anticipated, the other contending candidates and their managers set up a fierce howl in opposition. Al Smith said it was an attempt to change the rules in the middle of the game. Two other former presidential nominees of the Democratic Party, James M. Cox and John W. Davis, denounced the proposed change. Senator Carter Glass of Virginia called it a "short-cut" that should not be tolerated. Newton D. Baker, who was heavily backed as a "dark-horse" candidate, telephoned in his objection, declaring that a nomination won by changing the rules would have a "moral flaw" in its title.

We felt that all this talk about "sportsmanship" and "fair-play" was a trifle amusing, coming from experienced party leaders who were ganged up for the sole purpose of preventing the nomination of the candidate desired by the majority of the party. They had nothing else in common. Another ironic twist was the fact that no one questioned the obvious fact that more than a majority of the delegates favored Governor Roosevelt. Their only purpose was to put over a minority candidate, if possible.

We decided to stand firm, and with most of our leaders loyally standing by, I issued a statement to the effect that we proposed to drive ahead and abolish the rule.

I honestly believed at the time that we could muster enough votes to adopt a majority nominating rule because the figures showed that we could lose almost a hundred votes off our total strength and still win. But there is no question that many of the Southern delegates were deeply disturbed because they were bound by tradition to the old two-thirds rule. The South had felt in times past that the rule gave that section a veto power by which it could block the nomination of an objectionable candidate. Senator Pat Harrison of Mississippi, a loyal Roosevelt supporter, suggested publicly and privately that we ought to back down. The same sentiment was noticeable in other delegations.

The main weakness of our position was the fact that the proposal had come too early. It gave the opposition a rallying point and, what they needed even more than that, an argument to use against the Governor's nomination. Up until that time, they had failed to make a single dent in the Roosevelt armor. His record was able to stand up under every test. Now they had a chance to cry that they were being steam rollered.

We had to handle the situation carefully because it would have been fatal for us to be put in the position of repudiating those leaders who were leading the fight to change the rule. They were acting in good faith and sincerely trying to help the cause. The controversy raged all over the week end. Finally, after a number of conferences, we advised Governor Roosevelt that it was advisable for us to back off and that the best way to accomplish it was for him to issue a statement. That course was followed and we got out of a tight hole. I still felt that we were going to win on the first ballot anyway.

Roosevelt's statement was adroitly worded, and, while it suggested postponing a showdown on the issue, it also conveyed the implication that the question would be revived later on in the convention if the opposition persisted in forcing a deadlock. He said:

"The need of the nation—the need of the world—in these distressing days requires avoidance of personal animosities and discussion of procedure and calls for concentration and attention on principles and leadership.

"With this in mind I have been giving much thought to the subject of adopting a majority nomination rule instead of the two-thirds rule used by previous conventions.

"I believe and always have believed that the two-thirds rule should no longer be adopted. It is undemocratic.

"Nevertheless, it is true that the issue was not raised until after the delegates to the convention had been selected, and I decline to permit either myself or my friends to be open to the accusation of poor sportsmanship or to the use of methods which could be called, even falsely, those of a steam roller.

"I am accordingly asking my friends in Chicago to cease their activities to secure the adoption of the majority nominating rule at the opening of the permanent organization.

"I ask this of those delegates who are honoring me with their support and who number many more than a majority. I trust, however, that the committee on rules may recommend some rule to ensure against the catastrophe of a deadlock or a prolonged balloting."

James Hamilton Lewis Withdraws

One reason for optimism was an incident that happened late on Saturday, two days before the convention was to open. For a long time we had been making friendly gestures towards Senator James Hamilton Lewis of Illinois, who had the fifty-eight votes of that state pledged to his candidacy as a favorite son. That was the third-largest bloc of votes in the convention, and if they could be swung to the Roosevelt banner, the result would be inevitable. We knew that Senator Lewis did not for a moment regard himself as a serious contender and that he was extremely friendly to the candidacy of the New York Governor. After receiving a complimentary vote on the first ballot, we felt that he was willing to have the Illinois delegation switch, perhaps before the result of the ballot was announced.

I was in my hotel apartment putting on my clothes when Vincent Y. Dallman of Springfield, Illinois, came rushing into the room, breathless with excitement and exhibiting a telegram in which Senator Lewis withdrew his name and released the Illinois delegates. Louie Howe was in the room. Carried away with happiness and enthusiasm, I exclaimed: "Senator Lewis has withdrawn. This is the beginning of the end. Roosevelt will be nominated on the first ballot."

The always cautious Louie refused to get excited. He did not know Dallman and suggested that perhaps someone was "trying to put something over" and that the telegram was a fake. I assured him that Vincent had been one of our staunchest supporters from the beginning and that he and Senator Lewis had always been closely associated in politics. We tried to reach Senator Lewis by telephone in Washington, but failed. Dallman swore that he would take full responsibility for the authenticity of the wire. We hurried over to headquarters where the newspapermen were quickly assembled. I introduced Dallman who read the telegram. It said in part:

"I cannot see any adjournment until the end of the week. Please say to the Illinois delegation that has honored me with the choice for President, that I release each and all from any obligation. I send my grateful acknowledgment of the honor done me. I will not assume to direct or even suggest any individual or joint action for the delegation. I beg them to carefully weigh their responsibility and do everything that can serve the true demands of the democracy of America and meet the needs of the nation."

I was jubilant and felt that the band-wagon rush was on. But we muffed the ball badly on the Lewis telegram. It was released far too early, almost a week before the actual balloting got under way, and the result was that the opposition had plenty of time to muster their forces. We learned later that identical copies of the wire sent to Dallman had been sent by Senator Lewis to his campaign manager, William L. O'Connell, and to Mayor Anton Cermak. They apparently attempted to telephone him in Washington. In any event they were in no hurry to announce his withdrawal. The wire to Dallman had been sent to his newspaper office in Springfield and relayed from there to Chicago. This gave the other men plenty of time to act.

Although there was a large body of sentiment in the Illinois delegation for Roosevelt, the opposition forces used every stratagem to keep fifty-eight votes out of our column. This was finally accomplished by trotting forth another "dark-horse" candidate, Melvin A. Traylor, a Chicago banker, as the next favorite son after Senator Lewis. It is very seldom that a state is fortunate enough to have two favorite sons qualified for the Presidency, but the Illinois leaders were equal to the occasion. A few of the delegates came over to our side, although not at all the number we anticipated. The outcome was disappointing, but we had other irons in the fire.

Under Louie Howe's direction, the force at headquarters was doing a first-rate job of winning the good will of visiting delegates and keeping everybody happy. There is no more important work at a convention. Miss Mary Dewson of New York was in charge of the women's division and she did an excellent job among the feminine delegates. Miss Dewson had been carrying on a correspondence with most of them for months previously, thus building up considerable strength for us in those quarters.

Louie thought up one very shrewd scheme that helped considerably. The other candidates had a certain advantage, of course, in being on the ground. They could show their human qualities by strolling around and chatting with the delegates. To offset that, Louie rigged up a voice amplifier and had it attached to the private switchboard. Then he proceeded to call in groups of delegates for a talk with Governor Roosevelt at Albany. The Governor spoke to them as a group and often individually. These chats became very popular, and one or two delegations complained when they thought they were being left out. On one occasion, Governor Roosevelt spoke to a group of his campaign leaders and cautioned them not to indulge in personal attacks or bitter criticism of other candidates. He realized that tactics of that type do more harm than good in the long run, especially to the man who was going to win the nomination.

On the night before the convention opened, we had another general meeting at headquarters during which we organized our "field" forces for the convention floor itself. I wanted to make sure that the key men would be recognized immediately by all the Roosevelt delegates. As each man's name was called, he stepped down front so that all those in attendance had a good look at him. Those introduced included Floor Leader Arthur Mullen and his assistants. I also introduced Bill Howes of South Dakota, and a couple of other trusted lieutenants who were to act as emissaries in carrying messages and instructions. Those present were asked to have their delegations go along with whatever these men requested. We were anxious to ensure good teamwork and to avoid the mistakes, which often prove so costly, that come about because of the excitement and confusion on the convention floor. This precaution was worth while.

The Convention Opens

"The convention will please come to order. Delegates in the aisles will please take their seats."

The old familiar cry rang through the huge Chicago Stadium as Chairman John J. Raskob of the national committee raised his voice and pounded his gavel to start the convention proceedings. There is a carnival spirit, a touch of the sawdust and the sideshow, about a national convention that makes it unique among public gatherings. And we Democrats can always put a little more zest into it than our staid brethren on the Republican side. The truth is that the National Convention was invented by the Democrats in the days of Andrew Jackson, and ever since then it has been a favorite device of the party faithful. While these party conclaves may not always be successful, at least they are never dull.

The opening session of a convention is usually given over to routine matters, but the delegates at Chicago were in no mood to dillydally. They wanted "demonstrations"—a chance to parade their banners around the hall and to let off a little steam. Senator Barkley provided what was wanted by delivering a truly fine keynote address. He mentioned the expected "wet" plank, and they were off. Delegates tramped up and down the aisles, shouting and singing, banners were produced and flung out almost as if by magic, and a mighty pipe organ shivered and shook until the place was in bedlam. And when the pipe organ died away, a couple of bands were on hand to continue the din. The tunes were familiar, and each one had a meaning all its own—"How Dry I Am," "Maryland, My Maryland," "The Sidewalks of New York," "Hail, Hail, the Gang's All Here," "Happy Days." It was only the beginning; those tunes lingered on for almost a week, repeated over and over through long, hot, weary night sessions until most of the poor delegates wished they had the power to throw both the organ and the bands into near-by Lake Michigan. After all, it is possible to get too much of a good thing.

While the delegates were whooping it up at the opening session, we made public at headquarters the telegram addressed to me from Governor Roosevelt suggesting that we call off the fight against the two-thirds rule. Roosevelt's direct entry into the controversy was made necessary by the fact that, although those of us in charge wanted to back down, there were still a number of leaders, including Senators Long and Kremer, who insisted upon taking action. I assumed that the Governor's telegram would end the matter, but on the contrary those who wanted to abolish the rule declined to give way. As a result the rules committee decided to recommend the abrogation of the rule on the seventh ballot. In other words, if the first six ballots failed to produce a nominee, then a mere majority would be sufficient on the seventh.

It is easy to imagine the furor that kicked up. The opposition immediately accused us of insincerity and bad faith, and it was necessary for me to issue a statement disavowing the action of the committee. Then I hurried over and pleaded personally with Bruce Kremer, the Rules Committee chairman, to heed the Governor's wishes and let the matter drop. The committee after considerable wrangling finally did so, and the long headache was over at last. We had cleared another hurdle that might have proved disastrous.

The second day meant business. A series of test votes that would positively determine whether the Roosevelt forces or the opposing coalition had right of way in the convention. If we lost on any of the tests, we were through and we knew it. The first test was to come on the question of seating the delegation from Louisiana which was led, controlled, and completely dominated by that budding statesman, Huey P. Long, who modestly referred to himself in public as "the Kingfish." There was an opposition slate from Louisiana which included a number of outstanding Democrats, one of whom was former Governor Jared Y. Sanders; and just for his own amusement Huey provided a third "burlesque" delegation which went through the motions of pretending to oppose both the others. This third group was really composed of Long henchmen and during the preliminary hearings on the Louisiana contest they had done a lot of clowning for the purpose of making a farce out of the whole proceeding. Perhaps their antics amused some people but they disgusted a lot of delegates and in that way lost considerable support for Huey.

The question of which of the rival delegations should be seated revolved about the legality of the manner in which they were chosen. The point is considerably involved, and there is no occasion to discuss it here. The Roosevelt forces had decided that Long's delegation was actually entitled to be seated. When we decided to back the Kingfish, the opposition immediately united in favor of the Sanders delegation although it was unpledged. The rival delegates would have supported the Governor's cause had we agreed to seat them, but we honestly believed that the Long delegation was entitled to represent Louisiana. The Kingfish was never a shrinking violet—to use a somewhat mixed figure of speech and, like many other positive characters of his type, he aroused the most violent likes and dislikes. His followers idolized him while to others his habits of swagger and bluster made him obnoxious and odious to an intense degree. By a twist of fate, Huey suddenly held the center of the stage. The eyes of the nation were turned his way, and he loved it. He strutted up and down the aisles, issued instructions to his followers in a roaring voice, and engaged in verbal tilts with newspapermen or other delegates whenever it suited his fancy. Wherever Huey appeared, the temperature immediately shot up several degrees, and on one or two occasions he narrowly missed getting into fistic encounters. Our foes shook their heads in disapproval over the fact that we were supporting such a loud fellow but secretly they had made every effort to coax him off the Roosevelt band wagon. However, it was all in the game, and this business of self-righteous posing is more or less common in politics.

I recall that just before the contest argument was to get under way, I was on the convention platform engaged in conversation when someone gave me a hearty thump on the back. It was Huey. Without waiting for me to finish my conversation, he pointed to the New York delegation and asked me to identify some of the delegates.

"Who's that?"

"That's Mayor Jimmy Walker."

"Who's that?"

"That's John F. Curry, Tammany leader."

"Who's that?"

"That's John W. Davis."

Huey shook his head, "I never did like him."

Then he went on asking about each one in turn and adding his own personal comment on each.

The convention listened to considerable debate over the Louisiana contest before proceeding to ballot. During the course of the argument, Senator Long himself argued for his own delegation, and this occasion showed what a shrewd fellow he really was. He sensed the fact that it was time to cut out the horseplay and the oratorical nonsense. He delivered a reasoned, common-sense argument for his side that some thought was the best of the entire debate. His behavior won him considerable support.

While the debate was proceeding, I strolled over to the New

York delegation. Although a delegate, I had difficulty finding a seat because the majority were already giving me the cold shoulder on account of my connection with the Roosevelt forces. They had decided to go down the line for Smith, although the Tammany chieftains had never before shown any too much love for the Happy Warrior. I managed to find a place beside Judge Proskauer who was one of Governor Smith's closest admirers and supporters. We chatted a while, and I predicted how many votes the Roosevelt forces would muster.

The balloting commenced. As the roll of states was called, the tally was pretty close to what I had predicted. Mississippi cast its twenty votes for the Long delegation. Judge Proskauer was a bit surprised. He inquired:

"When did you win back that delegation?"

"We never lost it," was my reply. The opposition had been striving with might and main to break the Roosevelt strength in Mississippi but our lines stood fast. I shall never forget the look of disappointment on Judge Proskauer's face when the balloting was over. He knew that defeat was again looming for the Happy Warrior. We won the opening round by a vote of 638¾ to 514¼.

The next ballot was on the Minnesota contest. There was less difference of opinion on that because it was obvious that the Roosevelt delegation should be seated. We won that vote, 658¼ to 492¾.

Then came a sterner test, the battle between Senator Walsh and Mr. Shouse over the permanent chairmanship. The case for Senator Walsh was presented by Senator Clarence C. Dill of Washington and Senator James F. Byrnes of South Carolina, while the case for Mr. Shouse was presented by Mrs. Bernice S. Pyke of Ohio and John W. Davis, the party's candidate for President in 1924. The latter was a distinguished lawyer, and his address to the convention was a masterpiece of suave and eloquent pleading. But Mrs. Pyke really touched off the fireworks. She said that one of the "conspicuous candidates" had placed his approval on the plan of the Arrangements Committee to recommend Senator Barkley for keynoter and to recommend Shouse for permanent chairman. She pleaded with the convention to begin its proceedings in good faith, and while Governor Roosevelt's name was not mentioned, there was an imputation of bad faith on his part and everybody knew it.

While the thing was ballooned far out of proportion to its actual worth for political purposes, there is no doubt that a genuine misunderstanding had arisen, and the episode was causing considerable uneasiness in our camp. We rested our case entirely on an affidavit, sworn to by Bob Jackson, which Senator Byrnes read to the convention. In the affidavit Jackson pointed out that the Arrangements Committee had merely "commended" Shouse for the permanent chairmanship, instead of recommending him as Mrs. Pyke said—and he explained that this distinction in wording was all-important. He added that Governor Roosevelt told him personally over the telephone when the matter first came up at the Arrangements Committee meeting in April, that he was not in favor of Mr. Shouse for permanent chairman.

While the debate probably didn't change any votes on either side, we had an advantage in the fact that not a voice could be raised to question the fairness or the upright principles of Senator Walsh. With partisanship thrust aside, he was clearly the ideal man for permanent chairman.

But a great many of our delegates had pledged themselves to Mr. Shouse and they intended to go through for him. Probably every politician in the stadium was nervously jotting down figures as the roll was called. My own tally was kept on long sheets of common brown note paper, which are still tucked away among my keepsakes. I shall never forget the feeling of relief in my mind as the austere Senator Walsh, a slender man physically, strode down the center aisle from his seat in the Montana delegation to take his place on the convention platform. The vote was 626 to 528, and it marked the convention high-water mark for the opposition. One ominous sign for the opposition was Al Smith's failure to carry out his announced plan to take the platform for Mr. Shouse. He was sharp enough to realize that the tide was rolling the other way and that the time had not arrived for the supreme effort.

The battle for a "dripping wet" plank recommending outright repeal of the Eighteenth Amendment and modification of the Volstead Act, instead of a plank recommending mere submission, was a dramatic high-spot of the convention although it actually has little place in this story. The way in which repeal sentiment grew steadily in volume, like a huge snowball gathering size as it went along, seemed almost unbelievable even to those men and women who had been battling doggedly for years to end the Prohibition regime in America. The long debate which preceded adoption of the wet plank saw two outstanding candidates for the presidential nomination take the platform to urge its adoption. They were Al Smith, who received a friendly ovation, and Governor Ritchie, who was also roundly applauded.

Although many of the Roosevelt delegates in the South and West came from Prohibition states, we made no effort to dictate how they should vote on the wet issue. While Senator Hull took the platform to oppose the "dripping wet" plank and to recommend a milder one, he did so on his own responsibility and against the advice of some of us who urged him not to do so. The result was an overwhelming triumph for the wet forces, the vote standing 934¾ to 213¾. In view of the pussyfooting plank adopted by the Republicans, this bold action electrified the country. Governor Roosevelt had made known his desire for repeal on several occasions and the plank adopted was satisfactory to him.

Last-Minute Scramble for Delegates

The ballyhoo period was ended: the time had come to cut out the theatricals, to throw away the stage props, and to set in grim earnestness about the business of nominating a presidential candidate. I might almost say the business of selecting the next President, because even at that early date there was a feeling upon the part of everyone present that the Democratic nominee would be carried to victory in the succeeding fall election. This feeling added spirit to the contest, if that were possible, because there is no political prize in the world that excites the imagination of men quite as much as does the exalted position of Chief Executive of the United States. Even for those who play only a minor role, the experience is one that perhaps will never be forgotten, and for the actual candidates who feel the prize within their grasp, the suspense is terrific.

In the hours that preceded the actual balloting, the undercover

struggle for delegates was carried on by means of all the strata-
gems that human wit and ingenuity can contrive. I had only one
thought in the world: to hold our lines intact while we proceeded
to win over enough delegates from the wavering states to put over
the nomination of Governor Roosevelt on the first ballot. At the
same time the opposition was assailing us at every point, and we
had the longest line.

The nervous strain during this period of suspense was very close
to the limit of physical endurance. At a time when clear thinking
and cool judgment were needed as they never were before, I was
working eighteen or nineteen hours a day, conversing with hundreds of people, constantly consulting with other leaders, receiving reports from every delegation, and meeting at least twice daily
with several hundred newspapermen. I ate my meals, usually con-
sisting of sandwiches and milk, off a tray, and slept a few hours
just before dawn if the opportunity offered. To add to my burdens,
I was besieged on all sides for convention tickets, which I did not
have. Hundreds of other men were caught in the same dizzy
whirl and were trying to keep up the same maddening pace.

We had combined against us an alliance of resourceful men.
They knew when to be subtle and when to be daring. They knew
where it was wise to use flattery, and, above all, they knew when
to dangle a tempting prize before a potential candidate for the
Presidency or the Vice-Presidency. Every convention is full of
these gentlemen who nurse secret ambitions, and clearing them
out of the path is one of the hardest tasks of all.

Louie Howe had worked out an excellent system for keeping
us informed, and for that reason we were seldom caught napping.
A delegate from Iowa told us how he was called out of bed early
in the morning by a gentleman who wanted to know on how
many ballots he intended to stick by Roosevelt. A Southern delegate said his group were entertained all the way to Chicago by
a couple of gentlemen who were extremely generous with food
and drink but at the same time deeply distressed over their intention to vote for the New York Governor. We knew just where
pressure was being brought.

In the meantime, I was doing a little political footwork myself,
and so were other leaders in the Roosevelt camp. The test ballot-

ing had revealed that Illinois and Indiana were realigning almost solidly with the opposition even though I had every reason to believe that sentiment in those delegations was largely for Governor Roosevelt. Neither state had a serious presidential candidate. Indiana's position especially was disappointing, as the delegation had voted solidly against Senator Walsh; all our appeals were in vain. However, we had five or six men in the Indiana group who had been friendly to us from the start, and they kept us constantly informed on what was taking place. Our informants told us that Roy Howard, the extremely able manager of the Scripps-Howard newspapers, had conferred with Colonel Paul V. McNutt and promised that the Scripps papers in Indiana would support the Democratic state ticket if the delegation gave a minimum of eight votes to Newton D. Baker on the first three ballots. The Hoosier Democrats had just nominated Frederick Van Nuys for Senator and Colonel McNutt for Governor. Although the latter was not a delegate, he was in Chicago, and the chairman of the delegation was his close political ally, Frank McHale.

The Scripps newspapers had come out for Al Smith the previous week, but everyone took the announcement with a grain of salt as they had failed to support him in the 1928 race against Herbert Hoover when such support would have been tremendously helpful. It was an open secret that Baker was actually the candidate of the Scripps papers and that the Happy Warrior was being used as a stalking horse. Whether the dicker for the Indiana votes was ever suggested or not, Indiana actually did cast eight votes for Baker on the first three ballots. We had other reports of activities by Mr. Howard on Mr. Baker's behalf. Roy is one of the most brilliant newspaper executives in America, but he was a bit optimistic in assuming that he could take off a few afternoons from his newspaper duties to nominate a presidential candidate. The game is somewhat more complicated. However, he did succeed in keeping the Indiana votes out of our column just when we needed them badly.

Ohio gave us another disappointment. Earlier in the struggle it looked as though Governor Roosevelt had an excellent chance to get the vote of the entire bloc of fifty-two delegates after one or two complimentary votes had been cast for the Buckeye state's favorite son, Governor White. As I have indicated, the capture of such a large delegation would have been sufficient to ensure nomination. Before the balloting started, however, White announced that he would refuse to release the delegates because to do so would violate his understanding with Newton D. Baker and James M. Cox. Mr. Baker's name was bobbing up rather frequently at this stage.

We had arranged for Daniel C. Roper of South Carolina and Bruce Kremer to keep constantly in touch with William Gibbs McAdoo in the hope of winning over California's forty-four delegates, another bloc that was large enough to break the back of the opposition if the swing could be effected. There was perhaps more pressure being brought to bear upon the California unit than upon any other group in the convention. The delegates were pledged to Speaker Garner, but publisher William Randolph Hearst had been largely responsible for their victory in the preceding May primaries, and his associates were beginning to doubt the wisdom of his opposing Governor Roosevelt.

Mr. Hearst had long been a bitter political enemy of Alfred E. Smith, the spearhead of the opposition. And even more serious from his point of view were the undercover reports, constantly growing in volume, that if the convention was forced into a long deadlock, the compromise candidate was almost certain to be Baker. The one individual above all others who enflamed the wrath of the California publisher was the man who had served as Secretary of War in the Wilson Cabinet. Baker for years had been an ardent advocate of America's entry into the League of Nations, and, to Mr. Hearst, with his uncompromising isolationist viewpoint, that attitude made him little less than an enemy of his country.

There were a number of Mr. Hearst's representatives at the convention, and several of them were seriously worried over the Baker threat. In addition, a number of our leaders, including Joseph P. Kennedy who had been associated with him in business, called Mr. Hearst on the long-distance telephone to tell him about the Baker "dark-horse" movement and to ask his influence in getting the California delegation to switch. Damon Runyan, the noted Hearst writer, brought the publisher's secretary, Joseph

Willicombe, to see me, and together we called the Hearst ranch at San Simeon, California, to emphasize the menace of the Baker movement once again. I don't know how many other people did the same thing. The publisher listened very courteously and was outspoken in condemning the move to nominate Baker but beyond that he failed to commit himself.

During these negotiations, I used all the persuasive powers at my command and worked hand in hand with the other Roosevelt leaders in the battle to win over the deciding delegates. At the same time, if those negotiations failed, I had an ace in the hole to be played at the proper time, which to my way of thinking positively guaranteed us against failure in the struggle to capture the nomination. To explain about that, it is necessary to provide a little background.

Reaching an Understanding

Congress remained in session during the Chicago Convention, and on the Monday night of convention week Senator Harry B. Hawes of Missouri and Senator Key Pittman of Nevada were in the former's office in Washington discussing what was likely to occur. They are two of the keenest political analysts in the Democratic Party and they were deeply disturbed over the newspaper reports from Chicago indicating that a bitter deadlock would destroy the party's chances of success as it had in the past.

The two Senators decided to do something about it. To avoid misunderstanding, Senator Hawes called Governor Roosevelt at Albany by long-distance telephone and asked the Governor directly if Speaker John Garner would be satisfactory to him as a vice-presidential running mate. According to Senator Hawes, the Governor promptly replied:

"Senator, that would be fine; the Governor from New York and the Speaker of the House from Texas—clear across the country." Then he instructed Senator Hawes to get in touch with me at Chicago and relate what had taken place. Harry sent me the following telegram, the original of which is still in my possession:

GROUP BELIEVE WINNING TICKET WOULD BE ROOSEVELT AND
GARNER STOP NINETY VOTES OF CALIFORNIA AND TEXAS WOULD

ELIMINATE DISPUTE STOP AM ADVISED WOULD BE SATISFACTORY TO
PARTY HERE STOP SEE SAM RAYBURN TOM CONNALLY AND CHECK
MY OWN IMPRESSION STOP BEST WISHES.

Before Hawes and Pittman left the office, I was in touch with
them by long-distance telephone to thank them for their suggestion and to find out why they thought the Garner forces would
be willing to break away from the opposition. After the telephone
conversation, I immediately started on a hunt for Congressman
Sam Rayburn.

In the meanwhile, that same night, Harry Hawes got busy and
sent hundreds of telegrams to Democratic leaders, some in Chicago and some around the country, urging them to place the best
interests of the party above everything else and to do their best
to bring about a coalition of the Roosevelt-Garner forces. He got
an amusing reaction. Throughout his thirty years in Washington,
Congressman Jack Garner had remained true to his habit of retiring early at night and rising early in the morning. Someone
advised him of what was going on, and at 7:30 A.M. he called
Senator Hawes out of bed and in his high-pitched voice gave him
a sharp tongue-lashing for sending out telegrams to the effect that
he was willing to withdraw from the race and accept the Vice-
Presidency. The Speaker made it plain that he had no desire for
the Vice-Presidency and had authorized no one to entertain such
a proposition on his behalf.

Senator Hawes soothed him down by reading several of the
telegrams which had been sent out, the wires simply stating that
Roosevelt and Garner would make a winning ticket for the Democratic Party. The Speaker was somewhat appeased but still felt a
bit displeased, so later in the morning Senator Hawes called on
him in his office to discuss the matter again. He pointed out in a
joking manner that there was less work for the presiding officer
to do on the Senate side and then seriously urged Mr. Garner to
accept the Vice-Presidency as a great honor for his native state
of Texas and for the good of the party.

In the meantime, after constant scurrying through hotel corridors and a great many telephone calls, I managed to find Silliman Evans of Texas, whom I knew to be an exceptionally close

friend of Speaker Garner, and of Sam Rayburn as well. Silliman and I had become acquainted during the preconvention fight and had gotten together to discuss the way things were going on two or three occasions. He promised to get Sam and to bring him to my private apartment in the Congress Hotel. I hurried back there and was alone with Mrs. Farley when Sam and Silliman appeared. It was after 11:00 P.M. They had managed to slip in without anyone seeing them. The three of us went into the bedroom to confer.

In the ensuing conversation, I used all the salesmanship at my command to convince them of the necessity for a combination of the Roosevelt-Garner forces. I pointed out that the New York Governor would have a substantial majority over all his opponents combined on the first ballot and that by all the rules of the game he was entitled to the nomination without delay. A parallel situation had taken place at Houston in 1928 when Al Smith had a majority, and his opponents had graciously given way and permitted his nomination without further contest. I recalled that Governor Roosevelt and Speaker Garner were personal friends and had always thought highly of one another. I pointed out the obvious fact that the first delegation to see the light of reason would naturally be in a strategic position if it switched over to our side and assured the Governor's nomination. The Texas delegation with its forty-six votes was big enough to do the job even without California. And then came the big moment—I promised to do everything in my power to secure the vice-presidential nomination for Speaker Garner if Texas made the switch.

It was Sam's turn to talk. A slow-spoken Texan, who weighed every word, he had been chosen as campaign manager for the Garner forces because of his penetrating insight and level-headed attitude in political dealings. He had served for years in the House of Representatives with Jack Garner, and they knew each other's minds thoroughly. Sam measured out his words with a mixture of candor and caution that still remains vividly in my mind.

"We have come to Chicago," he said, "to nominate Speaker Jack Garner for the Presidency if we can. We are not against any other candidate and we are not for any other candidate. Governor Roosevelt is the leading candidate and naturally he must be headed off if we are to win. But we don't intend to make it another Madison Square Garden."

When he had completed what he had to say, Sam looked at Silliman who nodded assent. I was completely satisfied. Sam had made no promise; he did not even indicate that he was interested in the possibility of securing the vice-presidential nomination for his candidate. But a basic rule of politics is to "know your man," and both Rayburn and Evans had given me the impression that they were reliable, candid, and willing to listen to reason. The three of us solemnly agreed not to reveal the fact of our conversation to any living soul with the single exception that I was at liberty to tell the Governor and Louie Howe if I desired. There was a general realization that if the news of our meeting became generally known, it might prove extremely harmful for both sides and might defeat the plan in mind. We left with the agreement to meet again.

The day before he had left Washington, Rayburn had a long conference with his candidate in which the plain-spoken Speaker gave instructions on what he wanted done at Chicago. The delegations of Texas and California were pledged to him, and as a matter of good faith he wanted his name kept before the convention as long as there was a legitimate chance for his nomination. But he emphasized that the interests of the Democratic Party were to be considered first—his own interests second. He had no wish to jeopardize party success to advance his own political cause. While this attitude may seem unusual on the part of a presidential candidate, I think that in the years since that time the country has learned enough about the character of Jack Garner to believe the truth of the incident just related.

At the earliest opportunity, I whispered to Louie what had taken place in the meeting with Rayburn and Evans. He was unimpressed and, even after a long discussion and exchange of views, he was still of the opinion that it was a waste of time to continue negotiations with them. He pointed out that Texas had been committed to the Garner candidacy only after a spirited fight and that the Speaker was more than a favorite-son candidate. He emphasized the point that the meeting had been requested by me and that they had made no commitments, which was true. He expressed the belief that it would be smart politics for Rayburn and Evans to continue meeting me even if they had no intention of making the switch. This was really the first time during the entire preconvention campaign that Louis and I failed to come to an understanding on a major question of policy. Despite the logic of his arguments, I remained firm in the belief that Texas was our best bet.

Louis, at the time, was doing all he could to persuade the managers of Governor Harry Byrd of Virginia to give up the fight and to enter the Roosevelt fold. There was good ground for believing that what he had in mind could be accomplished because Governor Byrd had remained on friendly terms throughout the preconvention campaign and because, in addition, it was perfectly evident that he had absolutely no strength at all outside of his own Virginia convention. For him to stay in the race would serve no purpose except to help deadlock the convention, and Virginia's twenty-four votes would be of primary importance in smashing the opposition ranks. Louie felt so strongly about the matter that he took it up with Governor Roosevelt in one of the numerous long-distance telephone conversations between headquarters and Albany. After he had finished his story, I told the Governor my view of the situation. He told me to go ahead with the Texas negotiations, if it appeared the right thing to do, and also gave Louie authority to continue his talks with Byrd. With that assurance, I was determined to go ahead.

Meanwhile, the "Stop Roosevelt" managers were meeting constantly, planning their line of campaign and considering with painstaking care every possible place where a dent might be made in the New York Governor's forces. Although some of their movements were made public, there was one group of the real "high command" which met at least once a day in the utmost secrecy, and usually even the press failed to get wind of where they were or what transpired. We knew of these meetings, and in our camp the participants were usually referred to as "The Owls." Each of the coalition candidates for President was entitled to at least one or two representatives at these "Owl" meetings. Frank Hague or Jouett Shouse usually represented Governor Smith. Sometimes they met in the penthouse apartment of one of their number, which was located almost three miles from headquarters. Sam Rayburn later told me an amusing episode in connection with these meetings. He had returned to the Congress Hotel in the same taxicab with John Raskob. Upon getting out they separated immediately and they thought no one had seen them together. Ten minutes later he was in headquarters when the telephone rang and someone said, "Jim Farley wants to speak to Sam Rayburn." The fact that he had been seen with Raskob was already known at our headquarters. No doubt the opposition was just as cagey in checking up on our movements.

Swager Shirley, a former member of the House from Kentucky, was also extremely useful in connection with the Texas delegation. Shirley was an ardent supporter of Governor Roosevelt and had just come from a visit with him at Hyde Park. He was an old pal of Sam Rayburn's, a friendship which began when they were in Congress together. All during that week Shirley saw as much of Sam as he could, and of course he overlooked no opportunity to stress, in a diplomatic way, the strength of the Roosevelt case. His efforts were not without avail.

It was Thursday afternoon, and we were back in the Chicago Stadium listening to nine presidential candidates being placed in nomination by speaker after speaker, who unloosed what can only be described as a merciless and unholy flood of oratory. The afternoon wore on; there was a recess; we returned to another session at night; and still the hours were consumed by the endless chain of nominating and seconding speeches, to the accompaniment of the din, the uproar, and the unseemly noise which characterized the customary "demonstrations" for favorite candidates. Before it was ended, the delegates, the visitors, the campaign managers and workers, and even the candidates themselves were driven almost to distraction. I can hardly recall a more nerve-racking experience in my long association in politics.

During the recess, everyone went back to the hotel, presumably for dinner, but for those on the firing line it meant a fierce, last-minute scramble to corral more votes. We had our leaders pleading with the key men in California, Indiana, Illinois, New York, and other states. The opposition was working hard to crack the Roosevelt support in Maine, Michigan, Iowa, and Mississippi. I drifted over to the Garner headquarters for a "good-will visit" with his managers and supporters and to make a last-minute plea with Sam to make the break on the first ballot. I swapped good-natured banter with several Garner men who were at headquarters, and in the meantime Rayburn and Evans were arranging so that we could leave unnoticed and go into another room for a conference.

When we were alone, I recalled that at our last meeting I had promised to do everything in my power to secure the vice-presidential nomination for Mr. Garner if Texas would swing to Governor Roosevelt and had stated that, in my opinion, he could be nominated. "Now this time," I added, "I know positively that we can bring about his nomination for second place on the ticket."

Sam asked what I wanted him to do. "Have the Texas delegation record its vote for Garner on the first ballot," I urged, "and then before the result is announced switch to Roosevelt. I feel certain that some state will make the break after it becomes apparent that the Governor has a big majority, and Texas might as well be first."

Sam replied that he had more than 180 delegates and the same number of alternates who had come up from the Lone Star State for the purpose of backing John Garner for the Presidency, and that it would be unfair to them and to the state to agree to any such arrangements. He said that Texas was bound to vote for the Speaker for two or three ballots at least until it was shown whether he had a chance to be nominated. Then Sam asked me on how many ballots we could hold our lines without breaking. After pondering for a second or two, I answered, "Three ballots, four ballots, and maybe five."

"Well," replied Sam, "we just must let the convention go for a while, even if we are interested in the Vice-Presidency, and I'm not saying that we are."

Although it was a disappointment, Sam's position was reasonable, and there was nothing to do but to keep on plugging for the break.

The recess was over; it was a hot, sticky night; and the stadium seemed like a solid mass of steaming, yelling, cheering humanity, as the stream of nominating speeches rolled on and on. The powerful Kleig lights, placed at intervals for the benefit of movie cameras, added a touch of weirdness to the scene as they swept back and forth over the convention floor or were focused for a few minutes at a time on the convention platform. The galleries were crowded to capacity—and beyond capacity—with thousands of leather-lunged visitors, a great many of whom didn't even have tickets but were let in on "passes" supplied by friendly Chicago politicians. Most of these were hot rooters for Al Smith or Governor Ritchie, and they frequently displayed their feelings by booing seconding speeches for Governor Roosevelt. If those ill-mannered tactics did anything, they probably intensified the loyalty of our delegates from rural states.

I recall that on one occasion during the long evening I stepped out of the tiny gallery office, just over the platform, which we occupied as convention headquarters for the Roosevelt forces. A demonstration for Governor Ritchie was in progress, and the delegates and visitors were whooping it up with wild enthusiasm. A few feet away stood the Maryland Governor himself, watching the fun. I strolled over, put my hand on his shoulder, and said:

"Bert, it's a great demonstration, but it doesn't.mean a thing. We have the votes and that is what counts." He shrugged his shoulders, and responded with a smile, "Maybe you're right."

The unbearable pressure of the past few days was beginning to have its effects, and we knew it. The struggle for delegates had become so intense that honest rivalry was giving way to bitterness and ugly feeling. It was a dangerous spirit to have develop, and the chances were that the longer it went on, the more dangerous it would become. In such an atmosphere, men and women often give way to petty spite or hatred and take some action which they spend the rest of their lives regretting.

Balloting

Because the majority were for Roosevelt, the decision was up to us whether to seek an adjournment when the long speech-making session was over or drive right ahead with the balloting. I was nearer the point of mental and physical exhaustion that night than at any time during the convention. Throwing myself on one of the cots in the tiny gallery headquarters, I decided upon a council of war; the leaders were called in; I remained on the cot, too weary to get up, and questioned each one of them in turn as they came in. The verdict was that delay was dangerous; that time was bound to work for the opposition; that the only sensible course was to insist upon a ballot that night before adjournment. I agreed, and immediately telephoned Albany to inform Governor Roosevelt of our decision. The Governor sat through the night with his family and personal friends listening to every word of the convention over the radio, leaving it only long enough to talk by telephone with Chicago. He listened to the situation as I described it and quickly agreed that under the circumstances it was best to ballot without delay. Franklin D. Roosevelt is at his best in a crisis—cool, calm, clear-headed, and reveling in the thrill of combat. On that occasion, the sound of his strong, reassuring voice was like a tonic for jangled nerves.

Our "scouts" went hurrying up and down the long aisles of the stadium asking the chairman of each friendly delegation to visit the Roosevelt headquarters. When they arrived, we asked them to stand fast, to hold their delegations in line, and to be prepared to ballot no matter how late the hour or how much they disagreed with our program. The chairmen did as we asked, and their loyalty in standing firm was a great help.

The next step was to shut off the flood of oratory if we could. There were a number of Roosevelt seconding speeches still scheduled to take place, and we felt they would do the cause more harm than good because by that time it was after midnight and the delegates were getting restless. We felt that if our "seconders" yielded their time, the speakers for other candidates might do likewise. So we sent messengers around suggesting that it was time to get down to business. I learned something on that occasion that perhaps we should have known before: a thorough-going Democrat will give you his support, his loyalty, his vote, and his money —but never his radio time. When a Democratic orator has his throat cleared and ready, holds his manuscript in his hand, and knows the folk back home are there at the radio, it's too much to expect him to give way. Our appeal was in vain. The orators boomed away tirelessly. The first streaks of dawn were stealing into the stadium; the demonstrations had ended with a parade by the lassies in "Alfalfa Bill" Murray's kilted band; the secondings were over; and the clock showed the hour as 4:28 A.M. when Permanent Chairman Walsh banged down his gavel and announced: "The clerk will call the roll."

The convention by that time looked like a shambles. The galleries were mostly empty, and there were large vacant spaces in the area set aside for the delegates and alternates. The delegates themselves were wan and weary, petulant and ill-humored. Some were sound asleep, too exhausted even to notice the constant shouting and babble of the convention. It was a disagreeable job to ask this gathering of uncomfortable men and women to ballot on the choice of a presidential nominee; but politics is a deadly serious game. We knew that if a change of plan was announced, the opposition would immediately hail it as a sign of "weakness" on our part. Having said that the voting would take place, there was nothing to do but go ahead with at least one ballot. And to be perfectly candid, I was still absolutely convinced that the end of the first ballot would result in a break for the Roosevelt band wagon.

The first ballot took between an hour and a half and two hours before it was completed. Feeling was running high, and each side was straining for advantage. The delay was caused by delegates demanding a "poll" of each member of their delegation. That was done, of course, for strategic purposes, to show strength for some other candidate besides the one whom the majority was supporting. And Tammany Leader John F. Curry demanded a poll of the New York group, the largest in the convention. By that time, the Tiger was in the vanguard of the "Stop Roosevelt" movement, and leader Curry wanted to put the boys on record publicly. Mayor Jimmy Walker showed indifference to his approaching trial before Governor Roosevelt by casting his ballot for Al Smith. He got a cheer.

I sat on the convention platform, tense with eagerness and excitement, feverishly jotting down the vote of each state and territory as the long roll call went forward. Our delegates were standing by splendidly. Roosevelt was far out in front, and I was fairly beaming with happiness. The tally showed the New York Governor with a total of 666¼ votes, far more than a majority, and more than 450 votes in excess of his nearest rival. While the tellers were making their check and before Senator Walsh had made his official announcement of the outcome, I sat there fully expecting that some state would switch and announce its support for the majority candidate. In all the history of the Democratic Party, whenever a man received the huge vote that Governor Roosevelt did on the first ballot, he was nominated without delay. But nothing happened. I was bitterly disappointed, and the realization that almost two years of heartbreaking work was about to go for nothing sent me driving into action once more. There was no time to lose.

Dan Roper reported that McAdoo said California could not change without a caucus. I hurried onto the floor and pleaded with Mayor Tony Cermak of Chicago to use his influence to switch Illinois, knowing that Indiana would follow if that could be done. Tony was friendly, but the appeal was in vain because he insisted that the delegation had agreed not to switch without a caucus, which was impossible while the balloting was in progress. Had Illinois come over at the end of the first or second ballot, there is no doubt in my mind that under the customary practice at political conventions, the vice-presidential nomination would have gone to that state. Certainly I would have done everything possible to bring it about. There is an old saying in poker that a man frequently overplays his hand by staying too long. It happens in politics, also.

In the excitement, a delegate moved that the convention adjourn until nine o'clock that night; but the delay had been too great, and Senator Walsh ruled that the second ballot had already started and that the motion was out of order. The second roll call was largely a repetition of the first. By that time we had another job on our hands. It is an old axiom in politics that no matter how strong the leading candidate may be, a decline in strength on succeeding ballots is fatal. The arrow must go up and not down. We had held off a few votes on the first ballot and now we had to make certain that the second ballot showed a still larger majority for the New York Governor. The final tally showed 677¾ votes, a gain of 11½ votes. He was creeping upwards, and still the break failed to come.

Missouri gave us the largest increase, thanks to the friendship of Tom Pendergast of Kansas City and other Missouri leaders who were friendly. While loyal to Jim Reed, they knew he had no chance and were gradually coming over to the Roosevelt camp. In moving about the convention, I pushed my way past Daniel F. Cohalan, a New York delegate bitterly opposed to the Governor, as he was talking with Reed and urging the latter to stay in the race. The latter needed no urging; Missouri was breaking away simply because he was unable to hold the delegates in line.

After the second ballot our floor leader, Arthur Mullen, moved for adjournment, but that time the opposition leaders, feeling that it was good politics to blame us for wearisome night sessions, objected. They were also confident, as one of them expressed it, that they had Roosevelt "on the run." The motion to adjourn was withdrawn, and the third ballot got under way.

I was back on the convention platform by that time, my clothes wilted and wrinkled from the heat and my spirits down to a pretty low ebb. Turning to Bob Jackson, who stood there with me, I said, "Bob, watch this one closely. It will show whether I can ever go back to New York or not."

We narrowly escaped a serious set-back on that ballot. Knowing our intention to adjourn, Senator Pat Harrison had left the convention and was back in his hotel preparing for bed when he happened to turn on the radio. The announcer reported that the third ballot was about to start. Mississippi was voting for Roosevelt under the unit rule, and the delegation was held by the slim margin of 10½ votes to 9½ votes, with Governor Connor and other anti-Roosevelt sympathizers constantly trying to bring about a shift. Pat realized that his absence might prove disastrous. Only partially clad, he dashed out of the hotel, got into a taxicab, and was back in his seat in time to save the delegation.

Once again the voting showed the New York Governor slowly edging upward toward the two-thirds necessary to nominate. On that ballot he had 682 and a fraction, and still the break failed to come. By that time the limit of physical endurance had been reached, and both sides were ready to quit. The convention was adjourned until that night, and at 9:15 A.M. on Friday morning an army of disheveled delegates, unbathed, unwashed, unshaved, staggered thankfully forth into the sunshine.

The next few hours would tell the story. There was no rest for the weary. The coalition leaders were determined not to give in and they would be back that night fighting harder than ever. I told Pat Harrison that I wanted to see him at headquarters and then left the stadium in a cab accompanied by Mrs. Farley and George B. Hills of Florida. I had already asked Joe Guffey, Frank Walker, Ed Flynn, Vincent Dailey, and a few other trusted leaders to be there. To my mind, the mighty delegation of Texas was still the key to the situation. We went first to the private apartment occupied by Louie Howe in the Congress Hotel.

Others who were there have since recalled that meeting in conversation with me, it impressed itself so vividly upon their memory. Louie was lying on the floor in his shirt sleeves, his shirt open at the throat, and his head resting on a pillow. He had two electric fans blowing on him to bring relief from the oppressive heat. All night long he had remained in that same position, his ear glued to the radio, listening intently for the moment that never came, the nomination of his friend "Franklin" for the Presidency. Louie was actually a very sick man and he had never even visited the.convention itself. A chronic sufferer from asthma, he was attacked by frequent coughing spells that left him weak and gasping for breath. As a result of his all-night vigil, he was more haggard and drawn than usual and he made no effort to get up when we came in. He greeted us in a faint, husky voice, and his disappointment was self-evident. I recall Joe Guffey's expressing the view that Howe looked as if he wouldn't last through the day; but he had a spirit and a will to live that never gave way. He had only one thought on his mind: how to get the needed votes for "Franklin."

I asked the others to step back while I sprawled my long frame on the carpet to whisper in Louie's ear. We reviewed the situation rapidly; I told him that in my opinion Texas was the best bet and that it was my intention to stake everything on bringing over the Lone Star State to the Roosevelt banner. He agreed that it looked like the only course to pursue. In the meantime, at my request, Pat Harrison had succeeded in locating Sam Rayburn by telephone. They were friends of long standing in Congress, and, as a loyal Democrat, Pat pointed out that something had to be done and done quickly. Sam agreed to meet us in twenty minutes in the hotel apartment occupied by Senator Harrison and his intimate friend, George Allen, formerly of Mississippi and then a Commissioner for the District of Columbia. This neutral ground was chosen to avoid being seen.

I left immediately for Harrison's apartment. Upon arriving, I dropped into a chair, fell asleep, and was soon snoring peacefully. Allen tapped me on the shoulder and suggested that I lie on his bed until the others arrived, which I did and, according to George, immediately resumed my snoring. Rayburn brought Silliman Evans with him. The bargain we made to keep our previous meetings secret had been kept to the letter, even though other Roosevelt leaders had been constantly trying to get an agreement out of Sam. Without wasting time on shadow boxing, we got down to business. There was no disguising the fact that we had to have the Texas delegation to ensure victory for the Roosevelt cause. The balloting had shown that the only alternative to the victory of the New York Governor was a hopeless deadlock. Once again I stated my positive opinion that we could swing the vice-presidential nomination for Speaker Garner if Texas threw in their lot with us. Pat Harrison joined in eloquently to support my plea. Neither Sam nor Silliman needed much convincing. They were both realists in politics and they saw the situation exactly as it was. The conference lasted only a few moments. Not a thing was said by either of the Texans about the Vice-Presidency, and not a single promise was made by them. And yet I was elated. There wasn't a doubt in the world that they intended to release their delegates and swing the convention for Governor Roosevelt. As he stood up to go, Sam said: "We'll see what can be done." He had a hard job still ahead of him and he knew it.

Barely stopping to thank Pat and George, I dashed back upstairs to tell Louie the good news. Sleep was out of the question for him, and he was waiting my return. Pulling him over into the corner, I told him that Texas would come over, and F.D.'s nomination was assured. He nodded his head, and said, "That's fine." He had labored for years for just such a moment. Yet his face failed to change expression or to betray the slightest sign of emotion. What a man! Only those who knew him could appreciate what he really felt. I went off to bed for a couple of hours of needed rest.

Shortly after noon I was back in harness. The situation was somewhat humorous because for two hours various Roosevelt leaders had been frantically trying to reach me, either to learn what was going on or to enlist my help in winning over this delegation or that one. It seemed that the vice-presidential nomination was being held out as a lure in fifteen or twenty directions all at once. I assured everyone at headquarters that things were all right but decided at the same time to hold my own counsel. To spread the news too soon, hours before the convention reassembled, was to invite trouble. The early afternoon newspapers were carrying all sorts of predictions of what was to happen. The papers also carried a statement by Paul McNutt of Indiana saying that the Roosevelt vote had been disappointing and that otherwise Indiana would have led the band-wagon parade. McNutt was quoted as saying:

"Not only were we in a position to do Roosevelt some good with our own votes but our action would have brought half a hundred more."

Other opposition leaders were equally positive, and several of them were quoted as saying, "We have Roosevelt licked." Somehow, I wasn't disturbed.

There was one more ordeal to be faced. At four o'clock that afternoon, there was a press conference, and the main reception room at headquarters was packed with correspondents, some friendly and some unfriendly, but all demanding to know what about that first-ballot prediction of mine. There were a lot of wisecracks mixed in with a lot of good-natured "ribbing," and there was nothing to do but take it. I explained that under all the rules of the game Governor Roosevelt was entitled to the nomination after he had developed such strength on the first ballot and that his nomination was certain when the convention reassembled. Some reporters took this new prediction with a grain of salt, while others sensed something in the air and wanted to know what was taking place. I declined to say where the additional votes were coming from.

There was a wild scramble all that afternoon that almost defies description. The opposition leaders actually believed that they had Roosevelt "on the run," and of course each one of the rival managers was hoping the lightning would strike his candidate. As part of the campaign, they had our delegates deluged with telegrams from "back home" demanding that they quit the New York Governor and vote for someone else. To offset that propaganda Louie Howe had Roosevelt send our delegates a long message, urging them to stand firm.

Garner Breaks the Deadlock

Sam Rayburn was busy rounding up his Texas delegation and laying the groundwork for what was to follow. At about three o'clock in the afternoon he was informed that Speaker Garner wanted him on the telephone. The Speaker was in his office in Washington. They exchanged greetings, and then Mr. Garner told Sam: "I think it is time to break that thing up. This man Roosevelt is the choice of that convention. He has had a majority on three ballots. We don't want to be responsible for tying up this convention and bringing on another Madison Square Garden that might defeat the party candidate in November." Speaker Garner said positively that the nomination should be decided on the next ballot. Sam agreed fully but he asked the Speaker to be patient while he tried to see how it could be worked out.

Rayburn had already called for a caucus of the Texas delegation in the Sherman Hotel early that evening, and the California delegation was to caucus in the next room. The delegates were assembling, and Sam slipped out of the room to telephone Speaker Garner and to get an official release, the next and most important step in the proceedings. In the hallway he met William Gibbs McAdoo, the leader of the California delegation. The latter said: "Sam, we'll vote for Jack Garner until Hell freezes over if you say so." Rayburn replied that he was on his way to telephone the Speaker and for McAdoo to go back and release California. The ensuing conversation was a model of brevity. In keeping with a prior understanding, the Speaker was handy to the telephone waiting for the call. Sam asked him:

"Do you authorize me to release the Texas delegation from voting for you for the presidential nomination?"

"Yes."

"Do you release the Texas delegation from voting for you for the presidential nomination?"

"Yes."

Thus Garner broke the deadlock and ensured Roosevelt's nomination. Sam said good-by, hung up the receiver, and that was all there was to it. Rayburn went through this formality, carefully making sure of his ground, in order to be forearmed against those who might claim that he had no authority to release the Garner delegates. We had been making constant efforts to win over California through publisher Hearst and others without realizing that under their primary law the delegates from that state were morally bound to continue balloting for the Speaker until he released them or until it was shown conclusively that he had no chance for the nomination. In other words, the break could not be arranged without Garner's personal consent.

The struggle was not over yet. Rayburn found himself facing one of those curious and ironic situations which occur so often in politics. Early in the spring at the state convention, the Roosevelt forces in Texas had made an effort to capture the delegation. Despite their activities the Garner forces won easily and, naturally, in making up the slate of delegates, very few of the Roosevelt followers were included. That was bound to happen under the circumstances. Now Rayburn found himself confronted with the task of trying to rally a delegation to the Roosevelt standard, a large number of whom were generally known to be "bitter-enders" in their opposition to the New York Governor.

The scene that followed behind closed doors in the caucus room was as lively and exciting as anything that happened in Chicago. It was a kind of a miniature convention all over again. A sizeable portion of the delegates led by the irrepressible Amon G. Carter, Fort Worth publisher, wanted to continue voting for Garner even after Rayburn had announced that the Speaker himself wished them to go elsewhere. Carter and others made fiery addresses to the delegates, condemning the efforts to shift their support, and urging them to stand fast in the opposition ranks. The place was in an uproar; women were weeping hysterically; and, just to keep it boiling, a couple of delegates from Illinois managed to slip by the guards at the door and were circling about the room asserting that Garner would get thirty votes from their delegation on the next ballot. After a long delay, the Texas delegation got down to voting and by the narrow margin of fifty-four to fifty-one, with several absent, it was decided to swing behind Roosevelt. We had cleared the last hurdle—just by a hair's breadth. Silliman was instructed to find me and tell me what had happened.

Since there have been many conflicting stories told about what happened at Chicago in relation to the incidents just described, it might be well to clear away a few misunderstandings. In the first place, no one but Speaker Garner himself was in a position to release either the Texas delegation or the California delegation. While a great many people friendly to our cause tried to reach him by telephone in Washington, he positively refused to speak to anyone except Sam Rayburn with the exception of one occasion when he talked to a personal friend and then not about what he proposed to do. In keeping with our pledge to Rayburn, no one in our camp tried to telephone him directly. It was common knowledge at the convention that Al Smith kept a call in for twenty-four hours, vainly trying to reach the Speaker. Others in the opposition ranks were likewise making frantic efforts to reach him.

The impression was widespread at the convention, and it has been given currency since then, that publisher William Randolph Hearst was primarily responsible for breaking the deadlock. He and Mr. Garner had served in Congress some thirty years before the convention and, during the intervening time, they had never met and had never conversed with one another. The publisher made no effort to communicate with Mr. Garner while the convention was in progress, either by telephone, telegraph, letter or through an intermediary. To give the whole picture, it is only fair to say that, to my knowledge, Mr. Hearst never stated or intimated that he was instrumental in breaking the deadlock.

Completely ignorant of the fact that their cause was now hopeless, the managers for the other candidates continued their frantic efforts to "Stop Roosevelt" right up until the convention reassembled at nine o'clock that night. Some of their efforts were effective, and others bordered on the ludicrous. A friend of mine,

Ambrose O'Connell of Iowa, who afterwards became my executive assistant in the Post Office Department, was having dinner with Senator Walsh of Montana just before they were to leave for the stadium. Daniel F. Cohalan of New York, who had previously urged ex-Senator Reed to stay in the race, came over to their table where they were sitting. "We have Roosevelt stopped, Senator," said Cohalan, "and I'd like to have authority to present your name to the convention as a compromise candidate." The Senator glanced up in astonishment, thanked him rather coldly, and went on to explain that he had no presidential ambitions. Louie Howe had just told Senator Walsh what was to happen—in addition to which the Senator had shown conclusively at Madison Square Garden eight years before that he would never in any event take a nomination at the hands of a convention over which he presided.

Inducements to the Garner forces were being offered, along with the others, to stay in the race. It was hinted that the opposition might get together in his support and that his forces could expect up to three hundred votes on the fourth or fifth ballot. Frank Hague offered to switch his thirty-six votes to the Speaker.

As a result of their efforts, the coalition managers were in high glee because, it must be confessed, they had succeeded in cracking Mississippi and the chances were that on the next ballot, the twenty votes of that state would have gone to Baker or someone else. But, while they had been successful in opening a tiny crevice in our ranks, we had forced a split in theirs as broad as the Grand Canyon.

Having learned about the action taken by the Texas and California delegates, I knew positively that it was all over and the nomination was assured. I couldn't resist the temptation to tell some of the New York City leaders in the hope that they would see the light and join the band-wagon procession. Among those I called on were Curry, and John McCooey, the Brooklyn leader. The former assured me that he had just talked to the opposition manager and that they stated positively that Roosevelt was stopped. There was no use in continuing that effort. I started to eat dinner in the hotel dining-room but was so nervous that before the main course was served I jumped up, excused myself, and dashed out for a taxicab. Two enthusiastic Smith rooters, both friends of mine, were already in the cab and they argued all the way to the stadium that I should desert Roosevelt and go to the rescue of the Happy Warrior.

The scene that followed when William Gibbs McAdoo took the platform to announce that California had switched to the Governor of New York State, while the galleries howled their disapproval, has been told and retold until it is familiar to everyone. McAdoo had graciously offered to yield to Texas, but Rayburn felt that it might cause further ill feeling in his delegation to have the Lone Star State make the break first. When the galleries were finally brought to order by Mayor Cermak's appeal, the balloting started, and the stampede was on. I kept my own tally, and just the moment that the necessary two-thirds majority had been recorded for the New York Governor, I dashed to the headquarters room on the gallery floor and got Albany on the telephone through the private switchboard. I then experienced the greatest thrill of a lifetime of politics—the privilege of congratulating Franklin D. Roosevelt on his nomination for the Presidency of the United States.

On the fourth and final ballot, Governor Roosevelt had received 945 votes; Alfred E. Smith 190½; and 13 were scattered among other candidates. I regret to say it was not unanimous. Even though the outcome was a foregone conclusion, that last roll call was highly interesting because of the light it shows on the emotions that sway men's minds.

Perhaps there is no disappointment in the world equal to that which comes to a man who has had a chance for the exalted office of the Presidency, only to see it dissipated before his own eyes. The other candidates for the nomination had put up the hardest fight they knew how; they had used every legitimate means to win, but when the prize eluded their grasp, they accepted defeat like good soldiers and graciously yielded to the victor.

In this spirit of sportsmanship, and in keeping with the high principles that always marked his conduct in public life, Governor Albert C. Ritchie himself announced the switch of Maryland's sixteen votes from his own candidacy to the standard of the New York Governor. Ex-Senator Jim Reed took the platform to appeal for party harmony. Every candidate in the field released his delegates with the single exception of Al Smith, who had been twice placed in nomination for the Presidency by the man who now succeeded him as the standard-bearer of the Democratic Party.

The Smith delegates from New York, Massachusetts, and other states remained in opposition to the end, and the assumption is that they did so with his approval. The next day, ex-Governor Smith left his hotel quickly and started back for New York City without offering his congratulations to Governor Roosevelt who was flying to Chicago to accept the nomination. There was no doubt in the world that the Democratic nominee would be next President, and Smith had lost the coveted prize to one of his own lieutenants.

The excitement in the stadium was terrific all during the final balloting and it continued even after the outcome was no longer in doubt. While searching for me just before the balloting got under way, Silliman Evans had an amusing experience. He met Pat Harrison just in front of the speaker's platform and told him that everything was finally settled; that both Texas and California were going over to Roosevelt. Pat started on the run for the Mississippi delegation, then turned around and raced back to Silliman. He grabbed him by both shoulders and shouted, "Are you sure?" After being assured that it was true, Pat started on his way again at double-time to reach the delegation. He knew that Mississippi had recently caucused and had voted to leave the Roosevelt forces by the slender margin of one vote. What he didn't know was that the back-sliding delegate had been taken away from him through the efforts of the man he just talked to, Silliman Evans. The latter had turned the trick the night before while he was working with the opposition to break the Roosevelt ranks. Evans had brought pressure through a mutual friend to have the delegate change his vote.

All that night and the next morning, I was constantly busy trying to answer the anxious queries of delegates and others who wanted to know about the Vice-Presidency. Some of our most enthusiastic supporters were asking that we have a conference without delay to pick a man for second place on the ticket. There were a number of candidates being urged for the place, including Senator Dill, Governor Dern of Utah, and Senator Wheeler—

each one of whom had been a steadfast supporter of Governor Roosevelt from the beginning. I declined to call such a conference and avoided as many inquiries as possible.

Among those who called in the morning was Bernard M. Baruch, New York financier and lifelong Democrat, who wanted to know if it was too late to consider Governor Ritchie for the vice-presidential nomination. I replied that it was. My mind was fully made up that Speaker Garner was entitled to the nomination if he wished to accept, and, with the aid of several others, I had already started the job of swinging the entire Roosevelt strength behind his candidacy. This plan had been communicated earlier by telephone to Governor Roosevelt, and he told me to go ahead and do what seemed best. I told Sam Rayburn, who gave his approval.

Just before the balloting got under way, Rayburn called the Speaker in Washington, told him he was about to be nominated for Vice-President, told him that Governor Roosevelt was coming there to address the convention in person, and suggested that he also talk to the delegates over a voice-amplifying system connected with the telephone. This was the first time that the Vice-Presidency had been mentioned to him in the many conversations between Chicago and Washington. It was known to his friends that he had no desire for the office but preferred to remain in the Speakership. He had acted to break the deadlock, when his chances were just as good as those of the other opposition candidates, solely because he had in mind the welfare of the Democratic Party.

There was only one other candidate nominated for the Vice-Presidency, and he withdrew before the balloting commenced and moved to make the nomination of Speaker Garner unanimous. The nomination carried without a dissenting voice.

The Candidate and His Campaign Manager

We hurried out to the city airport by motor car and waited there several minutes, hemmed around by a pushing throng, eagerly watching for an airplane that first appeared as a tiny speck on the far-off horizon, grew steadily larger, and finally circled around the field to a graceful landing. Out stepped members of the Governor's family and after them the nominee himself, his face wreathed from ear to ear in the famous Roosevelt smile. We were jostled and pushed and shoved by cameramen, reporters, radio announcers, special police, and a host of curious citizens all headed for the same place. Somehow, I managed to get alongside. F.D. was on the lookout. He grasped my hand cordially, and exclaimed, "Good work, Jim."

On the motor ride from the air field to the convention hall, the Governor kept one hand constantly upraised in friendly greetings to the crowds along the route while with the other hand he made notes and marginal corrections on his acceptance speech. Louie Howe sat beside him with some material prepared at Chicago which he thought should be included. The Governor took the first page of Howe's material but the rest of the talk was his own manuscript. With his usual confidence and foresight, he had been busy at Albany during the convention week writing his acceptance speech!

A few minutes later the convention delegates were thundering their applause to the ringing words of a presidential candidate who promised to make war on the Republican Party, to make war on the Eighteenth Amendment, to make war on the economic depression, and who, above all, promised to bring about a "New Deal" for the masses of the American people. This was the first mention of the New Deal. The speech was a masterpiece of its kind, and the electric response it awakened was a tribute to the personal magnetism of Franklin D. Roosevelt, a useful political talent that has since made him one of the greatest vote-getters in the nation's history.

The proceedings at Chicago were not quite finished. After the convention adjourned, there was a meeting of the Democratic National Committee to elect a new chairman. It has been the traditional privilege of a presidential nominee to name the man who will be charged with the responsibility of conducting his campaign for the White House. Governor Roosevelt appeared at the meeting in person and very graciously recommended James A. Farley. I accepted the nomination.

III. The Birth of the New Deal

TAMMANY AND HAGUE FALL IN. SET-UP FOR THE NATIONAL
CAMPAIGN. BREAKING THE "FRONT PORCH" PRECEDENT.
JIMMY WALKER'S TRIAL. HUEY LONG AGAIN. LEHMAN
BEARDS THE TIGER. ADVICE FROM THE CRACKPOTS. FIRST
MENTION OF THE CABINET. THE ROOSEVELT LANDSLIDE.
GREEN INK. FORMING A CABINET. THE "BRAIN TRUST." RE-
PEAL OF THE EIGHTEENTH AMENDMENT. BESIEGED BY JOB-
HUNTERS. REWARDING THE FAITHFUL. HUEY LONG'S HAT.
LONG ASKS A SENATE PROBE. HUEY'S THIRD-PARTY THREAT.

THE intensity of the struggle which had to be waged to capture
the Democratic presidential nomination for Franklin D. Roosevelt
in 1932 was in reality a tremendous piece of good fortune—far
more effective than if he had won the honor without a battle in
a drab convention. The love of drama is age-old in the human
heart, and by the time the Governor of New York was flying to
Chicago to accept the nomination, the attention of every voter
in America was turned his way.

Roosevelt played the role with consummate skill, and the
country caught the picture of a smart and daring man who knew
what was wrong with the economic machine and what was needed
to set it right. His ability to discuss political issues in short, simple
sentences also made a powerful impression. We noticed shortly
after his acceptance speech, from reports of state and local leaders,
that he had gotten away to a flying start. He never lost that
advantage.

A political convention blows in and out like a ninety-mile gale.
The pressure and excitement at Chicago reached unbelievable
heights during the week while the Democrats were in session.
On Sunday, the day after adjournment, the city seemed as quiet
as a tomb.

I left for New York with Mrs. Farley and a number of intimate friends. Everyone was in a happy mood, ready for a little fun and frolic, and a party was soon under way in the dining car. Naturally, I was expected to join in and help celebrate the great triumph. But the effort was too much. After trying to answer a few questions on how the victory was won, I gave up and tumbled into the berth for an unbroken sleep of fourteen hours, the first really untroubled rest after months of constant nervous strain and furious activity.

The train arrived the following morning in Grand Central Station in New York City, and after bidding good-by to the rest of the party, I went to a near-by hotel barbershop to get shaved and refreshed for another ordeal which lay immediately ahead. It was July Fourth, a national holiday, and from time immemorial the day set apart for the annual patriotic gathering of the historic Society of Tammany which had its origin back in the stirring days when Thomas Jefferson was trying to forge the common people into an effective political weapon.

The Society of Tammany is purely a fraternal and social organization and for that reason must be distinguished from the Democratic organization of the Borough of Manhattan which is known throughout the nation as Tammany Hall. The majority of Democratic leaders, however, belong to both organizations, and the Fourth-of-July gathering is held in the Hall itself on Seventeenth Street. Even after taking residence in New York City, I had never become an active member of Tammany Hall, although the leaders of my assembly district named me as a member of the county committee in my election district.

Tammany and Hague Fall In

Nevertheless, I had only one purpose in mind: to swing a united party behind Governor Roosevelt in his campaign for the Presidency, and knowing the importance of capturing the vote of New York State, I was determined to smoke the pipe of peace with the Tammany leaders. A few friends of mine, who saw me that morning before the exercises got under way, were deeply disturbed and warned me against going to the Hall.

They pointed out that the Tammany leaders were still in an ugly frame of mind over the failure of the party to nominate

Al Smith at the Chicago Convention and that most of the blame was being heaped on my shoulders. "If you attend," said one friend, "you'll be hissed and booed and maybe something worse will happen. It may turn out to be an unfortunate beginning for the campaign, especially if it gets into the newspapers. The best thing is to stay away entirely until the ill feeling blows over."

The danger of a "Bronx cheer" didn't bother me, and I started off to see the thing through. The outburst of silence that greeted my entrance into Tammany Hall was really touching. A stranger being there might have assumed that a wake was in progress and that the corpse had just dropped in. Apparently my attendance was wholly unexpected, and those in the crowd were too astonished for a moment to believe their own eyes. Not a sound was heard as I moved out onto the platform from the wings—an unusual reception for a newly-made chairman of the Democratic National Committee. The suspense was broken after a few seconds by scattered hisses from the Braves in the gallery, but the Chieftains on the floor and the Sachems on the platform continued to look straight ahead in stony silence.

The exercises, lasting a couple of hours, consisted chiefly of straight, old-fashioned Fourth-of-July oratory with plenty of enthusiastic applause from the crowd. There was no mention of what had happened at Chicago. Al Smith was present, and when the exercises were over, I shook hands with him and all the other Tammany leaders who were on the platform. They were friendly enough, and I got the impression that it helped considerably to have me extend the olive branch first. A news writer in describing the incident said the good will of the Tammany Sachems was won over when I remarked, "Aren't we all Democrats?" It was a great line, and I certainly would have used it if it had occurred to me.

Before plunging into the campaign, which meant four more months of hustle and bustle and endless labor, I slipped over to Atlantic City, without revealing my whereabouts, for a week or so of badly needed rest and relaxation. The strain of the preconvention campaign had been terrific, and Louie Howe and other Roosevelt leaders were good enough to let me alone while the pleasant sunshine and invigorating sea air were helping me to get back a lot of badly-needed physical reserve.

During the Atlantic City visit, I received a telephone call from Frank Hague, the Mayor of Jersey City, who had acted as manager for the Smith forces and field marshal for the entire anti-Roosevelt forces at Chicago. He said there was no soreness on his part over what had happened, that he was whipped in a fair fight, and that if Governor Roosevelt would come to New Jersey to open his campaign, he would provide the largest political rally ever held in the United States. The Governor agreed and went to Sea Girt, New Jersey, in the month of August to address a monster outdoor rally, speaking from a platform erected in front of the summer home of Governor A. Harry Moore. Frank Hague kept his word. It was a lovely summer day, although a bit hot, and a flat field of many acres stretched out in front of the speakers' platform every square foot of which seemed to be filled with people. They were standing up, packed tightly together in solid ranks, and at first glance the crowd seemed endless. While it is very nearly an impossible task to estimate the size of a crowd like that, the chances are that the newspaper estimates, which varied from 100,000 to 115,000 people, were not far wrong. Certainly the throng was vast enough to cover the playing field of a couple of major league ball parks. If it wasn't the biggest rally in history up to that time, it must have been very close to it. In view of the turn-out which he engineered with the help of his Jersey City leaders, the recollection of Frank's dire threat at the Chicago Convention that Governor Roosevelt couldn't carry a single Eastern state, if he was nominated, brought a smile to those of us who accompanied the presidential nominee to Sea Girt.

Set-Up for the National Campaign

The campaign set-up of the Democratic National Committee in 1932 was whipped into shape and made to function with a speed that amazed veteran observers of political happenings, simply because the group around Governor Roosevelt were convinced all along that he was sure to be nominated and had already outlined a program, which was put into operation without delay. Headquarters were established in New York City, and while, in general, the campaign was run in much the same way as others before it, a few innovations were given a trial and proved highly successful.

There were two errors common in previous national campaigns which we were determined to avoid in the effort to put Governor Roosevelt in the White House. The first was the appalling waste of literature that usually took place through negligence and lack of foresight, a waste that not only cost a sizeable amount of badly-needed money but in addition detracted from the effectiveness of the campaign. We knew, for example, that huge bales of posters, pamphlets, and flyers were sent to state chairmen or county chairmen who, being too busy conducting meetings and doing other electioneering work, often left the literature to gather dust on the office shelves. A comprehensive check-up made by a field force convinced us that in some prior elections, less than 10 per cent of the campaign literature had actually found its way into the hands of voters who might be influenced by such propaganda. Another bad practice springing from carelessness was to send a mass of material about farm relief and related questions into crowded city voting precincts and to send material on labor conditions into rural areas.

The first step taken to correct this situation was to collect at headquarters a complete list of county and precinct workers for every state in the Union. The literature was sent directly to those men and women who were actually out trying to win votes, and always in small quantities. We learned that it was good policy to send a sample bundle or a small amount and have them ask for more, rather than to send too much without a request from them. The worker in the field who gets ten lithographs of the presidential candidate soon has them distributed, and he likes to "jack up" headquarters by demanding more and insisting upon prompt delivery. If he gets a huge bundle the first time without asking, for some reason it seems to cause him to lose interest.

The county or precinct worker also seems to feel that he has a new standing in his home community if he gets his orders directly from the "generals" who are directing the campaign against the political enemy. It gives him a sense of satisfaction to be let in as part of the show, and the degree of loyalty awakened by this simple gesture is truly gratifying. The fellow out in

Kokomo, Indiana, who is pulling doorbells night after night and respectfully asking his neighbors to vote the straight Democratic ticket, gets a real thrill if he receives a letter on campaigning postmarked Washington or New York; and we made sure that this pleasure was not denied him.

Perhaps the most effective innovation of the 1932 campaign was the expansion of the women's division into a major unit of the headquarters set-up. The effort to capture the feminine vote, of course, was not new, as it had been carried on after a fashion in previous campaigns, but the Roosevelt forces felt that it had been done in a haphazard manner and that a more intensive effort was needed to get the best results. Fortunately we had a group of women workers who had had long experience in political organization work in New York State and who were thoroughly familiar with the issues and public questions in which the women voters were interested. Among these were Mrs. Franklin D. Roosevelt, who had taken an active part in many previous Democratic campaigns, and Miss Mary W. Dewson, the head of the Women's Division. We knew what they could accomplish. In the gubernatorial contests of 1928 and 1930, they had gone over the Empire State setting up Democratic county units where none had existed before and the results were quite amazing. A comparison with past elections showed that the total party vote picked up anywhere from 10 to 20 per cent, after a women's organization had been established. We felt that the same kind of job could be done on a national scale. We also learned that the feminine workers took their job in deadly earnest and that they were apt to be more faithful than the men in distributing literature and doing the other little irksome tasks that are so necessary for victory.

The successful effort to cultivate the feminine vote was a large factor in the 1932 presidential election and in two subsequent national elections. The Roosevelt administration has remembered the lesson by appointing more women to really responsible positions, including one member of the Cabinet, than any previous administration. And the number of feminine delegates at Democratic National Conventions has continued to exceed the number at Republican conventions by a wide margin.

We had one tremendous advantage, even at the very beginning

of the 1932 campaign, which lent confidence to the entire organization and made the job of winning the presidential election far easier than it might have been otherwise. This advantage was a genuine conviction shared by Governor Roosevelt himself and those connected with him that his election to the Presidency was a foregone conclusion. Mr. Hoover, despite well-meaning efforts, was rushing from one mistake to another in his fumbling efforts to grapple with the depression, and it was apparent to all competent observers that public opinion had turned against him. The straddling plank on Prohibition adopted by the Republicans was too great a handicap for the Hoover-Curtis ticket to overcome in the East, while in the agricultural sections the depth of bitterness against the administration in power at Washington was wellnigh unbelievable. We knew at Democratic headquarters how the political tide was running, and this psychological factor was a big help.

Nevertheless, it was wise to avoid the danger of overconfidence, and realizing that national campaigning was new to me, I drafted an able corps of assistants to assist in the work at headquarters. One of these was Senator Claude Swanson of Virginia, who had the reputation of being one of the shrewdest hands at practical politics in the United States Senate. He was chairman of the Senatorial campaign committee. He had an office near mine, and I never recall asking his advice on one of those ticklish personal problems that are constantly bobbing up in a campaign without getting a clever suggestion on how to escape without offending anyone and without hurting the cause. Another invaluable helper was Senator Jack Cohen of Georgia, who had been a tower of strength during the preconvention campaign in lining up Southern delegates for Roosevelt at the Chicago Convention. Jack had a pleasant, matter-of-fact manner that made people feel at home with him. He was an assistant chairman of the committee, and when visitors from distant states came to headquarters to unburden their woes and worries, they went away perfectly happy after a talk with Senator Cohen. I brought in Joseph C. O'Mahoney, now a Senator, to act as first assistant chairman. Joe had a cool head, was a good organizer, and most of all he was intimately informed on the mining, farming, and livestock problems of the Western states, an invaluable asset. I was also fortunate in having the services at headquarters during the entire campaign of Arthur J. Mullen, Democratic National Committeeman from Nebraska who had a long and active career in the Democratic Party and whose knowledge of national politics was most helpful to me during that important period. Many previous Democratic campaigns had faltered badly because the officials at headquarters knew nothing about those problems and made no effort to learn. That was a notable blunder of the Smith campaign in 1928.

Of course, one of the most responsible tasks in the drive to win a presidential election is the process of determining what issues are to be stressed and what pushed aside, and what arguments are to be used in meeting the propaganda bombshells of the enemy. That is, in fact, perhaps the most important of all work in a campaign, and the choice of issues is decided upon only after the most careful and searching inquiry into the state of public opinion, into the attitude of industry, labor, and other vital groups; into the question of whether an issue has national or only local appeal, and above all others, into the question of guessing just where the foe should prove most vulnerable. It is easy to realize how a line of attack might fail to impress the public, or worse still, might rub public feeling the wrong way and in the end turn out to be a boomerang. That has happened on occasions too numerous to mention.

The publicity department has a big role to fill in setting the tone of a campaign, and our side had an advantage in the presence of Charles Michelson, the wise old fox who had the Republican spokesmen thrashing about in a fury because of the clever manner in which he exposed the ineffectiveness of the Hoover administration. In connection with publicity, there is an amusing side light on one of the propaganda barrages laid down by the penmen for the Republicans. They decided to sell the nation the idea that John Garner, Democratic candidate for Vice-President, was a Red, or at least had Communist leanings, because he had introduced a moderate-sized public works bill in the House of Representatives in the hope of providing employment and at the same time helping to relieve the depression. The Hoover administration plumed itself on its success in sidetracking the bill, and as a result was turning its heaviest siege guns on Garner. John Garner was about as unAmerican as the Mississippi River or the Grand Canyon. As I have indicated, he had been in Congress for years where he was known as one of the most reliable authorities in the country on such intricate problems as government finance, taxation, tariffs, and revenue bills. The effort to paint him as a Red seems so silly in retrospect that few people recall that it was done. It is important, however, in pointing out how a propaganda campaign can be used to distort a man's views and character in the public eye—that is, until the public has an opportunity to size him up on its own account.

Breaking the "Front Porch" Precedent

During the summer I paid a visit to Washington to consult with a number of Senators and Representatives on general problems, but most of all to get their views on the one question which was absorbing everybody's attention—what kind of a campaign should Governor Roosevelt conduct? Should he stay at home on the front porch mumbling a few homely platitudes while the world came to his door, or should he take to the stump and travel about the country flinging bold challenges at the Republican foe? That is a technical political question that always has been a plague to harassed managers and strategists, and probably always will be.

I talked with a number of Senators individually and with two or three groups. As I remember it, they were almost unanimous in recommending that Governor Roosevelt should stay in his own back yard, confining himself to radio talks with now and then a short visit to a near-by city to address a carefully planned rally. They argued that the campaign was won anyway, and why take a chance on a trip to the Far West that might prove disastrous?

The weight of evidence was on the side of those who were urging the traditional stay-at-home campaign. The refrain runs something like this: Bryan stumped the country while McKinley remained at home and was elected. Cox toured the country while Harding sat on his front porch and got elected. Wilson remained in the White House while Hughes went to California, snubbed Senator Hiram Johnson, and thereby lost the election. Davis stumped the country while Coolidge remained at home and the country kept cool with Coolidge. It was a tough nut to crack for anyone who favored a front assault on the enemy lines by the presidential candidate in person.

Many of the old-timers were familiar with the amusing and oftentimes tragic incidents that featured presidential barnstorming trips in prior campaigns. It frequently happened that the party candidate arrived in a city to make an address, only to find two rival groups of Democrats on hand to welcome him, each one wanting to take him in tow to the exclusion of the other group. Whichever faction managed to win out, the outcome was always disastrous because the defeated group would go away mortally offended and ready to do a little knifing on election day. No wonder that the political Nestors in the party said, "Stay at home."

A few days later I went up to Albany to talk with Governor Roosevelt himself on the advisability or nonadvisability of his embarking on a campaign trip to the Pacific Coast, with several major addresses to be delivered at strategic points on the way out and back. It was a sultry August day, and we sat in our shirt sleeves on the front porch of the Executive Mansion discussing whether he should stay there or take to the road instead. I told him what the Senators and Representatives thought and why they frowned on a long campaign jaunt as a foolish gesture that was tempting fate unnecessarily. It was rather a long story, and when I finished, F.D. was sitting there looking off into the distance, rubbing his hand on his chin, a characteristic pose when he is turning something over in his mind.

"Jim, what do you think yourself?" he asked.

"I think you ought to go and I know you are going anyway."

He grinned and nodded his head. "That's right. I have a streak of Dutch stubbornness in me, and the Dutch is up this time. I'm going campaigning to the Pacific Coast and discuss every important issue of the campaign in a series of speeches."

The trip appealed to Roosevelt because it was a daring thing to do. Once having made up his mind, after long consideration, the fears of other people would not deter him from doing something which he was sharp enough to see could be converted into a strong political asset. He went all the way to the Pacific Coast and back, and the net effect was to line up state after state in his column so solidly that nothing could shake them loose. Not only that, but later on he defied tradition again by going on a campaign tour into the states of the Solid South, something that no Democratic presidential candidate has done since the Civil War. He was sure of that territory but he wanted to build up a feeling of good will that would be helpful after he got to the White House.

The good old rock-ribbed, die-hard, steadfast states of Maine and Vermont got so much public attention as the result of a subsequent election that a word about the part they played in the first Roosevelt campaign might be interesting.

Roosevelt motored over to Vermont from Albany and delivered a series of outdoor stump speeches to the citizens of the Green Mountain State, who gave him a quiet but friendly welcome. The state was always looked upon as lost beyond redemption to the cause of the G.O.P. so that the visit of the New York Governor was regarded as nothing more than a gesture. Yet it was effective. The Republicans carried the state as usual, but the Democratic vote picked up in encouraging fashion in those areas where the Governor had talked.

Maine is always a bugaboo to campaign managers in national elections because the state ticket is elected in September, and knowing that it was almost always Republican, some sinister fellow had coined that irritating phrase, "As Maine goes, so goes the nation." It was an old tradition in Democratic circles that a few weeks before the state election, a delegation from Maine arrived at headquarters with the cheering news that if they were given financial assistance, the Pine Tree State was sure to electrify the country by deserting the Republican ranks. The delegation arrived as usual.

Being an optimist in politics, I directed the treasurer's office to give them a substantial sum of money to help in the state election. When Louie Howe learned of it later, he snorted in disgust. He said it was money thrown away, that Maine was certain to go against us, and that the funds could have been used to excellent advantage in some other place. Governor Roosevelt heard about it and also did a little kidding on his own account, intimating that a few shrewd gentlemen from the sticks had put one over on a city slicker. Nevertheless, I agreed with Bob Jackson of New Hampshire, who was at headquarters in charge of the speakers' bureau, that an uprising in Maine was very apt to occur if the Democrats were on the job and equipped for a good fight. When the returns from Maine came in, I had the last laugh. Victory for our state ticket had a profound psychological effect upon the campaign throughout the whole country.

There is nothing in politics—or out of it—that has the lure and fascination of a presidential candidate's special train. Getting the train fitted out properly is a job for experts, and the tiny details which have to be worked out in the most thorough fashion almost defy description. The right kind of living quarters must be provided for the candidate himself, members of his family who may be going along, and the staff of secretaries and assistants who help in preparing speeches, handling the press, and greeting visiting politicians. In addition, space must be found for dozens of newspaper correspondents, news photographers, movie cameramen, representatives of telegraph companies, and radio announcers. An invitation to go along is considered a high honor, and the person delegated to make up the list of guests must be as snooty as a society hostess in issuing invitations for a swank party. The trip usually develops into a "family party" with everybody becoming fast friends before it is over.

We were extremely cautious in making preparations for Governor Roosevelt's swing to the Pacific Coast and back. Men like Senator Thomas J. Walsh of Montana went along to make sure that the responsible party leaders in every state were let aboard to meet the presidential candidate and that the gate-crashers and those who had no business on board were kept out. I knew Roosevelt's skill in handling difficult political situations, and there was no fear in my mind that he would become involved in local, factional quarrels.

I started out a couple of days after the train and joined the party at Salt Lake City. Before leaving headquarters, Louie Howe gave me last-minute instructions to tell the Governor that his speech on the need for a balanced Federal budget should be one of the first to be delivered. I told Roosevelt who got a laugh at my description of Louie's serious and worried manner. He has a strong sense of the mischievous and I think he put off the speech just to have some fun with Howe. The budget speech was delivered much later in the campaign, at Pittsburgh, and it came back to trouble him more than any other speech he ever delivered.

Jimmy Walker's Trial

Before going West, Governor Roosevelt was called upon to play one of the oddest roles ever to fall to the lot of a presidential candidate. While the eyes of the entire nation were turned towards Albany because of the likelihood that he would be the next occupant of the White House, the Governor was compelled to forget about the political scene while he acted virtually as a trial judge in hearing the removal proceedings brought against Mayor James J. Walker of New York City. The dapper Jimmy, always jaunty and happy-go-lucky, was under serious charges of neglecting the city's business and of grave derelictions in his official duties, the charges going before the Governor as a result of sensational investigation conducted by the dour but thorough Samuel Seabury. Under the New York State Constitution the Governor was required to clear Jimmy or remove him from office.

With Martin J. Conboy, a well-known member of the New York bar to assist him in sifting the evidence, Governor Roosevelt sat day after day listening to the host of witnesses called by Seabury to discredit the Walker administration. The "trial" was good headline news because of the important personages involved, and there was a feeling that the outcome might prove to be one of the key factors of the presidential campaign. It was one of the few bright spots on the Republican horizon, and the G.O.P. leaders were gleefully hoping that the presidential nominee would get himself all tangled up in a muddle with Tammany Hall. Quite a number of them were openly predicting that he would lack the courage to oust Walker, thus causing the whole country to lose confidence in his character. They didn't know their man at that time.

All during the trial I was the center of a fierce tug-of-war which, in addition to the thousand and one other duties of the campaign, caused me plenty of grief. In the first place, I had known and liked Walker for a great many years, and his friends assumed that the only thing necessary was for me to call up Albany, tell the Governor to call off the hearings, give Jimmy a clean bill of health, and the whole thing would be over—just like that. It is next to impossible to argue with people who have such a short-sighted point of view, and their number is legion. Then there were the people with a little more breadth of vision, who felt that the New York Mayor had a big following in certain New England cities and over in New Jersey and that his removal might cause us to lose a number of pivotal states, in addition to New York State itself. I told those people as patiently as possible that if the evidence warranted such action, Roosevelt would remove the Mayor and that no power on earth could stop him. And I added that courageous action of that kind would help him in the estimation of voters throughout the entire United States, not hurt him. On the other hand, I pointed out also that there was no disposition to make Walker a martyr solely to help the Governor politically and that if he were entitled to be exonerated, he would be.

I mentioned the case to Roosevelt personally on two occasions only, under the following circumstances. Early in the summer Jimmy telephoned and requested me to meet him at the Casino, a restaurant in Central Park. I went there and John F. Curry, the leader of Tammany Hall, was with him. The Mayor pointed out that the Governor had announced the selection of Conboy as special counsel to help him and that the hearings would shortly be under way. He wanted his attorney, John J. Curtin, to have a talk with the Governor or Conboy so that he could be informed on the procedure to be followed, what witnesses were to be called, and so on. I agreed to lay their request before the Governor, which I did subsequently on a visit to Albany. Roosevelt said that they were entitled to the information and that he would see that they were properly advised and given their rights in every respect. I can truthfully say that Walker never asked me to intercede with the Governor on his behalf. Moreover, as I have pointed out, at the Chicago Convention a few weeks earlier, he voted against nominating Roosevelt for President, even though he knew then that he was going to face removal charges before him.

The Albany hearings had been going on for a few weeks when the Mayor's brother died. Some of the leaders in New York City felt that it might cause a sympathetic reaction in his favor if the

hearings continued without postponement for a week or two. I
went to Albany with Edward J. Flynn, leader of the Bronx, and
a few others to discuss the campaign generally and also to ask the
Governor's view on postponing the hearings. Upon reaching
Albany, I received a report that Walker had resigned, a report
which proved to be true. The resignation ended the entire controversy, and the conspicuously able manner in which Roosevelt had
conducted the hearings enhanced his reputation around the entire
country.

A lot of people got the impression that the case was "pre-
judged" and that the Governor had determined to oust the Mayor
anyway. I did not discuss it with him again until several months
later when he was President-elect. Motoring down from Albany
to Hyde Park, he told me that Conboy and he had never once
exchanged views on what they thought the evidence indicated,
either before or after Walker's resignation. He spoke of his personal fondness for the Mayor and expressed regret.

An incident happened during the summer months that had a
humorous touch and helped to relieve the tension around headquarters. I had a visit from Norman Mack of Buffalo, one of the
old field horses of Democracy, who had been active in the party
for generations and at one time had been chairman of the National
Committee. He had been national committeeman for New York
State until the Chicago Convention, when the honor was taken
away from him by the action of a few narrow-minded leaders who
resented his support of Roosevelt for the presidential nomination.
Norman was meticulous in his personal appearance and always
wore well-tailored clothes of the finest quality. He also carried a
cane, which added a touch of dignity to his appearance. On this
day, Mack was deeply agitated over Al Smith's glum silence and
his refusal to come out openly for the party ticket. He said, "I'm
going down there and tell Smith that he should come out for
Roosevelt, and I'm going to talk right up to him." Until he
started out the door, I hadn't noticed that in his nervous excitement, the grand old man had kept on his bedroom slippers instead
of putting on shoes. I didn't have the heart to tell him. About
an hour later he returned from the Empire State Building, still
wearing the slippers.

"Did you get Al over to Roosevelt?" I asked.

"No one can talk to that man in the frame of mind he's in now," replied Norman, deeply disturbed over the failure to accomplish his mission.

Huey Long Again

Sometime along in the torrid summer months, before the big guns of the campaign had really begun to boom, we had a call from another distinguished visitor who likewise was noted for the splendor of his sartorial raiment. Huey Long was in again. The Louisiana Senator was itching to perform a stellar role; he wanted to steal the national spotlight; and there is no doubt on earth that, in the back of his mind, he was already looking forward to the day when he himself would be a candidate for the Presidency. When he telephoned headquarters to ask about an appointment, a secretary promised to let him know right away and asked where he could be reached.

"I'm at the Waldorf-Astoria," replied Huey, "in rooms 1220, 1222, 1224, 1226, 1228 and 1230," naming a string of room numbers that left the impression he must have taken over at least one floor of the hotel for himself and his retainers. A short time later he came over to see me and to outline the plan he had in mind. He wanted the National Committee to provide him with a special train, equipped with loud-speaking devices and other paraphernalia, in which he would travel all over the United States, going to every one of the forty-eight states, promising immediate cash payment of the soldiers' bonus. He fairly beamed as he outlined the grandiose scheme, which apparently had tickled his imagination and fired the flame of his ambition. The prohibitive cost of such a venture never troubled him for a moment and neither did the fact that it would be a fatal mistake of policy to have the presidential candidate outshone by a mere campaigner in the ranks. And, of course, he didn't bother to inquire whether Roosevelt favored cash payment of the bonus.

The scheme was unthinkable, but it would have been the blunder of the year on my part to say so bluntly or to hurt his feelings in any way. I promised to take it up with the other advisers at headquarters, one or two of whom almost dropped over in a swoon when they heard what Huey had proposed. A day or so later, I called Huey back to headquarters and explained that his original plan had been modified and a substitute speaking schedule worked out which we were most anxious to have him fill. He knew that he was being given the "run-around" and he received the bad news with a mixture of disgust, disappointment, and rage. There was no doubt that he had his heart set on that special train.

He strode up and down the room in swift strides like a panther, stopping every now and then to pound his fist on my desk, all the time voicing a lot of very unflattering remarks about the "pin-heads" who were trying to run Roosevelt's campaign. "I hate to tell you, Jim, but you're gonna get licked," he finally wound up. "Yes, sir, Jim, you're gonna get licked. Hoover is going back into the White House, and that's all there is to it. I tried to save you, but if you don't want to be saved, it's all right with me."

After a while Huey calmed down and listened to reason, agreeing to fulfill the speaking tour we had mapped out. At the time, there was a disposition to regard him as somewhat of a freak who was far more apt to hurt the cause than he was to help it. The part he played at Chicago was still remembered vividly, and most of the old-timers at headquarters were frankly afraid that he might upset the apple cart. So they had very carefully worked out a schedule which would take Huey into states believed already lost or so firmly committed to Roosevelt that he couldn't possibly do any harm.

I don't hesitate to say that we underrated Long's ability to grip the masses with his peculiar brand of public speaking, which was a curious hodgepodge of buffoonery and demagogic strutting, cleverly bundled in with a lot of shrewd common sense and an evangelical fervor in discussing the plight of the underprivileged. He put on a great show and everywhere he went, especially in the larger cities, we got the most glowing reports of what he had accomplished for the Democratic cause. We talked it over later at headquarters, and it was generally agreed that if we had sent Huey into the thickly populated cities of the Pennsylvania mining districts, the electoral vote of the Keystone State would have gone to the Roosevelt-Garner ticket by a comfortable margin. We never again underrated him.

Lehman Beards the Tiger

As I have said earlier, because New York has the largest electoral vote of any state in the Union, it is always looked upon as a pivotal state in a national election and for that reason gets an unbelievable amount of attention from both Democrats and Republicans—in fact, a degree of attention usually out of proportion to what the situation really calls for. It was so in 1932. The factional hard feelings engendered at Chicago were gradually petering out as the campaign wore on, and Democratic prospects of capturing the state looked pretty good. We decided that Lieutenant Governor Lehman was entitled to succeed Roosevelt in the gubernatorial chair. The Tammany Hall leaders were forgetting their wounds from Chicago and were sincerely supporting the national ticket, but their pride had been injured, and they were casting about for a chance to regain a lot of lost prestige. When the idea gets about that a political "bigwig" no longer has a finger in the really inside things, he has already started on the toboggan and he knows it. The Hall leaders decided to reassert their independence and show their power by backing a rival candidate, Mayor John Boyd Thatcher of Albany, for the gubernatorial nomination. Thatcher had a good record in office; he came from one of the oldest and finest families in the state; he was backed by the powerful O'Connell brothers who controlled Albany county politics; and all in all it was a pretty good choice for the test of strength.

I was nominally state chairman but being busy with the national campaign, had delegated the job of looking after New York State to Vincent Dailey, a trusted assistant. He did a thorough job on his own account, traveling all over New York State into every county in the hunt for Lehman delegates, in much the same way that I had traveled across the continent looking for Roosevelt delegates the previous year. The state convention met in Albany in late September to nominate the state ticket, and a rapid count of noses showed that only the slender margin of a few votes would decide the issue—with control of New York State hanging in the balance.

I was a registered voter in New York City but was denied the right to attend the Albany convention as a delegate—perhaps the only time in history that a national chairman and a state chairman combined failed to make the grade. This petty gesture was maneuvered by John F. Curry, the Tammany Hall leader, whose blundering and shortsighted leadership during this period laid the groundwork for the subsequent downfall of the Democratic organization in New York City and the loss of the mayoralty to Fiorello LaGuardia. Curry was about the opposite of the popular conception of a Tammany leader; he was a quiet-spoken, well-groomed man, kindly and honorable in his personal relations. But he was way over his head in trying to decide party politics, and his successive errors were really tragic.

Tammany actually controls only a part of New York City, and there was no reason under the sun why that organization should have opposed Roosevelt at any step in the game. Ed Flynn, the Bronx leader, always stood loyally by the Governor, at Chicago and elsewhere, and as a result of his stand was endorsed time and again by the voters of his district in overwhelming fashion. But the Tammany leader seemed to get a lot of satisfaction out of putting his own neck in the noose, a habit that finally lost him his political head.

The atmosphere at Albany, just before the state convention got under way, was crackling with excitement. There was a rumor around that Al Smith had promised Curry and John McCooey, at a secret meeting several weeks earlier, that he would go along in supporting Thatcher for Governor, an extraordinary thing, as Lehman had always been one of his most generous campaign supporters. There was no way to confirm or explode the rumor, but the Happy Warrior was on his way to Albany. His attitude on the Governorship would tell the entire country whether he intended to swing into line behind Roosevelt for the Presidency or go the whole way and bolt the Democratic ticket. We had positively no inside knowledge on the subject because, just after the Chicago Convention, we had decided to let Smith alone while his own friends endeavored to win him over. And all during that period he had maintained a complete silence on national politics.

A final check-up revealed that, thanks to the missionary work of Vince Dailey, we had a margin of about eleven votes for Lehman—with more than eleven hundred accredited delegates in attendance. There were a couple of upstate delegations in doubt, but Vince met them at the railroad station early in the morning and promptly escorted them to the Executive Mansion for an intimate chat with Governor Roosevelt. The chance to rub elbows with the man who would probably be the next President had a magical effect because the delegations stayed put from that time on. Roosevelt's personal appeal swung the tide for Lehman. As a matter of fact, if it was not for Governor Roosevelt's personal assistance and driving force, Lehman would never have been nominated.

Al Smith arrived promptly and gave the key to the course he intended to pursue by throwing himself with his customary vigor into the battle to secure the gubernatorial nomination for Lieutenant Governor Lehman. The usual behind-the-scenes bickering and bargaining got under way, and this time a few funny things took place because the rival factions were meeting in suites only a few floors away from each other in the De Witt Clinton Hotel. A delegate would receive all kinds of flattering attention in one suite and perhaps receive a call to visit the other side on his way out. That made it pretty easy to check up on what was going on. I walked in on one of the opposition meetings to say "Hello," but the leaders turned away and refused to let me hear what was going on. There was no doubt about it; I was being snubbed by the Tammany boys.

We held our lines fast and the Tammany leaders, sensing that another defeat was in prospect, determined upon a really smart piece of strategy that very nearly upset the entire slate and might have had a tremendous influence on what has happened in national affairs since then. They suggested a compromise whereby Robert F. Wagner, then in the United States Senate, would be the party candidate for Governor and Lehman would run for his vacated seat in the Senate. Wagner would have consented because the threat to party harmony was so great, although his ambition was to remain in the Senate and push the relief and labor legislation in which he was vitally interested. There was no doubt that a vast majority of the delegates were ready to flock to his standard if the plan wasn't halted in rapid-fire order.

We went up to the suite occupied by Lehman in the De Witt

Clinton to discuss the best way out of the dilemma. He was getting a raw deal, being the victim of a cruel thrust really aimed at Roosevelt and me, and we felt sorry for him. Al Smith was there, and so were Ed Flynn, Vince Dailey, Herbert Bayard Swope, and a number of others, including Judge Lehman, a brother of the Lieutenant Governor. We telephoned the Executive Mansion a couple of times to inform Roosevelt of what was going on and to get his opinion on how we should proceed. It was early in the evening, the convention was to meet an hour or so later, and the nomination had to be made that night because it was the last date for filing under the primary law.

We finally decided that the best course to pursue was to have Lehman himself go downstairs, beard the Tiger in its den, and serve notice straight-from-the-shoulder in the fewest possible words that he would have the gubernatorial nomination or nothing. There was a real threat behind that plan because it could only mean a record vote in the convention itself, and neither Curry nor McCooey wanted to offend the large Jewish vote in New York City by ruthlessly tossing overboard a faithful public servant who deserved the honor, simply to satisfy a grudge against a third person. It was a move designed to out-fox the Tammany leaders at their own game.

The weather was unseasonably hot, and the air in the over-crowded room was stifling by the time this plan of action was agreed upon. Lieutenant Governor Lehman had spent most of his adult life in banking and financial circles, and the rough and tumble of backstage politics with its accompanying nervous strain was still comparatively new to him. He was a man of medium height, rather shy, reserved in manner, and with the most intensely serious mental attitude of any man I had ever met. He didn't have the faculty of easing the strain now and then with a hearty laugh or a good outburst of anger. On this occasion, he was visibly disturbed over the twist of fate that seemed destined to rob him of the Governorship just when it was within his grasp. The perspiration was rolling down his face. Some suggested that Smith and I and one or two others should accompany him on the visit to Curry and the other Wigwam chiefs. But Lehman had plenty of nerve. "No, I'll go by myself," he replied, and he did. He went out the door and was gone some time, during which he served warning on the group opposing him that he had enough votes to nominate him for Governor and that he intended to go through. He came back and said they had given him no answer. A short time later, word came up that Tammany had yielded to the threat and was willing to support Lehman for Governor. The stage was set for the great drama of reconciliation between Roosevelt and Al Smith, the big event to which everyone had been looking forward with the keenest anticipation for days.

The affair took place after dinner in the vast old armory where the state convention was in session. A more spectacular setting could hardly be imagined, especially in view of the grim pulling and hauling over candidates that preceded the meeting. A mob of people had stormed the doors early, eager to be in on the show, and the armory was packed so tightly that it seemed about ready to bulge. The usual trappings of a political convention were in evidence—a band or two, plenty of bunting, and a lot of gaily colored streamers festooned about on anything that would hold them.

Governor Roosevelt came in, proceeded at once to the platform, and received a rousing ovation from the crowd. Governor Smith was down on the floor in his seat as a delegate. Someone motioned him to come forward. He strode up the aisle to the platform, pushed out his hand, and said, "Hello, Frank, I'm glad to see you." The Governor responded, "Hello, Al, I'm glad to see you too—and that's from the heart." I came in with Roosevelt and was standing side by side with the two men when this conversation took place. Immediately the place was in a bedlam as the crowd went to it with a "whoop and a holler" that almost blew the roof off the armory. There was a dramatic touch in the reunion of these two stalwart leaders, whose years of close association had been broken by the bitter-end struggle between them for the presidential nomination; and the sight brought forth a sentimental response from the thousands of yelling and cheering delegates and visitors. Al and Frank stood there grinning like schoolboys for several minutes, with hands clasped together, while the excited photographers took picture after picture.

Smith made only a brief reference to the national ticket in his speech nominating Lehman for Governor, but it was apparent to everyone that the breach was healed and he intended to remain loyal to the party.

Later Smith took the stump for the Roosevelt-Garner ticket, but his first speech in New Jersey soured a lot of people in the South and West because he raked over the unpleasant issues that had led to his own downfall when he ran for the Presidency four years before. His other speeches, especially the one in Boston, were very effective and helped us considerably in New England and all along the Atlantic seaboard.

The act of reconciliation at Albany helped us more than anybody could have foreseen at the time, due to a flight of fancy on the part of a very clever member of the corps of journalists. The reporters were seated in the press box at the armory, just in front of the platform, ready to dash off color stories for the press of the Nation on the public hatchet-burying ceremony between Smith and Roosevelt. It was a "natural" for human interest, and the reporters were straining forward trying to catch every word or glance or change of expression that might betray the actual feelings of the two men. With the place in an uproar and excited partisans scrambling back and forth on the platform, I don't know how they were able to find out anything, let alone write about it in good, readable, newspaper style without waiting a minute.

But the reporters were equal to the occasion—and especially one member of the group, big Fred Storm, who was covering for one of the wire associations. Fred is noted for his ready wit and quick thinking. He sent out a bang-up story of the meeting between the two men in which he related how Smith reached out first for the Governor's hand, pumped it up and down like an old pump-handle, and exclaimed, "Hello, you old potato." Fred must have had a personal microphone attached to the Happy Warrior's lapel because I was the closest man there and I certainly heard nothing like it. However, it was the exact type of whimsical expression that Smith often used, and his legion of admirers throughout the country were delighted with that version of the meeting. Lengthy letters were written to the newspapers, telling how the phrase of "old potato" really got its start, and the expression became a classic of the campaign. It was one of those things that sounded truer than what was really said, and it went a long way in dissipating the ill feeling that existed previously. Fred did us a very good turn with that story.

The manner in which Governor Roosevelt's rivals at Chicago were coming into the field ensured a united party for the November election, and, on top of that, the Hoover campaign was unable to get going. The Republicans themselves became extremely worried over the outlook, and the President, abandoning his early plan to spend most of the time in the White House, scheduled a number of speaking tours. We felt more and more confident as the campaign went along.

Advice from the Crackpots

While a political campaign in retrospect seems like a lot of fun and gloriously exciting, during the heat of the moment, when the pressure is on, it is about as nerve-racking and exhaustive as anything humanly could be. A typical campaign organization is thrown together with lightning speed, and it grows overnight like a mushroom until it attains a size which astonishes even those in charge. In the campaign of 1932, which was relatively light for a presidential year, we had over five hundred persons employed at headquarters in New York City, and a few hundred more could have been employed without in any way wasting money or engaging in useless activities. There are a number of work divisions which are simply indispensable, for example, the publicity bureau, the radio bureau, the speakers' bureau, and the financial division. In addition there are a number of other offshoots, such as the labor division and the Veterans' division, which no sensible or worthwhile campaign organization could afford to do without. Trying to co-ordinate those different activities is a considerable undertaking in itself without attempting, in addition, to confer with hundreds of leaders and to assist in drafting campaign strategy.

And the real work is only part of the story. The trouble is that a political campaign is everybody's business, or so everybody seems to think. From the time headquarters are opened until the electioneering is over and the ballots are in, there is a steady stream of people flowing into the offices, each one of whom is anxious to unburden his or her soul of a stupendous idea that will positively blow the opposition sky high and win the election in a walk. Most of these well-meaning zealots are suspicious—they won't give up the colossal idea except to the head man himself, which makes it always a bit awkward and very often annoying. In addition to the "big idea" men, there are people who want a job, and last, but certainly not least, are the song-writers. Hundreds of the latter always show up lugging copies of a new melody that will surely "wow" the populace and often they sing the song whether you like it or not. I recall one occasion when a composer, who brought along a portable victrola and records, succeeded in getting by the guards and planting the music box on my desk. The song he composed was terrible.

The poor, misguided persons who bring in half-baked notions have a persistence worthy of a better cause. A great many of them apparently believe in the old selling slogan, "Never take no for an answer," because they refuse to be put off and hang around headquarters for days on end. There was the Indian Chief who professed a great love for Governor Roosevelt and the Democrats, and said he had hiked all the way from the tribal reservation in the Far West just to do his bit for the cause. He wanted to don his battle regalia and stand around headquarters to show the world that the Indian vote was committed to us. Of course he wanted a little something in return and was highly indignant when we refused to put him on the pay roll. He came back time and again, finally threatening to go over to the opposition unless his demands were met. The Chief made good. The office workers glanced out a few days later and saw the Chief going by on a float in a Republican parade, arms akimbo and dressed in his finest feathers and war paint.

Another steady customer was a stout, good-natured colored woman who wanted us to provide a free steamboat excursion ride around Manhattan Island every day that summer for members of the Negro race. A few of the disappointed ones got ugly, but that didn't happen very often.

The best way to meet the situation is to keep calm, cool, and collected and to put up with the annoyances and interruptions as good-naturedly as possible. A sense of humor is the best thing in the world to keep a person from going into a rage or into a nervous breakdown. I recall a few incidents that happened in 1932 out of which we got many a good laugh and which helped us keep a sense of balance when the excitement was at its peak.

The outer gate at headquarters in the Biltmore Hotel, leading to the suite of offices occupied by the assistant chairman and by myself as national chairman, was under the supervision of Senator William C. (Wild Bill) Lyons of Texas, a lifelong Democrat who won the distinguished title of Senator by serving in the Colorado legislature—or at least running for the job. Bill's recollection is that he actually served one or two terms in the State Senate, but an impression still persists among his old-time friends that he was merely a candidate. Bill had moved to New York several years earlier and was engaged in the clothing business when I met him through Damon Runyon, noted sports writer for the Hearst newspapers, and Jack Dempsey, former heavyweight champion of the world, both of whom were pals of his in Colorado. We became friendly. When the campaign opened, Bill more or less took over the job of head gate-keeper, appearing at headquarters before we were fully organized, and going to work without being asked. I thought it was commendable zeal and put him on regularly. Bill had a keen eye for the time-wasters and the cranks and he did a good job of shooing most of them away.

The Senator had, and still has, a speaking voice noted for its high pitch and unusual volume and he could whisper louder than the average man talks. Being a self-made man, Bill also constructed his own rules of grammar as he went along. His favorite way of discouraging an unwanted visitor was to boom:

"Mr. Farley ain't got no time to see you. He's busy seeing important people. You're just wasting your time around here because you ain't going to get in."

Once in a while he varied the formula by saying, "No luck, the Kid is out," an offhand reply that surprised and perhaps shocked one or two distinguished visitors who didn't understand that Bill looked upon me as a sort of protégé.

The Senator likewise had a habit of blunt speaking, of saying what was on his mind in plain words, a trait he had acquired during his long years in the open country; but unfortunately a great many people didn't appreciate that fact, and he was often misunderstood.

One day Bill was tending the gate when a short, slender man, quiet in dress and quiet in manner, approached the rail and asked to be let in to see Mr. Farley. Somehow he failed to impress the Senator, and despite the visitor's entreaties, the entrance was barred. He had to take his choice of seeing someone else or going away without seeing anyone at all.

The first I knew of the incident was a few minutes later when the telephone rang, and a voice at the other end of the wire said: "Jim, how can a man get in to contribute $10,000 to the campaign? That fierce fellow at the gate won't let me by."

It was William H. Woodin, a leading industrialist of New York City, one of our most generous contributors and later Secretary of the Treasury in the Roosevelt Cabinet. Unassuming and good-natured, as usual, Woodin merely chuckled over the incident and thought it was a great joke on himself. I suppose many other individuals would have been mortally offended under similar circumstances.

On another occasion the Senator met his match—and a little more. Among those who sought admission was the austere and dignified ex-Senator James A. Reed of Missouri. Recognizing him as he approached, Bill sprang forward, slapped him on the shoulder, and said, "Hello, Jim, come right in—you're always welcome." But a slap on the shoulder was too much familiarity for the stern and unbending Reed, who growled, "You insolent so-and-so," pushed his way by, and continued on in. It left Bill speechless for the first time in his life.

Louie Howe, although he had a priceless sense of humor, was a sworn enemy of Senator Lyons, and with his usual dogged persistence, he was determined to unloose him from the job of gate-tender. He felt that Bill's rough and ready mannerisms and his constant assaults on the King's English were giving visitors the wrong impression. When I went West to join President Roosevelt on the trip to California, Louie thought the chance had come; he immediately called Joseph C. O'Mahoney, assistant chairman in charge, and said, "Joe, fire Bill Lyons." Joe advised me by long-distance telephone that night what was happening, and I advised him to stall Louie off until my return. Joe managed to do so, although with considerable difficulty, because Howe checked up time and again to see if his orders had been carried out.

Shortly after my return, Louie telephoned that he was coming over to see me right away. He still maintained his offices a few blocks away in the rooms used for the preconvention campaign. I saw a chance to have some fun with Howe and to get even with him for trying to discharge Bill. A new fellow was put on the gate with positive instructions not to let anybody in. When Louie appeared a few minutes later with his customary slovenly clothes, his hat pulled down over his eyes, and a bunch of papers under his arm, he looked exactly like a typical campaign "bug" who had an idea to sell. The gate-keeper refused to let him in, and Louie hopped up and down and threw his hat on the floor, he was so enraged. While this was going on, Bill Lyons was in an adjoining room hardly able to contain himself, he was so happy to see his arch-enemy being kept out. Finally, Howe had to telephone me, and I strolled out and let him in. After a few moments I explained that he had been "framed," that he wanted a new gate-keeper and now he had him. Louie took the joke in good part, as he always did, but one of the first things he said was, "Bill Lyons ought to be fired anyway." He never gave up. Neither did Bill, and he was still on the gate when the campaign reached its finish.

First Mention of the Cabinet

Between his lengthy electioneering jaunts, Roosevelt attended to the duties of the Governorship at Albany. He liked to be informed on how the campaign was progressing from our point of view, keeping a line on things by means of the telephone and of lengthy reports which were sent to him constantly. Occasionally, I went up to Albany for a personal chat. Roosevelt liked the excitement of campaigning; he is never so happy as when, surrounded by a few men who know the business as well as he does, he is figuring out ways and means of capturing public sentiment and beating off the enemy's attack. He keeps pencil and paper handy on those occasions and he often jots down his ideas to make them plainer or draws diagrams and charts outlining in graphic fashion the plan he has in mind. One of these meetings at Albany took place on the night of October 10, a date fixed in my mind ever since because something was said that made the occasion worth remembering for me.

We were in the small study of the Executive Mansion which he used for an office, just the two of us, going over in detail the reports on public sentiment which came in to me from all parts of the country and discussing other phases of the campaign work. After the business of the night had been disposed of, we sat there for quite a while just talking over personal things and looking ahead a bit to what might happen after the election. F.D. is a great fellow to chat in a friendly manner about individuals he knows and to show an interest in how they are getting along. A number of names entered into the conversation, especially of men who were connected with the campaign, and we mentioned their strong points and their weak points and the little foibles that tended to distinguish them from one another. The line of conversation brought something to the Governor's mind because he said to me, "Jim, keep an eye on the men around headquarters and those who come in from time to time, and tell me later on what you think about appointing them to positions in the Administration."

This was the first time a mention of Federal appointments ever passed between us, and naturally it was a subject that had an unusual degree of interest for me. As he had brought up the subject voluntarily, I thought it was a good chance to reassure him about a matter that had been on my mind for some time. I told him that I had been most careful not to embarrass him by promising positions or appointments to anyone, either during the Chicago Convention or after it. He told me that he appreciated that attitude and that he had pursued the same policy himself. He added that, although he constantly reflected on the grave problem that would be his after he got to Washington, he had only definitely determined upon three appointments—Louie Howe for his secretary, George Dern of Utah for Secretary of the Interior, and myself for Postmaster General. It was a very nice way of letting me know. The appointments were later made, except that Dern was shifted to the War Department.

The Roosevelt Landslide

As the campaign moved down the homestretch into the last month before election, it was as certain as anything humanly could be that the American electorate was getting ready for one of those periods of drastic upheaval which result in the "ins" being tossed out rather unceremoniously while the "outs" take over the government. The political pendulum in the United States, once it starts moving, can swing faster and farther than it does in almost any country on earth, a wholesome thing which has a tendency to keep those in office a little bit more on their toes. The Democratic Party, after three successive and crushing defeats in presidential elections, was about to ride back into office on the crest of a landslide. The signs were unmistakable. President Hoover was out on the stump frantically endeavoring to regain the magic of his lost prestige and trying to ward off the unhappy fate which he realized at last was about to overtake him. President Roosevelt was moving about on a leisurely schedule delivering a series of campaign speeches in which he did little more than "shadow-box" with the main issues, taking no chances of losing an election that was sure to go his way. As the campaign progressed, larger and larger crowds flocked to the Roosevelt rallies to get a glimpse of him, one of the best signs that popular sympathy was running in his direction. Another sign, rarely in error, was the fact that the "fence-sitters" and the gentlemen who love to bet on the winner were flocking into headquarters to congratulate me and others on the manner in which the campaign was conducted. There are always large numbers of those folks, whom I once heard described as invincible in victory and invisible in defeat.

Knowing the victory psychology was in the air, we helped it along whenever there was an opening for doing so—and very often when there was no opening at all. In response to the query which always comes from newspaper correspondents about the probable outcome of the election, I responded on all such occasions that we declined to concede a single state to the Republicans. That, of course, was exaggerating the situation just a trifle. We never had any hope of capturing Maine, Vermont, or Connecticut. However, it is often bad policy to concede a state in advance of the election, not only because it might contribute to the defeat of state officials on the same ticket, but also because it is unfair to the party workers in those states who must get out the vote and do the other routine electioneering work. And the truth was that in 1932, we were feeling very cocky and inclined to be over-optimistic in view of the expected party triumph following on twelve long, lean years out of office.

The people around headquarters were fairly bubbling over with excitement during the week before election. By long tradition the candidate of the party always concludes his campaign with a giant rally in Madison Square Garden on the last Saturday night of the campaign so that Governor Roosevelt's presence in town added to the excitement. The Republicans made a few efforts to get him involved in last-minute controversies, especially on Mr. Hoover's prediction that grass would grow on the city streets if we got into power, but Roosevelt was too old a hand at the game to be caught in that fashion. He ignored the enemy and gave the country the picture of a confident man who knew what he intended to do when the reins of government were passed into his hands.

The arrangements for receiving returns at National Head-quarters in the Biltmore Hotel on election night itself were en-trusted to the competent care of Louie Howe who had consider-able experience in that line from past state elections. The set-up had to be taken care of with extraordinary pains even down to the last, minute detail. In the event of a close election, the manner in which voting returns came into headquarters might be of the utmost importance in guiding the actions of those in charge, and while there was no anticipation of anything like that, at the same time there was a determination that no precaution should be over-looked.

Howe arranged to receive a direct all-night report from each of the three great newspaper wire services over at his own office a few blocks away, and these reports were shifted and sent to head-quarters without delay. The facilities provided by the telegraph companies were taken care of in the same manner. In addition, at headquarters we had a staff of more than a dozen telephone girls, selected for their intelligence and general ability, who sat around a long table and did nothing else but receive reports from key

Democratic leaders in all parts of the country who were instructed in advance to phone us at regular intervals. I sat at the head of the table and in numerous instances talked with these leaders personally when they called in. Their reports were immediately condensed into short typewritten statements to be handed individually to a few of the most important leaders and also to be enlarged and projected on a screen for the several hundred others who were present.

The only pessimistic note around headquarters while these preparations were going forward was sounded by Louie Howe himself, who, as the critical time drew near, seemed to get gloomier each moment in his attitude about the final outcome. Never a very optimistic soul, Louie persisted in looking upon the dark side of things and, in keeping with his customary practice of keeping out of the limelight, he decided to remain in his own little hide-away office on election night and to stay away from headquarters entirely. Even when the first returns started trickling in, showing a positive swing to F.D.R., Louie was still unhappy over the outlook; in response to my kidding remarks over the telephone, he responded that it was always a bad sign to take an early lead. Laughing at his fears did no good; he refused to buck up and look on the cheerful side. I recall that later on in the night, about 11:00 P.M., when the worst pessimist in the world could no longer question the outcome, Mrs. Roosevelt and I left headquarters and went over to visit Howe. He was overjoyed at what was happening, but he declined to accompany us back to headquarters. He preferred to congratulate F.D.R. over the telephone while he continued to pore over the returns like a little miser inspecting his gold. Louie's one great desire was to see the telegram from President Hoover conceding defeat and congratulating his successful opponent. It failed to come over the wire until about 2:00 A.M. the following morning, and Louie remained on the job until it arrived.

An election-night party is always an intimate family affair, and that year it was made even more so because of the faculty possessed by Roosevelt of cutting away stiff and pokey formalities and making other folks enjoy themselves by the simple formula of having a good time himself. Naturally, it was a gala night, and, while he perhaps had a clearer insight than anyone else into the years of trial and work that lay ahead, he thrust all that aside for the time being to enjoy a few hours of fun and frolic with his friends. The outcome was definitely known early in the evening, and as a result there was really no feeling of tension at all. All the members of the Roosevelt family, including his wife and mother, were there for the celebration, and the sight of a mother fortunate enough to see her son elected to the highest office in the land was so unusual that she attracted almost as much attention as the President-elect himself.

We had a room set apart for Roosevelt where he could receive returns without being bothered by the mob of people milling around in the other offices. He sat there with me and one or two others. At first, we were deeply interested in studying reports to see how the balloting was going in various sections of the country, but after a while that became too tiresome. We gave it up for a lot of good-natured bantering and joking. I remember Roosevelt got a laugh by remarking in a mournful tone, "I don't seem to be doing so well in Pennsylvania." Under other circumstances, it might have been mournful but it was hardly so when he was sweeping the country by a majority unprecedented for the Democrats.

When the result was certain and President Hoover had issued a statement acknowledging defeat, the new President-elect suggested that we let in the hundreds of people who were outside the doors almost literally bursting with the desire to see him and to offer their personal congratulations. The handshaking occupied quite a while, and among those who called to wish him well were Al Smith, John J. Raskob, Senators Wagner and Copeland, Governor-elect Lehman, and a host of other friends and acquaintances. Kermit Roosevelt, the son of Teddy Roosevelt, was one of those who came in to offer congratulations. They shook hands cordially and F.D. said, "Give my regards to all the family." Kermit responded that he would and then added, "But I don't know how welcome this news is going to be." He was referring to the election and the fact that Teddy's family were still ardent Republicans.

When Mrs. Farley came along in the line of those congratulating him, Roosevelt leaned over and whispered, "Get ready to move to Washington." Bess said she didn't want to go to Washington. "Well, get ready anyway," he added, "because Jim is coming down there after the Fourth of March."

Before going home, hundreds of campaign workers gathered together in the Biltmore ballroom, where Roosevelt made a brief address of thanks, during the course of which he very generously said that the major credit for his election belonged to Louie Howe and me.

To put it rather mildly, the outcome of the election was highly pleasing to me personally, and so were the thousands of telegrams which poured in from all parts of the country from Democratic workers and others praising the way in which the campaign had been conducted. Having invested about two years of my life in the job, working almost literally night and day, I found deep satisfaction in realizing that it was a success and not a failure. I put a tremendous amount of study and work into the campaign and, while unworried about the way in which the election was going, I honestly never considered that there was anything exceptional about the electioneering methods which we followed. For that reason, it was all the more pleasing to receive the unstinted praise of men in public life to whose opinion I had come to attach the deepest significance. Senator Hiram Johnson, the California Progressive who helped win the West for Roosevelt, telegraphed, "I take my hat off to the greatest political general of our times." Senator Carter Glass also was kind enough to wire that I was "the greatest campaign manager of them all."

One of the letters which I have come to cherish was received from James M. Cox of Ohio, a thorough-going Democrat and the party standard-bearer in 1920, who was considerate enough to sit down a few days before election to write me his views. The letter was composed so cleverly and the words of wisdom it contained are so true in politics, that I think it is worth quoting verbatim. He said:

"You know human nature as well as I do. If we should win on Tuesday, and I think we will, you will be regarded as a sort of political king; if we lose, the king's hostler. But with me, my dear fellow, the thought is this—whether win or lose, you have made a magnificent leader. You brought a party that was pretty badly torn at Chicago into an harmonious unit. You have been kind, considerate, far-seeing, and indefatigable. Not one of these words, in my humble inventory of things, will be erased if our portion on Tuesday is a defeat. I am glad to have known you better."

Another letter with a humorous twist was sent by Governor Albert C. Ritchie of Maryland, who said I was his "ideal" of a campaign manager, "particularly a preconvention campaign manager," referring to the good luck we had had in winning the presidential nomination away from him at Chicago.

On the morning after election, I went up to Governor Roosevelt's house on Sixty-fifth Street in New York City to talk over a few things in connection with his future plans that had to be taken care of without delay. The victory spirit was very much in the air, and dozens of people were dropping in to pay their respects while hundreds of idle curious were milling around outside eager to see what was going on. Roosevelt and his aides posed for pictures for the news photographers times without number.

Louie Howe said he wanted to see me on something very important, and at his request I dropped into his campaign office at 331 Madison Avenue on the afternoon of that same day without having the slightest idea of what he had in mind. For a few minutes we talked about the election generally and did a little joshing on how different it would have been if the election had gone the other way. Then Louie walked slowly over to the door, peered up and down the hall very mysteriously, locked the door, came back to his desk, and sat down. This was Louie's way of impressing me with the fact that he attached the deepest significance to what he was about to say. He had been observing the behavior of human beings throughout a long lifetime and as a result had adopted certain little mannerisms that gave emphasis to the ideas he wanted to get across.

Sitting down again, he cupped his face in his hands, pondered for a second or two, and then said, "Jim, has Franklin ever told you what he wants you to do in his administration?"

"No, he hasn't," I replied. "I have had a marvelous experience during the past two years helping him get elected to the Presidency. The election itself was reward enough, and even if he feels that he has no place for me at all, I shall be completely satisfied."

We were both sparring around a little, of course, hoping that the other would open up first. The truth is that if F.D. had gone to Washington without me I would have died, and the same was true of Louie. However, I couldn't be certain whether Louie had been instructed to tell me something or whether he was merely trying to ferret out a little information for himself.

The conversation proceeded, and Howe told me he was convinced, although nothing had been said, that the President-elect would offer me the post of Postmaster General in his Cabinet. However, he added, that it might be far wiser for me to turn down the Cabinet post and to suggest an appointment as Collector of the Port of New York, which, because of the fees attached, is one of the best-paying positions in the Federal Government. My private business had been badly neglected during the two years while I was dashing around the country on political errands, and Louie pointed out that by remaining in New York I could keep an eye on it, along with the other duties, and perhaps build it back into a paying proposition.

Then we discussed other men who were being mentioned in the press as probable appointees to the Cabinet, diplomatic posts, and other high-ranking positions in the Federal Government. Because of our work in the campaign, Howe and I had a pretty good line on almost all of those individuals being mentioned, although we made it a rule not to make comments on candidates unless the President-elect asked our opinion.

Finally, I asked Louie if he knew what he was going to do himself after the new administration started business in Washington, and he replied in the negative. "Well, please accept my congratulations," I said. "You are going to be the Secretary to the President of the United States." Then I told him about the conversation between Roosevelt and myself which took place on the previous October 10. Louie beamed all over when he heard the story, and it was perfectly apparent that he had been trying from the outset to find out if F.D. and myself had discussed him. Although his appointment was a foregone conclusion, Roosevelt had never bothered to mention it to him, even when they were living together in the same house! My own view is that F.D. took it so much for granted, and he had already formulated so many plans in his own mind centering around Howe as secretary, that it never occurred to him to mention that fact. Under the circumstances, Louie got a big kick out of hearing it first from a third party.

Throughout the campaign against the Republicans, Howe and I had worked in harness with the same close understanding that we had in the preconvention campaign which resulted in Roosevelt's nomination at Chicago. Only once during the summer did anything occur that might indicate that we were drifting apart. On that occasion, I had a visit from Mrs. Roosevelt who told me in a very diplomatic way that Louie felt he no longer enjoyed my confidence to the same extent as formerly and that as a result he was considerably upset. The news disturbed me also, and I at once pointed out to Mrs. Roosevelt that if I had failed to consult Louie it was due to an oversight or to overwork and that there was no intention in the world on my part to leave him out of the picture. She suggested that we get together for a good talk and in that way iron out any misunderstanding that might exist. I was glad to do this and called up Howe at once. We chatted amiably, and I was never able to find out whether Louie actually felt he was being overlooked or whether he took that very shrewd way of letting me know that it would be disadvantageous to both of us to break up the team.

Green Ink

When the campaign of 1932 wound up in a blaze of glory for the Democratic cause—a landslide for the national ticket that eclipsed anything the party had known since before the Civil War—it was only natural that people should begin to sit up and take notice of the men and women who were charged with manipulating the mechanism of the campaign. There is a nerve-tingling air of excitement about a presidential election, much as there is about a good football game or some other outstanding sporting event, and the whole country usually catches the fever before the spielers and the spellbinders conclude their final appeal for votes. I suppose, also, that the existence of this sporting instinct, deeply imbedded in the national character, is the real reason why the defeated side generally takes a licking with such good grace.

Having gotten a kick out of trying to guess the outcome of an election, the public, after it is all over, as a rule wants to be let in on the "inside" of things; the men and women who buy the newspapers want to know who pulled the wires and how it was done. This curiosity is the reason why so many straw votes, test votes and nationwide "polls" continue to flourish while campaigning is in progress, no matter how far off these predictions may subsequently prove to be. The fellow who makes a bad guess about the outcome, or the chap who sees his favorite poll go "haywire," comes to the conclusion that politics is a pretty mysterious business after all and he listens eagerly to the man who explains, or pretends to explain, just why things happened the way they did.

In the fall of 1932, the newspapers started to gratify the public taste for the personal side of folks in the limelight by running a number of feature stories concerning the men around Governor Roosevelt, many of them to the effect that Farley was a huge man, possessed of unbounded energy, who loved to spend his time writing thousands of letters and signing them with green ink. The stories were carried in such a widespread fashion that I got perhaps more than the usual share of inquiries from puzzled people who apparently had the impression that I did nothing else.

Why do you write so many letters—and why do you sign them with green ink? What good do they do? Why don't you go on the radio and talk to those people all at once? How can you possibly pay attention to other matters if you spend all your time signing letters?

Well, in the first place, I'm an old-fashioned fellow who was brought up in a small town, who learned his politics in a small town, and who still believes that the only way to get ahead in public life is to understand people and to sympathize with their viewpoint. It doesn't hurt my feelings when some sophisticated gentleman of the writing craft describes me as the kind of fellow who likes to go back to the old home town and salute the neighbors by their first names while they greet me in return with a hearty "Hello, Jim." The radio is a wonderful thing—it has been a tremendous factor in promoting the success of the Roosevelt political fortunes—but, to my way of thinking, there is no substitute for the personal touch and there never will be, unless the Lord starts to make human beings different from the way he makes them now.

So here's the reason why I write a letter. The receiver knows that it was intended for him personally and no one else in the world and, far more important, he can keep that letter telling about the fine help he rendered in electing the President of the United States, or the Governor, or the Senator, until his dying day. I know because I've seen them time and again—frayed, soiled, and tattered from being exhibited on a thousand different occasions but still holding together somehow or other. In fact, in the early days, I kept one or two such communications myself and was proud of them.

Now, why the green ink? Because years ago, it occurred to me that it would be wise to have some little distinguishing mark that would induce the receiver to remember me as an individual, something that would stick in his mind perhaps long after the contents of the letter itself had been forgotten. Green ink did the trick so well that it was given the job permanently.

To whom do I write? There are more than 150,000 loyal men and women in this country who are connected with regular Democratic organizations ranging from "bigwigs" like national and state committeemen, down through precinct and district captains and canvassers, to the local committee workers and other humble folk who pull the doorbells, distribute the literature, and haul the voters to the polls on election day. An army is seldom stronger than its infantry forces, and a political army is never stronger than its corps of workers. Having come up through the ranks from the lowest rung on the political ladder, I know and appreciate fully what their efforts mean to the success of the Democratic ticket. The names of all of them are on file at headquarters in New York City, and at least once during the campaign, frequently more often, a letter is addressed to each individual telling about the campaign plans and setting forth the kind of teamwork that is desired and expected. After the campaign is over, you may be sure that the worker gets another letter praising his efforts, and in nine cases out of ten the letter is richly deserved. After the campaign of 1932, the first time it was done on a wholesale scale, we learned that approximately 86,000 of these toilers in the ranks had never before received a letter from National Headquarters, and they were both pleased and appreciative.

After that particular campaign was over, Howe and I estimated that from the time the preconvention campaign to nominate Roosevelt had gotten under way a couple of years earlier to the end of the national campaign, we had sent out a total of nearly 3,000,000 pieces of mail, several hundred thousands of which I signed personally. That meant an untold amount of drudgery; at times, the grind was almost killing, but a man gets out of life only what he puts into it. The work had to be done by someone; if I didn't like it, it was always my privilege to step aside.

This general correspondence of course is only part of the work. Besides those letters sent to all workers in the campaign of 1932 and again in 1934, I sent out thousands of others to leading political workers who knew just how the political tides and drifts were going in their home districts. I had one such list of about 2,000 men and women, each one of whom was a seasoned political observer, with whom I corresponded at regular intervals, and upon whose judgment I relied in determining how the Democratic candidates were faring. The information gained in that way was of inestimable value in helping me to determine the probable outcome.

In addition to the work just described, I try to be very careful in my personal correspondence, which is exceptionally large. I have a staff of trained and capable stenographers and sometimes I call in from four to six at a time. Sorting through the mail quickly, I can indicate in a sentence or two the kind of reply I wish to have prepared and the stenographer in each case composes the answering letter. In going over the completed draft, if the salutation is Dear Mr. Jones, I scratch out the Mr. Jones and substitute Dear Bill, or whatever the first name may be, and frequently I add a postscript. Most of the letters are signed just plain Jim.

A few newspaper correspondents have described me as the nation's most prolific letter-writer, and from my experience as the nation's number-one mailman, the designation seems to be correct. The letter-signing is ordinarily left until the close of the day when appointments and other unfinished business have been disposed of. If there is a particularly heavy batch of mail, the letters running up into the thousands, I frequently sign for hours on end—usually the procedure takes me from six to eight hours.

I have been asked if my hand gets cramped or tired from steady letter-signing. On occasions it does, but not often. When that happens, I hold it under the cold water for a few moments, then flex the fingers back and forth, repeating each process until the circulation returns and the hand is normal again. After five or ten minutes, it is usually possible for me to resume without any ill effects. If there were no interruptions, I have been able to sign very close to 2,000 letters in an hour, although the pace is usually much slower. The best time for that kind of labor is at night when the telephones are quiet and there are no other distractions.

Occasionally a letter is addressed to the wrong person, or it turns up in the wrong state, and while a few such instances have been embarrassing, for the most part the practice of letter-writing has been extremely helpful. Every kind of precaution is taken to avoid errors. For example, my secretaries read the death notices every day to guard against the always embarrassing error of sending mail to deceased persons. It is quite surprising how many candidates for office die right after the elections are over, due perhaps to excitement or disappointment.

We had one mishap a year or two ago which caused me to groan inwardly and wish that green ink had never entered into my thoughts or into my fountain pen. I signed about 9,500 commissions for post-office appointees—had them sent out in regular order—and was flabbergasted sometime later when they started to pour back into the department because the ink had faded. There was no choice but to go through those hours of toil all over again. You may be sure that black ink was used the second time—although the green ink as a rule has held up pretty well.

The majority of folks who are accustomed to receiving communications from me apparently expect to have them signed in green ink because very often I get word from individuals who want to know why they received a letter signed with black ink. For some reason or other, they seem to feel cheated.

Some of the letters have resulted in humorous incidents. One of these got countrywide attention and caused me quite a little grief. When I was traveling in the Far West late at night several years ago, the train stopped in the station of a small city, and I stepped out on the platform. There were a number of people on the platform, but the night was dark, and when a voice out of the crowd shouted, "Hello, Jim," it was impossible for me to distinguish the face of the speaker. However, I recalled having correspondence with a fellow from that city and I took a chance, replying, "Hello, Joe, how are you? How are political conditions out this way?" Fortunately, it was a bull's-eye and the man was delighted because it demonstrated to the neighbors that Jim Farley actually called him by his first name and wanted his advice on political matters. Unluckily, the story got into print, and two or three rather chagrined persons wrote in to ask if he or she was the person described in the incident. Not liking to hurt the feelings of the others, it was a source of regret to me that the story had become public.

If anyone supposes from the foregoing that political letter-writing on wholesale principles was invented by me, or by anyone else now living, the impression should be corrected at once. The business was started a great many years ago when the Republic was young, and it was developed into an incredibly fine art by some of the early patriots who are now revered in the nation's schoolbooks. Thomas Jefferson was a master of the practice, fashioning the framework of a powerful political party by means of a skillfully conducted letter-writing campaign carried on by himself and his associates.

A few years ago, I happened across a letter sent to Samuel J. Tilden when he was about to begin his campaign for the Presidency, written by Horatio Seymour, one of Tilden's ablest lieutenants and campaign managers. In the letter, Seymour outlined a proposed plan of action for the approaching campaign, based upon letter-writing to precinct workers, that was so splendidly conceived it could be used as a model today with very few changes in wording. Seymour knew human nature and he knew politics. Among other things, he suggested a personal letter from Tilden to each volunteer worker, and he laid down a formula for checking on what workers were actually out on the firing line and what ones were lying down on the job. In conclusion, he recommended that Tilden announce the plan to the public as an adaption of "Van Buren's Old Campaign Methods," referring, of course, to Martin Van Buren, the Red Fox of Kinderhook, who made a name for himself by outlining a similar campaign plan back in the days of Andrew Jackson. So letter-writing has a pretty good tradition behind it in Democratic ranks. I always keep Seymour's letter close at hand and reread it frequently.

There are two fallacies about this letter-writing which are quite common. The first is that as a result of it, it is possible for me to call every person I ever met by his or her first name. The other fallacy is that the letters merely go out to a list of names, and a rubber-stamped signature would do just as well. The truth lies in between; I don't know all the workers by name but there is hardly a fair-sized city or town in the country that hasn't at least one individual known to me personally. And every national chairman of a political party should aim for the same thing, because it is impossible otherwise to do a good job.

People often inquire, "Why do you continue all this letter-writing? Aren't you satisfied with what has been accomplished?" The answer is that it is my ambition to turn over to my successor the best-functioning political party in the history of this country.

I am a firm believer in party politics—so much so, that in my opinion it would be a tragedy for Uncle Sam if either the Democratic Party or the Republican Party were to pass from the scene. There is a belief in some quarters that, with the radio and the other kinds of high-pressure propaganda methods now available, the old type of political organization is bound for disuse or decay. Not to my way of thinking, and if it is true, the fact should be deplored by every thoughtful American because the steady climb up through party ranks is still the best training ground for American officials under our democratic system of government.

The great contribution of the political party is that, except on a few occasions, it has allowed the United States to avoid the destructive blight of government by minority. No one has ever explained how that can be accomplished without political parties national in scope; and no one will ever explain it because it can't be done. We don't want three major parties in this country.

The two great political parties help to make the United States a nation because they promote national unity. Without them, it is easy to see how a lot of geographical or sectional political movements might spring up. Few people ever reflect that often a public man has no other way to become a national figure except through the medium of party politics. A United States Senator has a chance to get into the headlines and to command a following, but the Governor of a medium-sized or a small state has no such chance unless he blows up the State Capitol or does something equally spectacular. However, through the medium of party politics he can become known, and his talents for public office are made a matter of interest to leaders of the same political faith in other states. In that way, he comes into prominence and he begins to feel, and those around him feel, that he has a fair chance to become a factor in national political affairs.

If party government, and especially the two-party system, should crumble in this country, something which seems to me very unlikely, then the United States will be at the mercy of every organized minority, every ambitious demagogue, every radio spellbinder, and every political crackpot who comes along. They will spring up overnight and get control of things. And when that happens, it will be a sorry day for the majority of wholesome and fair-dealing American citizens.

The Democratic Party has existed for over a century, and its contributions to the upbuilding of the American nation as we know it, can never be overestimated. If green ink helps me to cement that party into a greater and stronger political unit, then I shall be perfectly satisfied and feel amply repaid for the untold hours of monotonous and tiresome letter-writing.

Although the incoming mail is seldom as heavy as the outgoing, I get plenty of it, including an oversized collection of post cards, notes, and other assorted missives from the misguided individuals who feel the urge to write me for no other reason except that they see my name constantly in the public prints. This type of mail is common to all men and women in public life, but I seem to get a particularly heavy dose of it. The letters may be divided roughly into three different classes, those that are threatening or abusive, those that beg for money or other favors, and those setting forth some harebrained scheme on political or governmental problems. The communications range all the way from the humorous and curious to the pathetic, and a great many of them are so pointless that perhaps only a psychologist could explain why the writer went to the bother of putting such thoughts on paper.

For some odd reason, an appeal for funds to help purchase a set of false teeth, or some other kind of dental work, seems to be a very popular form of request. I have had several of them. Then there was a man, obviously sincere and worried, who said he spent $150 for a Mexican divorce and wanted to know if the police would arrest him as a bigamist if he got married again. He was beginning to feel that someone sold him a spurious document and he asked me to set him straight. Another chap suggested that I was pretty good at picking election winners and should be just as good in picking winners at the race track. He proposed that we establish a partnership on the ponies. There was a lady in the Far West who wanted to be shipped to Shanghai as a package via the China Clipper, dressed in "an Uncle Sam suit made out of Clipper stamps." She said the idea came to her in a dream and was too good to pass up. The abusive and threatening letters are usually unsigned and seldom make coherent reading.

Some individual in New York, obviously a dyed-in-the-wool Republican, used to send a post card whenever he heard me make a grammatical slip, or some other kind of a mistake, in a radio address. He sent a post card, of course, so that the postal employees would have a chance to read about their chief's error. The observations in some instances were rather keen, and as a man often has peculiarities of speech that he knows nothing about until they are pointed out by someone else, I always tried to profit by the lessons of my anonymous teacher.

Forming a Cabinet

There is an old saying that to a Roosevelt life has never a dull moment. Whenever one of the clan is around, an experience or event that might seem commonplace to another person immediately takes on an air of excitement and adventure. That was especially true of the "in-between" period, covering the few months from the election of 1932 to the inauguration in March, 1933, when Roosevelt merely possessed the honorary title of President-elect and was marking time until he formally took over the reins of government. Under normal conditions, the sense of suspense and anticipation would be strain enough for any man. But conditions just before F.D.R. took office were far from normal. In fact during President Hoover's brief "interregnum rule," while he was working out his term of office, the flow of events quickened to a pace that now seems almost unbelievable. The industrial depression, already about three years old, very rapidly widened and deepened into a financial and business panic of nationwide proportions. The feeble efforts of the administration in power to bring about financial and economic stability had merely postponed the inevitable.

The fact that something grave and far-reaching was about to happen did not become evident at once. The magnitude of the industrial and financial paralysis unfolded itself gradually, and, as he had sources of information not available to the average person, it was only natural that Roosevelt should realize what was happening and sense the danger somewhat in advance of the great bulk of the population. I saw him frequently during this "in-between" period when his mind was fully occupied with the heavy duties of forming a Cabinet and deciding upon the general lines of policy which he proposed to pursue after entering upon life at the White House. He paid a visit to his old retreat at Warm Springs, Georgia, in the fall of 1932, and another visit in the following spring, because down there he found it possible to get much more of the solitude and time to think which at that critical period was vitally necessary. As the imminence of a major collapse impressed itself more and more upon his mind, he found it necessary to discard a great many of the things already tentatively decided upon and to substitute new, and in some cases vastly different, plans in their stead. This ability to make whatever adaptions were necessary was made easier by the fact that he had wisely refrained from making commitments on the Cabinet or in other important regards.

I had literally thousands of people pressing me, as Chairman of the National Democratic Committee, to lay their claims for this or that Federal post before the President-elect, but most of those people were advised to wait until he had completed the all-important task of deciding upon the make-up of his official family. I had another hint of my own coming appointment as Postmaster General several weeks before inauguration. Frank Walker and I went up to keep an engagement with F.D.R. at his New York City home where he was staying temporarily. It was a morning appointment, and he was still in bed when we arrived so he sent down word for us to come up. He was reading the newspapers and had them spread all over the bed. There was a dispatch from Washington which caught his eye. The story said that Postmaster General Walter Brown had purchased a costly new limousine out of department funds, although the government had already provided one, simply because the roof of the old car was too low for the silk hat which he wore to official functions. One paper had a cartoon showing Brown's head, plus the silk topper, sticking through the roof of a swanky limousine. F.D.R. remarked with a chuckle, "Frank, did you see this picture of Jim's immediate predecessor?" An opening like that was too good to be overlooked, and I promptly replied, "Thank you, sir, for the appointment." He never really notified me officially that he wanted me in the Cabinet, except in off-hand conversations such as the one just described. He employed the same way of breaking the news to a lot of other folks, whom he knew well, and who were given places in the new administration.

Cabinet-making is a delicate piece of political business, not only because of the men and women who must be given consideration but also because many deserving individuals must be left out, thus tending to make them bitter towards the new administration right from the beginning. Roosevelt had an especially difficult problem because he had captured the Democratic presidential nomination from a number of strong rivals, and the country was waiting to see if he appointed any of them to Cabinet positions. He did not—and I think most people who are experienced in public life would agree that it would have been a mistake for him to do so. I doubt, also, if any of the men who competed for the nomination against him would have liked a Cabinet post. They were shrewd enough to realize that Cabinet work requires too much "team-play"—that the individual very often must give up his own views in order to carry out the orders of the President— and they were hardly the sort to submerge their own viewpoint and personality in that of another man. This highly important matter of difference in viewpoint cropped out very early during the period while Roosevelt was pondering over Cabinet selections.

One of the first moves made by the President-elect was to indicate to Senator Carter Glass of Virginia that he would like to have him serve as Secretary of the Treasury, a position the elderly Virginian had filled with honor and distinction several years earlier under President Woodrow Wilson. The two men had become acquainted during the Wilson administration and had come to have a liking for each other. Glass had also impressed the country during his service in the House of Representatives by his able work in helping to formulate and enact the legislation setting up the Federal Reserve System. The American people had a wholesome respect for his ability, and Roosevelt felt that his presence in the Treasury would lend an air of confidence and stability that would prove pleasing to the country. Glass took the offer under advisement. Very early in 1933, however, it became evident from reports reaching the President-elect that the financial and banking conditions were far worse than most people realized, that a crisis was approaching, and that measures far more radical than at first anticipated would have to be undertaken. He felt that, under the circumstances, it was only fair that his ideas on the gravity of the subject should be communicated to Senator Glass. I was entrusted with the task and went to Washington early in January for a talk with the Senator. Realizing that mine was a very delicate mission, I solicited the aid of Rear Admiral Cary Grayson, a close friend of the Senator, in arranging the appointment. Grayson was present at my meeting with the Senator, which took place at the latter's apartment in the Raleigh Hotel.

I had met Glass only once before for a brief visit, and knew nothing about him personally except that the newspapers always called him the "fiery Virginian" and gave the impression that he could shrivel a man to a brown crisp by his burning words whenever he became aroused or angry. That knowledge made me about as ill-at-ease and nervous as a man could be when our conversation opened. I informed Senator Glass about the President-elect's attitude and then unbosomed myself of a few very learned sentences about the gold question and related monetary questions which, it was apparent, would become matters of the most vital importance as soon as the new administration came into power. This was the nub of the whole conversation as the orthodox views of Senator Glass on monetary matters were well known to the entire country. I was hardly what one might call an authority on the gold question and was scared to death for fear that Glass would let go with a tirade of strong language on the subject or, worse still, ask me a few technical questions concerning the views of the President-elect.

My fears were groundless, and as in so many cases, I found that the public impression of Senator Glass as a hot-tempered, intolerant fellow who enjoyed roasting other people on the spit was a bit overdone. He was courteous and kindly in his reply, expressed sympathy with the President-elect because of the overwhelming burden of duties which he was about to take up, and said he appreciated Roosevelt's thoughtfulness in letting him know what was the probable attitude of the new administration on financial and monetary problems. His charming manner put me completely at ease, and I came away with a more pleasant understanding of his personality and character. The way had been smoothed considerably by the tact and diplomacy of Admiral Grayson who, in later years, helped me over many a rough spot with other people in the same gracious manner. Sometime later Senator Glass informed the President-elect at a personal interview that he would be unable to assume the grave responsibilities of the Treasury. He felt that the strain would be too much for a man of his age. There was no doubt that both men realized their conflicting views on financial questions would soon lead them far apart.

Henry Wallace was chosen Secretary of Agriculture because of his broad knowledge of farming problems and the fact that his ideas on what should be done to relieve the industry corresponded very closely to the views entertained by Roosevelt himself. It was decided early that the post of Secretary of the Interior should go to a progressive Republican because of the substantial support which that class of voters had given to the Roosevelt-Garner ticket during the campaign. When Senator Cutting of New Mexico declined the post, it was given to Harold L. Ickes of Illinois who had been a big factor in the success of the Roosevelt Progressive League. Later, when we were Cabinet members together, Harold told me that he had visited Democratic campaign headquarters during the course of the campaign to see the chairman, and I had kept him waiting in the outer office for two hours. His name wasn't very well known at the time, but the country came to know him later in a big way. The selection of Miss Frances Perkins as Secretary of Labor—the first woman ever to hold a Cabinet post—was a personal choice on the part of Governor Roosevelt who had formed a very favorable opinion of her views and ability while she served as Industrial Commissioner of New York State in his administration. She had first been appointed a member of the Industrial Board, which exercises a broad degree of jurisdiction in labor matters, by Governor Al Smith.

During the course of Roosevelt's spring visit to Warm Springs, I went down there to talk over a number of appointments and to report to him on a number of things which he had commissioned me to do. Among the visitors who came to the pleasant resort at the request of the President-elect was Senator Cordell Hull of Tennessee, who had proved to be such a wise and faithful lieutenant in the preconvention battle to win the nomination. Before he paid his scheduled visit to the "Little White House," as the Roosevelt cottage had come to be known, I dropped over to see Hull at old Meriwether Inn and suggested that we take a walk. For more than an hour, we strolled around the graveled and winding roads of Warm Springs, under the large shade trees, while I endeavored to impress upon him that the President-elect was about to offer him a most responsible post in the new administration and that it was his duty as a good citizen to accept. Roosevelt had intimated that he wanted Hull in the Cabinet and was afraid he might decline. While he did not say just what place he intended to offer the Tennessean, my own notion was that it was either Secretary of the Treasury or Secretary of State. Hull, of course, was pleased to learn that the man about to enter the White

House held him in such high esteem, but he was genuinely reluctant to give his consent. As I have said before, Hull had been in public life for a long time and he had the common sense to realize that while the glitter and power of high administrative posts may attract a lot of men, a majority of them soon after taking office find themselves worried and tormented by the strain of official duties and the constant criticism of an unsympathetic public. For this reason, plus the fact that he knew the cost of official entertaining would prove another severe drain upon his slender financial resources, he had no desire to enter upon one of the most responsible Cabinet posts. While appreciating his position, I knew that Roosevelt wanted him. I pointed out the opportunity that it would give him to promote the acceptance of the economic views to the study of which he had devoted a lifetime, and emphasized that his long years of experience in public office and his even temperament would make him an invaluable aide in the troubled days that lay ahead. We discussed the matter almost until the time Hull left for the Little White House. During the visit, Roosevelt tendered him the Secretaryship of State, the most important place in the Cabinet.

During the crowded years since that peaceful meeting in the tiny village of Warm Springs, I have had an opportunity of the kind denied to most men to observe Cordell Hull and the other men whom Roosevelt brought to Washington in the effort to make the United States a better place to live in and a more secure place for the bulk of American citizens. I have seen the key men of the New Deal at the White House, at Cabinet meetings or at other meetings called for the purpose of discussing government business. Because of the fact that relief and public works and other urgent questions occupied the spotlight during the early days of the New Deal, Hull was in a kind of eclipse in the sense that he did not become known to the public as quickly as some others in the Cabinet. In the fall of 1933, however, I jotted down a note, intended only for my own use, to the effect that Cordell's accomplishments in office would be appreciated by future generations rather than his own and that his record of accomplishment would stand out long after the rest of us were forgotten. I'm still ready to stand on that prophecy. To a fellow who worked his way up through the ranks, it always appeared to me that Hull conducted himself as a statesman should. He was tenacious in his views, perhaps at times a bit too stubborn, but he always knew his subject well and he gave the impression that his views were founded on long-time needs and were based solely on the premise of what was best for the public good. When decisions went against him, Cordell knew how to accept the outcome graciously, without a show of temper or disappointment.

Shortly after my talk with the new Secretary of State at Warm Springs, the same kind of "missionary work" had to be done to persuade William H. Woodin, prominent New York industrialist, to accept the other important place of Secretary of the Treasury. On that occasion, the job was delegated to Basil O'Connor, who had been Roosevelt's law partner before the latter became Governor of New York, and who was also an intimate friend of Woodin. The latter was quiet to the point of shyness, and although he had been a generous campaign contributor, it was literally true that there was absolutely nothing that he wanted in return. Roosevelt wanted him in the Treasury because of his recognized ability and his wide knowledge of the problems of finance and industry. O'Connor called for him one afternoon early in February, and together they motored back and forth through Central Park in New York City for an hour and a half while Basil argued that it was Woodin's duty to accept the Cabinet post. Woodin finally consented to serve, even though reluctantly, because he saw the logic of O'Connor's argument that under the grave conditions which prevailed, the responsibility of accepting was far less serious than the responsibility of refusing, if it compelled Roosevelt to take some man he didn't want. The President-elect, shortly afterward in a special announcement, revealed that Hull and Woodin would be in his Cabinet.

Just about two or three weeks before Inauguration, there was an ominous rumble in the banking world that was to be the forerunner of a collapse unprecedented in American history. The banks were beginning to give way under the pressure of years of bad business and the heavier burden of worthless stocks and securities in their portfolio. The loud boom of the late twenties was about to wind up in a louder bust. Lines of anxious and frightened depositors started to form in front of banks, and while the runs were comparatively few, they were too widespread to be dismissed as unimportant. The pressure became too strong in Michigan, center of the key automotive industry, and the Governor was compelled to call a bank holiday to protect the state's savings institutions from a worse disaster. Now the news was in the newspapers, and the fear psychology spread wider and wider. The shadow of the bank line started to spread itself clear across the country, touching every state as it went. The depositors were insisting on cash withdrawals, and the wiser ones, those who knew what panic meant in the past, were demanding gold. And the banks were beginning to run out of gold, the drain was so great. Other states followed the lead of Michigan and closed the banks. At his Hyde Park home, waiting for the special train that would take him to Washington, Roosevelt was constantly advised of what was going on and he never for a moment underestimated the deadly seriousness of what was taking place. He had a chance to confer with Woodin and other well-informed persons and thus to prepare himself for the emergency. When he went aboard the train that was to carry him to the Nation's Capital, a couple of nights before the Inauguration, Roosevelt was facing the most serious crisis to confront a new President since the critical day when Abraham Lincoln took over the burdens of the White House almost three-quarters of a century before. Lincoln then looked out on a nation threatened with permanent disruption because of the ugly menace of a civil war; Roosevelt looked out on a still greater nation threatened with financial panic and economic chaos because of blind, unreasoning fear.

As a member of the incoming Cabinet, I was invited with my wife and three youngsters to ride to Washington on the Roosevelt special. The group on the train included members of the President-elect's family, Louie Howe, several other intimate friends, and the usual quota of newspaper correspondents and photographers. It was a late afternoon run from New York to Washington, and during the course of the journey I was invited to go back to the last car for a chat with the President-elect. F.D.R. was seated in a chair alongside the wall of the living-room, facing across the car. I dropped into a chair beside him.

Some folks came in from time to time for one purpose or another, but during a good part of the visit we were alone. Although in good spirits, as he usually was, he was fully conscious of the gravity of the moment at hand and for this reason was inclined to be serious in his mood and thoughts. He knew the entire nation was looking to him with anxiety and hope as the only way out. For several hours before boarding the train, he had received call after call from Governors and other high officials around the country who wanted his advice or who wanted to suggest what he should do after reaching Washington. To add to the burden of his troubles, the beloved Senator Thomas J. Walsh of Montana, who was slated to become the new attorney general, had died suddenly that morning making it necessary for him to appoint a substitute without delay. After consultation with Howe and a few other intimates, he had tendered the place to Homer Cummings of Connecticut, knowing that the Attorney General would have a major role to play in the program he had in mind. Under the circumstances, it might seem as though Roosevelt would be too full of the subject in the minds of all to think of anything else. On the contrary, I recall that he spent most of the time chatting about religion. He said that a thought about God was the right way to start off and he told me about his own religious training as a child. He expressed the view that, in a crisis like the one approaching, the faith of the people was far more important than any other single element and that the fundamentally religious sense of the American people would be a great factor in seeing the nation through. Then he revealed his intention to begin Inauguration Day by attending divine services at the Episcopal church which he had attended as a young man during Wilson's administration. He talked for some little time in the same vein, saying that in the end the salvation of all peoples, including our own, would depend upon a proper attitude toward God.

The conversation remained in my memory because it gave me a fresh insight into Roosevelt's way of thinking and the manner in which he approached problems of overwhelming magnitude. There is no doubt that he already had his mind made up on the fundamental policy to be pursued in handling the complex banking situation. Retaining a clear mind and a cool head, he reasoned that the question of what particular measures were to be adopted, whether legislative or executive, was far less significant than the need for restoring the shattered confidence of the American people. And after reaching that decision, he had the courage to adhere to it without wavering and without letting doubts and divided counsel sway him into doing something else. His attitude, in my judgment, was not that of a man who was carried away by conceit or overconfidence; it was the straightforward attitude of a man who sincerely believed that his fellow countrymen could be rallied to meet the test.

After the inaugural ceremony at the Capitol and the customary parade down Pennsylvania Avenue, the members of the new Cabinet and the White House secretariat were instructed to gather in the Oval Room on the second floor of the White House for the swearing-in ceremony, the first time in history that all were to take the oath of office at the same time. The spacious old home set apart as a dwelling place for the Presidents has come to acquire through the years a magical quality that stirs the imagination of every youngster in America, and this feeling came back with renewed force as I entered the stately portals of the White House for the Cabinet ceremony. It was the first time I had ever been there. The brief exercises in the Oval Room were witnessed only by the families of those being sworn in and a few friends of the Roosevelts. The new President sat at his desk, a beaming smile on his face, and read out one by one the name of each member of his official family, beginning with Secretary of State Hull. The oath was administered to each separately by Justice Benjamin N. Cardozo of the United States Supreme Court. After the swearing-in was over, Roosevelt made a happy little talk to the assembled group, bidding us welcome to the new administration and expressing the hope that we would be able to pull together without friction and to work shoulder to shoulder for the common good and the best interests of the nation. By this informal little touch, the Chief Executive had successfully converted what is usually a stiff and pompous ceremonial into a friendly, happy occasion that was appreciated by everyone present. A man who wouldn't feel pleased under the circumstances would have to be either a humbug or a stuffed shirt.

The nation saw another side of Roosevelt the next day when he first summoned Congress into special session and then boldly issued his proclamation closing every bank in America until the fierce financial gale had a chance to pass over. The events of that week seem almost like a dream. The thing that stands out above all else like a shining star was the flaming courage of the man who dared to shut off the nation's financial life because the emergency demanded it, and then calmly sat down to the microphone to ask his fellow Americans to have faith and confidence in what was transpiring.

In my opinion, Roosevelt's banking address will go in history as one of the greatest utterances of an American President. If we are to measure the effectiveness and worth of an address by the response which it calls forth, it may be the greatest of all because no other talk in history ever called forth such a wave of spontaneous enthusiasm and co-operation. He risked tremendous odds in following such a course. We know how successful it was, but it is just as easy to imagine the economic and financial chaos that would have resulted if the people had given way to fear and panic instead of resolutely regaining their lost confidence. With a flash of inspiration, he accomplished a miracle of wise government.

There is no occasion for reviewing the steps which Roosevelt took for reopening the banks on a sound and stable basis. In some quarters, he has been criticized for not co-operating with the outgoing President, Mr. Hoover, who wanted to do something about the banking situation at the last minute. Roosevelt was wise in refusing. It would have been extremely bad judgment on his part to exercise authority without legal right. And even more compelling was the knowledge that Mr. Hoover never would have gone straight ahead, as Roosevelt was prepared to do, to meet the situation head on. The outgoing President was too inclined to make a lot of fuss and feathers out of such emergencies and to miss the popular approval that springs up in response to prompt and courageous action.

The three months or more that followed, during which Roosevelt held the imagination and approval of the country by recommending a broad series of relief and recovery measures to Congress, will also take its place in the history books as an outstanding example of democracy working at its best. The thing that had paralyzed the country during the few previous years was not that the measures undertaken by the Hoover administration were wrong but that they were done timidly and in half-hearted fashion and failed to go far enough. The program put through by Roosevelt and a Democratic Congress saved the nation an enormous amount of stress and trouble and it also saved the private fortunes of a lot of those individuals who later became the President's severest critics.

Putting aside the measures that were temporary in character and designed only to meet emergency conditions, the genesis of the entire Roosevelt program may be traced back very easily to the policies and the principles of government which he advocated throughout his public life and particularly during his four years as Governor of New York State. The idea that these reforms were born of expediency on the spur of the moment is erroneous; and any man who makes a thorough study of Roosevelt's record prior to his entry into the White House will reach the same conclusion. True it was that these reforms were put before Congress and enacted into law with far greater speed than originally seemed possible, yet this was simply a case of a great leader, with a proper sense of political "timing," who realized that the temper of the country gave him a unique opportunity to accomplish constructive reforms that otherwise might have taken a generation. The financial group that later took up the hue and cry against the New Deal were silent because the chill of the depression was still upon them and they feared for the fate of their own vast properties.

The paralysis and fear which gripped some of the minority groups during the depression proved a boon to the people of the United States because, while they were still recovering from their fright, the Chief Executive was able to get across the measure insuring bank deposits, the Social Security Act, the Farm Relief Bill, and a number of other acts that were vitally needed. Recalling the anguished outcry about "dictatorship" that arose over the President's simple plan to reorganize the executive departments in the spring of 1938, just imagine the din that would have been raised to defeat the Bank Deposit Insurance Bill if the minority groups had only had the courage to oppose it at the time when the bill was before Congress. They would have plastered the nation with four-sheet posters at every corner proclaiming that Roosevelt was trying to ruin the banks to satisfy his Communistic friends. They don't dare ask for its repeal now for the simple reason that they realize the people would never stand for it.

The "Brain Trust"

I have been asked time and again who were the persons around Roosevelt upon whom he leaned the heaviest for advice and counsel during that baptismal period of the New Deal. The general impression was that he was advised wisely and well and, as is usually the case, the public was prone to think that there was some mysterious person behind the scenes who actually pulled the strings. The press, in very accommodating fashion, supplied the missing link by printing a great many readable pieces about the "Brain Trust," meaning the younger men around Roosevelt who had been called in for technical assistance in handling technical problems.

In the first place, I should be able to qualify as a dispassionate authority because no one ever charged me with being the big "inside man," and I certainly never tried to take on the role. Banking and financial problems were unfamiliar to me, and so were a number of the other very complex matters that had to be considered and legislated on in a hurry. Yet, all during this period, I saw Roosevelt frequently on other business, and in that fashion it was fairly easy for me to form an opinion of what was going on and to get a picture of what was taking place behind the scenes. At his invitation, I dropped over to the White House morning after morning to talk things over, especially about important Federal appointments.

On a good many of these occasions, F.D.R. would be still in bed, reading the morning newspapers after having finished his breakfast. Louie Howe was usually present, and we would chat perhaps for a half hour or an hour on what was transpiring and how the public was reacting. In those conversations, the President was more interested in getting a line on public opinion and on the political effect of the New Deal program than he was in discussing specific measures. These "bedroom" conferences were later banned, to a large extent, by the White House physician, Dr. Ross McIntyre, who very wisely felt that the Chief Executive should begin his day in more leisurely fashion.

Of course, in offering my opinion as to what persons were influential in getting the administration off to a good start, I am not attempting to talk for Roosevelt. Whether he agrees with me or not, I don't know, because I never asked him. But in my humble judgment, there were two men who did magnificent work in putting their shoulders to the wheel, and whose wise and effective counsel made the going a whole lot easier. Those two were Attorney General Homer Cummings and the late William H. Woodin, Secretary of the Treasury. Like the old wheel horses that they were, they labored tirelessly and quietly, and for that reason the public rather overlooked them in the search for more glamorous heroes. Nevertheless, Cummings rendered invaluable assistance by the manner in which he cut through the knotty legal problems bound up in the bank closing and other difficult questions. He provided Roosevelt with the legal opinions which he had to have, and have in a hurry, in order to deal effectively with the situation that confronted him. Speed is a nightmare to most lawyers; but, even though he knew his professional reputation was at stake in every single opinion that he gave, Cummings forgot his own interests for the good of the cause. It is not an exaggeration to say that if he had insisted upon moving with more time and caution, the whole job might have been badly bungled. Woodin was likewise just as self-effacing and just as swift in seeing what was needed and in suggesting a way to do it. While others were acquainted with the theoretical phases of the problem, Woodin had a firm grip on the practical side, and his cool judgment prevented a number of serious errors that would have been very damaging.

I know there were dozens of people who were consulted on the banking legislation, and also on relief and recovery problems, the NRA, public works, and the other great measures that occupied so much time and attention during the early months of the New Deal. In praising Cummings and Woodin for their efforts, it is not my purpose to say the final word or to take away any credit from the young fellows in the "Brain Trust" and many others who gave truly important help.

The story of the formation of the so-called "Brain Trust" has been rehearsed many times. It resulted simply from the fact that when Roosevelt was running for President he needed the assistance of people who could give him detailed information and technical assistance on specific problems. For example, while he knew far more about agriculture than most men in public life and knew that it was vitally important to raise the income of the farming class, he needed a lot of statistics on grain exports, the volume of various crops, the relief efforts made by other administrations, and a raft of similar information on which to base his talks. The same was true of banking, relief, and other issues.

The first man brought in was Raymond Moley, a professor at Columbia University, who helped Roosevelt in a study of judicial problems while the latter was still Governor of New York State. He knew his subject thoroughly and was called in time and again when information was needed on other subjects with which he was familiar. When the campaign got under way, a number of others were likewise employed for the same purpose and they met in a group in order to collaborate and to exchange information. The group included Rexford G. Tugwell, another Columbia University man, who was first brought in by Moley—if my memory is correct, Adolph A. Berle, an authority on banking and corporations, Judge Sam Rosenman, long a close friend and adviser to Roosevelt, and Hugh S. Johnson, who later attained nationwide fame as the dynamic head of the NRA. Basil O'Connor, Roosevelt's former law partner, sometimes acted as an intermediary between the group and Roosevelt, and a number of others, experts on individual subjects, were called in from time to time. The group was wholly informal, and perhaps no one would ever have noticed it except for the fact that an enterprising newspaperman, who, I believe, was James Kieran of the New York *Times,* tagged it with the name "Brain Trust," which stuck and immediately made the group front-page news. Later most of these men came to Washington to assist Roosevelt in the same capacity. Another young man who received a lot of notice in the same way was Lewis W. Douglas of Arizona, who was made Director of the Budget.

In view of the fact that the "Brain Trust" was roundly ridiculed by a large section of the press as a bunch of "starry-eyed visionaries" and "crackpot reformers," it may surprise a lot of people to know that my good friend Hugh Johnson, the ex-cavalry officer and newspaper columnist, was a member of the original group. But the fact remains that he was, and I insist upon giving him full credit (even though he probably won't want it). Some folks in a position to know said Hugh was the ablest of them all.

After Moley, Johnson was the first member of the select inner council to brave the cold political breezes in person, which he did by endeavoring to fill the difficult and discouraging role of director of the National Recovery Administration. In the comparatively short period during which he attempted to set up a few rules to govern businessmen in their relations with labor and in their relations with each other, I think Hugh hit the front pages more often than any other individual on record except the President himself. He was denounced from the Atlantic to the Pacific as a ruthless dictator, and to put it in the words of his own brusque prophecy when he took over the job, "dead cats" were soon being hurled at him from all directions. There is no doubt, however, that the NRA under Johnson's direction tried to take in too much territory, or that a different story might have been told if fewer regulations had been set up and its efforts at supervision had been restricted to fewer industries.

The public, naturally, has always been interested in knowing how much influence, intellectually and politically, these men of the so-called "Brain Trust" have exercised in determining the basic policies of the Roosevelt administration, allowing for the gross exaggeration of hostile newspapers and Republican spellbinders. It was good tactics for the opposition to picture Roosevelt as a President wholly surrounded by men inexperienced in national government; and I have been too long in politics to find fault on that score. Neither is it my purpose to detract from the contributions made by some of these men to the liberal and progressive policies of the New Deal administration.

But the so-called "Brain-Trusters" never exercised as much in-

fluence in shaping Roosevelt's policies as the public imagined—
and certainly not as much as they thought themselves. I have been
amused many times at worried friends who came to whisper in my
ear about dinner parties at which the guests were held "spell-
bound" by one of the "bright young men" explaining the ideas
and the philosophy behind the New Deal program. The inference
was, of course, that the philosophy and the basic ideas actually
originated with the gentleman who was doing the expounding. I
suppose that things like this do no permanent damage.

The humane policies which Roosevelt has endeavored to apply to the nation did not enter his mind in a flash some weeks
after he got to the White House. They were basically the same
as the legislation which he and other forward-looking Democrats
like Robert F. Wagner, Alfred E. Smith, and a number of others
had been sponsoring in New York State for a quarter of a century. They put all kinds of legislation on the statute books to
protect working men and women from exploitation, to guard them
against long hours and underpay, and to save them from being
compelled to put up with unsanitary working conditions.

The first Roosevelt farm policy, as I recall it, followed in very
large measure the recommendations of a group of farm organization leaders who were called to Washington for that purpose—
and no distinction was made between Republican and Democratic
recommendations. The idea of a huge public works fund to relieve
unemployment had its strongest advocates in William Randolph
Hearst and Al Smith, while the NRA was put through as a substitute for a drastic bill, providing a thirty-hour week on a national
scale, which had already passed the Senate. The task of framing
the NRA legislation was done with the assistance of some of the
best-known business leaders in the nation—even though some of
these gentlemen jumped out from under at a later date when they
felt things were not going as well as they should.

The best test of the influence of the "Brain Trust" is the fact
that virtually all the original members of the group have dis-
appeared while a new crop of men is at hand to do the same kind
of very necessary spade work.

Moley at first was used as a symbol for the entire group. He
had Roosevelt's complete confidence, and, although the opposition

started shooting at him as a "red," the same people would hardly call him that now. Moley's departure from the picture was made necessary by a series of unfortunate incidents that happened during his attendance at the World Economic Conference at London in the early fall of 1933. These incidents precipitated a break between himself and Secretary of State Hull, Robert W. Bingham, Ambassador to Great Britain, and other high officials in the nation, and obviously the President was bound to defer to the latter group to prevent a Cabinet break. Moley's trouble was the usual trouble that afflicts men inexperienced in public life. He was inclined to be temperamental and to imagine that every man who took issue with his viewpoint did so because of personal dislike and not because of a basic disagreement in outlook and political philosophy. For that reason he found it hard to work in harness with other people.

The fact is that any man who aspires to cut out a place for himself in public life must have a hide as thick as a rhinoceros and be ready to bear all kinds of discourtesies, disagreements, and at times the flick of rank injustice without letting it poison his outlook on men and events. And above all things else, he must learn to trim his views to meet the opinions of others, even when he is convinced that the wiser course would be to drive right ahead with his own ideas.

I always felt that Moley's departure was a matter for real regret because in some respects he was one of the most valuable men ever around Roosevelt. He had a keen mind, was a terrific worker, never sounded off on a subject unless he had explored it fully, and he made a good "funnel" through which a lot of technical information could be poured on its way to the President. He could also consider public questions without rancor and without letting his personal prejudices influence his judgment on what measures should be adopted to correct the situation. I think if Ray had had a little more political experience at his command when he tackled the job, he would have been the ideal man for the place he occupied.

I saw Lewis Douglas frequently because a Cabinet officer naturally comes into contact with the Federal budget officer and because Roosevelt did the unprecedented and gracious thing of let-

ting him sit in at Cabinet meetings. Later Douglas broke away
from the administration and became one of Roosevelt's severest
critics because he disliked the fiscal policies of the New Deal, especially the idea of spending to promote relief and recovery.

Without questioning the sincerity of his views, I was never impressed with Douglas as a public figure. His ideas on questions
of government were the orthodox ideas of those who seem to
think that government has done its duty if the budget is balanced
and that nothing else matters. To put it bluntly, he had what is
commonly called the Wall Street point of view. He was against
spending because it put the budget out of balance and tended
to raise taxes but he never, as far as I could discover, had anything definite to offer on how to feed the millions of people
who were suffering from loss of jobs, loss of income, and loss of
savings. The idea that things would improve if the government
did nothing was not the kind of philosophy that the people wanted
to hear or that the nation would accept in those troubled days.

I think a fault common to many of the "Brain-Trusters" and
other inexperienced men who have been trusted with high responsibilities and given ready access to the White House is a tendency to forget that Franklin D. Roosevelt is President of the
United States. It is well-nigh impossible for a young man to
get close to the seat of power without imagining that he himself occupies the place at the head of the table. This tendency
for a man to link himself with the presidential power may not
be conscious, but nevertheless it exists. There is a tremendous
thrill in being allowed to sit daily at the elbow of the individual
who is shaping policies and measures which influence the lives
of 130,000,000 and to be asked for opinions on the wisdom of
these measures. The individual at first may attempt to sway the
judgment of the President because he honestly thinks the Chief
Executive is making a mistake and he wants to protect him, but
more and more there is a tendency for a man to insist upon his
own views because he wants to see them adopted as administration
policy. I have no doubt that in the case of Douglas he resigned
because he had deep convictions against the fiscal policies which
Roosevelt was following. Yet, I cannot help thinking that in some
of the statements which he issued later, he was apt to overlook

the important fact that Roosevelt made him a national figure and that he did not make Roosevelt. James P. Warburg was another individual who, to my way of thinking, was altogether too harsh in his personal remarks about the President after the latter had been kind enough to honor him with a place of trust and responsibility.

Public interest in the "Brain Trust" reached its peak during the 1936 presidential race when the monotony of campaigning was varied by a unique Republican slogan which might be epitomized and paraphrased to read, "Turn the Professors out." In the old days, it used to be, "Turn the rascals out." The brunt of the attack was borne by Rexford G. Tugwell, head of the Resettlement administration, who, in the absence of the departed Moley, Johnson, and Berle, was used as a symbol for the group. While I was described in G.O.P. literature as the "spoilsman" who had fastened "Farleyism" on the country to suit the wishes of an ambitious Chief Executive, Tugwell was described as the head of a cabal, composed of dreamy-eyed intellectuals, who had taken away from the President the actual control of governmental policy. It was a paradoxical picture which never failed to charm those who drew it.

I conferred with Tugwell on a number of occasions and got the impression of a man who was reasonable, honest, and sincerely interested in improving economic conditions. Apparently he was unhappy in public life and at a loss to know how to meet the verbal shafts aimed in his direction. Never having read the books written by him (neither did most of his critics), I am not in a position to say whether his views were radical or communistic. In his discussion with me, he was sensible in his approach to particular situations and never arbitrary. There is no question that Tugwell was close to the President, that he enjoyed the full White House confidence, and that the Chief Executive got a genuine pleasure out of hearing his views on such subjects as land conservation, the rehabilitation of stranded farm populations, and the improvement of agricultural conditions. Yet, despite his closeness to the President, Tugwell never took advantage of that position and he was careful to stay in his own back yard. He kept his fingers out of politics and tended to his own knitting, an example that could have been followed with profit by some of his successors. In view of the real situation, I think that the abuse heaped on him was too raw and uncalled for.

As I shall point out in more detail later, many of Roosevelt's troubles have arisen from the fact that he is too easy-going with subordinates. He permits them to take in too much territory and even when they assume the functions of other officials, he is inclined to look on the situation with amused tolerance. He will overlook mistakes and shortcomings if he likes a man. This tendency to leniency is the reason why the public often gets the impression, from reading dispatches out of Washington, that the administration is torn and ripped by conflicting factions and cross-currents of interest. During the early days, people often went to the White House with whispered warnings that Moley was exercising too much power, that Hugh Johnson was getting too much publicity, or that this or that official was tending to put him in eclipse. Roosevelt simply smiled away those complaints. He seldom brings himself to the point of giving a subordinate a sharp going-over.

Roosevelt positively hates to "fire" a man or woman he knows, even when the provocation is severe. He put up for a long spell with a sharp disagreement between Secretary Wallace and George Peek over farm policies when the latter was with the Triple A administration. Later Peek was shifted to the Export-Import Bank Corporation where he carried on a campaign against the trade policies of Secretary of State Hull. The President knew about it but was reluctant to act. Secretary of the Interior Ickes and Under-Secretary West were both on intimate, personal relations with Roosevelt. Their affection for the President was not extended to each other. Ickes and West were badly in need of a political divorce for incompatibility of temperament long before the President got around to doing something about it. Being fond of both men, he disliked the idea of siding against either, even though he realized a quarrel of that kind was bad for the administration.

After all, Roosevelt has made a sincere and honest effort to strike a happy balance between the theoretical knowledge gained by the professors and schoolmen and the practical knowledge gained by men who spend their lives in the busy world of finance and industry. This bridge must be erected if we are to have the complete answer to our problems. Even if the results in some instances have been disappointing, he should be given credit for making the effort and attempting to do something that will have to be done eventually.

People often point to the "Brain-Trusters" who were formerly with Roosevelt, and who are now gone, and try to cite that as an illustration of the fact that the President is headstrong and self-opinionated and hence hard to get along with. That is overdoing the picture. Up to this time, well along in his second administration, he has not had a single resignation from his Cabinet. It remains the same as when he took office except for a few changes made necessary by death. That shows the other side of the picture, due in large measure to the fact that his Cabinet is composed mostly of persons long experienced in the wear and tear of practical politics. An old hand at the game like Homer Cummings, for example, would hardly make the mistake of confusing himself with the President simply because he had a big part in the bank holiday program.

There have been numerous occasions when Cordell Hull might have packed his bags and walked out of the State Department in a huff because of some incident in connection with the tense and delicate foreign situations which he has had to handle. He remained because he realizes that those incidents are inevitable in public life and because he sincerely believes in the ultimate triumph of his policies.

I have been sitting across the table from F.D.R. for more than a decade now, dealing with him constantly on political and governmental matters of the most controversial nature. It would be idle for me to give the impression that we have never had a disagreement or that I was fully satisfied with everything he has ever undertaken. But I always reflect upon the fact that the people elected him President, not I, and upon the further fact that whatever position I have been fortunate enough to attain in public life has been due to him and not vice versa. As a result, my political health is still pretty good, despite reports to the contrary, and in the meantime I have seen literally dozens of others come and go.

Repeal of the Eighteenth Amendment

During the hot summer months of 1933, while public attention generally was focused upon the recovery efforts of the Roosevelt administration, I was busily engaged in making sure that another very essential part of the program was put into effect without a slip-up. My efforts were largely centered on trying to make certain that enough states voted for repeal of the Eighteenth Amendment to ensure its demise, a position written into the party platform by a vast majority of the delegates at the previous year's convention. Sentiment for repeal was still very strong, but Roosevelt and I, and a number of other party leaders, were afraid that the tide might start turning the other way before definite action was taken. That was especially true of the Southern states where dry sentiment had been particularly strong. At the request of local leaders, I stumped a number of these Southern states, asking the voters to stand by Roosevelt in his recovery program and to help it along by voting for repeal. We felt that this line of argument would be most effective in getting the desired action. The President entered into the drive personally by sending a letter to Leon McCord of Alabama, in which he pointed out that he was most anxious to see the Eighteenth Amendment taken out of the Constitution. The result was that before the end of 1933, the necessary three-fourths of the states had voted to remove the Prohibition amendment from the organized law of the land, a show of speed that even those connected with professional repeal organizations believed impossible a few months earlier. We have always looked back with pride upon this ending of the Prohibition era as a major accomplishment of the Democratic Party. I know that my efforts helped a trifle, at least, because one disgusted fellow in Pennsylvania wrote in that, although he was a lifelong dry, he was going to support repeal just to get me off the air. He said that every time he turned the dial, I was appealing for repeal votes.

I had an amusing experience in the winter of 1934 which demonstrates that, once politics get in the blood, it's almost impossible to eradicate the germ. I had gone to Sarasota, Florida, to dedicate a post office and was chatting with Karl Bickel, President of the United Press, when he told me that Harry Daugherty was wintering in Sarasota and was anxious to see me. Daugherty had been Attorney General during the unfortunate Harding administration, finally being compelled to resign as a result of a sensational investigation into his department conducted by Senator Wheeler of Montana. I had no idea why he wanted to see me, but told Karl it was perfectly all right to arrange the appointment. Bickel later introduced the two of us on the porch of the hotel. Daugherty pulled me off to one side and said, "It's none of my business, and perhaps I shouldn't ask. But at what stage of the Chicago Convention did you enter into an agreement with the Garner forces?" As a political trooper, that's all he wanted to know. It was Daugherty who, in 1920, was given the lion's share of the credit for putting across Harding's nomination which also took place at Chicago. While the two of us were conversing, a couple of news photographers were snapping pictures. Daugherty asked them to destroy the plates, saying it would be unfair to me because people might misunderstand the reason why we were conversing. I thought it was a very generous gesture from an unreconstructed Republican.

Besieged by Job-Hunters

Patronage is a term used to describe government jobs filled by men and women appointed as the result of political recommendations. A job, for example, held by a young man who was endorsed by his Senator or Representative in Congress, or by some high official in the party, is a patronage job. Although the word has behind it a long history of honorable usage by men and women in public life and by political historians, a great many people apparently never had heard of it before 1933 and seem to think the practice itself was invented by me in a diabolical scheme to replace faithful government employees with deserving Democrats. In fact, the whole business of patronage was pumped up into such a major campaign issue in the 1936 election that the word came to have a sinister meaning in the public mind.

So let us begin at the beginning by laying down the proposition that dispensing jobs under the patronage system has been followed by both major political parties since time immemorial, and that when it comes to doing a thorough job of it, the Republicans, on occasions, can make us Democrats look like so many amateurs. There is no room for argument on that score because I have the records.

The patronage controversy naturally centered around me because the national chairman of a political party is looked upon as the final arbiter in matters of that kind, and he is the man who must place party recommendations and endorsements directly before the President. After a close study of the records, I decided that the only difference between myself and the gentlemen who performed similar services in the past for the G.O.P. was this—I frankly said I believed in the patronage system and intended to follow it, something which they never did. In fact after Roosevelt's first election in 1932, I even let the public in on the secret by announcing to the press how patronage questions would be handled and by writing the exact methods to be followed in job distribution in a special article written for the *American Magazine*.

The furor kicked up by these matter-of-fact announcements was really amusing. It seems my policy of candidly espousing the idea of patronage violated all the known rules of the game—the thing to do was to employ patronage methods but never say so publicly. In other words, the sin was not in doing it, but in getting caught. However, that rule of conduct never has appealed to me, and it never will. It was really laughable to hear some of my good Republican friends in Congress dolefully predicting that Farley would ruin the Federal service by introducing the "spoils system" when all the time the Post Office Department files were filled with their own job-hunting appeals sent in under the previous administrations. Some of them have gotten writer's cramp from penning so many appeals.

I recall an incident that happened in 1934. Robert W. Moses was the Republican candidate for Governor of New York, although he had previously held responsible posts under the Democratic administration of Al Smith, being at one time Secretary of State and at another time State Conservation Commissioner. He was acting in the latter capacity in 1928 when I wrote him a letter asking him to appoint a Democrat whom I knew to a minor position in the Conservation Service. Al Smith was running for President at the time, and I often saw employees hired by Moses driving to work in Bear Mountain Park near my home with "Vote for Hoover" signs on their motor cars. I felt that it would be a good idea to give employment to a few Democrats. Moses refused to comply but he kept the letters and in his gubernatorial campaign, being somewhat destitute for issues, he flashed them upon the public. Apparently he thought the voters were going to rise up in horrified wrath upon learning that I believed in appointing party members to office, although most of them knew it all the time. The newspapermen dashed in and wanted to know if the letters were "authentic." I replied in the affirmative, adding that I was "no hypocrite," and still believed in the sentiments expressed in the letters. As a campaign issue, the Moses "exposé" was a complete dud because the voters very sensibly buried him under an avalanche of votes for the Democratic gubernatorial candidate, Herbert H. Lehman.

This discussion of patronage, however, is not intended to be controversial because an entire book could be written on this subject alone. Neither is it my purpose to deny that grave abuses can creep in because every individual old enough to read and write is familiar with the fact that political appointees often fall down on the job.

A number of sincere people believe that when men and women are appointed under the patronage system, the Civil Service must go out the window because the two cannot exist side by side. That is not true either; and it is my intention to go into this question a little more fully in discussing the Post Office Department.

This space is being given to the patronage question because a great many Americans would like to know what happened when we turned the political complexion of the Federal Government from Republican to Democratic and how it was done. It was an interesting process, and this is merely an effort to touch on the high spots and to relate some of the interesting and comical things that happened.

The Republicans had given us a good lesson on how to do a thorough house-cleaning job. No doubt Woodrow Wilson must have had some Democrats around in his day, and it is reasonable to assume that a few of them at least must have been efficient, but they were among the missing by the time we got to Washington. Talk about weeding out the politically unfit! The men who swung the scythe in the Harding, Coolidge, and Hoover eras must have been experts at the trade. If there were any Democrats in the Federal service at the end of 1932 except those stipulated by law on by-partisan commissions, they were so few and far between that no one recognized them when they were discovered. It was a government of Republicans, by Republicans, and very largely for Republicans.

I soon discovered after settling down to the job in Washington after the Inauguration in 1933 that only a "green horn" in politics would have talked so freely about patronage and job-filling. I was delighted at the opportunity to participate at Cabinet meetings and to try out some of my notions on how to introduce better and more efficient business methods into the Post Office Department which had been operating at an annual loss for several years. With the exception of major appointments, which would have to be discussed directly between the President and myself and other high government officials, I had made arrangements for taking care of other job applicants over at the headquarters of the Democratic National Committee. The set-up there was in competent hands, and there was no reason in the world why it couldn't be handled in that way.

But the stories in the press had stirred the imagination of the men and women who wanted to serve under the new administration, and each one arrived at the logical conclusion that the surest way to cinch the matter was to see me personally. I had anticipated quite a rush of deserving patriots who were willing to help F.D.R. carry the burden. But, to be frank, I had never had the slightest conception of what was about to happen. They swarmed in and flocked in by the hundreds and thousands until it seemed as though they must have been arriving by special trainloads. They hurried to the headquarters of the National Committee and, when they learned that it was impossible to see me there, they hurried over to the Post Office Department to demand an audience with me at once. I may as well confess—because everyone knows it to be a fact—that for two or three months I was compelled to hand over the running of the Post Office Department to my worthy assistants, Joseph C. O'Mahoney, William C. Howes, Clinton B. Eilenberger, Silliman Evans, and other capable aides.

There was no use in taking up headquarters at the National Committee because it was physically impossible to handle the crowd. Fortunately, there was a fair-sized room in the old Post Office Building that could be used for reception purposes, and there was nothing else to do but see them there. The persistence of a job-hunter who has an eye on the job he wants is truly a marvelous thing. My poor assistants were run ragged trying to keep them pacified even long enough to take down names and addresses and to find out what they wanted. The rules of etiquette were forgotten temporarily while they struggled with each other for favorable places in line. At the time, J. Austin Latimer was acting as my secretary, and about five or six times a day, in an effort to keep things in order, he and I braved the lions by walking out into the packed reception room. We went swiftly about the room, followed by a male stenographer, taking the name of each individual, and a brief description of the type of post he wanted. This was really the only way to get rid of them. It is easy to imagine the clamor and uproar that arose when Austin and I put in our appearance.

Quite often, before we started the rounds, Austin would shout out in a loud voice to inquire if there were any Senators or Representatives present. If so, they were immediately taken inside for a private audience. That simple gesture caused a lot of ill feeling because national and state committeemen and other officials from "back home" felt that they should outrank mere members of Congress, or at least be given equal consideration.

The unfortunate thing was that most of the poor people present misunderstood entirely what was taking place and had not the slightest chance in the world of landing a position through our recommendation. There was one old man from Alabama who said he had been a Democrat all his life, and it was about time he got something in return. He actually came there day after day for weeks. Paying not the slightest heed to discouragements or rebuffs, he always carried a bundle of newspapers under his arm and sat there reading for hours on end. Evidently he had decided to wait us out. Another poor old man who had come all the way from Idaho did very much the same. While job-hunters are usually looked upon as potentially lazy loafers who merely want to get on the government pay roll for a soft snap, the fact is that the Roosevelt administration came into office in the midst of a bitter depression, and many of these men and women were driven to the point of desperation in the effort to find something to do. Even now in looking back upon those days, while many unpleasant incidents occurred because of the antics of selfish individuals, it is impossible for me to think unkindly of the job-hunters. The sorry plight of many of them was almost beyond description. I cannot think of any more heart-rending experience in the world than the sight of a crying woman begging for a job to help support her family, when as a matter of fact she didn't have a single qualification in the world to entitle her to an appointment. There were literally scores of those cases because it was the era before Federal relief and the women had no place else to turn. And, unhappily, most of them felt that if they only saw me personally to tell their story, all I had to do was to say the word and employment was assured.

Untold dozens of the job aspirants discovered where I lived and haunted the hotel corridors in the effort to catch up with me. As a result, even though my working day usually extended to midnight or even after, I virtually had to slip back and forth to the office like a man dodging a sheriff's writ. When the pressure let up a bit, I was about the happiest individual on earth.

The only fortunate break in the whole thing was the fact that in their diligent pursuit of me, the job-hunters for the most part stayed away from the White House and left President Roosevelt undisturbed in his heroic efforts to lead the country out of the depression. It wasn't so in the old days. Andrew Jackson found huge hordes of them on his doorstep, while some historians say that the death of William Henry Harrison was hastened by the unceasing and unreasonable demands of the patronage hunters. President Polk got so worked up on one occasion that he confided in his diary that he felt a good Colt pistol was the only thing that would enable him to clear his office of job-hunters and get back to public duties.

In view of what happened, it is reasonable to ask why the patronage system was employed at all and what it was that the Roosevelt administration tried to do in regard to Federal positions. The answer is that there are thousands of jobs in Uncle Sam's service that touch very closely the daily lives of the American people, and the way in which those jobs are administered has a deep influence in determining the attitude of the public toward the administration in power. This, of course, does not include the still greater army of clerks, stenographers, technicians, and other workers who hold office by virtue of the Civil Service and who compose the vast majority of Federal employees. Naturally no effort was made to displace them, and none could be made under the law.

Nevertheless, it was proper and essential that the jobs which closely touched matters of policy should be filled by individuals in sympathy with the aims and purposes of the Roosevelt administration, and that program was carried out. It was not done in a hurry and it was not done in 100 per cent of the cases, as many of our political opponents would like to have the public believe. Neither were all the new employees all Democrats. On the contrary, President Roosevelt chose two men in his Cabinet who had previously been identified with the opposite political party and he perhaps appointed more men and women who were not members of his own party than any President in recent history. During the campaign of 1936, I recall that many conservative Democrats left our ranks on the plea that Roosevelt had handed over the Democratic Party to "Brain-Trusters" and "Republicans like Wallace and Ickes." In other words, this talk about weighting down the Federal system with Democratic time-servers was just so much campaign fodder which everyone recognized as such.

However, as Chairman of the Democratic National Committee, it was my duty to recommend Democrats for these key positions, whenever and wherever they were available, and I proceeded to do that to the best of my ability. The rules we followed can be boiled down to a few essentials, as they were in the article written by me for the *American Magazine*. They were:

First, is the applicant qualified? Second, is he loyal to the party and sympathetic toward the program of Franklin D. Roosevelt?

I said at the time that "patronage is the test by which a party shows its fitness to govern" and, after watching the system in operation for more than five years, I am more than ever convinced that it is a true watchword of government. It is simply impossible for a President of the United States, or a Cabinet member, or the head of an independent government establishment, to put his policies into operation with the maximum of effectiveness unless his key employees are fully in sympathy with what he is endeavoring to accomplish. Take my word for it, no matter how conscientious an employee may be, or how loyal he thinks he is, if he is basically at odds with the policies of the department in which he works, that fact will show itself in his labors sooner or later.

That was notably true of the Treasury Department in the earlier days. For some time before his resignation, Secretary Woodin was physically unable to run the department in the manner in which it should have been run. He wanted to resign earlier, but the President said no. Some of the officials under him held economic views similar to those of Budget Director Douglas and were actually averse to carrying out President Roosevelt's direct orders. That situation was corrected when Henry Morgenthau, Jr., a close friend of the Chief Executive, who believed in his policies, took over the department. And it may be well to point out, also, that the situation never would have developed if Mr. Woodin had been able to perform his duties fully. There never was a more loyal soldier than he was when he was able to handle things in person.

And, while we are on the subject, it is truly inspiring to find out how many individuals disagree entirely with President Roosevelt's views and the program he is trying to put across but are perfectly willing to hold well-paying and responsible positions under his administration. Patriotic fervor that goes to such lengths is not in the least uncommon.

I recall that early in 1934 a group of Congressmen called on me to protest against what they said was the discourteous and inconsiderate treatment accorded .them when they called at certain government departments. They said that in a great many cases the same individuals who were running things under Presidents Coolidge and Hoover, and who always looked out well for their Republican colleagues, were still on the job. It is a recognized fact that a member of Congress simply must go to departments of government when matters concerning his district are at issue. That's the democratic way, and whether those in executive positions like it or not, the Representatives really represent the people and are entitled to courteous consideration. On complaint of the Congressmen, I took the matter up with the White House and elsewhere, and after investigation we found that the complaint entered by the Congressmen was true in a great many cases.

The Post Office Department receives constant inquiries from Senators and Representatives who are interested in the extension of the air mail, the rural-carrier service, or some other phase of the department's work. These inquiries are handled by my secretary, William J. Bray, who has worked on Capitol Hill from the time he was a youngster, beginning as a page boy in the Senate. His years of experience enable him to direct most of these inquiries into the proper channels without bothering to consult me. Bray understands the importance of handling these matters promptly and efficiently for the Congressmen and Senators, and his efforts avoid a great deal of useless conflict and criticism.

I firmly believe that if the Republicans should win the Presidency and Congress in the year 1940—which they won't—they should proceed to place in office individuals who approve and sympathize with their policies. In fact, there's no need of handing out such advice because every sensible person knows they would do it anyway. Can anyone imagine the G.O.P. stalwarts coming in and working side by side with Harry Hopkins' social workers, or Harold Ickes' public works men, or my corps of dyed-in-the-wool Democrats. An administration that attempted a hybrid alliance like that wouldn't last long.

In connection with this patronage business, it is well to keep in mind two things. First, while I transmitted a great many recommendations for appointment to the White House and to other Cabinet officials, only a small part of them actually were approved. That does not mean that the applicants were double-crossed. It simply means that the applicants in those specific cases failed to show the qualifications wanted or that someone else was believed more capable and hence got the job. In the second place, it should be borne in mind that it is just as important to keep out undesired applicants as it is to put in friendly appointees. For example, it would be very bad for the Roosevelt administration to appoint an official to an outstanding position in New York, Illinois, or some other state if the person designated happened to be unacceptable either to the Senators and Representatives or to the people of that state. That has happened on occasions, and, no matter how capable the individual may be, the reaction is certain to be very bad.

When he was first appointed a Director of the Tennessee Valley Authority, Dr. Arthur E. Morgan came over to see me, at the suggestion of the White House, to talk over his plans for making appointments. He was a very earnest man, and I think he was truly desirous of making an outstanding name for himself in developing the government's plant at Muscle Shoals. We chatted amiably for a while, and I suggested it would be wise to avoid appointing people down there who would be unacceptable to the Senators and Representatives from that area, pointing out that simple things like that often bring about their defeat and that after all it was a smart practice in government to avoid antagonizing the men who vote the appropriations. I didn't suggest that he appoint anyone.

Dr. Morgan, however, got very exercised and promptly replied in what seemed to me discourteous fashion that he would appoint whom he liked and that he had no interest whatever in politics. I pointed out in return that President Roosevelt would never have landed in the White House if someone hadn't thought about politics and that he himself was a political appointee. He got a bit more wrathy at that, and so did I. The upshot was that I arose from the chair, thanked him for coming over, and told him that for all of me he could go out and do what he pleased. I never saw him after that and never tried to help him or hurt him in connection with the TVA. However, when he got into trouble later, it was perfectly apparent that Dr. Morgan simply didn't understand how to get along with other people, and that's an indispensable quality in public life. Moreover, he never consulted Democratic Senators and at first they were not inclined to go to his defense or to give him a lift in presenting his side of the case to the public.

Rewarding the Faithful

Politics is a co-operative business. Even a lone wolf needs help at times. I believe a man should listen to the recommendations of others in the party because they helped him attain his own position. Not only that, but men like Dr. Morgan, who think they are pursuing the only pure course by refusing to accept recommendations from Senators and Congressmen, usually wind up by appointing only their own friends and confidants. And that is a far worse kind of spoilsmanship than any other kind.

During his first visit to Warm Springs shortly after the election of 1932, I went over with F.D.R. this question of patronage, especially as it affected policy-making positions in the government, in a very careful way. As a result of that meeting, he made out a list of competent people throughout the various states whom he thought had rendered loyal and valuable assistance and were entitled to be considered for administration posts. I made out a list of my own along the same line. This procedure did not mean that only those who supported Roosevelt in the campaign or in the preconvention drive for the nomination were to receive consideration. Far from it. On the contrary, he subsequently appointed dozens of people who had never been active in politics or who supported someone besides himself for the presidential nomination.

Nevertheless the lists we compiled were very helpful. Those were stirring days during the convention at Chicago, and with high stakes at issue the loyalty of men and women was tested to the limit. We knew who stood fast and who yielded to promises or threats and went over to the enemy. We never had any quarrel with an individual who frankly said from the outset that he was on the other side. But after the election of 1932, when Roosevelt was preparing to enter upon his duties at the White House,

I got a broad smile out of watching some of the folks who came along to remind us how they had fought and bled for his cause on the political battlefields. Some of these gentlemen may have appeared to do so—as far as public appearances went. But I was acquainted with what went on behind the scenes during the critical time when the "coalition leaders" were doing their best to "Stop Roosevelt" by breaking up his delegations from within. I knew who stood for Roosevelt and who weakened for reasons best known to themselves.

I've been in politics for the best part of a lifetime and during that period I've learned a few things that are helpful in the effort to see things in their proper light. After the Chicago Convention, I was well pleased with the outcome but I thought it might be well to have a better understanding of what took place there. So I arranged for a series of confidential reports from thoroughly reliable people telling me the inside story of what went on in every delegation, particularly in those delegations that showed signs of breaking. Believe me, those reports are most interesting. Very often on a cold winter evening, when there's nothing else to do, I just browse through them again to brush up a bit on past history. I've never shown them to anyone else in the party, but they have given me many a hearty laugh, in addition to much useful information.

In a great many instances, in regard to individual appointments, I merely transmit to President Roosevelt the recommendations of Senators and Representatives and other outstanding figures in the party. Very often I know nothing about the person recommended and frankly say so to the Chief Executive. In that event, he indicates that the person recommended has a chance for appointment, whereupon a thorough investigation of his qualifications is immediately undertaken, or he says to do nothing further about it. In the early days of the administration, never having been in Washington in an official capacity, I placed before President Roosevelt numerous recommendations for positions, the duties of which were wholly unknown to me. But the Chief Executive, because of his former connection with the Wilson administration, had an excellent grasp of the needs of the Federal service and he very quickly pointed out the type of man or woman that was needed for each place. He knew what type of lawyers would be helpful to the Justice Department—positions that are always much sought after—and he knew the qualifications that were needed for little-known but responsible positions like Comptroller of the Currency and head of the Bureau of Indian Affairs.

Of course, I recommend many persons for Federal positions because of my own personal knowledge of their qualifications and their sincere efforts to bring about the success of the Roosevelt program. These recommendations, however, are based upon national and party considerations and not upon mere friendship to me. Frequently, I go over to the White House and discuss with President Roosevelt as many as twenty Federal appointments at one time. The list may include a judgeship, a few United States marshals and attorneys, and other positions of a like nature. The President goes into each case with extreme care. Very often I bring out the name of a person recommended, and he says at once, "Not big enough for the job." He never seems to grow weary of routine matters of that nature and he insists upon carrying out his own responsibility without delegating it to others.

I know a number of people who sincerely think that this appointment system is wrong simply because so much reliance is placed upon members of Congress and other elected officials. To my way of thinking that is the most democratic way of all and, in the long run, the best way of getting competent people. I'm not blind to the fact that Senators and Representatives often suggest the appointment of unfit persons. That is a fault common to everyone. But it is well to remember that during my few years in Washington, I have had hundreds of other people make recommendations to me, as national chairman. These recommendations have come in from people in all walks of life, prominent industrialists, newspaper publishers, lawyers, economists, and also from civic and professional organizations. Some of the individuals urged upon me for appointment were worthy of appointment, and a great many more were not. As a rule, there is a tendency on the part of people not active in politics to recommend personal friends or acquaintances rather than people who are well known and widely respected in their own communities. On the whole, I think the people who come in through political endorsement stand up better under the hard test of performance in office. Certainly, I think the majority of men and women who were appointed to high positions under the Roosevelt administration through Democratic connections have made a very impressive record, despite the few who failed to measure up to their responsibilities.

It is a demonstrated fact, too, that the residents of smaller states have a better chance under the appointment system now in operation. Whenever any other method is attempted, experience has shown that the list is apt to become top-heavy with appointees from the bigger states because those folks have a better chance to get into the news and hence to build up for themselves a national reputation.

Once again, I think it should be pointed out that the system we use is substantially the same as that which the Republicans employed when they supervised the direction of Uncle Sam's government. Call it the "spoils system" or anything else, the fact remains that down through the years many eminent men and women got their start in public life as the result of a political appointment. Hanging on the wall in the outer office of the Postmaster General's office in Washington is a copy of the commission issued many years ago to Abraham Lincoln, appointing him postmaster at New Salem, Illinois. He was a political appointee, and it always seemed to me that he turned out to be a pretty good citizen. Lincoln knew politics from the ground up, and his knowledge of men, gained in that way, stood him in good stead when he took over the heavy burdens of the Presidency.

I think the objection of most people to the present system is that patronage jobs are used to build political machines. That is a fact, and it would be a senseless falsehood to deny it. Moreover, I am perfectly conscious of the fact that when political organizations begin thinking about jobs and nothing else, when they forget that the public business should come first, they have commenced their own death chant without realizing it. History shows very plainly that a lust for jobs on the part of shortsighted leaders has broken up more political organizations, both Republican and Democratic, than any other single cause. That is a danger that must be guarded against; in fact, it is something that is inherent in every kind of organization. The protest of the public is the best way to discipline an organization against that sort of thing.

But those people who are inclined to imagine that patronage, and patronage alone, is the only thing that keeps a political party knit together are off on a tangent that is about as far wrong as anything humanly could be. I am convinced that with the help of a few simple ingredients like time, patience, and hard work, I could construct a major political party in the United States without the aid of a single job to hand out to deserving partisans. In fact, untold thousands of loyal soldiers in the Democratic army have been toiling for years without receiving tangible reward for their services and without asking for any such reward.

To put it plainly, people who think that individuals become active in politics merely for the sake of being "in on the spoils" underestimate the idealism of their fellow citizens. Politics is the national sport of the American people—not baseball, or football, or any other athletic game. In fact, it is more than a sport, it is a matter, with most people, of the deepest sincerity and conviction. We know the huge gatherings that are assembled year after year in the big cities to hear men and women discuss public questions. The interest in rural sections is, if anything, even more intense, although the folks there must provide their own show or listen to the radio. People are just as selfish, and just as unselfish, in politics as they are in any other human endeavor.

The United States is crisscrossed from ocean to ocean and from Canada to the Gulf with thousands upon thousands of civic and professional organizations, luncheon clubs, and fraternal orders, and the amount of effort and labor which individuals invest in them without hope of material or monetary return is truly amazing. There are federations of women's clubs, many of which are constantly concerned over political and civic problems. If people will work so unselfishly along these lines, why won't they do the same in politics? The answer is that they do. The Democratic Party was kept alive for many many years when carping critics thought its demise was inevitable, merely because devoted bands of men and women were committed to its principles and had the will and the courage to keep it alive. It will remain alive and healthy if Congress should decide to place every single job in the Federal Government, with the single exception of the Presidency, under Civil Service.

Huey Long's Hat

It would be an unforgivable oversight on my part to discuss the question of Federal patronage without considering the relationship between the Roosevelt administration and the Honorable Huey P. Long, late Senator from Louisiana, who in a brief span of years built himself a place of power in national politics that was equaled or exceeded by few men of his generation. The meteoric rise of Huey as a factor in political affairs might seem like the theme of a motion picture scenario, except for the fact that it really happened. Starting from scratch, without wealth, family prestige, or influence of friends to set him going, Long climbed into absolute control of Louisiana while still a comparatively young man and he proceeded to wield that power with a vigor and ruthlessness that really startled his fellow countrymen. I doubt if a parallel for his case exists in the history of America.

While he was on his upward climb, Huey employed sensational tactics to attract attention and to get himself a following. The same method was used before him by other men who wanted to coalesce the poor and oppressed into a political unit because they had no other avenue of entrance into the columns of the newspapers and magazines. Unlike many of his predecessors, however, Long did not follow the usual pattern and became more cautious and conservative as responsibilities came his way. On the contrary, he shrewdly sensed that the identical tactics which brought him into the seat of authority in Louisiana, and made him the idol of countless followers, could be employed perhaps with greater success on a national scale. While still dominating the affairs of Louisiana through the medium of his political henchmen, Long went to Washington during the tag end of the Hoover administration to take a seat in the United States Senate. Disdaining the hoary old precedent that Senate newcomers should be seen and not heard, Huey immediately launched into a series of personal and political tirades that left some of his colleagues aghast and both amused and amazed the American public.

Huey and I bumped into each other almost constantly during the few years that followed when President Roosevelt was first writing history with his New Deal program, and for a time it seemed as if we were destined to be in a state of permanent collision. That was not at all due to the fact that there was any rivalry between us or that we had fallen victims to the kind of mutual dislike that frequently springs up between men in the political business. Quite the contrary; I had no dislike for Long, and on frequent occasions he told people that there was no personal ill feeling on his part. Even when he was attacking us, I could always get a chuckle out of Huey's rantings.

Huey first crossed my path at the Chicago Convention where, as previously related, he started and kept alive the unfortunate and premature effort to do away with the two-thirds nominating rule, a move that very nearly disrupted the Roosevelt forces. He was sincere in taking that position, and there was no thought in his mind of causing embarrassment for me. But I happened to be presiding at the meeting when he put over the scheme, and if the thing had ended in disaster for the Roosevelt cause, that would also have been the end of Mr. Farley's political career.

During the campaign Huey stayed in line and supported Roosevelt for the Presidency, even though the effort was apparently irksome to him. Once Congress reassembled in special session early in March, 1933, however, Huey could no longer restrain himself and he was off the reservation before the first month was over. It was a time of extreme tension and excitement, and the imagination of the country was inflamed by the manner in which Roosevelt was handling the banking situation and related problems. The eyes of 130,000,000 Americans, or so it seemed, were focused as a unit on Washington. Long saw a chance to get back into the spotlight. He attacked the administration's bank-opening bill and also several other measures, whooping it up in characteristic style. The country was in no mood, however, for that peculiar brand of opposition, and the bills passed handily either over his opposition or despite his failure to help.

During this trying period, President Roosevelt was wholly engrossed in the mass of work attendant upon his relief and recovery program. He was literally working sixteen and eighteen hours a day on the problems before him, and, naturally under the circumstances, the task of considering Federal appointees in the various states was delayed for a few months. This was not done to whip recalcitrant members of Congress into line—it was simply that there was no time for it. Most of the Senators and Representatives appreciated the situation and were patient. But Long wanted action and, as a result of several years' habit, he was accustomed to getting what he wanted without delay.

We knew before the first of the month was out that a conflict with Long and a straight-from-the-shoulder settlement was inevitable, sooner or later. The root of the trouble lay in the fact that Huey was by nature a solo singer. It was impossible for him to take a place in the chorus. He tried teamwork for a while, but it was soon apparent that he had to be the lead horse or nothing. Even in his attitude towards the President, Long had to be the dominant mind. Right from the beginning he started telephoning me and the White House, insisting that the men he recommended for appointment as U. S. marshals, attorneys, and so on in Louisiana would have to be appointed without delay.

Roosevelt was quick to appreciate the problem at hand and he decided on a course of action without delay. Hundreds of pleas and petitions were pouring in from citizens in Louisiana who said their rights were being invaded by the policies written into law by the Long regime. The President was determined not to accept the Senator's recommendations and was ready to let him know that fact. We talked it over one day late in June and decided to have a meeting with Long himself two days later. The Chief Executive instructed me to be at his office in the executive wing of the White House for the meeting.

It was a morning appointment; the day was hot; and Huey came charging into the White House in his usual breezy and jaunty manner. He was nattily dressed in light summer clothes and wore a sailor straw hat with a bright-colored band. Before he left, the hat proved to be the most significant thing at the meeting. He was ushered into the President's oval office without delay and took a chair beside the desk, facing the Chief Executive. I was seated near by.

The conversation opened in easy and good-natured fashion, although Huey lost no time in giving the impression that he was actually responsible for Roosevelt's nomination at Chicago. According to his modest conception of what happened, he not only delivered Louisiana but also brought along several other Southern states which would otherwise have gone over to the opposition. That was a little too much for me, and I pointed out that while he was responsible for Louisiana's support of Roosevelt, and had helped with Mississippi when that delegation started to crack, he had nothing to do with the other Southern states. Furthermore, I reminded him that we could have seated the rival delegation from Louisiana, which was also committed to Roosevelt, and that would have left him out of the convention entirely.

Huey had come in with a chip on his shoulder, and although his words were courteous enough, it was obvious from his attitude that he was there for the purpose of testing the mettle of the President of the United States. He kept his hat on during the conversation. At first I thought it was an oversight, but soon realized it was deliberate.

It made me decidedly ill at ease for a moment until I glanced at Roosevelt and saw that he was perfectly aware of what was taking place and, furthermore, was enjoying it immensely. The cue was to say nothing and let him handle Huey. Roosevelt leaned back in his chair, perfectly relaxed and composed. He had a broad smile on his face which never changed for a moment, not even when Huey leaned over to tap him on the knee or elbow with the straw hat to emphasize one of his finer points, a trick which Huey pulled not once but several times.

While this performance was going on, Marvin H. McIntyre, the White House appointment secretary, came into the room on a couple of occasions and he was visibly incensed at Long's failure to show the customary respect for the Chief Executive. On one of these trips, I saw McIntyre standing there with his teeth clenched and I thought for a moment that he was going to walk over and pull the hat off Huey's head. Later he told me that was exactly what he started to do. Mac was a trifle light physically, but his Scotch ancestors left him plenty of courage and he would have acted without hesitation except that he wanted to avoid embarrassing the President. After a while, Huey sensed that he had made a blunder. He took off the straw hat in another of his gestures, and kept it off.

Throughout the entire interview, the conversation was pleasant, without an ill-tempered or hasty retort, despite the hat drama being enacted on the side. Long contended that he had supported the President's program better than a great many other Senators on Capitol Hill and for that reason was entitled to be recognized in the distribution of patronage. Roosevelt insisted that his sole interest was in seeing that worthy men were appointed to public office and that he intended to attain that end. There was nothing said that could give offense to Senator Long and, at the same time, there was nothing said that could be construed as a promise even to consult him on patronage matters.

One of the things Long complained about bitterly was the fact that Arthur A. Ballantine, a hold-over from the Hoover administration, was being held in office as Under-Secretary of the Treasury. That was merely a temporary arrangement to help the new men become acquainted with their duties, and it was recognized as such by the Treasury officials and by Ballantine himself. However, the Internal Revenue Bureau had entered tax suits against Long and some of his followers during the Hoover administration, and as a result he was very bitter against Republicans. It is only fair to add that he never mentioned the tax suits to us or suggested that anything be done.

When the meeting broke up, Long and I left the President's office together. We were standing just in front of the executive offices before separating when Huey said, "What the hell is the use of coming down to see this fellow? I can't win any decision over him." He kept his word. It was the last time he ever went to the White House, and it was the last conversation I ever had with him.

That last meeting between President Roosevelt and Huey Long has always had a special compartment off by itself in my memory. I think each one of us present knew at the time that it would have far-reaching consequences. Huey was already nationally known; his "share the wealth" plan was becoming a household byword; and we never for a moment assumed that he could be tossed aside lightly without political consequences. There is no doubt in my mind also but that Long himself welcomed the split and was pleased to have it originate on the other side. He was already dreaming dreams of conquest and looking far beyond the political horizon to the presidential campaign of 1936 and after. To play "second fiddle" to any man was foreign to his nature.

After watching both men intently at close quarters, I honestly believe that, casting prejudices aside, Roosevelt was entitled to the decision. He was far and away the stronger man. In that test of strength which both of them recognized as such, meeting elbow-to-elbow and eye-to-eye, F.D.R. showed himself to be all back-bone and brain. He had the situation in hand at all times, and his cool manner and well-chosen words and phrases had Huey fenced in completely. Long presented his case very well but after a time he seemed to lose his fire, and as the end drew near, he was perfectly willing to call it quits. Huey had been having a gorgeous time pushing around some of his colleagues in Senate debate, but I doubt if he had ever before tackled a man quite as sharp and strong as Roosevelt. He gave me the impression that he didn't like to "take it" any too well. A fellow of his character is at his best when things are going to suit him and not when someone else is giving better than he sends.

Long Asks a Senate Probe

Old-time employees around the White House said later that they never recalled another instance when a man consciously kept his hat on while visiting a President. Huey did that, of course, to steal the show. When it failed to work, he realized that it had placed him at a disadvantage.

The Louisiana firebrand never forgave President Roosevelt for the fact that he was worsted at that meeting. I know that after-wards he told newspapermen that F.D.R. was the "toughest" fellow he had ever met, and his manner left no doubt that he was looking for a chance to get vengeance. We were to feel his wrath a short time later, and once again it so happened that I was the gentleman in the middle.

Early in the winter of 1935, Long decided that the time had come to begin his political assaults on the Roosevelt administration and the Democratic Party and he made up his mind that the most effective way of accomplishing it was to make me bear the brunt of the attack. He had already worked out his own peculiar method of proceeding under such circumstances, and the Senate was well acquainted with his plan of action. Two or three members of that body had incurred his anger on prior occasions. Huey had crushed them by the simple process of delivering violent harangues, during the course of which he repeated and magnified every petty charge that he had ever heard against them. It was a complete reversal of the rules of courtesy that prevail in Senate debate, but that fact meant nothing to Long.

I was a fairly easy target for his shafts because for some time the press, which was hostile to the administration, had been carrying articles criticizing me for acting in the dual capacity of Postmaster General and National Chairman of the Democratic Party. As a rule, I made no effort to answer those criticisms. Huey, however, was quietly gathering together everything he saw in print on the subject and he knew just how an article could be turned to give it a sinister insinuation. Early in January or February, I forget which, he formally presented charges against me, and demanded a Senate investigation. The charges were placed before the Committee of the Senate for preliminary investigation and to determine whether a full investigation should be authorized.

Long's move failed to worry me. I was completely innocent of the charges which he brought, and he knew very well that he was assailing my character unfairly simply to further his own political ends. What he had started was a fishing expedition in the hope that something unexpected might hook onto his line. I had been working at a terrific pace for months on end and decided to go to Florida for a vacation, paying no attention to the Long charges at all. I had hardly arrived in Florida when Marvin McIntyre called me from the White House and said he thought it best that I should return to Washington at once. Huey had opened one of his circus performances in the Senate, and some of the people in the administration who were a bit inexperienced politically were getting jittery. Day after day during the month of February, Huey took the Senate floor to delight the packed galleries with his threats that he was going to "blow the roof off the Capitol" by his sensational exposé of the wickedness of the Roosevelt administration. He thrashed his way up and down the aisles, reading excerpts from newspaper articles and bellowing out that what he read was nothing compared to what he was going to prove when the investigation itself got under way. As usually happened under such circumstances, Long's charges made the newspaper headlines, and interest in everything else was forgotten temporarily in the expectation of the spicy drama that was to follow.

When Mac asked me to come back to Washington, I was peeved and resentful. I was physically exhausted and needed a vacation badly. Long's charges didn't disturb me in the least, and the prospect of returning at once to plunge into the laborious job of replying to a lot of unjust accusations didn't improve my frame of mind. After a lengthy discussion, Mac and I reached a compromise. I agreed to return after one week in Florida and no sooner.

I returned to Washington on February 17 and went immediately to the White House for a conference with the President, which was attended also by Secretary of the Treasury Morgenthau and Secretary of the Interior Ickes, the latter two being present because Long's charges involved matters concerned with their departments. The conference was held in the White House proper in the Chief Executive's private office on the second floor. We had another meeting the following day.

While Long's "charges" were vague and indefinite, he sought to leave the implication in his Senate speeches that I was profiting through my private business connections on government contracts for the construction of post offices and on other buildings being erected with public works funds. Ickes was public works administrator and the Treasury Department also had a large voice in the awarding of post-office contracts. Both men told the President that they had called for the papers in the cases which Long mentioned and that there was absolutely not a shred of evidence to support the Senator's charges. We talked it over for some little time, and later, after the two Cabinet members had gone, Roosevelt and I continued to discuss the best way to handle the situation.

The Chief Executive was anxious to have my name cleared. He knew the charges were without foundation and he realized also that it was really a thrust aimed at himself by an ambitious and unscrupulous opponent who wanted to smear the administration. He suggested that perhaps the wisest procedure was for me to ask voluntarily for an investigation and to appear personally and refute the charges. He felt that this would end the matter for all time and prove a boomerang to Long because the facts showed that the charges were wholly unwarranted. But for once I disagreed with the President of the United States. I had done nothing wrong and had no intention of acting the part of a scapegoat to help keep Long in the headlines. My own inclination was to do nothing at all unless the Senate requested my appearance. I realized that the very fact that a man goes before a committee to answer charges and submits himself to cross-examination leaves an unpleasant impression on the public mind. Even questions, if asked by an unscrupulous man, can leave a bad implication when seen in cold print, no matter what answer is given in reply. Huey would have liked nothing better than to stage a Roman holiday at my expense, and I had no wish to be the helpless martyr.

The President, however, pointed out that the Long accusations had been given nationwide circulation and that the public might get the wrong impression entirely if I made no answer at all. The logic of what he said was apparent. It was finally decided that I should make no public statement but should send the Senate Committee a detailed and specific answer to everything said by Long. I followed that course, taking up one by one everything alleged by the Louisiana Senator in his speeches and also referring to the implications contained in his resolution calling for an investigation.

The charges at the time seemed highly important, but, as with everything of that nature, interest in them has since faded away and it would be tedious to set them all forth in detail. Some of the things Huey said implied grave wrong-doing on my part and some of them were merely funny and would have no significance even if true. Huey had a genuine sense of humor, and I think it was his ability to mix up the important and the ridiculous that gave him such crowd appeal. For example, he cited the fact that the Texas legislature had passed a resolution approving my work and he charged that I was personally guilty of inspiring the resolution. It was a bit of clowning, but I had to answer it.

Another charge, far more serious, was to the effect that a gentleman had come to Washington to inquire when we would be ready to set up the organization for disbursing the $4,800,000,000 relief and public works fund which had recently been appropriated by Congress. Long quoted me as replying, "I shall be ready to set up organization in about two weeks." That was a fictitious conversation entirely and serves to give a typical example of Long's "shot-in-the-dark" methods. He wanted to prove wrong-doing in connection with the distribution of relief funds, and having no evidence he simply invented it. In response to that charge, I informed the Senate Committee that no such conversation ever took place, that I had absolutely nothing to do with the expenditure of work relief funds, and that I never had attempted to assume jurisdiction over such expenditures. That statement is still true.

In addition to making this formal statement of fact, which went before the committee, I also did something else. There were several members of the Senate personally friendly to me who never entertained a moment's doubt about my honesty but who were disturbed over Long's charges and wanted to be in a position to refute them accurately if it came to a showdown. I showed these gentlemen my checkbook, copies of my income tax returns, and every other paper that had a bearing on my personal financial situation. These papers completely refuted the charge that I was profiting, directly or indirectly, from government business and they showed also that after spending all my mature years in politics, the only thing I had accumulated in a financial way was a collection of debts running into thousands of dollars. That is a common occurrence in politics, despite the cynical disbelief of some people, and the Senators were well aware of that fact. The knowledge that this evidence was available, and had been seen, was a decisive factor in influencing the action taken by the Senate.

Long's resolution was brought to a vote, and by a wide margin that body decided that he had failed to establish even "prima facie" evidence of wrong-doing. Hence the proposed investigation was squashed. Before the final vote, the facts were placed before the Senate on my behalf by Senator Josiah W. Bailey of North Carolina, who had the courage to tackle Huey on his own ground at a time when a number of his colleagues were content to steer shy of him. Bailey's frank and full exposition of the entire matter was tremendously important in influencing the Senate vote, and I have always been grateful to him on that account.

During the entire Huey Long controversy no one rendered more intelligent, efficient or loyal services in my behalf than Senator Kenneth McKellar of Tennessee, Chairman of the Senate Post Office and Post Roads Committee. He frequently entered into debate with Senator Long and was at all times more than generous in my defense in handling the situation. His many acts of kindness and his generous support of me at all times places me under everlasting obligation to him.

The vote was largely along party lines. Even if personal elements were involved, I realized that it was essentially a political move, and consequently there was no ill feeling on my part when regular Republicans such as Senators Vandenberg of Michigan and Austin of Vermont voted to investigate. However, I was pleased at the fact that such outstanding and upstanding members of the Senate as Hiram W. Johnson of California, William E. Borah of Idaho, and Henrik Shipstead, Farmer-Laborite of Minnesota, voted to dismiss the charges without investigation. I appreciated their vote of confidence, and the name of each one of them has since had behind it a golden star in my private book of accounts. The excitement kicked up over the charges was soon forgotten, and the Louisiana Senator began looking for grist for his political mills in other directions. During the time when the thing was in full blast, a friend of mine talked to another widely known gentleman who was annoyed with me politically because of my activity in behalf of Roosevelt. It was Al Smith of New York. My friend mentioned the Long charges, and Al replied, "Huey is barking up the wrong tree; he won't get anywhere because Jim is an honest man." I appreciated that remark, when it was repeated to me, very much.

Several months later when the incident had blown over and Huey was busily engaged in some of his other hobbies, I was leaving a Washington hotel with a few friends when I saw him standing just inside the entrance. I was still a bit nettled at his conduct and looking for a chance to see what he had to say for himself. To attract his attention, I said, "Hello, Huey, how are you?" He was engaged in conversation and hadn't seen me up to that time. Turning around, he merely said, "Hello," and then resumed his conversation. I saw he wasn't ready to talk so I went along.

A short time later an acquaintance of mine was talking to Long and he asked what inspired him to bring the charges against me. "Oh," said Huey, "Jim was the biggest rooster in the yard, and I thought that if I could break his legs, the rest would be easy." He said candidly that he had hoped his daily speeches on the subject would bring in a number of anonymous communications that would help him to sustain his charges, but none came. That is a common method of procedure in fishing expeditions of that character.

During this period in 1934 and 1935 when Senator Long was waging a kind of private war on the Roosevelt administration, we never had any illusions as to the real purpose which inspired his actions. By the same token, we never underestimated his ability to do us a large measure of political damage. The times were still far from normal, and countless voters were in the ugly frame of mind brought on by the hardships of the depression. They were ready for rash action under a reckless leader, if for no other purpose than to show their displeasure at what had taken place. Sensing the temper of the times, Long was preparing to make a bid for national power. It was evident that he had in mind the formation of a third ticket for the presidential election of 1936.

Huey's Third-Party Threat

I've always made an effort not to let personal bias warp my political judgment. We kept a careful eye on what Huey and his political allies, both in office and out of office, were attempting to do. Anxious not to be caught napping and desiring an accurate picture of conditions, the Democratic National Committee conducted a secret poll on a national scale during this period to find out if Huey's sales talks for his "share the wealth" program were attracting many customers. The result of that poll, which was kept secret and shown only to a very few people, was surprising in many ways. It indicated that, running on a third-party ticket, Long would be able to poll between 3,000,000 to 4,000,000 votes for the Presidency. The poll demonstrated also that Huey was doing fairly well at making himself a national figure. His probable support was not confined to Louisiana and near-by states. On the contrary, he had about as much following in the North as in the South, and he had as strong an appeal in the industrial centers as he did in the rural areas. Even the rock-ribbed Republican state of Maine, where the voters were steeped in conservatism, was ready to contribute to Long's total vote in about the same percentage as other states.

While we realized that polls are often inaccurate and that conditions could change perceptibly before the election actually took place, the size of the Long vote made him a formidable factor. He was head and shoulders stronger than any of the other "Messiahs" who were also gazing wistfully at the White House and wondering what chance they would have to arrive there as the result of a popular uprising. It was easy to conceive a situation whereby Long, by polling more than 3,000,000 votes, might have the balance of power in the 1936 election. For example, the poll indicated that he would command upward of 100,000 votes in New York State, a pivotal state in any national election; and a vote of that size could easily mean the difference between victory or defeat for the Democratic or Republican candidate. Take that number of votes away from either major candidate, and they would come mostly from our side, and the result might spell disaster.

Not only that, but private reports indicated to us that Long would be financed in a substantial way if and when he decided to enter the conflict. A number of very wealthy people who hated Roosevelt, according to what seemed to us reliable information, were ready to put up the cash for the Louisiana Senator, if he wanted it, in the hope that his candidacy would split the Democratic Party. It would be playing with fire for them to finance such a scheme, but they later attempted it with other third-party aspirants, notably former Governor Eugene Talmadge of Georgia. A Senate committee revealed that thousands of dollars were pumped into the Grass Conventions at Macon, Georgia, organized by Talmadge, and most of the money came from prominent members of the Liberty League and "Wall Street" operators. Long had another added advantage in the fact that he was bound to receive a huge share of newspaper publicity because of his natural flair for news-making. When his untimely death removed him from the scene, none of his followers or imitators were able to carry on with the same threat.

I never agreed with the people who felt that the Republican Party would be a hopeless minority in 1936 and that the real opposition would come from the "left," or third party. Neither did I think that Long's strength would increase measurably as the election approached. On the contrary, my personal opinion was that he was nothing like a match for President Roosevelt on the stump and that, while he might dazzle the populace for a while as others had done before him, his popularity would dwindle away just as rapidly.

After the death of Senator Long and the election of Richard Leche as Governor, the feud between the Roosevelt administration and the state of Louisiana gradually ended. Funds were awarded for a number of public works projects in Louisiana, and the state was also given its proportional share of other relief funds. The tax suits entered against some of the Long followers which had not already been disposed of, were dismissed by the Justice Department. This was attacked by the opposition as a political bargain and described by some news writers, hostile to the Roosevelt administration, as the "Second Louisiana Purchase."

I am not hoping that those who feel that way about the Louisiana situation will change their views as the result of anything written here. In the first place, I had absolutely nothing to do with the tax cases, which were originally started by the Hoover administration and not by New Deal officials as constantly charged. The Roosevelt administration, to my mind, took the only fair course that could be chosen. The tax cases were not dismissed to placate Long, despite his power. Long was not given the opportunity to recommend the appointment of income tax officials or of a Federal district attorney who might be disposed to favor him. Neither were the cases turned over to his implacable foes in Louisiana, who, because of their hatred, might wish to do him harm unfairly. An outstanding attorney, who had neither bias nor prejudice, was brought in to handle the cases solely on the basis of justice. My recollection is that some of the cases came to trial. Not being a lawyer, I am not competent to pass on the final action of the department in dismissing the suits.

The question of allotting Federal funds to Louisiana was another grave matter. Some people have the mistaken impression that the state was denied funds for public works because of the administration's quarrel with Long. On the contrary, when he was not allowed to name the Federal officials who could supervise the projects, Long had a series of enactments put through the state legislature which virtually took all control of Federal monies, expended in Louisiana, out of the hands of Federal officials. Under the circumstances, the public works administrator could hardly spend funds there when he was denied the right to see that they were expended honestly. Later when Governor Leche came into power those restrictive enactments were removed by the state legislature. The people of Louisiana were paying Federal taxes and they were entitled to a fair share of recovery and relief funds. The Roosevelt administration did not punish governors who were on the opposite side of the political fence, despite statements to the contrary. Governor Landon was the Republican candidate for President in 1936, and even though it was known a couple of years earlier that he would be in the race, no effort was made to penalize him on that account. He was allotted his full share of Federal funds and frankly said so.

However, as I said before, I am not hoping to convince anyone who holds the opposite view regarding the Louisiana situation. If there was a "purchase," it is only fair to ask what was purchased? As soon as Senator Long died, thus ending the threat of him running on a third ticket, it was apparent to everyone in politics that Louisiana would vote the Democratic ticket in 1936. It was just as surely in the Roosevelt column as its neighboring Southern states. There was no need to "purchase" the state in that respect. And I think that every citizen who examines the facts will agree that the Roosevelt administration did not attempt to make a deal or compromise during the hectic days when Senator Long was very close to being the "balance of power" in American politics.

IV. The Post Office Department

ENCOURAGING THE PHILATELISTS. REPUBLICAN STAMP
GIFTS. CANCELING THE AIR-MAIL CONTRACTS. BUILDING
NEW POST OFFICES. POSTMASTERS AND POLITICS. SAVING
AUNT EMMA'S POST OFFICE. THE POSTAL INSPECTORS.
ABUSES OF "FRANKING."

THE Post Office Department has the rare distinction of being one form of "government in business" provided for in the Constitution itself. Although they were rugged individualists in the best sense, the sturdy men who fashioned the framework of the American Government recognized that an efficient, nationwide system of mails was vitally necessary to the ordered growth of the new Republic. The Constitution thus having made provision for the establishment of a postal system, George Washington showed himself to be an executive of discrimination and judgment by selecting the wise and industrious Benjamin Franklin as the first Postmaster General.

The expansion of the department into one of the mammoth business organizations of the modern world was perhaps one of the things that Benjamin failed to foresee, although he was shrewd beyond his generation in understanding how the physical sciences could be developed to meet the needs of man. In Franklin's day, the postal service was a puny affair, with annual revenues of less than $100,000, depending for its mail delivery upon horseback riders or upon slow-moving coaches that jolted for days over rutty roads. Today, the department has annual revenues in the neighborhood of $730,000,000; it employs more than a quarter of a million men and women to perform many and far-flung activities; and its mails move forward with streamline speed.

The Post Office Department is also, I am compelled to confess, one of the most efficient publicly owned business organizations in the world, and the service it renders is seldom eclipsed, or even matched, by private industrial organizations comparable in extent. The cost of mailing a letter is down just about to a minimum,

deliveries are regular and prompt, and the department performs
its functions with a minimum of friction and with very little
criticism, public or private. The credit for this superb record of
public service is due in large measure to the "esprit de corps,"
which has been built up through the years among postal workers
themselves, and to the contributions of many able Postmasters
General who have held office under both Democratic and Republican administrations.

The history of the department is closely interwoven with the
growth and expansion of the United States itself, and from its
annals could be unfolded a thrilling and romantic tale of the
heroic men and women who constructed the mighty nation which
now spans the continent. In the early days, especially in the Far
West and Southwest, the Federal mail was the only communication linking the outside world with mining and lumber camps in
out-of-the-way places, with newly formed agricultural communities in the Great Plains states, and with struggling settlements of
fisher folks and others in the Pacific Northwest. The pony express
rider often arrived with his precious cargo, to be greeted by a mass
of cheering men and women who could hardly wait for letters
and newspapers telling them what was happening to their friends
and relatives in distant places. The department records tell of
intrepid men who year after year carried Uncle Sam's mail
through the wilderness and in sparsely settled regions, braving the
menace of hostile Indians and other perils, not because the pay
was large, but simply because the work furnished the sort of
excitement which satisfied their adventure-loving souls. Heroism
was not uncommon in the pioneering period, in fact it became so
common that the story of a mailman who lost his life in line of
duty was accepted as a matter-of-fact happening.

The department records disclose step by step the growth of
great states and cities from the tiniest beginnings. They also reveal the tragic fate of agricultural and mining settlements which
quickly grew into prosperous and flourishing communities only to
wither away and die when both people and industry moved elsewhere. Some of the early places listed in the Post Office Department records are now missing from the map entirely.

The mail service is the one activity of the Federal Government that reaches into every hamlet in the land. In thousands upon thousands of rural settlements, the local post office has come to be regarded as a social center and a friendly meeting place where men and women come each day, not only to ask for mail but to exchange greetings and gossip with their neighbors. The business of trying to decide whether a small post office should be abandoned on cold economic grounds alone or permitted to continue its existence because of its value as a social institution is a perplexing problem which the department is called upon to face almost daily.

The postal service has always utilized the most modern methods available in the all-important task of mail transmission. Letters are now whirled through the sky by the air-mail flyers from ocean to ocean in about the same time that it formerly took a horseman to pack the mail fifty to sixty miles. In the large cities, besides the thousands of delivery trucks in use, air tubes are employed to hasten the dispatch of letters between strategic points such as the post office and the railroad stations. The China Clipper Service, the first transoceanic flying service ever to link the United States with foreign soil, was made possible by the generous subsidies provided by Uncle Sam through the Post Office Department. Handling the operations of such a huge enterprise and directing the many other services which it is called upon to perform, in addition to delivering the mail, is a task of major proportions. Since taking over the duties of Postmaster General in the Roosevelt Cabinet, I have had a good opportunity to study the postal business, to find out how it compares in efficiency and costs with similar organizations elsewhere, and to introduce a number of innovations and alterations that seemed desirable. This work has been done gradually during the past five years. The net result has been gratifying, and it can be stated without fear of contradiction that the department has never functioned in better order, both from the standpoint of the taxpayer and the postal clients, than it functions today.

The recounting of what was undertaken to promote efficiency might interest people in commerce or industry but to the average person, unfortunately, information along that line makes pretty dull reading. Consequently, I shall skip over the many excellent reforms instituted in the accounting division and elsewhere to discuss those things connected with the department which have often been "front page" news and have provided a great deal of interest for the general public, even when they were not very significant in themselves.

The Post Office Department has done very well in the matter of publicity since the Roosevelt administration has come into power; and, in one respect at least, this publicity has helped to bring large sums of added revenue into Uncle Sam's Treasury. The occasions which brought the department into the headline news of the day were the cancellation of the air-mail contracts, the issuance of a few sheets of ungummed postage stamps which excited the attention of collectors, and the general charges hurled by spokesmen for the opposition that the department was being converted into nothing more than a convenient dumping ground for Democratic job-holders. This last charge especially provoked a wealth of indignant comment from G.O.P. Congressmen and hostile newspapers who never raised an eyebrow at revelations of unsavory practices in the department during the prior period when it was under the supervision of the Republicans.

I intend to discuss all of these questions in this chapter, giving the other side of the picture for the first time. I also intend to point out that millions of dollars have been saved for the government in postal operations that might have been saved earlier by a little more diligence on the part of previous Republican administrations, especially in regard to the air-mail contracts. It is perfectly all right for Uncle Sam to be generous and reasonable with private contractors who fly the mails; yet there was no excuse on earth for the fat figures at which air-mail contracts were let before the contracts were canceled by the Roosevelt administration. The act of cancellation, which was severely criticized in some quarters at the time, has since effected substantial savings for the Treasury without injuring the service in the least, and I wish to make that exceedingly plain right at the outset.

Encouraging the Philatelists

A person who collects stamps put out by the United States Government or by any other government is described by the high-sounding title of philatelist, a rather heavy word to describe a person engaged in such a peaceful and pleasant hobby. The practice of gathering and preserving stamp issues has been going on for a long time both here and abroad, in fact philately is an old and venerated avocation in which kings and emperors and commoners have long indulged. Philately became fairly widespread in this country at an early date, and a few years ago the art was encouraged in a minor way by the Post Office Department which established, in 1921, a special agency to promote the sale of stamps directly to collectors. It was estimated that in 1933 there were about 2,000,000 individuals in this country who could be classed as stamp collectors.

For a great many years, in fact, ever since his boyhood days at Hyde Park, New York, F. D. Roosevelt has been a serious-minded philatelist and he has managed to acquire an enviable collection for an amateur at the trade. He has subscribed to journals of philately and has formed many pleasant friendships by exchanging correspondence with others who were devoted to the same hobby. Others in the new administration who genuinely liked stamp-collecting were the President's secretary, Louis McHenry Howe, and Secretary of the Interior, Harold Ickes. With such keen interest shown in high places, it was only natural that philately should be given far more than the cursory attention usually accorded such details of government, and that we should see an opportunity to turn this public interest to the advantage of the department which, after all, is a form of business and should be run with that thought in mind.

Special stamp issues had been put out by other administrations down through the years to commemorate noteworthy occasions. However, no administration on record ever put out as many issues as the present Roosevelt administration has during the past few years, the total running between seventy-five and a hundred. The first one was a stamp to commemorate the proclamation of peace in the Revolutionary War, the design picturing the crude headquarters which General Washington used while his army was wintering at Newburgh, New York. The site of the Newburgh headquarters was across the Hudson River and not very far away from the site of the present Roosevelt homestead at Hyde Park, so that the first commemorative stamp had a personal touch for the Chief Executive.

Noticing an awakened public interest on the part of the public towards stamp-collecting, we extended very early the facilities of the philatelic sales agency, set up a large exhibition room where the stamp issues of the United States and of two hundred foreign governments were placed on display for the benefit of visitors, encouraged the formation of stamp clubs, and participated to a greater degree than ever in the annual conventions of the three major philatelic agencies. This stimulation of interest has had remarkable results, and the number of stamp clubs in existence at schools and elsewhere throughout the country has grown with leaps and bounds. It is now estimated that there are approximately 9,000,000 people who have taken up the hobby of stamp-collecting, in contrast to the 2,000,000 collectors of a few years ago.

This encouragement of the stamp-collection business has proved to be a real boon to the finances of the department. Whereas the receipts from the philatelic agency formerly amounted to around $300,000 annually, the total is now close to $2,000,000 annually with favorable prospects for further increases. The greater part of this income is profit for the government because the agency is operated at a low cost, and the expense of producing the stamps themselves is negligible in comparison to the revenue received.

The department's activities in relation to new stamps was first brought to the attention of the general public in a manner that no one had anticipated. When the special issues were first put on general sale for the public, I was informed that it had long been a custom in the department for the Postmaster General to present proof sheets and specimens of postage stamps for souvenir purposes to high-ranking officials in the government and to other persons. On the basis of long practice, I purchased a number of these specimen sheets, some of which I autographed, paying the postage costs in each instance.

One sheet of Mother's Day stamps was presented to a personal friend in New York City, who had been a collector for many years and who naturally appreciated being remembered when the issue was placed on sale for the first time. He wrote me about another the specimen sheet, thought it was interesting, and wanted to acquire one if possible. I agreed to send it after receiving the $6 in payment for the stamps. Being unacquainted with the man, I should have been careful to explain that it was intended solely for inclusion in a private collection and must not be used for commercial purposes under any circumstances. A short time later he went to the bank and tried to negotiate a loan, offering to put up the specimen sheet as security on the theory that it was worth several thousand dollars. The bank declined to make the loan, but the story got into print and it aroused much unfavorable comment from philatelic journals and from the press generally. The business of determining stamp values is complicated to a high degree, and the public got the impression that the department had commenced the doubtful practice of giving away stamps of unusual value instead of selling them.

I acted quickly to clear up the situation and to disabuse the public of the idea that an individual had been placed in a position to profit handsomely at the expense of the government. The department was directed to run off an adequate supply of specimen sheets of the Mother's Day issue, similar to the one which had gotten into the possession of the gentleman from Virginia. At the same time, specimen sheets of nineteen other special issues, including the National Parks Series, were run off and these specimen sheets were sold over the counter to every collector who wanted one. The sales continued for three months from March 15 to June 15, 1935, and during that period these sheets to a total value of $1,467,972.70 were disposed of for cash. In other words, the widespread publicity given to an honest error on my part finally resulted in a net profit to Uncle Sam of at least $1,400,000. From a business standpoint at least, the outcome was highly satisfactory.

Republican Stamp Gifts

The excitement over the specimen stamp sheets was really a tempest in a teapot and apparently was regarded with amused tolerance by the general public, most fair-minded people accepting at its face value the straightforward explanation of the department as to how the incident had occurred. However, a number of people who saw an opportunity to make political capital out of the affair continued to keep it alive and to clothe it with insinuations that gave it a sinister twist. That was true of a couple of reactionary Republican newspapers which looked upon collusive bidding for air-mail contracts with complacency and without criticism, but became highly incensed over what they professed to believe, and tried to have the public believe, was a doubtful practice started by me to enrich a few friends. It was nothing of the kind, and I propose now to set forth how outstanding Republican officeholders received gifts of stamps, some of them extremely valuable, on occasions without number. A record of stamp gifts was compiled in 1905, reaching back into previous administrations, and the records since then have been kept in detail.

I judge from the Post Office Department annals that stamp collecting must be an old Republican custom because certainly the G.O.P. statesmen of former years treated themselves very generously in the distribution of free stamps, especially when new issues were first placed on sale. These gifts were always made by the Postmasters General, and the recipient paid nothing. The reader will bear in mind that I paid postage charges in connection with the sheets distributed by me, even though it was not in accordance with precedent in the department.

A record, which the department compiled, of stamp gifts under the G.O.P. is seventy or eighty pages deep with names and facts so that naturally this is no place to recount all of them. The most comprehensive picture of how the stamp specimens were distributed on other occasions may be had by recalling the story of the albums containing specimen issues which were distributed in the period from 1903 to 1905, a total of seventy-three albums being given out gratis by the department.

The gentlemen receiving the albums included a notable list of distinguished Republican statesmen, who then dominated the affairs of government, including President Theodore Roosevelt, Senator Henry Cabot Lodge of Massachusetts, Elihu Root, a member of the President's Cabinet, "Uncle Joe" Cannon, G.O.P. Speaker of the House, Senator Chauncey Depew, of New York, Senator Philander C. Knox, of Pennsylvania, and George B. Cortelyou, another member of the Cabinet.

The albums were richly bound and tastefully gotten up, each one containing approximately 140 die proofs of the stamps issued by the United States from the time of the first issue back in 1847 up until 1902. It was said that the albums had considerable value at the time they were distributed free and, according to reliable catalogues, they should have a minimum value of $1,000 apiece at the present time.

The album distribution gives a pretty apt illustration of the way in which special stamps were passed out under former administrations, but that was far from being the only distribution. Mark Hanna, then Senator from Ohio, who compiled quite a record as a G.O.P. political manager in his prime, was remembered on several occasions. He was given a complete set of the ordinary stamps issued in 1902, and a similar favor was bestowed upon Senator Lodge and Mr. Cortelyou, the latter apparently being an active collector as his name appears more often than any of the others.

Complete sets of "Pan-American proofs," a special series of six different stamps issued in 1901, were presented to twenty-three Republican members of the House of Representatives and to ten members of the Senate, the latter group including Hanna and Senator Boise Penrose, the Republican leader of Pennsylvania. The Pan-American inverted stamp was likewise given to a number of Senators and Representatives, and the stamp catalogues now estimate that each one of the stamps is worth $1,200. Six complete sets of Cuban "overprints," put out by the department in 1899, were bestowed upon the Republican Secretary of War. The worth of individual stamps in this series now varies between fifteen cents and $600. Die proofs of the Trans-Mississippi postage stamps, issued in 1898, were passed out rather liberally, the recipients including Honorable Charles Curtis, later Vice-President of the United States, and several other members of the Senate and House.

The late Anthony Comstock, noted reformer and crusader against vice, must have been an avid philatelist because the G.O.P. leaders very thoughtfully remembered him on more than one occasion with a stamp gift for his collection. He got a set of the Cuban overprints among others.

On various dates, between 1923 and 1929, a total of 470 die proofs were given to the successive incumbents who acted as Postmaster General and forty die proofs were given to the late President Coolidge who was then in office. Mrs. Warren G. Harding received one set of die proofs and Mrs. Coolidge received three, showing that the practice persisted down to very recent times. The "die proof" is a sample of the new stamp to be issued, cut in the size and color wanted and then sent over by the Bureau of Engraving and Printing to the Post Office Department for final acceptance. Naturally these die proofs are rare.

The foregoing recital is only a very meager record of the big-hearted way in which souvenir stamps were passed out to the faithful during the long years when Republican worthies sat in authority over Federal affairs, and the forlorn Democrats were left out in the cold entirely. To my knowledge, this history of stamp issues has never before been published. The question naturally arises, why did I neglect or overlook the publication of these facts during the time when the souvenir stamps distributed by me were under fire? It is obviously true that the Republican spokesmen who managed to work up such a degree of synthetic indignation would have forgotten the incident at once if the full story had been made public.

The reason why the records were not revealed then was closely tied up with my own notion of how a public official should act under criticism and, wisely or unwisely, I followed the only course of conduct which seemed fair under the circumstances. In the first place I had done nothing unethical and nothing that was to cost the government money, and therefore it was against my policy to apologize, to beg off, or to seek refuge behind any kind of an excuse. The simple record of the transaction was made public and that was enough. In the second place, it has always seemed to me that the weakest kind of a defense is to point to another person and say, "He did it too."

Nearly all of the public men mentioned here in connection with stamp gifts, such as Theodore Roosevelt, Henry Cabot Lodge, Elihu Root, Mark Hanna and "Uncle Joe" Cannon, have passed away from this earth long since; and it would have been rather shabby tactics on my part to hide behind their names when they had no opportunity to defend themselves. Those gentlemen received high honors at the hands of the American people in their generation; they conducted themselves honorably; and the public would hardly appreciate seeing them dragged into a controversy in which they rightly had no part.

And above all other reasons was the fact that there is no evidence in the world to suggest that any of these gentlemen profited even a penny's worth from the comparatively few souvenir stamps which they received as gifts. As a matter of fact, I assume Senators Lodge and Hanna and other men of that caliber were given the die proofs without solicitation and that they never for a moment considered that the transaction would ever be open to criticism. While the incidents are recorded here, they are mentioned merely as an interesting sidelight on an amusing controversy and in the sincere belief that the readers will regard them in that way. It is not my intention to cast aspersions on these gentlemen— even though they were distinguished members of the opposite political party.

The discontinuance of the issuance of die proofs and uncut sheets was ordered by me after the furor over the Mother's Day stamps, even though to my mind there was nothing reprehensible or blameworthy about the practice. However, as long as the critics felt that I should be purer than the pure Anthony Comstock in regard to souvenir stamps, I had no wish to disappoint them. President Roosevelt now buys his stamps over the counter like other collectors.

The department's philatelic business continues to thrive, and, with President Roosevelt's personal help in designing new issues, there is a pretty good chance that some day no home in America will be without its stamp-collector. All of which means more revenue for Uncle Sam. The hobby is still looked upon as rather mild by a lot of individuals who like to think of themselves as too "red-blooded" to indulge in so simple a pastime. Yet, it is a matter of record that most people who start collecting stamps keep on doing so, and that it is one of the most pleasurable and fascinating of indoor pursuits. The stamps can be kept in very attractive form and on top of that they can be of real assistance in the study of history, geography, and other subjects.

A genuine, honest-to-goodness stamp-collector will never let pass without loud protest anything about a new model which displeases him. We have had a number of heated protests during the past few years from earnest philatelists who questioned the stamp designs selected by the administration for new issues. A few artistic folks complained at the disappearance of the feet of Whistler's mother in the Mother's Day stamp, and another shower of protests came in over the fact that, on the four-cent stamp in the Army series, General Robert E. Lee had only three stars on his uniform instead of four, leading to the mistaken suspicion in the case of some of Lee's ardent admirers that an effort was being made to deny the Confederate General his full rank.

Canceling the Air-Mail Contracts

The Post Office Department down through the years has been given the unique function by Congress of virtually handing over funds to private concerns for the purpose of enabling them to stay in business. These subsidies have been passed out in the form of liberal payments for carrying the mail to steamship lines and to air passenger lines, the object being the perfectly legitimate and necessary one of keeping them in operation when otherwise it might be impossible for them to do so. The American flag would have vanished from the high seas long since except for the mail subsidies, and the air passenger lines would never have reached their present state of development if it were not for Uncle Sam's help. Very few people question the wisdom of the subsidy policy; in fact, it is looked upon as a matter of national concern and continued in force regardless of what political party is in power.

It always happens that when large sums of money are available in the form of government grants, a fierce form of competition springs up between rival organizations endeavoring to get a share of the available funds. Under the circumstances, it is difficult to draw a line between the unscrupulous and those who have a legitimate interest. That has always been true in the case of subsidies, and the rigid chalk-line which a government official must walk to avoid entanglements is appreciated only by those who have observed it first-hand. Individuals seeking government contracts, which mean financial profit for them, will always endeavor to curry favor with officials, and the dangers of such contacts are all too obvious to need recital here.

The foregoing is merely by way of a preface to recalling one of the most disputed acts ever taken by the Roosevelt administration, namely the cancellation of domestic air-mail contracts during the month of February, 1934. The cancellation was based upon evidence brought out by a Senate investigating committee, and it was actually ordered only after the most painstaking examination of that evidence by postal officials, Department of Justice officials, and by President Roosevelt himself. While the facts are too lengthy and too much involved in legal questions to warrant detailed repetition, the general basis for the cancellation was the conviction that the contracts had been let by my predecessor, Postmaster General Brown, without the kind of competitive bidding stipulated in the law and at figures that were wholly unjustified by the services rendered. The files of the Post Office Department, as made public by the Senate Committee, revealed that Brown had called the representatives of the leading air transport companies in to a meeting at the Post Office Department on May 19, 1930, and that a virtual agreement on the division of the air-mail contracts had been entered into at that and subsequent meetings. In the minutes of the Senate Committee, the original meeting on May 19 was always referred to as the "Spoils Conference," and the revelation that such a gathering had been held stirred up public indignation and excited the wrath of other companies that had been frozen out of the bidding.

After being advised by the solicitor of the Post Office Department that the contracts were illegal, and after consulting Attorney General Cummings, I issued an order canceling the contracts on February 9 to be effective ten days later. I also issued a statement, explaining why such action was taken, which said in part:

"I do not believe Congress intended that the air-mail appropriation should be expanded for the benefit of a few favored corporations, which could use the funds as the basis of wild stock promotion resulting in profits of tens of millions of dollars to promoters who invested little or no capital. Nor was it intended to be used by great corporations as a club to force competitors out of business and into bankruptcy. Nor should appropriations and contracts be given to a few favored corporations by connivance and agreements."

Before this cancellation order was actually issued, we had checked with officials of the War Department and were advised that the flyers of the Army Air Corps would be ready to carry the mail on a temporary basis over several selected routes, beginning February 20, thus ensuring against interruption of service on the more important lines. The first air mail ever flown had been carried by the Army flyers sixteen years before, and it was assumed that with the advancement in plane design and technical equipment, the corps would have no difficulty in maintaining service over the strategic routes agreed upon. The outcome was tragedy—unforeseen and unavoidable—and the unhappy fate of the brave military aviators who perished in line of duty served to overshadow entirely the question of whether the private contracts had been let on a just and equitable basis.

Nature seemed to conspire against us during the comparatively brief period in which the Army flyers carried the mail. The United States, from the Atlantic to the Pacific, was swept by an almost unprecedented wave of adverse weather that included blinding snowstorms, heavy fogs, perilous sleet, extreme cold, and other conditions of the type that made flying extremely hazardous. A majority of the Army men piloting the planes were young; with a brave disregard of danger, prompted only by a desire to do the job well, they continued to make flights with the mail even in the teeth of such desperate conditions. The result was a shocking series of accidents. Disturbed at this unexpected turn of events, President Roosevelt issued an order, under date of March 10, ordering the Air Corps to effect a drastic and immediate curtailment of service. In his order, after recalling how the Air Corps had taken over the mail service on February 9, the Chief Executive said:

"Since that time ten Army flyers have lost their lives. I appreciate that only four of these were actually flying the mail, but the others were training or were proceeding to the mail route. I appreciate also that almost every part of the country has been visited during this period by fog, snow, and storms, and that serious accidents, taking even more lives, have occurred at the same time in passenger and commercial aviation.

"Nevertheless, the continuation of deaths in the Army Corps must stop.

"We all know that flying under the best conditions is a definite hazard, but the ratio of accidents has been far too high during the past three weeks."

The Army Air Corps suspended all service temporarily in response to the President's order, resuming it about a week later when weather conditions had improved. About two months later the service of the Army flyers was discontinued. War Department officials said later that the air-mail experiment had been of definite military value because it revealed a number of unsuspected weaknesses in the equipment and training of the Army Air Corps. Nevertheless, even those lessons hardly compensated for the loss of fine young American officers, and the unfortunate and unforeseen outcome of the experiment was deeply regretted by everyone in the administration, including myself.

Realizing at the outset the need for handling the air and ocean subsidies with scrupulous care, I first selected William W. Howes of South Dakota as Second Assistant Postmaster General in charge of that phase of department work. Later, when Bill moved up to be First Assistant, the man chosen to succeed him was Harllee Branch of Georgia, who was promoted from the position of Executive Assistant. Branch was a newspaper correspondent throughout most of his adult life and, before coming to the department, had represented the *Atlanta Journal* in Washington. The wisdom of the choice has been demonstrated many times since then by the efficiency and honesty with which the duties of the Second Assistant's office have been discharged.

The task of determining how large contracts should be let in order to ensure a fair return for the operator, a just break for the government, and adequate service for the public is a hard and worrisome occupation, the reward for which is hardly in keeping with the energy and brain power expended on the job. Branch is one of the most conscientious men I have ever met in the public service, and the measure of what a fine job he has done can be given by quoting a few significant statistics on the administration of his office.

In the fiscal year 1937, two and one-half times as much air mail was transported as in 1932, yet the cost to the government was $7,000,000 less!

In 1932, the department was paying nearly $20,000,000 to private contractors for carrying the mails while revenues were only about $6,000,000. In 1937, the department paid out less than $13,000,000 to private contractors, and revenues were more than $12,000,000 despite a drop in postage charges. In other words, the service has been developed almost to a self-sustaining basis, and in a year or two, due to the steady increase in volume, the air mail should be paying its own way. Thousands of additional route miles have been added to both the domestic and the foreign air-mail service.

The foregoing figures prove beyond the shadow of a doubt that the Roosevelt administration was amply justified in canceling the old air-mail contracts. And they demonstrate also that previous Republican administrations were lax in looking after the financial interests of Uncle Sam. During the three and a half years ending December 31, 1933, excess payments under the old contracts amounted to $46,800,000.

For those people who think that all government posts are "sinecures," requiring little work and worry in return for good pay, the true story of how much labor a majority of responsible officials put into their work would be revealing. The department recently observed "National Air Mail Week" to commemorate the first flight of the mails, twenty years before, and a nation-wide campaign was put on to stimulate interest with the one thought uppermost of doing more business for the postal service. Mr. Branch and dozens of other officials worked overtime for months to make the celebration a success, and as a result it was roughly estimated that an extra revenue of about $1,000,000 would flow into government coffers from the stimulated use of the air mail during that week alone. This is cited merely as an example of how conscientious officials work hard and produce results for Uncle Sam without getting an additional penny for themselves.

Congress enacted a law setting up a United States Maritime Commission, and the ocean-mail contracts were turned over to this body on October 26, 1936. From March 4, 1933, until the date of transfer, the Post Office Department had effected savings of more than $10,000,000 on these ocean-mail contracts.

Because of the spectacular elements involved, the furor over the mail-subsidy contracts awakened a high degree of public interest, especially in the Senate hearings and investigation which continued during the period while the Army flyers were engaged in carrying the mails. Senator Hugo Black (Democrat), of Alabama, was Chairman of the Investigating Committee. One morning, early in 1934, the Senator called at my office without having made a previous appointment. When he came in he said: "Mr. Farley, I have examined every bit of the testimony before the committee and in addition I have examined the private files of the companies involved, which were brought before the committee as evidence. There are numerous references to visits paid you by company officials and about the conversations that took place. Yet there is not a scrap of evidence to indicate that you or anyone in your department ever compromised the government's interests or tried in any way to interfere with the Senate hearings. I thought you were entitled to know that and I came down simply for that purpose." Naturally, I was gratified at what Senator Black had to say and for his kindness in coming down to tell me.

Building New Post Offices

There is another official position in the department, the activities of which have been stepped up to unusual proportions during the past few years, and that is the office of the Fourth Assistant Postmaster General, which has jurisdiction over post office quarters, equipment and supplies, motor vehicle service, and the maintenance and upkeep of many Federal buildings throughout the country.

As part of the general plan of the Roosevelt administration to provide work and wages for the worthy unemployed during the business depression, Congress authorized a substantial program for the erection of new post office buildings. The virtue of such a plan consisted mostly in the fact that it provided better facilities for government business, saved rental expenditures in hundreds of cases, and, in addition, provided employment locally where it was most needed.

The total sum appropriated for these post office buildings, which were to be passed on jointly by the Postmaster General and the Secretary of the Treasury, was $255,000,000. Out of 1,525 projects authorized, the program was 70 per cent complete in the late spring of 1938. The new buildings house, in many instances, not only the post office but the Federal courts, the customs service, and other Federal agencies. They have been constructed with a view to preserving the type of architecture prevalent in the section where they were erected, and the vast majority are really excellent buildings that will last for years and save money for the government.

Silliman Evans of Texas, a businessman of wide experience who had played an important role in nominating Roosevelt, first occupied the position of Fourth Assistant Postmaster General. He did a good job but resigned in June, 1934, to accept a more lucrative position in private business. I selected in his place Smith W. Purdum, a tried and experienced government employee who had proved his mettle by working his way to the top rank from the humble post of substitute railway mail clerk, to which he was appointed in 1898.

Purdum is a short, gray-haired man who speaks with a delightful Southern drawl, chews big, black-looking cigars, and arrives at his office about 8:00 A.M. daily to remain there until about eight at night. On occasions without number, the records of the building custodians disclosed that he was the last one to leave the building at the end of the day.

Purdum is a completely honest man, and it is a matter of genuine mental relief to know that, as long as he is in charge of expenditures for new buildings, no man will ever be able to raise the finger of slightest suspicion against the financial operations of the department in that respect. He is fair but unyielding in what he considers to be the proper conduct of his office. For more than two years, I have been trying to have him approve the erection of a post office at the City of Orangeburg in my home County of Rockland, New York. The receipts at Orangeburg justify a new building, and its erection would enhance my prestige considerably.

But Smith insists doggedly that other villages in the congressional district are more entitled to a new building than Orangeburg, and it looks as though I am waging a losing battle.

On a few occasions, I have been privileged to designate Purdum to represent the Post Office Department at meetings of President Roosevelt's Cabinet, and he was the first person who has come up through Civil Service ranks to be so honored in this administration. In fact, very few Civil Service career men in the country's history have attained minor Cabinet rank. Naturally, it was a great pleasure for Smith Purdum to sit in at Cabinet meetings under the circumstances, and it gave me just as much pleasure to accord him the privilege.

The rural mail service is another branch of the department's work in which real savings have been effected while at the same time the service has been expanded and made more efficient. Since March 4, 1933, more than 7,000 consolidations have been made in rural routes, saving $8,415,000 in the annual cost. Approximately $1,600,000 of this saving has been spent for new routes and extensions. The service is now bringing the mails to 300,000 people more than it did in 1933, at a net reduction of about $6,250,000 in expense.

Postmasters and Politics

Ever since the Roosevelt administration has been in power, the Post Office Department has followed the practice of accepting the recommendations of Democratic members of the House of Representatives in nominating candidates for first, second, and third class postmasters. If the vacancy occurs in a Republican Congressional district, the department accepts the recommendation of some other leading Democrat in the state, perhaps a United States Senator or the Chairman of the Democratic State Committee.

First, of course, all candidates must take a Civil Service examination to become eligible for the job. The commission certifies the three candidates receiving the highest rating in the examination to the department, and the department in turn asks the Congressman which one of the three he wants appointed. In some instances, the Representative may decline to endorse any one of the three but may prefer instead to ask for a new Civil Service examination, a procedure which he has a right to follow under the present law.

The policy of following the recommendations of Congressmen on postmasterships has been in force for many years and has been applied in practically the same manner by Republican and Democratic administrations. While to a person unversed in politics, the appointment of a postmaster may seem a very simple thing that could have no possible bearing on an election, the opposite is true. The voters keep rather a sharp eye on the man they elect to Congress. If something turns up which convinces them that he has no influence at Washington and is regarded with indifference by those in power, they usually prepare to give him a quick political burial. The privilege of recommending postmasters, of course, is not without its perils. When there are four or five candidates for the job, and the Representative finally backs one of them to fill the place, he loses the support of the other four candidates and perhaps also the votes of their families and friends. On the other hand, that is very little compared to what he would lose if a person hostile to himself should be given the job. Under the latter circumstances, the voters might soon decide that the Congressman had lost his influence. This is particularly true in the case of a postmastership in a small city or in a rural area. That fact probably accounts for the practice of letting Congressmen have a voice in the selection. Then, too, Congressmen should know more about the qualifications of an applicant than officials in Washington.

The method of selection just outlined was followed in substantial form by the previous Republican administration, although for some reason officials in charge seemed ashamed of it and tried in every way to keep the fact hushed up. It is easy to know how the appointments were made because naturally the records are still on file in the department. However, when I took over the duties of Postmaster General I found that permanent employees of the department were cautious in discussing the appointment of postmasters. They never inquired about the wishes of the Senators and Representatives in respect to a given case but phrased it differently by asking what "advisers" the department intended to follow in making the nomination. The word "adviser" has a soft sound, and apparently it soothed the nerves of the G.O.P.

postal officials who hated to have the public think that there was the slightest hint of politics in what they were doing. The word "adviser" was one of the first Republican holdovers to be dismissed under the new administration.

The final test of the administration for any official is the record of his service in office. I was well aware of that fact from the first day, and with that in mind, I devoted my efforts and energies to the job of making substantial improvements in the postal service and to saving money for Uncle Sam rather than bothering about petty criticism in regard to details which, after all, were not extremely important. There was no effort at concealment made in regard to post office appointments and none should have been made. The public was entitled to know the facts.

And yet, simply because I made it a policy to tell the truth, the business of post office patronage was exaggerated into a major campaign issue—or rather, an attempt was made to make it so—and the practice was tagged with the title of "Farleyism" by spokesmen for the opposition and by a large part of the daily press which had become hostile to the Roosevelt administration. An effort was made to picture the whole Federal Government as weighted down by time-serving employees foisted on it by the "Farley regime," although the vast majority of such employees never had been endorsed by the Democratic National Committee.

I know that many sincere people dislike the method of having postmasters nominated by members of Congress and believe that the entire matter of appointment should be turned over to the Civil Service. With those folks, I have no quarrel at all. They are entitled to their views, and criticism of that type is legitimate and honest.

Believing that the final test would be the actual record of accomplishment of the Post Office Department, I made no effort to answer partisan Republican critics in regard to patronage because their protests were obviously insincere. There was one gentleman who voiced a very earnest and honest protest to me personally against the appointment practice being followed by the Roosevelt administration soon after we came into power, and I answered him at length. This exchange of letters took place in 1933, and the letters were never made public because neither of us was seeking to gain political advantage at the expense of the other. Although he had been nominally affiliated with the Republican Party throughout a long life in public affairs, Senator George W. Norris of Nebraska found it necessary on many occasions to bolt the national ticket named by the Republican Party because he was unable to digest the reactionary and shortsighted policies advocated by its nominee. He supported Senator LaFollette of Wisconsin for President on a third-party ticket in 1924, and four years later he urged the election of the Democratic nominee, Alfred E. Smith, over his G.O.P. opponent, Herbert Hoover. When President Roosevelt was first a candidate in 1932, Senator Norris was one of his loyal supporters and he has continued to support the New Deal policies in the Senate and on the stump.

Senator Norris is an outstanding example of an independent in politics who has been able to remain in office, regardless of the support or opposition of the party organization, because the public likes his views and relies on his rugged honesty. He is against the patronage system on principle and he has never attempted to apply it during his many years in office. On many occasions in Congress, he has denounced the appointment of postmasters by Senators and Representatives, usually while the Republicans were in power.

When the Roosevelt administration came into office, Senator Norris was against my holding the dual posts of Postmaster General and Chairman of the Democratic National Committee, making several speeches against it in the Senate. First, however, he wrote me a long letter from his home at McCook, Nebraska, under date of September 22, 1933, setting forth his views and telling why he was opposed to the method being followed. This letter was easily the strongest and most sincere arraignment of the patronage system ever brought to my attention, and I intend to quote most of it and my letter in reply. Because of its length, the Norris letter has been deleted in part, although nothing has been left out that gave force to his argument. The Senator said:

"Ever since President Roosevelt has been in office, I have tried to keep out of the patronage difficulties. I would not write you now if it were not for the fact that I feel as deep an interest in the success of President Roosevelt's Administration as you do.

"What I am about to say has particular reference to the Post Office Department although in a general way it applies to all the other Departments and Bureaus. I want to be on record as protesting against the policy which is being pursued. In my judgment, the Post Office Department is being built up into a great political machine. I have made similar protests when my own party was in power. I have called attention many times to what I thought was dangerous to the party in trying to run the Post Office Department as a sideshow to a political party. My protests have always been unheeded—I presume this one will be.

"Nevertheless, I want to clear my own conscience, and go on record as opposing the indiscriminate and universal discharge of Republican postmasters for political reasons. Many of the postmasters in my own State are not now my political friends. They were appointed, and I have permitted confirmation to go through without objection in hundreds of instances where I knew the appointee was my political enemy, so that I cannot be said to have any selfish ax to grind, or that I have any political motive in mind. I have long advocated the placing of the Post Office Department upon an efficiency basis, and the entire obliteration of partisan politics.

"I have openly on the floor of the Senate and elsewhere, condemned the activities of the Republican Postmasters General, and their assistants, in trying to inject politics into the Post Office Department. I have not made much impression upon the Department, but I firmly believe that the rank and file of the people, regardless of politics, are nearly 100 per cent in favor of running the Post Office Department as a business institution rather than a political machine. It is painful to me to get news almost daily of efforts which are being made, and apparently successfully made, to put postmasters out of their positions before they have finished the terms of their appointments. It is openly asserted that the object is to put Democrats in office.

"The great popularity which President Roosevelt enjoys is in spite of the fact that the Post Office Department is apparently trying, the same as its Republican predecessors have done, to get partisan advantage out of the appointment of Postmasters. OUR POST OFFICE DEPARTMENT ALSO SUFFERS ON ACCOUNT OF SUCH

PARTISAN POLITICAL ACTIVITY—EXPENSES ARE INCREASED, AND
EFFICIENCY IS DECREASED. [Capitals mine.] People are not paying
any attention to it now, but I want to warn you that the time will
come, even within the present Presidential term when they will
think of these things.

"It is almost common knowledge that as Chairman of the
National Democratic Committee, you have emissaries in all the
Departments in Washington passing on applications for office, and
the first qualification necessary is a partisan one. Investigation,
I think, would show that this course has surpassed the partisan
activities of any of your predecessors. You are riding on a high
wave of success now, and my words will probably go unheeded,
but the time will come when you will remember what I have said.

"I want President Roosevelt's Administration to be successful,
and as a friend of the Administration, I desire with courtesy and
respect to enter this my protest, and without any reflection upon
you, Mr. Farley, I want to say frankly I do not believe the Chairman of the Democratic National Committee should be Postmaster
General on account of the moral effect upon the country, and
for the good of the Roosevelt Administration, you should have
resigned your chairmanship when you went into the Post Office
Department.

"People generally are taking it for granted you are there for
the purpose of putting Republicans out, and Democrats in. There
are many of the Republicans who should have been put out, there
should be some removals made which have not yet been made,
but when it comes to a clerical position, particularly when it comes
to a great Post Office Department, politics should have no stand
whatever—we should have an administration of postal affairs which
is entirely non-partisan."

I replied to Senator Norris under date of October 23, 1933.
My letter said:

"I have read your very interesting letter of September 22nd,
and I want to assure you that I was very glad to receive your
frank expression. No one appreciates more than I the effective
and able support which you have given to the President. I have
always admired your sincerity of purpose and I want you to know
that your views will always be welcome. Indeed, I should like to

have an opportunity to sit down with you and discuss at length the subject-matter of your letter, particularly the expression of your belief that I should have resigned the chairmanship of the National Committee when I entered the Post Office Department.

"Let me say, however, that I see no conflict between the two positions and I hope that when my term of office shall have been finished, it will be possible to say that efficiency has been increased and expenditures decreased. You may be interested to know that at the outset of this administration, I announced that no postmaster who is rendering loyal and efficient service need fear being removed just because he happened to be a Republican. That policy has been followed to date. Of the 702 postmasters who have been removed since the 4th of March, 652 were removed for positive infractions of postal laws and regulations, and only 52 for what has been termed 'pernicious political activity.' In all of these cases, including the latter 52, I am satisfied the record will sustain the test of any fair-minded examination.

"Let me also add that when I assumed the duties of this position I found two major law posts in the Department: a Solicitor at $9000 a year and a Special Assistant to the Attorney General for the Post Office Department at the same salary. Both positions were exempt from the Civil Service. An investigation of the work performed in the two offices convinced me that one of them was unnecessary, and I promptly abolished the position of Special Assistant to the Attorney General and placed all the work of the Post Office Department under the Solicitor. This, I think, was a step which would meet with your approval.

"You say that 'when it comes to a clerical position, particularly when it comes to the great Post Office Department, politics should have no stand whatever—we should have an administration of postal affairs which is entirely non-partisan.' Let me assure you that this principle has been followed in the administration of the Post Office Department. There have, of course, been changes of personnel at the heads of the various bureaus, but no clerk has been dropped from the rolls of this Department because of politics.

"It may be, as you say, that 'people generally are taking it for granted' that I am holding this office for the sole purpose of putting Republicans out and putting Democrats in. Of course, I cannot help what assumptions are made. The record will eventually speak for itself. As indicated above, efficient and competent Republican postmasters have not been removed. I may also add that in conformity with the direction of the President it will be my purpose to submit to the next session of Congress recommendations for the management of the Post Office Department which I hope will have the effect of vastly improving the service."

This exchange of letters took place five years before the writing of this chapter, and yet I am still ready to stand on my reply to Senator Norris who, incidentally, was fair enough to point out that the Republicans always followed the same policies pursued by the present administration.

The prediction that department expenses would go up has not proved true. There have been reductions in expenses and increases in revenues. Senator Norris, in writing his protest, was under the impression that even clerical positions in the Post Office Department were handed out on political lines. That was a mistaken assumption. I can say that no Civil Service employee can truthfully claim that he or she was passed over for political reasons. All appointments and promotions in the postal service have been made strictly in accordance with the Civil Service laws and rules. The recommendations of permanent subordinate officials in the department have been followed without exception in that regard, and the rights of the Civil Service employees have been scrupulously observed. In addition to Smith W. Purdum, the Fourth Assistant Postmaster General, more than twenty-five career employees are now holding supervisory positions in the department, a greater number than ever before. The length of time these supervisors have been connected with the postal service in various capacities averages more than thirty years. A number of career classified postal employees have been appointed to postmasterships in large cities, the list including Baltimore, Maryland; Cleveland, Ohio; Washington, D. C.; Atlanta, Georgia; Memphis, Tennessee; Knoxville, Tennessee; Springfield, Ohio; and Dallas, Texas.

There are nearly 14,000 postmasters in the first, second, and third classes, and under the old law, they were appointed by the President for a four-year term, subject to confirmation by the Senate. Since the Roosevelt administration has been in power, the

Representatives and Senators, with relatively few exceptions, have designated the person they wanted from the eligible list of three so that practically all the presidential postmasters are now Democrats. Under the law enacted by Congress at the last session, the postmasters in future will be appointed without term and, after being confirmed by the Senate, will be in the classified service, removable only for cause under the regulations of the Civil Service.

Under this new legislation vacancies occurring in presidential offices may be filled in one of three ways:

1. By the reappointment of the incumbent upon the expiration of his term, provided he passes a noncompetitive examination.

2. Or by the promotion of a classified postal employee, who must have been a resident for at least one year prior to the closing date for receipt of applications, of the office for which he is an applicant.

3. By an open competitive examination held by the Civil Service Commission, in which event the department may select any one of the first three eligibles.

The forty-hour week for postal employees was recommended to Congress by me and subsequently enacted in a bill sponsored by Representative James Mead (Democrat) of New York, and Senator Kenneth McKellar (Democrat) of Tennessee. The bill would have been defeated except for the fact that it was sponsored by the administration.

A great many people have come to look upon me as a symbol of the patronage system. Senator Norris is regarded by many progressive and liberal people as the classic example of an independent who has always scorned political organization. I realize that neither of us could ever be converted to the views of the other. I appreciate the many excellent things Senator Norris has done for the American people during his long years in the Senate. Yet I cannot help feeling that if he had affiliated earlier with a liberal, forward-looking organization, like the Democratic Party, that was national in scope and influence, he could have played an even greater part in American affairs—and perhaps been chosen for the Presidency. He would have filled that office with distinction. The development of Muscle Shoals and many of the other reforms he fought for over a long period of years had to wait for fulfillment until the Roosevelt administration took office, and the program was made successful largely through organization methods. I still believe in organization.

Trifling things are often magnified into major happenings in politics. A great hullabaloo was raised by a couple of New York City newspapers over the fact that the Post Office Department was preparing to appoint a new postmaster at West Point, New York, where the U. S. Military Academy is located. The incumbent was a woman appointed in 1927 through partisan Republican politics although she was not a resident of West Point. At the time of her appointment, she had been third on the eligible list submitted by the Civil Service Commission with a rating of 74:80. The top man on the list was Jacob L. Hicks, a veteran of the Spanish-American War and the World War, who received a rating of 91:60. Hicks was passed over simply and solely because he was a Democrat.

When it was reported that the department was preparing to ask the Civil Service Commission to hold an examination for the West Point office early in 1936, the incident was given big headlines in a metropolitan newspaper which described the incident as a brazen "instance of 'Farleyism' in the Post Office Department." The presidential campaign was in full swing at the time, and the newspaper was an uncompromising opponent of President Roosevelt. The incumbent who held office was pictured as a "war orphan," meaning that her father had been killed in military service, and the impression was given that she would be left destitute if displaced as postmaster. The truth was that she had been receiving a salary of $2,800 annually for several years and, in addition, a pension of more than $100 a month as a retired New York City schoolteacher. The latter sum would be paid her until her death. The pension made her ineligible to hold a state or municipal job.

A number of United States Army officers throughout the country were induced to write to the department in her behalf, although the same officers had been singularly quiet eight years before when a War Veteran, who suffered disabilities overseas, had been trying to secure the position. He and several others wanted to take the examination in 1936. The part played by the Army officers was simply another case of men acting with good intentions but doing an injustice to others because they were not aware of all the facts. I fully believe that 98 per cent of the American people would have acted as we proposed to act under the circumstances.

I have visited more post offices during the past few years than any of my predecessors, the total number running into the thousands. Frequently I embark on a trip of several days' length, participating at the dedication of several new buildings and paying brief visits to other postal offices in between. The experience gained on these trips is of great assistance in the proper understanding of intricate problems pertaining to the mails.

It is common knowledge that in traveling about the country in that fashion I also talk to state and local party leaders in regard to political conditions. Even if I had no wish to do so, it would be impossible to avoid mixing the two. Under the circumstances, people often inquire how it is possible for me to charge the government for expense in connection with postal business when politics also enters into the picture. That is a fair question. The answer is that I have never charged Uncle Sam for a dollar of expense in connection with my travels. I have never submitted an expense account. The Postmaster General has a pass which entitles him to ride free of charge on all railroads. The Pullman charge is paid by the Democratic National Committee, and other incidental expenses are paid either by the committee or by myself, depending on what they are.

Saving Aunt Emma's Post Office

The human equation touches the business of the Post Office Department so intimately and at so many points that on occasions even a Solomon would be perplexed in trying to rule whether Uncle Sam's pocketbook or the interests of worthy and patriotic citizens should be given first consideration. This is particularly true in connection with the reallocation of rural routes. The population of the United States is shifting constantly, sometimes from rural areas into the urban centers and sometimes the other way, while individual communities in isolated places are constantly drying up because of changing economic conditions.

There has to be a reasonable ratio, of course, between the amount of money expended on mail service and the number of people served. Very often we find it expedient to close up branch offices in large cities; and again we find it wise to close up small offices in country areas and substitute rural carrier service. The latter course usually causes a storm of protest because very often local pride is touched to the quick when a post office is to be abandoned if for no other reason than the fact that the village or hamlet will then, for all practical purposes, disappear from the map. The Congressmen and Senators are quickly urged to the rescue and the department hears about it in no time.

Early in 1935, the department decided to abandon the little office at Lincoln, Indiana, and to substitute home carrier service once a day from a near-by town. Lincoln happened to be the home town of Everett C. Watkins, veteran Washington correspondent for the Indianapolis *Star* and one of the best-known and best-liked newspapermen in the Nation's Capital. In response to appeals from his Aunt Emma and other residents of Lincoln, Watkins wrote me a letter, half in jest and half in earnest, which impressed me as perhaps the finest picture ever penned of how a post office is converted by the neighborly inhabitants of a small community into a pleasant social center. The letter said:

"Dear Mr. Farley: This is a serious matter. The village of my birth—Lincoln, Jackson township, Cass County, Indiana—is threatened with humiliation—the loss of its post office.

"Indignation meetings are being held at Lincoln, according to special delivery letters that are popping in on me every hour of the day. Our best village orators, including my Aunt Emma, are voicing mighty sentiments. That's the reason your ears have been burning. We are all heated up on the subject. You have opportunity to become the hero of my birthplace if only you spare our post office. But if you fail us—well, you would be pretty sure to lose the last of the few remaining hairs on your head.

"The Lincoln post office was established in 1856. Going to the post office to get the letter that seldom comes has given us great pleasure during all these years. There would be no chance for the 'abundant life' if you deny us our long-established habit of the daily trip to the post office, established in the general store, a few minutes after the mail train, which never stops, tosses off the mail bag. Indeed, our village of Lincoln would lose its identity if you, Jim Farley, put us on a rural mail route out of a neighboring town. We've fought all these years to keep Lincoln on the map.

"We don't ask for a Federal building. We are content with what we have—a humble post office on the grocery counter—but we would feel humbled if we lost our P.O.

"We appeal to you to save our pride; to spare us the hurt we would suffer if our village is swept off the post office map. Think how you would feel if your birthplace, Grassy Point, N. Y., should have its pride trampled on by some heartless P.M.G.

"In Lincoln we have no Rotary Club; we have no Elks Lodge; we have no court house; no city hall; no poolroom; no bowling alleys; no ping-pong parlor; no airport. All of which increases the importance of our post office. Take away our post office and we would have no place to go. Take away our post office and we would have no forum where the mighty questions of the day could be discussed. Our barbershop is open only one day a week so the post office gives us our only meetingplace for the village debating society. Right now, Jim Farley—they call you Jim out there—is the chief topic of the debates that are raging.

"My Aunt Emma is the chief debater. She is a citizen with pride in Lincoln and she loves going to the post office just to look into an empty lockbox. It would be taking away her personal liberty to deny her the privilege of going to the post office. So, in the name of my Aunt Emma, I appeal to you to be bighearted and spare our post office.

"We may not be able to erect a Jim Farley statue, but if only you save our post office from rural route oblivion we promise to hang your best photograph in the post office and to hold a Praise-to-Jim mass meeting. What do you say, Jim?"

I surely couldn't resist such an eloquent appeal and the post office at Lincoln was saved through an order issued personally by me. The grateful citizens later erected a billboard sign reading "Lincoln Post Office. Thanks to Jim Farley." I saw the sign on a subsequent visit there and also had the pleasure of meeting Everett's Aunt Emma.

The incident had an amusing aftermath. In one of his appeals,

Everett promised to help preserve the post office in my own native town of Grassy Point, N. Y., if I would do the same for Lincoln. Unfortunately, the Grassy Point Post Office had to be abolished late in 1937 because the income was so small; no one in the village would be bothered having the job. It was perhaps the first case in history where a Postmaster General abolished the office in his native town.

The Postal Inspectors

There is one branch of the department which has been permitted from the beginning to function without a shadow of interference, political or otherwise, and that is the Post Office Inspection service which is truly one of the great organizations of its kind in the entire world. The persons in that service are all career men who have won their advancement entirely through the merit system. Shortly after taking office, I called in Chief Inspector Kildroy P. Aldrich and gave him my pledge that the postal inspectors would never be interfered with or "called off" no matter what they were investigating and that there would be no effort to retaliate for anything they ever uncovered. That pledge has been kept.

The postal inspection service has a long and honorable record of achievement, and its accomplishments are always guarded with the strictest secrecy so that the public knows little or nothing about it. For a long time, it was a common warning among thieves and crooks not to meddle with the Federal mails because Uncle Sam "always got his man." The inspectors never let up, and many a mail robber has been brought to justice years after he thought the theft had been forgotten entirely. Even during the past few years when other kinds of violent crimes were increasing at a rapid rate, the number of mail robberies was surprisingly small simply because the bandits preferred to operate in other ways. And there was a high percentage of recoveries and convictions when such robberies did occur.

A notable case was the theft of $233,411 in cash, securities, and jewelry which occurred in 1933 at a loading platform in the rear of the main post office at Sacramento, California. Possessing virtually no evidence and only a meager description of the armed bandits, the inspectors kept on relentlessly until finally their efforts led to the arrest and capture of the notorious Touhy Gang of the Midwest, perhaps the most desperate band of murderous criminals in the country at that time. Not only were the ringleaders apprehended and convicted, but the inspectors recovered 85 per cent of the missing loot and solved at least two other mail thefts at the same time, one amounting to $78,417 and the other to $7,443. This remarkable feat of crime detection was based entirely upon a laundry mark found upon an abandoned glove, the trails from that single clue leading into the underworlds of half a dozen large cities. The postal inspectors have been just as amazingly successful in other instances.

The quiet and efficient manner in which the postal inspection service performs its duties is best illustrated by the handling of the Treasury Department's vast gold shipments in 1934 and again in 1937. The postal service was called in by the Treasury Department in both cases and given the job, the arrangements being worked out after long negotiations between officials of the two departments.

In 1934, a huge quantity of the yellow metal was shipped from the U. S. Mint at San Francisco to the U. S. Mint at Denver. In the latter year, the largest gold shipment in history was made from the Philadelphia Mint and the U. S. Assay Office in New York to the depository at Fort Knox, Kentucky. Both shipments were given the protection of the registry service and a detachment of soldiers from the regular Army was sent along in each instance to "guard the mails."

This transfer of gold, especially the one in 1937, reads like a fantastic tale from the Arabian Nights or some other highly romantic piece of literature. Owing to the tremendous amount of gold to be moved, several special trains were used, while the transport of the metal from the mint to the trains, and again from the trains to the depository was carried on by the motor truck service of the Post Office Department.

Actually, the amount of gold handled in the San Francisco-Denver shipment amounted to $2,290,504,382.79, weighing more than 2,375 tons, which gives an idea of the magnitude of the shipments. Twenty-five special trains were used in the handling of this shipment and altogether there were 97 carloads of gold transported.

If coupled together these cars would have made a gold train of more than one mile in length. The trains moved on separate days at regular intervals, and no one but persons actually concerned in the handling of the shipments were permitted even remote access to the trains en route.

The 1937 shipments to the Fort Knox, Kentucky, depository reached even larger proportions, aggregating $5,523,706,546.45 in gold bullion. This mass of gleaming metal was transported from New York and Philadelphia to Kentucky by means of 38 special trains, involving in all the use of 215 railway mail cars. There were 445,501 bars, representing 11,430,430 pounds, in these shipments. They were made over a period of months, the movement having been delayed by flood conditions along the Ohio River Valley.

This 1937 shipment was the largest gold transport in history, and it represented about one-quarter of the world's supply of twenty-one billions, and one-half of the eleven billions held in the United States.

The Postal Inspection service earned new laurels by its transportation of those extraordinary cargoes. It also performs just as clever a job in diligently bringing to justice a post card thief or some other petty offender who thought he could trifle with Uncle Sam's mails.

Abuses of "Franking"

The various units of the Federal Government are privileged to transact their business through the mails without paying postage under what is known as the "franking" privilege. This free use of the mails, of course, is confined very strictly to official business, and violations are comparatively rare. The members of the Senate and House of Representatives are also allowed by law to "frank out" copies of a speech or other printed material, provided it has first been inserted in the *Congressional Record*. Naturally, the members of Congress make use of the privilege freely in order to get their views before their constituency. The speeches are printed at the Government Printing Office, and the actual cost must be paid by those who order them.

Although the franking privilege is about as old as the government itself, it is frequently attacked and demands are made for its complete abolition. These complaints come to the Post Office Department, which carries the mail free, and my opinion on the subject has often been requested.

In the first place, if to send out copies of a speech is to "abuse" the franking privilege, which I deny, then I have "abused" it more than any other individual in the administration. During the past several years, I have spoken in all parts of the country, and my remarks have subsequently been distributed on a wide scale after having been inserted in the *Congressional Record* by members of the Senate or House.

I look upon the franking privilege, which is given to members of Congress regardless of party, as a close link to the right of free speech. It was so looked upon in the early days of the Republic, and it is true today. We noticed its value especially in the campaign of 1936 when in some sections of the country the entire press was hostile to the Roosevelt administration. We received constant complaints from individuals in those areas who said it was impossible to get our side of the story, and for this reason copies of franked speeches were eagerly sought. With the press and radio in private hands, I think it would be a grave error to end the franking privilege for members of Congress. Most of them certainly would not have the funds otherwise to pay for the necessary publicity. While it may cost the government money, the cost is more than offset by the resultant benefits to good government. If newspaper publishers are permitted to have their editorial views go through the mails at less than cost, then why should the same privilege be denied to men and women who have been elected to represent the people of the United States?

The bulky mass of press releases and "hand-outs" sent through the mails under the franking privilege by the government departments and bureaus is another story. A vast increase in press material was inevitable under the New Deal because of the emergency relief activities that were undertaken. The public wanted to know what projects were being approved by the Public Works Administration or the Works Progress Administration, and what the Home Owners' Loan Corporation and the Farm Credit Administration were doing to relieve hard-pressed mortgagees. The same type of information was carried on by the government under previous Republican administrations, particularly by Herbert Hoover who established a record in that respect while serving as Secretary of Commerce.

It is obvious that this sending out of press material has been overdone, resulting in waste for the government and placing an unnecessary burden upon the postal service. There is always a tendency on the part of an employee to be more liberal in the use of public funds for such purposes than he would be with the funds of a private concern. The aggregate of publicity material has become so great that it tends to defeat its own purpose, and some way should be found to cut it down.

In summing up the work of the Post Office Department under the Roosevelt administration, I think it can be stated with fairness that the department has been operated with the three-fold purpose of watching out for the financial interest of the government, providing the maximum service for the public, and guarding the morale and physical well-being of the employees. The service provided by the department has been extended considerably while costs have been materially reduced in many important respects. By advertising the added facilities of the air mail and by issuing commemorative stamps, the part played by the postal system in modern life has been brought home to the American public far more intimately than before.

The test of the ability of an individual or of a political party to govern is the record made while in office. I am willing to stand on the record.

V. The 1936 Election

A COMPETENT critic of public affairs, who thought he knew
something about United States elections until the 1936 landslide
left him breathless, was kind enough later to describe the drive
for President Roosevelt's re-election as the "campaign without a
mistake." It was a pleasing compliment and necessarily exaggerated as such generalities usually are, because there never was a
campaign waged without a mistake and there never will be one.

Yet in looking back upon those stirring days, the campaign takes
on a perfect aspect in one sense because the Democratic Party,
which less than a decade before had been looked upon as a hopeless
minority party, was able to capture forty-six out of forty-eight
states in the presidential election and at the same time virtually
destroy the grip of the Republican Party both in Congress and
in the administration of state affairs.

The size of the plurality was unprecedented and, to a great
many people, unbelievable as well. What makes it all the more
remarkable was the fact that during his first term of office President Roosevelt had collided head-on in dispute after dispute with
the most powerful economic groups in the country, and they had
banded together to oppose his re-election. The bankers were
against him solidly because they disliked his bank reform program;
the financial interests and "Wall Street" were almost frenzied
in their opposition; the manufacturing and commercial interests
were strongly opposed to him; and last, and perhaps most powerful of all, the big metropolitan newspapers were almost a unit in
the fight to bring about his overthrow.

In the light of past history in this country, it would seem as
though the combined weight of this money power and propaganda
would have been irresistible; on the contrary, it was ineffective

and impotent. Those once mighty forces were licked to a stand-still by the overpowering personality of one individual. This clash of opposing forces, and the unexpected result, is the one thing which still gives a deep, underlying significance to the 1936 election.

The wave of popular enthusiasm that swelled up in 1933, in response to President Roosevelt's masterly handling of the bank crisis and his gallant attack upon the depression, carried through the Congressional elections of the next year and resulted in a remarkable victory for the Democrats—although the fact was generally overlooked as the presidential campaign got under way two years later. Even though it was soon forgotten, the 1934 election was a fairly accurate test because the same powerful forces that later made such a desperate effort to unseat the Chief Executive were arrayed against him then. Shortly before the balloting got under way that year, I sat down and dictated a lengthy report to the President, discussing in detail the political conditions in state after state, and indicating what seemed to me to be the probable outcome. It was a very optimistic report, indicating that the Democrats would have greater success, and not less, than they had had in the previous presidential election.

At a Cabinet meeting held a few days following the election, President Roosevelt diverted attention from the business at hand for a few moments to make a very generous reference to the pre-election forecast. Upon first reading the letter, he said it made him "mad" to think any person in his right mind would be foolish enough to let his hopes and enthusiasm run away with him in such fantastic fashion, especially in that part of the letter in which I predicted Democratic victory in Pennsylvania. Then, he said, he reread the letter after the election, and, considering what actually took place in the various states mentioned, he felt it was the most remarkable prediction he had ever read. The fact that F.D.R. had a tendency to underestimate considerably the strength of the New Deal with the public may surprise a lot of individuals who have the opposite impression; yet he continually underestimated his own popular strength as I shall reveal again later in this chapter.

There is no doubt, however, that the year 1935 marked a recession in the Democratic tide, due to a number of causes. First, a reaction of that kind is natural and inevitable and, in the sense that it must come, it is actually welcome in an "off-year" politically when elections are few; secondly, the Roosevelt recovery program was not in full swing; and thirdly, a powerful opposition had been welded together by men of wealth and influence to destroy the President's hold upon the public, if they could. The Democrats fared rather badly in a few of the state elections that were held that year, and naturally those minor victories were hailed by the opposition as a trustworthy sign of shifting political winds.

There was a statewide contest in New York to elect an assembly, and realizing that the outcome would be looked upon all over the country as an important barometer, I worked exceptionally hard, along with others, to ensure a victory for the Democratic ticket. I was confident until about seven o'clock on election night when the fact that no telephone calls were coming into headquarters proved very disturbing indeed. It is an unvarying rule in politics that when things are going well in the balloting, the leaders will call up early full of enthusiasm to break the good news. When they fail to telephone—that's an ominous sign indeed. It means that first returns were unfavorable and that leaders are holding off hoping for something more favorable a little later on.

The Republicans captured the New York State Assembly that year, and the outcome was gleefully hailed by opposition spokesmen everywhere as a repudiation of the Roosevelt New Deal. The truth was that the Democrats carried the state by more than 250,000 votes, yet due to the way in which assembly districts had been gerrymandered in the past, the Republicans were still able to retain their grip on the assembly. There was no disputing the fact, however, that the Democratic pluralities had been substantially reduced for the first time since 1932, and under the circumstances the New Deal foes had a right to be jubilant. The outcome in the Empire State lent encouragement to the anti-Roosevelt forces, and as the New Year got under way an intense propaganda campaign was directed against the Roosevelt policies, and against him personally—a campaign unprecedented for generations back. Much of it was marked by ill will and hatred; and seemingly there was no end limit to the publicity power of the opposition, no bottom to the financial war chest which sustained it.

The attack was given a potency which it might not have had otherwise because it was participated in, and to a very large extent directed, by men and women well known to the public to have been associated with the Democratic Party for a great many years. This breach in party ranks looked very promising to its sponsors, and they initiated a shrewd and determined campaign to make its influence felt in the approaching election.

Exploding the Liberty League

Hoping to give a nonpartisan tone to the war against the administration, and being unwilling at that juncture to join hands openly with the Republican Party, the wealthy foes of Roosevelt banded together into a private organization which they called by the resounding title of American Liberty League. They filled its coffers with stacks of cash, hired an imposing array of publicists, economists and political strategists, and then began a frontal assault to undermine the confidence of the American people in the purposes and accomplishments of the New Deal. The new organization received a sympathetic press, and at the beginning of 1936 its backers were thoroughly convinced that the American Liberty League would wield the balance of power in the election of the next President, particularly in view of its Democratic backers. The League subsequently did wield quite an influence, but not in the way its sponsors anticipated.

While there was never any doubt that the League would eventually support whatever Republican candidate was nominated, the strategy at first was to deny an open alignment with the G.O.P. and to cause trouble and dissension within Democratic ranks. It was a formidable threat, and with confidential reports reaching us constantly from state leaders we had a fairly accurate idea of what was going on. Former Governor Alfred E. Smith of New York was allied with the League and so was former Governor Ely of Massachusetts, both of them nominally Democrats. In addition, a number of other party leaders were preparing to show their hostility. The members of this group confidently believed that they could muster as many as two hundred delegates, and maybe more, in opposition to the renomination of President Roosevelt at the Democratic National Convention—and in that way engineer a serious party split to take place after the convention was over. A stream of publicity along that line issuing from the convention would have been embarrassing and hurtful. We talked over the strategy being pursued by the opposition on many occasions, and as national chairman, it was my duty to head it off.

I started off the preconvention campaign in 1936 with three definite things in mind: first, to bring about the unanimous renomination of President Roosevelt; second, to make certain that the platform adopted was thoroughly in line with New Deal views and principles; and, third, to ensure the abolition of the two-thirds nomination rule, a course of action which had been recommended by the previous national convention.

The challenge of the opposition came our way in a novel form. Late in January, at the sumptuous Hotel Mayflower in Washington, there was a memorable gathering of the pompous plutocrats who signed the checks which kept the Liberty League operating as a high-geared political unit. For an hour they sat chortling and chuckling while former Governor Smith belabored and ridiculed the New Deal policies and accomplishments of his old political ally, Franklin D. Roosevelt, who was spending the evening a few blocks away at the White House. As a piece of oratory, the Smith speech had the customary entertaining sparkle, but, considered as a political effort, it was one of the major tactical blunders of modern politics.

A few nights later, the late Senator Joseph T. Robinson, of Arkansas, answered Smith in a nationwide radio address, during the course of which he effectively punctured the arguments of the former Governor and demonstrated that Smith had completely reversed himself in regard to the very policies which had won him the title of the "Happy Warrior." Robinson received literally thousands of letters praising his speech, and it was evident that the force and logic of his reply had struck home with the public. But apart from the argument in the case, even a novice could see how incongruous it was for the man who had risen from the "Sidewalks of New York" to be announcing his political stand before an audience of wealthy potentates in white tie and tails, most of whom had bitterly opposed him when he ran for the Presidency eight years before. There is no doubt that the "billion dollar dinner" of the Liberty League moguls and its "dozen Du Ponts" ruined the Happy Warrior's influence with the great mass of his former followers.

The most effective way to meet the challenge of the opposition, in our opinion, was to throw the issue before the voters and let the primaries determine whether the anti-Roosevelt forces should be given a voice in the convention. The conservative group, allied with the Liberty League, was openly boastful of its ability to pick up a substantial number of seats in New York, Massachusetts, Connecticut, Rhode Island, New Hampshire, Pennsylvania, and Maryland. It was predicted that Governor Eugene Talmadge would capture the Georgia delegation and, in the effort to bring that about, he was heavily financed by the identical wealthy gentlemen who were sponsoring the Liberty League. Florida was said to be in open revolt, and the same condition was supposed to exist in a few Midwestern states, notably Ohio and Minnesota. If the opposition captured all the convention seats they set out to get, or even a substantial part of them, the result would have been a very serious situation indeed.

After a thorough canvass of political conditions in the spring of 1936, we arrived at the conclusion that a gaping hole existed in the battle-lines of the opposition. Wishing to take advantage of that, the Democratic National Committee's first "battle-order" was to ignore the Republican Party and to concentrate fire on the Liberty League. The latter organization seemed to be one of the most vulnerable ever to appear in politics, and our campaign was developed on that theory. Our analysis was correct. In January, the Liberty League was a sensation. The utterances of its spokesman and director, Jouett Shouse, were given front-page presentation in the press of the nation day after day while League pamphlets, denouncing the New Deal, were given wide circulation and League orators were speaking to capacity audiences. A few months later, even before convention time in June, the League was a discredited political outfit, marked with the indelible brand of selfish partisanship, and the Republican Party was frantically trying to denounce and disown it. In point of fact, the G.O.P.

never did recover from the initial blunder of permitting the Shouse organization to direct the firing during the preliminary skirmishing.

The collapse of the Liberty League, while astonishing and humiliating to its wealthy backers, was inevitable. The individuals who financed it might just as well have given their very generous donations directly to further the campaign of President Roosevelt because the result would have been the same. The American people resented the idea of a league formed by organized wealth to further its own political interests, regardless of what happened to other classes in the nation. The League went too far in its vicious criticisms of the Chief Executive, causing a reaction in his favor, and above all else its directors made a major error in assuming that volume alone is a prime factor in political publicity as it is in commercial advertising. They discovered that influencing public opinion differs widely from selling a commodity.

It has always been a habit of mine to set things down in writing. This writing process is helpful in clarifying ideas and in a campaign it has the advantage of making it easier for those in charge to gauge conditions as election time draws nearer. The opposition was setting up a terrific clamor during the spring of 1936, and many otherwise keen observers were so deceived by it that they actually believed that the Republicans might defeat President Roosevelt, or at least give him a close race. On April 20, I dictated a lengthy memorandum summing up the private reports coming to me from state leaders. I wrote down the opinion, based upon what these reports disclosed, that the Democrats could carry all the states but Maine and Vermont "if the right kind of a campaign is carried on." This did not mean that the party was that strong at the time when the memorandum was written, but it did express my conviction that President Roosevelt would grow constantly stronger as the campaign progressed. There were numerous reasons why that was true, one of them being his unparalleled ability as a stump speaker, which at that time was not generally appreciated.

A Tragic Figure

In considering the type of campaign to be waged, I had frequent discussions with President Roosevelt and with other key men in the Democratic set-up, including Majority Leader Joseph T. Robinson of the Senate, Director of Publicity Charlie Michelson, White House Secretary Steve Early, and numerous others. There was another consultant whom I saw frequently although the public had virtually forgotten that he existed and our meetings were never recorded in the press or elsewhere. I am referring to Louis McHenry Howe, first secretary to the Chief Executive, who was lying virtually at the point of death in the Naval Hospital, a few blocks away from the White House.

The story of Louie is a story of tragedy—the story of an intelligent, brave, and faithful individual who devoted the best part of a lifetime to advancing the public career of a close friend, only to have chronic ill health rob him of the fruits of victory just as soon as his ambition was realized. From the day he took up residence in the White House, a privilege given him by his equally faithful friend Frank Roosevelt, Louie Howe's physical condition grew steadily worse. His wheezing and coughing spells grew longer, and his step became slower and slower. He was compelled to stay away from his office for days at a time. He rendered yeoman's service to the Chief Executive during the first stormy period of 1933, especially in helping to placate the somewhat truculent leaders of the various "bonus marchers" and "hunger marchers" then converging on Washington. He was helpful in a great many other ways, yet it was inevitable that the part he performed as an active figure should dwindle and dwindle as the ravages of ill health made further inroads upon his frail body. He was compelled to step aside, in a sense, and to watch new men, young, eager, and active, step in to perform the role which he himself had performed so well and so willingly. It was particularly hard in his case because work alone, and the opportunity to be a factor in the wise administration of public affairs, was the only thing that interested him or satisfied him. He had few hobbies, other than collecting stamps and reading detective stories, and golf and other forms of stimulating action were out of the question. Under the circumstances, it was only natural that Louie should feel downhearted and depressed at times as he contemplated the influence and position in the Roosevelt set-up, which he had worked so hard to attain, slipping from his fingers through no fault of his own.

On one or two occasions when attending a brilliant dinner or reception at the White House, I recall thinking that, while hundreds of us were there enjoying the pleasure and thrill which a function at the White House always brings, Howe was perhaps off by himself in an upstairs room poring over a book or working on some business in connection with his office. Although he never cared much for formal society, he loved to chat with people and to observe what was going on until his poor health finally made even that simple pleasure a difficult task.

However, no matter how much he suffered and no matter how his vital energy drifted away, Howe clung to the realities of his office and to life itself with a fierce tenacity that was almost superhuman. He kept abreast of developments at all times. He let everybody know that he wanted to be considered an active participant in what was going on, and he never gave his brain a moment's rest from trying to see through and solve political problems. It was this grim persistence that kept him alive.

I remember when I went to the White House in 1934 for a conference in connection with the Congressional elections of that fall, my secretary, Mrs. Jane Duffy, brought a package down from New York especially for Howe. We were in the study on the second floor of the White House which was known at one time as the "Lincoln Room." After a while Louie came shuffling in, clad in bathrobe and bedroom slippers. The black hollows under his eyes contrasted with the ashen whiteness of his skin, and it seemed to me that he had never looked so badly. Yet he took the package and insisted upon opening and going through it himself, even though one of the others there could have done it in one-tenth the time. We then went on with the political conference in which he participated. Another man as sick as he would never have made the effort.

Howe was always able to think out the situation that confronted him, sum up his own strength and weakness without prejudice, and then map out a course of action that would be most effective in getting the results that he wanted. In that way, time after time, he was able to turn a handicap into an advantage. He took stock of his position after reaching the White House and through the effective use of the talents at his disposal he maintained himself in power to a degree that would have been impossible to most men under similar circumstances. Realizing that he could not go out and meet people on equal terms, he decided to stay in the background more than ever and to be known to most people in the far-flung set-up of the government only as a "telephone voice." Yet it was a potent voice, as the listener always knew, and in that way Howe became a shadowy figure in the early days of the first Roosevelt administration, a sort of "mystery man," whom everybody respected and many feared. Far from trying to dissipate the impression that he was a "mystery man," Louie derived satisfaction from the idea and he knew very well that it measurably increased the effectiveness of his position.

I called on Louie frequently, while he was at the White House and later after he went to the hospital, both because I was under deep obligations to him personally and because I had a sincere respect for his political judgment. He retained almost to the end the striking ability to consider a situation "in the abstract" and to render a wise opinion concerning persons and events about which he knew nothing except what was told him by others. He was always frank to the point of being cold-blooded in discussing either my own faults or the faults of others with whom we were in close association. Yet he was able to hear the same frank criticism of himself without taking offense or harboring ill will against the critic. He had a good appreciation of a joke and he never expected to hear sympathetic talk regarding the state of his health. He wanted to be consulted for his political judgment and for no other reason.

After lying critically ill in the White House for many months, Howe had been removed by doctors' orders to the Naval Hospital where better facilities were available for treatment. The doctors held out no hope at all for his recovery, and the manner in which he survived and continued to dabble in politics, seemingly in defiance of the laws of nature, was to his physicians a never-ending source of wonder. During his illness at the hospital, Louie grew a small mustache and Vandyke beard, which gave him an appearance indescribably odd and made him almost unrecognizable. He explained to me that his father had worn such a beard and, as they resembled each other closely, he felt that a beard would likewise look well on him. Maybe—but I always had the feeling that he conceived the idea while lying there on the hospital bed, that it tickled his sense of humor, and that he got a real "kick" out of watching the faces of astonished visitors who saw the beard for the first time.

Before calling upon Howe, I usually had my secretary telephone the hospital and make an appointment, designating some hour that would fit in with the remainder of the day's schedule. If my secretary suggested 2:00 P.M. as a convenient hour, the answer would invariably come back from the hospital that Mr. Howe would be glad to see Mr. Farley at three o'clock, or at four o'clock, or at some time other than the one suggested. It was one of Louie's whimsical ways of reminding me that I was calling upon a person who still occupied an important place in the political picture, and not merely paying a hurried visit to a sick friend in the hospital. He did the same with Mrs. Roosevelt, who was most faithful in visiting Louie, and the two of us, understanding him perfectly, enjoyed observing this bit of byplay.

Howe was always inclined to be suspicious of Democrats who opposed the nomination of Roosevelt at Chicago and, even though some of them later occupied places of responsibility in the administration, he was never able to give them his complete confidence. His attitude was that of the watchdog who had been instructed to regard the new visitor as a friend, but who nevertheless kept a sharp eye out to see what might happen.

During the preconvention period in 1936, Howe shrewdly surmised that the opposition, led by Jouett Shouse of the Liberty League, never seriously anticipated a chance to block renomination of the President but intended to concentrate instead on a strenuous effort to have a voice in shaping the party platform. He felt that Shouse knew a number of influential Democrats around the country, because of his former connection with the National Committee, and that he would endeavor to have them placed on the Resolutions Committee. I assured him that the situation was being watched carefully and that the delegation leaders were being requested to guard against such a contingency. Howe also distrusted Al Smith and, when the latter finally delivered his blast against the administration at the Liberty League dinner, he felt that his suspicions had been justified.

On one occasion I had planned a vacation trip to Hawaii to begin early in the summer. That was before Louie had become seriously ill. Congress, however, had remained in session longer than anticipated, and Howe suggested at a meeting in his White House office that, in view of what was going on, it would be better for me to postpone the trip and remain on in Washington. It seemed unnecessary to me, but Louie persisted, saying, "Jim, I've done those things for Franklin for years—postponed vacations, canceled engagements, and everything else too numerous to mention. I wish you would do what I ask." He spoke the truth, and I did as requested.

I think the thing that upheld Howe most of all was the warm friendship and unswerving loyalty of his friend, F.D.R., during the closing days when he himself realized, deep down in his heart, that his days of usefulness were at an end. Roosevelt very seldom gives praise by word of mouth but he has a way of showing appreciation by gracious little acts that are far more effective than words in conveying his attitude. His devotion to Louie was shown in that kindly manner. Louie had the title of Secretary to the President, with Mac and Steve designated as assistant secretaries, and that relationship was never disturbed, even though at times it was a serious inconvenience to the Chief Executive not to have the White House fully staffed.

During the last month or two, even the iron will of Louie Howe had to yield to the harsh reality of his illness, and there were days when he was in a coma-like condition, barely able to recognize those around him, and totally oblivious of what was going on in the political world. To the wonderment of those in attendance at the bedside, he was able to rally from those sinking spells and to resume immediately his former duties, always assuming that the busy world in the meantime had stood still. He would call government officials, or the White House, or the Democratic

National Committee, offering instructions and at times giving orders that were wholly impossible in view of existing circumstances. It was the last gallant stand of a dying man.

Yet F.D.R. had anticipated those orders and suggestions. He had given positive instructions to everybody that, no matter what Mr. Howe said, he was to be treated with full respect and courtesy. If something was done that had to be countermanded, then the instructions to that end would be issued from the White House. The Chief Executive was not too busy to attend to that. And so the telephone remained by Howe's bed and he continued unhindered up to the last. F.D.R. went to see him frequently at the hospital, and those visits had a most cheering effect upon Louie. The Chief Executive's attitude demonstrated that nothing could ever alter the close bond between them, and that assurance was what Louie wanted more than anything else.

The difficulties under which the President labored at the time were hard and heavy. A myriad of petty problems crossed his desk daily in addition to the grave responsibility of keeping the United States on an even keel in a disordered, topsy-turvy world. A campaign for re-election, involving the fate of his administration, was just around the corner. The opposition was in full cry, and he was being pictured by the Liberty League and that part of the press which was hostile as a cold and cynical "dictator," plotting and grasping for more power. He was none of those things to those who saw his tender solicitation and thoughtful consideration for a dying friend.

I conferred with Louie on the same basis that had always existed between us, except at the tag end of his illness when it was hardly possible for him to carry on a conversation at all. There was no effort made to conceal from him anything in regard to the campaign for the President's re-election and above all, no effort was made to deceive him. Howe could detect an untruth quicker than any man I have ever met, and the individual who lied to him would never again enjoy his confidence or his friendship. Some of his suggestions for the campaign were really excellent. The original suggestion for the Good Neighbor League came from him. He knew that a number of people interested in Roosevelt's re-election would not work directly through the Democratic National Committee because they disliked to affiliate with any political party. That was true of a large body of independents and of socially minded people who felt that a partisan tag might prove a handicap. So the Good Neighbor League idea was worked out and it bridged the gap in splendid fashion.

For months before the end came, Howe's mind was obsessed by the thought of what was going to happen in the 1936 election, and he could talk or think of little else. Just as four years before, he was inclined to be pessimistic about the outcome, crediting the opposition forces with far greater strength than they really possessed. I remember one visit to Louie at the hospital late in 1935. Shortly before going, I talked to one of the doctors who advised me that, while the patient was comfortable and it was all right to converse with him, there was positively no hope of his recovery. Yet when I talked to Louie himself, I discovered that he had his plans for the next year's campaign all worked out. The headquarters of the Democratic National Committee are in the Biltmore Hotel in New York City. He explained that he would go to New York, take a suite of rooms in the Biltmore, and help direct the campaign from there. Of course that was wholly impossible in view of his condition, but I agreed with him that it was the best way to handle the situation. He also advised the President of his intention to help run the campaign from a hotel bedroom.

My devotion to Howe was based on the simple fact that I probably never would have achieved a place of prominence in the Roosevelt Cabinet and with the Democratic National Committee except for his constant confidence and unfaltering loyalty. Every man needs a "lift" on the way up; he needs a chance to demonstrate his talents. Otherwise success may never come. My own chance came largely through Howe. Back in 1930, it was his firm insistence that was largely responsible for my being named Chairman of the Democratic State Committee just when a hitch in the plan seemed about to develop at the last moment. That was the beginning that made possible my later entry onto the national scene.

During the preconvention campaign of 1932, a number of complaints were sent secretly to Albany by old-line Democrats who branded me an "amateur" in politics and said my activities were hurting Governor Roosevelt's chances for the nomination. A number of those complaints went to Howe himself; instead of agreeing or losing confidence in me, he came to my defense on every occasion and insisted that the campaign set-up should remain as it was. He always had the courage to stand firm on his own judgments, and he sincerely believed that I was necessary to the Roosevelt cause.

Very few people are aware that my decision to continue the dual role of Postmaster General and Chairman of the Democratic National Committee was based in part upon advice given me by Howe. At a White House meeting between the two of us, he told me that he greatly admired the way that I had stood up under a terrific "drubbing" from the opposition without becoming soured and embittered. "I anticipated a number of times," he said, "that you would come over here and insist upon throwing up the whole thing." Then he explained why he thought it would be wise for me to continue. He said the excellent manner in which the affairs of the Post Office Department were being administered would answer criticisms on that score while a resignation would be misinterpreted. In regard to politics, he pointed out that, in a sense, the Democratic Party was just being rebuilt into a national political unit. In many states, particularly in the highly important Farm Belt, where the Republicans had been winning for years on end with monotonous regularity, the job of constructing an effective Democratic Party was just getting under way. He thought that the continuance of that work was vitally necessary if the party was to continue as the dominant party in national affairs. Howe said that if another man took over the job, the task of rebuilding might be carried on successfully or it might be bungled entirely. He felt that the only safe thing for the Roosevelt administration was for me to keep on functioning as chairman, remembering always that in the end our course of action would be justified by the results. I was guided largely by his judgment in the matter.

The only tribute I can pay him is to say that, as long as I live, I shall never ask for a better friend than Louie Howe.

The Philadelphia Convention

The policy of endorsing a straight-out slate of delegates pledged to the renomination of President Roosevelt in every state where opposition threatened was a primary factor in revealing the vital weakness of the Liberty League. The League was like a huge bass drum, impressive to look at and noisy to hear, and yet nothing else but a hollow shell. It had no popular support at all, and those Democratic leaders who were foolhardy enough to associate with the League, soon found that their influence had vanished entirely. The Georgia primary resulted in a crushing defeat for Governor Talmadge; former Governor Ely dropped out of the race for convention delegate in Massachusetts; and everywhere else the story was the same. In New York, Governor Smith was satisfactory to all factions as a delegate, because he was entitled to that honor as a former presidential standard-bearer. He had no influence, however, in selecting the rest of the delegation.

As the tom-tom beating of the Liberty League gradually died away from a thunderous volley to a faint tick-tick, hardly louder than a clock, the public turned more and more to see what the Republican Party had to offer in the way of candidates for the presidential nomination. The field was slim, for a variety of causes; even the G.O.P. spokesmen admitted that to be true.

The Old Guard was still ready to die rather than to surrender an inch to the advancing force of liberal and progressive government, and that element of the party was under the acknowledged leadership of former President Herbert Hoover, who, as everyone knew, was a receptive candidate for the nomination. A challenge to battle coming from his direction would have been most welcome because it would have made possible a clear-cut contest between the conflicting political philosophies of Roosevelt and Hoover. We helped all we could by making frequent mention of the former Chief Executive in speeches and pamphlets, but, as convention time drew closer, it became evident that the party leaders had no intention of nominating him. The field was narrowed then to Senator Vandenberg of Michigan, who gave the impression that he did not want the nomination; Frank Knox, the Illinois publisher; Governor Alfred M. Landon of Kansas; and Senator Borah of Idaho.

At the headquarters of the Democratic National Committee, we were taking very careful note of the strength and weaknesses of these Republican candidates. This task was made easier because for once, at least, the party of Jefferson was not facing a probable internal scrap over the presidential nomination. The records of the G.O.P. candidates were carefully combed, and in the light of the information disclosed by this research work, it was fairly easy to form an estimate on how each would run, if nominated.

At first, the Democratic strategy was to say nothing about the contending candidates for the Republican nomination, with the exception of Mr. Hoover, in the belief that it was wiser to let them fight it out among themselves. About a month or so before the convention, it became apparent that Governor Landon was going to carry off the prize. That was reassuring news as his lack of experience and record in office made him extremely vulnerable. We felt that it might be a good idea to aim a blow in his direction—but not too hard a blow, just a mention to convey the impression that his candidacy was a source of worry to the Democrats.

In line with that policy, I delivered a speech in Michigan during the course of which a very mild attack was directed at the Kansas Governor. The tenor of the attack was to the effect that he had compiled a very ordinary record in office and that his only claim to fame was the balancing of the relatively small Kansas budget, something required by law, and something which had been done in several neighboring states by Democratic Governors. It was a matter-of-fact argument and not intended to be sensational.

In delivering the speech, I pointed out that the fiscal and economic conditions prevailing in Kansas were those of a typical prairie state and that, like its neighbors, the state had made progress because of the spending and agricultural policies of the Roosevelt administration. The word "typical" was pounced upon at once by spokesmen for the opposition who twisted it into a reflection upon the fair name of Kansas, which, of course, it was never intended to be, as a glance at the context would quickly show. The incident contributed to Governor Landon's publicity drive, although the hubbub soon died down and it had no effect at all on the subsequent campaign.

President Roosevelt and I were exchanging ideas frequently, part of the time in writing, regarding the conduct of the campaign. The Chief Executive sent me a long memorandum shortly after the Michigan speech, touching upon a number of matters. During the course of it, he said: "Another good rule which should be passed down the line to all who are concerned with speech material is that no section of the country should be spoken of as 'typical' but only with some laudatory adjective. If the sentence had read, 'One of those splendid Prairie States,' no one could have picked us up on it, but the word 'typical' coming from a New Yorker is meat for the opposition." The incident is related to show how an unintended and meaningless phrase may be puffed into a major political pronouncement and how, as the Chief Executive pointed out, it could have been averted by a little more care in the selection of an adjective. There is no business on earth where a man's words are held against him to the same extent as in politics.

Because it lacked a vigorous contest for the presidential or vice-presidential nomination, and hence lacked drama, the National Convention of the Democratic Party in Philadelphia late in June was looked upon as a sort of humdrum affair and was soon forgotten by the public, especially in view of the general interest awakened by the Republican ticket. Both Governor Landon and Frank Knox were newcomers in the national field, unknown to most people, and fresh faces always stir up fresh interest. All the same, the Philadelphia Convention was a highly important gathering, both for its effect in that campaign and for its effect on future conventions.

It was the kind of meeting we had hoped and planned for, a "harmony" gathering, devoted mostly to one long eulogy of the manifold accomplishments of the Roosevelt administration. We could have finished the business in a couple of days, but the proceedings were strung along for two reasons. First, F.D.R. is a sentimentalist and he wanted to deliver his acceptance speech on Saturday, as he did four years before at the exciting Chicago Convention. And secondly, we had the full use of the radio and we took advantage of it to hammer home effective points for the administration for hours on end, a tiresome process yet one that was particularly helpful in view of the volume of criticism then being hurled in the direction of the Democrats by hostile forces.

The convention itself, if a bit of self-praise may be pardoned, was a fine piece of political architecture. The three major objectives were accomplished without a slip-up. The renomination of President Roosevelt took place by acclamation without a single voice being heard in opposition. An excellent platform was adopted, full of ringing New Deal phrases, pledging a continuation of the humanitarian legislation of the Roosevelt administration. And the obnoxious two-thirds nominating rule, by means of which the party had on so many occasions in the past strangled itself into suicide, was finally abandoned as a parliamentary rule of procedure after more than a century of existence. A long and intense campaign had to be carried on to bring about the elimination of the two-thirds rule. Senator Bennett Clark of Missouri was chosen as chairman of the committee to bring in the recommendation, a fitting selection in view of the fact that his father, Speaker Champ Clark, had lost the presidential nomination in 1912 because the rule was then in force. The Speaker obtained a majority of the delegates but never the necessary two-thirds.

A convention has to be watched with extreme care to prevent it from getting out of hand. One or two budding statesmen planned to have themselves nominated for the Vice-Presidency at Philadelphia, a move that would have gotten nowhere and would have been highly undesirable in view of Vice-President Garner's record in office and his popularity with the party. We managed to learn of these self-advertising stunts in time and to choke them off. If any man entered the lists against Garner, we were determined to press it to a vote and the landslide of votes for the Texan would have buried his opponent. The threat alone was enough to bring about the hasty withdrawal of other aspirants.

The Liberty League Democrats failed to put in appearance, although they sent a long telegram to the delegates, just before the proceedings got under way, urging them to repudiate the Roosevelt administration. They acted something like small boys who wanted to spoil the party because they were not invited. Their telegram was answered in a single sentence reply, and after that no one paid them any more attention.

The acceptance speech delivered by President Roosevelt at night to an audience of more than 100,000 people in Franklin Field was a magnificent effort. Carried by radio to an unseen audience of millions, it was a strong opening gun for the most effective stump-speaking campaign in American history.

Governor Landon's Weakness

The campaign set-up of the Democratic National Committee was organized and functioning a few weeks after the Philadelphia Convention while the Republican National Committee was forced to go through the tedious process of rebuilding its fences in state after state where two successive defeats in national elections had done devastating damage. This necessary rebuilding process left the rival outfit at a severe disadvantage although the G.O.P. standard-bearers, Landon and Knox, were receiving an exceptionally good press and the public generally assumed that their campaign was going along in splendid fashion. Very often, in politics, appearances are deceitful. The fact that the Republicans actually thought they were going to win during the early days of the campaign has now been forgotten.

The main campaign force of the Democrats, assembled in New York at the Hotel Biltmore, included the various subdivisions such as Labor, Veterans, Foreign Language, Business, Publicity, and so on. We had a small staff in Chicago, concerned mainly with the agricultural states, and we also maintained a few writers and economists in Washington. Early in July, I embarked on a policy developed in previous campaigns. I sent a personal letter to about 2,500 leading Democrats in towns and cities throughout the whole United States asking their frank opinion on how conditions stood at the moment and what they expected their home localities to do in the November election. This letter was sent to a restricted list—to Democratic leaders whom I knew to be in close touch with actual political conditions. The majority were known to me personally. Every one of them replied. On three separate occasions later, this group was again canvassed for opinions.

The first flood of answers brought the revealing information that Governor Landon reached his peak as a presidential candidate during the period immediately following the convention at Cleveland where he was nominated. The advance publicity had been cleverly handled. The public was interested in this new Plumed Knight of the Republican Party, and the opinion was widespread that an appealing political figure was about to come forward to challenge President Roosevelt on equal terms. The interest in Landon was especially keen in the agricultural states adjoining Kansas and in some of the Eastern industrial centers. His ability as a "budget balancer" had traveled before him, and people really believed that he would be able to cut out this "wasteful Federal spending" and at the same time continue to make benefit payments to agriculture and take care of the army of the unemployed. This attractive picture of Landon as the new dragon-slayer was first presented in able fashion by the Hearst press and then imitated by the other Republican newspapers. Unfortunately, they "oversold" their man, a very common habit with people unskilled in politics, and for that reason the let-down that came in its wake was greater than it otherwise might have been. The downward spiral started with the flat and uninspired acceptance speech delivered by the Republican nominee and it never stopped.

The fact that the press was overwhelmingly against President Roosevelt in pivotal areas such as New York, Pennsylvania, Illinois, Ohio, and New England was a serious handicap that had to be met right at the start. The effectiveness of the Chief Executive as a radio speaker was generally known, but it would have been impossible to use that means of communication from the beginning because of the prohibitive cost. From a Democratic standpoint, therefore, the campaign had to be separated into two distinct parts—Roosevelt off the stump and Roosevelt on the stump. During July, August, and September, the President busied himself with those duties which kept him before the public in legitimate fashion without indulging in direct political action. He traveled through the drought states and at that time met Governor Landon, an occasion that made front-page news which the newspapers had to carry whether they liked the Chief Executive or not.

The able manner in which Roosevelt handled that Des Moines meeting with his distinguished rival, the Republican nominee, led a number of people to suspect that it was all a deep, dark plot hatched by the conniving Roosevelt to gain an advantage over his competitor who had less experience in handling such politically acute occasions. Actually it was nothing of the kind. It was the result of an unforeseen situation that for a time threatened to prove very embarrassing. After the President had decided to visit the blighted areas of North and South Dakota and adjacent states, the White House invited the Governors of those states to meet the Chief Executive while on the trip, a custom usually followed on such occasions. The invitations had been prepared and, if my memory is correct, had already gone out when someone recalled that Kansas was also suffering from the drought and that the omission of Governor Landon's name was sure to be regarded as highly significant. Did it mean that Kansas was to be ignored and only states with Democratic Governors would get relief funds? Was it intended as a deliberate snub to the Kansas Governor? A way out had to be found. The President could hardly travel through Kansas, as that would have been interpreted as taking an unfair advantage of Governor Landon. The Des Moines meeting was happily decided upon as a practical solution for the problem. It worked out very well and was carried through both by the President and the Governor in good faith. In the light of what actually occurred, the subsequent "inside stories" telling how the incident was deliberately planned were rather amusing.

Governor Landon was too vulnerable a candidate to fight the Roosevelt administration successfully. He had been too close to the New Deal in the administration of state affairs in Kansas for his attacks to carry conviction. As I have said earlier, his budget balancing had been made possible by generous financial aid from the Federal Government; he had sought even more funds; and he had endorsed a number of New Deal policies. He had suggested the "iron-hand of a dictator" during the 1933 crisis, and many of his state acts had been declared unconstitutional by the Kansas Courts. And overtopping other reasons was the fact that he was too unacquainted with Federal affairs to discuss them in convincing fashion. While President Roosevelt was giving a good positive picture of public leadership during the summer of 1936, the Democratic National Committee was engaged in the task of puncturing the Landon "myth" and thus preventing the Kansas Governor from making gains.

The Republican National Committee made a questionable and shortsighted effort to conduct the campaign of 1936 on a plane of personalities instead of principles, and a unique feature of this attempt was that, beside attacking the party candidate, the committee directed a large share of this mud-slinging at me as party chairman. The master minds who worked out the G.O.P. strategy in the back room apparently recalled the success of the "Tammany" campaign against Al Smith in 1928 and felt that the same sort of tactics could be employed again with similar results. During the Hoover-Smith campaign, however, the shabby business was craftily turned over to a special "whispering department" set up for that purpose, whereas in 1936 it was made a part of the regular Republican strategy. Chairman John Hamilton traveled extensively about the country, delivering petty and unfounded attacks against me when his time might better have been employed at worthwhile accomplishments for his party. I think it only fair to point out that many outstanding Republicans deplored tactics of that sort and never indulged in them.

I never replied to personal attacks directly or indirectly. The only issue in the campaign was Franklin D. Roosevelt, and if the opposition spokesmen saw fit to inject extraneous matters, they were simply wasting valuable time on something that in the end might prove to be a boomerang. In other words, it was a case of taking a personal drubbing for the good of the party, and the pluralities piled up everywhere for Democratic candidates in November proved that to be the right course.

I have always believed that efforts to drag a man down personally are apt to prove more harmful than helpful because public sympathy is very often swung over to the person under attack. We had a minute study of Governor Landon's record compiled at headquarters, and a vigorous fire was directed constantly at his official acts. This study of the Governor's record revealed that a very serious bond scandal occurred during his first term, yet the scandal was never referred to by Democratic orators or in the party literature. In the first place, Governor Landon had acquitted himself well once the scandal had been brought to public attention. In the second place, he was a man of good reputation and excellent character, and the public would have resented an attempt to link him with unsavory financial dealings.

Taking the Rap

My only reason for mentioning this phase of the campaign here is that I have been asked upon innumerable occasions why the accusations of the opposition were allowed to stand unchallenged. A few newspapers and magazines were far more vicious than the Republican high command in the stories which they printed about me. If any doubt lingers in the public mind regarding those petty tales, I wish to state here and now that they were unqualifiedly false.

There is an impression in some quarters that these unwarranted charges and attacks fail to disturb me in the slightest. That is not true, although I make an effort not to let them destroy my peace of mind or outlook on public life. Yet, it is an unpleasant experience for any man, particularly if he has a family. The most malicious tale, repeated often in a chain of newspapers, was to the effect that I was "bribing" millions of voters with relief and public works funds, the stories and editorials always stating without qualification that those funds were being expended under my supervision. Many of the stories went even further in reputing personal dishonesty. I had them collected by competent attorneys, along with several magazine pieces, with the purpose in mind of starting libel actions when the campaign was over, a course of action urged by several intimate and trusted associates. The whole business was so unpleasant, however, that I decided to drop it rather than keep it alive even in my own mind.

This suggests the far broader question of assuming responsibility for actions taken for the benefit of the Democratic Party, which the press has popularized under the clever phrase of "taking the rap for the Roosevelt administration." Within the meaning implied in that phrase, I have "taken the rap" for many, many things with which I had no connection at all, for many things in which the responsibility was only partially mine, and for many things in which the sole responsibility was mine and mine alone. The volume of criticism heaped on me has been far heavier than on most officials in public life; and yet my shoulders are broad, and I have made an effort to "take it" without crying aloud and without endeavoring to have the load shifted to other shoulders.

Do I feel that I have been compelled to "take the rap" unfairly for President Roosevelt? Should the criticism have been directed at him instead of me? I know, and every thoughtful person knows, that the late Senator Huey Long aimed his fire at me in the hope of destroying the political power of the President of the United States. The outcry raised against cancellation of the air-mail contracts was intended to hurt the Roosevelt administration. The malicious and baseless charges of "vote-bribing" with government funds was really intended to impugn the honesty and good faith of the Chief Executive. The list might be extended indefinitely. The talk of "spoilsmanship," as I have pointed out in a previous chapter, was a false accusation raised by the very people who used the same method to select job-holders when they were in office.

It was not pleasant to be the target for barrages of that character. On the other hand, what could President Roosevelt do about it? He was in no position to defend himself against such attacks, let alone me. When a general is directing his troops in war, he knows that the enemy is going to fire missiles against his subordinates whenever the opportunity presents itself. He has no option in the matter. I have "taken the rap" for President Roosevelt on numerous occasions, and so has he "taken the rap" for me and other officials in the administration. If a Cabinet member falls down on the job in handling his duties, the blame falls back on the President because his administration is at fault. In the handling of the 1936 campaign, we had numerous close political decisions to make, and everyone knows that those decisions were considered very carefully before public action was taken. In one or two instances, as in the decision to support Senator George Norris of Nebraska, we had to abandon the cardinal principle on which we were endeavoring to build up a sound, Democratic organization in every state in the nation.

This endorsement for Norris reacted against the Democratic

Senatorial nominee and naturally, having preached the doctrine of rigid party regularity, I was singled out for most of the criticism. We had no alternative course because it would have been unthinkable to oppose a liberal statesman like Norris for mere party reasons.

I deliberately remained silent in the face of many unjust attacks in the belief that it was expedient to do so for the best interests of the party. That was my own choice. The only possible way in which President Roosevelt could be open to criticism would be in the event that he permitted me to "take the rap" and then sought to evade responsibility by disowning what was done or by failing to show appreciation either publicly or privately. The answer is that President Roosevelt has been most generous and appreciative both in his public utterances and in his private conversations, as I shall endeavor to show before this record is completed. The problems facing us have been common problems, and the actions taken were taken with the realization on both sides that they implied joint responsibility for the final results.

Roosevelt on the Stump

The entire campaign, from the Democratic standpoint, was based on the proposition that Roosevelt, and Roosevelt alone, was the issue before the voters. In the literature prepared for distribution by the committee, and in all the party oratory, the central theme was always the "gallant leadership" of the Chief Executive, the underlying idea being that people think first in personalities in connection with politics, and secondly in terms of issues. The opposition unwittingly helped the Democratic campaign by carrying its criticism of the President to outlandish lengths. It was almost certain to cause a reaction in favor of the President, as it did. If the Republicans had concentrated on a constructive platform of their own, they would have done much better.

This obvious fact that the American people were determined to form their own estimate of what President Roosevelt had done and was doing, regardless of campaign oratory, was recognized generally by men who had long experience in observing national politics. Some of the newspaper publishers, who were so bitter against the Chief Executive that they lost their judgment, were unable to see it, and yet the fact was always there. Of course, we continued to put forth every effort, just as though it were a "nip and tuck" battle for control of the nation's political affairs.

I started writing early to Vice-President John Nance Garner, who had gone to his home in Uvalde, Texas, after Congress adjourned, to have him come North for a visit to campaign headquarters and also to have him deliver at least one campaign address. There was really no reason why such a speech was necessary except that, if he failed to talk, an effort would be made immediately to construe it as an indication that the Vice-President was disgruntled and dissatisfied with the way things were going. In one of his replies, dated August 22, the Vice-President wrote a chatty note, in which he described the fine time he was having at Uvalde, and then he summed up his estimate of the campaign in a few words, saying:

"As I told you yesterday, I will come to New York or go anywhere you tell me, where I can be helpful. I don't see how I can do anything calculated to get new votes or even retain the ones we already have. You boys talk it over and if you can possibly let me ride down here please do it.

"Jim, after all, the people in this country are going to vote for or against Roosevelt and it doesn't make a great deal of difference just what is done by the campaign other than get our votes to the polls. The personality of the Chief is the principal issue in this campaign and I don't believe the Republicans or anybody else can change that. If your organization functions and gets our votes to the polls, the 'Boss' is going to be elected by a larger vote than he received in '32, regardless of the desertion of some of our so-called Democratic statesmen."

We kept urging the Vice-President to come North, which he did like a good soldier obeying orders, but he always insisted that it was a "mistake" for him to be making campaign speeches. In one of his notes, he said: "I don't want to come up to New York any earlier than I can be of service. If you need me I will come up and work from seven o'clock in the morning until seven o'clock in the evening, cleaning up the offices or doing anything to be helpful, but I don't want to make any mistakes and it may be a mistake that Frank [Walker] is arranging for."

The Vice-President delivered the speech which Frank Walker wanted him to deliver, despite his protests to the effect that it might be a "mistake." On the contrary, it was an extremely effective speech. Yet Garner's philosophic attitude towards the campaign, expressed in his prophetic observation about the probable size of the vote, was just as true as if it had been made several months after the election instead of two months before.

President Roosevelt did not "take the stump" until the last part of September, opening with an address before the New York State Democratic Convention at Syracuse. This left him little more than a month in which to refute the arguments of his numerous foes and to combat the effects of an unprecedented onslaught against his administration and his motives which had been going on without interruption for almost three years. It was a sizeable task for a man whom the opposition was describing as a "visionary" without a realistic grip on practical matters.

Roosevelt's "one month" on the stump deserves to be recorded as the greatest piece of personal campaigning in American history. The radio, of course, gave him an advantage over those early giants of the Republic who might have done the same under similar circumstances, and that should be given due consideration. Yet it does not detract from the magnificence of his accomplishment.

This estimate of Roosevelt's effectiveness as a campaigner is not based on blind hero-worship or on the mistaken notion that he is a superman without faults or blemishes. He has made errors in electioneering, like everyone else, and he is not free from the faults that are common to all human beings.

Yet my work was that of a political manager, and a political manager must strike a balance of his assets and liabilities in much the same way that a man would in any other profession. Manager Joe McCarthy of the New York Yankees could hardly be expected to underrate the playing power of Babe Ruth who was perhaps the greatest baseball player of all times both in the box score and at the box office. Coach Zupke of Illinois made no mistake in exploiting the gridiron talents of the incomparable Red Grange. The records show that I have always rated Roosevelt's effectiveness even higher than he did himself.

In between campaign years, the President has taken a number of jaunts across the continent and has visited practically every part of the country at one time or another. I have always urged him to make those journeys, even when he was inclined not to do so. The people like to see their Chief Executive and they should have the opportunity if at all possible. Someone asked a Republican politician in North Dakota how the election was going in his state. "Roosevelt has been across North Dakota three times," he responded, "and those visits sewed up the State. Some of our Republican candidates never even knew North Dakota was on the map, let alone paying us a visit."

I urged the Chief Executive to include Vermont in his campaign tour in 1936, a fact which he revealed after the election when the Green Mountain State was one of two states to go against him. Maine elected a state ticket in September. If the national election had been held at the same time, and the Chief Executive had gone there to campaign, the chances are at least even that he would have swung the tide.

Early in the summer, President Roosevelt made his decision to remain off the stump and to confine his speech-making to a home-stretch drive of four or five weeks, and although many of the party leaders were nervous and urged him to start sooner, he wisely held to that decision. The throngs of people who greeted him in Chicago, Detroit, Boston, and other key cities were fully described in the press at the time, and even hostile newspapers gave adequate coverage because of the news value of what was occurring. Only a person who traveled with the Chief Executive could appreciate the magical effect of his presence and his voice upon the crowds who came to listen. It escapes description, yet it was there. The state of Connecticut, which was doubtful territory, was landed in the Democratic column because of his motor ride through a number of Connecticut cities on the New England tour.

The reasons that make one individual pre-eminently successful at the art of mass campaigning have never been set forth lucidly, although without that talent a man is apt to be a failure in politics no matter how good a citizen he may be otherwise. By the same token, no one has ever put his finger on the indefinable elements that go to make up the prescription for a successful candidate, and it has been attempted times without number. Men halting in speech and manner have been elected to public office with unfailing regularity while others who were firebrands on the stump could never make the grade. The only answer is that the public has confidence in some men who aspire to office, in much the same way that the public has confidence in a good doctor without knowing much about the science of medicine. The quality is "felt" rather than understood. Roosevelt has it to an exceptional degree.

A series of readable volumes could be gotten together from the material written by competent newspapermen and journalists to describe the power of Roosevelt's speech-making, his clarity of expression, simplicity of words, clear tone of voice, and the other qualities that make his public utterances so noteworthy. He outranks most of his contemporaries simply as a speaker.

Yet, the basis for his appeal lies in the faith the majority of people have in him and in his sincerity. One reason is that the President never "talks down" to an audience, a habit widely used by "rabble-rousers" and other demagogic types who hope to vault into prominence by saying what they think the public wants to hear. The truth is that most voters respect a dignified and grammatical appeal far more than they do clowning and ranting, provided they are convinced that the speaker has a genuine regard for their rights and political interests and is not simply putting on a show to advance himself politically. The people also suspect the "reformer" type, the fellow who, unconsciously perhaps, gives the impression that he regards himself as a little bit above the ordinary mortal. The successful man must demonstrate that the opportunity to rub elbows with other men is a real source of pleasure, not an irksome task to be put up with for what it brings. Roosevelt is successful in that respect because he so thoroughly enjoys campaigning and mixing with his fellow mortals. He rode for hours in the 1936 campaign in motor processions, waving constantly to people along the roadsides, shaking hands with hundreds, and delivering often ten or fifteen speeches a day. He never gave the impression of working hard; on the contrary he was stimulated and exhilarated. The husky voice and worn-down look was noticeable by its absence.

I have already said that the influence of the radio in determining the outcome of the 1936 election can hardly be overestimated. Without that unrivaled medium for reaching millions of voters, the work of overcoming the false impression created by the tons of written propaganda put out by foes of the New Deal would have been many times greater than it was, and, to be candid, it might conceivably have been an impossible job. Yet no matter what was written or what was charged, the harmful effect was largely washed away as soon as the reassuring voice of the President of the United States started coming through the ether into the family living-room. The full effect can be realized only by pondering on the fact that the Chief Executive was able to reach directly every voter in the land who had a radio and whose mind was sufficiently open for him to turn over the dial. Those who refused to listen, and there were many, were hopeless anyway.

I have never seen a complete analysis of the part played by radio in national elections since broadcasting has become an accepted and standard part of campaigning for votes. It is my recollection that broadcasting was first employed to any considerable extent in the 1924 presidential race which was a three-cornered affair between President Coolidge, John W. Davis, the Democratic nominee, and the late Senator Robert M. LaFollette of Wisconsin running on a third-party ticket. Coolidge won in a landslide. In the 1928 race, between Herbert Hoover and Alfred E. Smith, the landslide was even bigger for the Republicans. In 1932, the pendulum swung back and the Roosevelt majority, unprecedented for a Democrat, swept Mr. Hoover out of power. In 1936, occurred the greatest landslide of all. In other words, there has been a landslide in every national election since the use of the radio became general. What does that suggest?

My own belief is that it shows the determination and the ability of the individual voter to pick his own candidate, regardless of what he sees or hears to the contrary. The elections have not resulted uniformly in victories for the same party but they have tipped the scales to a marked degree in favor of individual candidates. My belief is that the day of the "front-porch" candidate, the man who stays at home and says nothing, while others carry the burden of campaigning for him, is about over. The voters want to see the candidate for office, and make their own estimate of his qualifications, before marking the ballots. This is no place to speculate on what may happen in future elections because of the vital political power bound up in the effective use of the radio. My only point is that under the conditions pertaining today, Franklin D. Roosevelt stands without a peer or a close rival as a political campaigner and that it may be decades before the country sees his equal again.

While the campaign was hot, a number of well-known Democrats went over to the Landon-Knox ticket, and many other persons equally well known came over to us from the opposition. It is impossible to say accurately how these "conversions" affect the voting public. As a general rule in politics, they have very little effect. I have had individuals come to me and try to strike a bargain, going on the assumption that if they were given what they consider "proper recognition," they in turn could "turn over 10,000 votes to the Democratic ticket." That is a common error in politics. The labor vote, the Legion vote, the "machine" vote, the foreign-language vote—all of them are important. Yet I doubt if a leader could "turn them over" to any candidate unless the candidate and the cause he represented happened to be popular with the group in question. Voters are very independent people. I never took it for granted that I could deliver any votes to anybody, not even the votes of the members of my own family. We had an amusing case in a recent election of a party official who couldn't even deliver the vote of his own wife. It almost caused a family rumpus, but she voted the opposition ticket; there was nothing he could do about it despite his chagrin. There was a former Republican Governor in a Western state who was willing to come out for Roosevelt in 1936 if he could, in effect, dictate the farm policy of the administration. He was supposed to have the balance of power in his own state. We declined to make the bargain, and we carried the state without his help.

On the Saturday before election, President Roosevelt visited headquarters in New York to thank the several hundred workers engaged in the re-election drive. During the course of his speech, which was covered by the press, he took occasion to answer the campaign of personal vilification which had been directed against me, saying:

"I am proud of the fact that our information has been kept at a pretty high level. One reason for that is the fact that we have at the head of this campaign a man who has always been square.

"I have known Jim Farley for a great many years and I have never known him yet to do or think a mean thing.

"For a long time now—a good many years, he has been taking it on the chin—taking it with a smile and not batting an eyelid, because, I think in the back of his head he has had the idea that in spite of all kinds of unfair attacks, the American people, just like you and me, will read him for what he is, absolutely on the level.

"And incidentally, of course, I get reports not only from Jim but from lots of people—about what has been going on here in New York and, after experience with many headquarters dating back to 1912, I have come to the very definite conclusion that the national headquarters this year has been what we call in the Navy 'a happy ship.' No crossed wires, everything clicking, and the result is going to bear that out next Tuesday.

"And I am very grateful, grateful to all of you from Jim down to the office boy. And maybe the office boy will be national chairman or President about thirty years from now."

The Landslide Begins

While there never was any doubt in my mind about the final outcome, it became apparent a few weeks before the polling day that the American public was preparing for one of those astonishing uprisings at the ballot box that are the constant marvel of popular government. "A landslide" is still the best description of a one-sided election because when the mass of the electorate starts to move in one direction, it carries everything before it. The thing grows and grows. Once the slide is on, nothing can be done to stop it, and very little, if anything, can be done to help its progress.

In the 1936 campaign, recognition of the fact that a "slide" was on became general among those people who were experienced in politics. Even a great many "insiders" in the Republican campaign organization, who had been through such things before, realized what was happening even though it was impossible for them to say so publicly. Naturally, on our side of the fence, the evidence was overwhelming. While a few hostile newspapers of wide circulation were still carrying banner lines to the effect that Governor Landon was headed for the White House, the private reports streaming into headquarters indicated that he was to be one of the worst-beaten candidates of a major party in the country's history. For example, in Pennsylvania, we were informed of cases where Republican Clubs, with memberships running up into the thousands, formally abandoned the national ticket of their party and declared for Roosevelt and Garner. The thumping plurality achieved in New York State was presaged among other things by the strength of the Democratic Party in "upstate" industrial areas, or areas above New York City, where the G.O.P. in other years had been relatively strong.

In view of the situation, how is it possible to explain the ridiculous forecast of a Landon-Knox victory by the widely read and highly regarded *Literary Digest* poll, which thousands of people looked upon as infallible, and by other polls of lesser repute which forecast a similar result? To attempt an answer, of course, is to do so on the supposition that the so-called straw votes indicating a Republican victory were "honest." There is certainly no reason to believe that the *Literary Digest* poll was subsidized by G.O.P. money—although a few others were. Yet I believe that a poll can be made to show any desired result, and that those behind the *Literary Digest* poll hoped for the election of the Republican candidate. We were wary of straw votes from the beginning of the campaign. The truth is that the *Literary Digest* was "off" in one or two forecasts made in the 1935 elections, a fact that was generally overlooked at the time.

A gentleman connected with a national broadcasting company wired me for a statement extolling the significance of the *Digest* poll, the wire to be read over the radio in connection with the reading of the first returns. He said that Governor Landon and other outstanding Republicans had given him similar wires. It would have been a blunder on my part to do such a thing because, as the results were announced indicating a Landon victory, my telegram praising the *Digest* poll would have been quoted over and over again. So I wired the gentleman:

"The only poll I am interested in is the one to be held on November third. If there is any method of telling in advance the full percentage of our majority I'm naturally for it."

On a few occasions in New York State, when the Governorship and other important state offices were at stake, we took a sample of the electorate in the fashion usually adopted by straw vote operators for the purpose of discovering just how accurate such sampling methods really were. We took the polls with all the customary precautions, and the canvassers employed were positively trustworthy. We also took polls by post card and other means of communication by mail directly with the voters. On some occasions, the straw vote indicated the ultimate election outcome with surprising accuracy. On other occasions, the poll went completely crazy for reasons which could never be determined. That conclusion will be hotly disputed, no doubt, by poll operators who are completely sold on the accuracy of their own forecasts. To such individuals, the only possible answer can be, "Just you wait and see." Polls go wrong, and that's all there is to it.

We had a parallel experience with the Democratic National Committee. During 1932 and 1934, we had a number of test votes taken under the supervision of Emil Hurja, a statistician then in the committee's employ, and they were accurate and helpful in a great many respects. Hurja was still with the committee and resumed his ballot sampling in 1936. His polls showed a heavy Landon drift in many areas, and having unshaken belief in his figures like all poll operators, he disregarded my constant warnings that the figures were so far wrong as to be positively worthless. Yet he operated on precisely the same principles that he did in his earlier efforts which were accurate. At the fag end of the campaign, the newspaper reporters covering both Republican and Democratic headquarters in New York City operated an election "pool," asking campaign officials to participate as well as themselves. I split the winning honors with Senator Joe Guffey of Pennsylvania and George Morris, political writer for the New York *World-Telegram* and a great personal friend, each of us predicting 523 electoral votes for Roosevelt. In that poll, Hurja predicted only 376 electoral votes for Roosevelt although everyone around Democratic headquarters was predicting 480 votes. A number of news correspondents predicted over 500 votes.

The vast majority of voters who helped to roll up the enormous plurality for the Chief Executive never in the world imagined that the outcome would be so one-sided. Consequently, even after the ballots were in, they looked upon my pre-election prediction that the Democrats would carry all but Maine and Vermont either as a lucky guess or as the usual wild victory claim put out by a campaign manager endeavoring to bolster the courage of his workers. Being somewhat jealous of my reputation as a political prophet, I think this is an excellent opportunity to demonstrate the fact that the statement issued to the public coincided exactly with my own inner convictions about the election.

All But Maine and Vermont

In every campaign in which I have participated as manager with Roosevelt as top candidate on the ticket, it has been my practice to send him a complete, documented report on the probable outcome, usually on election eve. Elections are held on Tuesday, as everyone knows, and on the preceding Monday night in 1936, President Roosevelt motored from his Hyde Park home to the near-by city of Poughkeepsie for a final rally with the home folks, a sentimental practice of long standing which really has no bearing on the election outcome. Returning from Poughkeepsie, the Chief Executive telephoned me at the headquarters in New York that the messenger carrying the report had not arrived, although I had informed him several hours earlier that it was on the way. The young man carrying the report arrived shortly thereafter.

I am going to quote briefly from the covering letter which said:

"My dear Mr. President:

"I am sending you by special messenger a book which will contain copies of letters from leaders in every state. You will note that I have made a brief summary of each state, quoting from each letter. I have also sent copies of the letters I have received up to and including this morning.

"As you will note, these letters are from Congressmen, Senators, State Chairmen, Campaign Directors and influential Democrats

I have communicated with in every state. These letters are not a week old. In other words, the latest information I have in my possession except that which will come to me over the telephone today. I am telephoning every state leader north of the Mason and Dixon line this afternoon for last minute reports, and if I get anything worthwhile I will pass it on to you this evening.

"After looking them all over carefully and discounting everything that has been given in these reports, I am still definitely of the opinion that you will carry every state but two—Maine and Vermont. The following states are likely to be close and, in my judgment, if you lose them, and I question very much if you will, it will be a very narrow margin: New Hampshire, Connecticut, Michigan and Kansas. My personal opinion is that you will win both Kansas and Michigan, and if you lose any states at all, in addition to Maine and Vermont, it is likely to be New Hampshire and Connecticut."

After going into a number of state situations in detail, the letter concluded:

"I have dictated this letter rather hurriedly, as I am rather pressed for time today, and the reports I am submitting from each state tell the story sufficiently for your information. I am risking all the reputation I have, IF ANY, as a prophet, but I am very sincere about it, because as you know we discussed this situation many times. P.S. I forgot to mention that I have every reason to believe that we will beat Dan Hastings in Delaware. I know this will be pleasing to you."

The report to Roosevelt included literally hundreds of letters from party leaders. They were held together by a black leather cover and indexed. In addition, I spent hours on Monday afternoon and night telephoning to Democratic campaign workers, and new information disclosed in that manner was relayed to Hyde Park. A check-up disclosed later that the number of phone calls exceeded one hundred.

It will be noted that in the letter to the President, I listed a few doubtful states and then expressed the view that they would be found in the Roosevelt column. It is a pretty good rule to remember that in the case of a national landslide, states generally singled out by the leaders of both parties as "doubtful territory" are more than apt to fall into the winning column. The sweep takes care of those situations, moving across state lines almost without anyone's realizing it.

The news correspondents who cover the President regularly also had an election pool at Hyde Park, and the Chief Executive participated as he had in the past. The slip dropped into the hat, carrying his election forecast, revealed that F.D.R. anticipated his re-election by a poll of 360 electoral votes for himself to 171 for his opponent, Governor Landon, or, in other words, he was just 163 votes short of his actual majority. Once again, as in 1934, he had widely underestimated his own popularity and the popularity of the New Deal with the American voters, a trait quite rare in political candidates.

A few people were of the opinion that President Roosevelt deliberately put a low total into the newspaper pool in order to avoid possible criticism on the score of being conceited. I don't think so. Every individual loves to guess an election contest accurately, and in the past the Chief Executive had been remarkably close on more than one occasion. The real reason was that with the duties of the Presidency and the job of campaigning, it was impossible for him to stay close to the management of the campaign, and as a result he lost touch with conditions and was not in a position to gauge the drift of the electorate to the Democratic ticket. His estimate of the electoral vote, made in the Hyde Park pool, was submitted before my report reached him.

Asked by the newspaper correspondents, on the day following election, for a comment on the outcome, I suggested that in future years the slogan should be, "As Maine goes, so goes Vermont." If the campaign of 1936 did nothing else, I hope it has ended for all time the old shibboleth, so vexing to the Democrats, that "As Maine goes, so goes the nation." It was an annoying slogan, and a mental hazard to Democratic workers, despite the fact that we always hated to admit it.

After the blizzard of mud-balls hurled in my direction during the long months of the campaign, it was gratifying to read of the enormous pluralities piled up for Democratic candidates in all parts of the country and to receive a few kind words of approbation from friends and disinterested observers who appreciated what the election meant in terms of national politics.

John D. Rockefeller, Jr., wrote me that my election night statement over the radio, promising that "no reprisals" would be instituted against those opposing us, was an example of the "finest kind of sportsmanship."

A letter which pleased me beyond measure came from the witty and forceful Senator Carter Glass of Virginia; in it he said:

"Permit me to thank you cordially for your telegram of November 2nd wishing me well at the election. It was exceedingly fine and thoughtful of you to wire me a word of encouragement. Whatever may have been said or done in the past, as whatever may ensue hereafter, I shall always cherish my personal friendship for and association with you. Often have I said that no member of the President's Cabinet has a greater share of my respect and personal devotion. You are always perfectly frank and in the open, without concealment of any description. I have never known you to fail to keep a promise.

"I take leave to congratulate you on the incomparably effective way in which you conducted the campaign. None of the Old Testament prophets had anything on you. When you predicted that Roosevelt would carry 46 of the 48 states everybody, including myself, was incredulous; but you hit the mark precisely, as you did in 1932."

They say a prophet is not without honor, save in his own country. While I have no illusions about being able to live up to such a patriarchal and distinguished role (elections are too uncertain), it was cheering to discover that, at least in the Democratic Party, it was felt that my electioneering work may have been helpful in paving the way for the November triumph. A few months later, in Washington, the party leaders very kindly gave in my honor a dinner, which is mentioned here only because President Roosevelt and Vice-President Garner took the occasion to tell the country that the campaign "charges" made by the opposition were so much political smoke which failed to accomplish its purpose.

VI. F.D.R.

ROBINSON AND THE SUPREME COURT. HOW F.D.R. WORKS.

A FIGHTING EXECUTIVE. HIS OUTLOOK ON PEOPLE. ROOSE-

VELT AND A THIRD TERM. MRS. ROOSEVELT.

WITHOUT a drop of exaggeration, it is possible for me to say that thousands of people during the past decade have asked me, "What kind of a man is Franklin D. Roosevelt?" By that I do not mean to imply that they have asked me the question in exactly that form or in those precise words. Yet his name always bobs up in conversation, and it is evident that the person conversing with me is attempting, consciously or unconsciously, to form an accurate picture of Roosevelt in his own mind. This intense curiosity about the personality of the man in the White House has been noticeable over a long period, and the volume of questions increased in 1938 when the press began carrying reports out of Washington to the effect that a rift has developed between the President and other high-ranking Democrats on fundamental issues.

Because of the many avenues of information now open to the public, including the daily press, the radio, countless magazines, and critical journals, I suppose Roosevelt has been talked about and written about during his own lifetime about as much as any man who ever lived. Yet the public is still dissatisfied and anxious to know more because conflicting stories tend to blur the picture and to raise doubts about his real character. Like many other forceful and positive individuals, F.D.R. has the faculty of stirring up intense loyalty and devotion among his legion of followers, amounting to a sort of unquestioning hero-worship, and of arousing the most bitter hatred and distrust on the part of those who dislike his program and policies. He isn't a neutral figure and he never brings out a neutral point of view.

I have had an unusual opportunity to observe Roosevelt because close political association has brought the two of us together on occasions without number under the type of circumstance that sheds a clear light on a man's true character. We have conversed on trivial things and routine governmental matters and we have also sat down to discuss and to make decisions on far-reaching problems that touched his political future and his career in the most intimate manner. On times like that, when personal interests were closely tied in with public questions, the opportunity was there to set a gauge on his motives and aspirations because politicians are realists and never hesitate to say what they really mean when engaged in private conversation on serious business.

Like everyone else around him who knows him intimately, I have found Roosevelt extremely interesting, so much so that for a long time I have made it a habit to study closely what he said and how he acted under the pressure of the man-killing role he is attempting to fill. Naturally, this close-up picture of the President differs in many respects from the common conception both of his friends and his enemies. It would be impossible to write about the New Deal without writing about the Chief Executive. Therefore, this chapter will be devoted to a discussion of Roosevelt as a human being—not about his philosophy of government, or his stature as a public man, or his handling of policies and measures—but about the way he talks and acts with the men and women around him and with those who are privileged to have a part in his administration.

In setting out to discuss in this manner the President of the United States, who happens also to be the head man of the Democratic Party, I realize that it is an undertaking in violation of all the known conventions of political conduct. Ordinarily to concede that the President gets mad once in a while, or that he may get peeved by the stupid actions of subordinates, is to run the risk of having it blown up by the political opposition into the tale of a Chief Executive who spends his days and nights in a blind rage, cursing and condemning everyone who disagreed with him. By the same token, to say that he may have been mistaken in some policies is to risk a story that, "Roosevelt's chief political lieutenant admits his blunders have ruined the country."

However, I feel that for several years now the furious foes of F.D.R. have been attacking him with everything in the political armory from pop-guns to two-ton bombs, and as this barrage has failed to shake the confidence of the great mass of Americans in his character, nothing that is written here can be distorted unfairly into something that will do him harm. Due to the eminence of the position which he occupies, the President of the United States is at a disadvantage in dealing with those who oppose him, and particularly so in this instance because such a large percentage of the daily press is violently against the present administration. It isn't always possible for the Chief Executive to tell his side of the story, especially where individuals are concerned. When a number of government officials have broken with the Chief Executive on matters of policy and left the administration, only their side of the story appeared in print. That is inevitable.

My own experience has been—and certainly more than the normal quota of criticism has come my own way—that the stories which hurt the most are those that are not true at all, particularly the petty little tales that throw a false light on a man's motives. Most of them are too small to be dignified with a denial and yet they live on and do harm. In Roosevelt's case I have seen numerous brief items concerning his relations with other men in the government, either in Congress or the Executive Departments, that were simply not true at all. That does not mean that the items were printed deliberately to put him in a false light or to assail his motives, but unfortunately they did so and nothing could be done about it. I know a number of men who have left the government service and who have since been quite bitter in their personal attitude towards the Chief Executive. My own observation has been that I have never known a broken friendship of that kind—and Roosevelt always puts his helpers on a close basis of friendship—where Roosevelt struck the first blow. In fact, in every case his side of the argument was certainly as convincing as the other fellow's, even though there was no way in which he could get it before the public.

Based upon the common knowledge that he sees the newspaper corps of Washington twice a week, and upon the additional fact that he has an extremely able secretary, Steve Early, whose sole duty is to handle public relations, the assumption is widespread that the Chief Executive is in a position at all times to put his views and opinions on disputed questions before the public in the best possible light. Unfortunately, that is not the case, due to the peculiar limitations that surround the man in the White House, whether it happens to be Franklin D. Roosevelt or some other man.

Robinson and the Supreme Court

An incident that illustrates how the President is often placed in a false light by happenings beyond his control occurred during the hotly waged legislative struggle over the Supreme Court reorganization bill in the spring of 1937. The measure caused a sharp cleavage in Democratic ranks which augmented the bitterness of the battle because a "family quarrel" is often far more acrimonious than any other kind. A valiant effort to pilot the court bill to passage in the Senate was being made by Senator Joseph T. Robinson of Arkansas, majority leader, who had established a unique record of success in the handling of other New Deal legislation, a record eclipsed by few of his predecessors in the difficult role of party leader. The Arkansas Senator was the key man in the dramatic struggle from the administration viewpoint, due to his long years of leadership and the esteem in which he was held by his Senate colleagues, regardless of their attitude towards the court bill.

While the controversy was raging at full blast, in fact, on the very day that the Senate Judiciary Committee issued its report on the measure, Supreme Court Justice Van Devanter sent in his resignation to the President. He had been a constant member of the "Old Guard Bloc" on the Supreme Bench, the bloc that had consistently voted to throw out as unconstitutional the major legislative enactments sponsored by the Roosevelt administration and numerous state statutes that were designated to protect working men and women against exploitation. The "timing" of Justice Van Devanter's resignation, despite denials, was interpreted everywhere as an adroit move by the conservatives on the Supreme Bench to weaken Roosevelt's drive for the reorganization bill by voluntarily breaking up the opposition bloc, an effect which it probably had.

It was a long-standing desire on the part of Senator Robinson to round out his lengthy career in public life by service on the Supreme Bench, a fact that was known to most of the other Senators, and an ambition which many of them shared. The reading public has a warm and legitimate interest in appointments to the highest court in the land, and the newspapers naturally gratified that interest by speculating on possible nominees to succeed Justice Van Devanter, the name of Senator Robinson being prominently mentioned in most news dispatches.

It was President Roosevelt's intention from the beginning to nominate the Arkansas Senator for the vacancy. There was never any question on that score. Yet Robinson was badly needed in the Senate to lead the administration fight, and his removal from that body before the reorganization bill was disposed of would have been an insurmountable handicap. There was no hurry about the appointment as the new Justice would not sit until the fall term of court.

Attorney General Homer Cummings and I talked the situation over with the President at a White House luncheon, just prior to a Cabinet meeting and a couple of days after Van Devanter's resignation. The Chief Executive found himself in a dilemma. The Court foes had been quick to seize upon the vacancy and the ensuing complications as an opportunity to win a strategical advantage and to improve their position in the Senate. Already two opposing versions of the affair were being printed. Some critics said the President was about to show his ingratitude by failing to bestow the Court appointment upon Robinson, who was making such a brave stand for the administration measure. Others said it was being held out as a "bribe" or bait to keep the Arkansas Senator active in the fight. In view of the latter stories, the President said he disliked asking Senator Robinson to the White House to discuss the appointment, fearing that his motives would be misinterpreted.

It was finally agreed that I should telephone Senator Robinson, tell him how much we appreciated his loyalty, and give him assurances that his lifetime ambition would be gratified. Early the next day, I talked with Senator Robinson on the telephone and delivered the President's message. He was pleased at the news and understood perfectly why it was being handled in that way. In the normal course of events, the appointment would have been made in a couple of weeks and the incident would have passed away without further significance.

Then came the unexpected and unforeseen death of Senator Robinson, an event deeply mourned by his associates in the councils of the party because a more loyal and sincere man had never trod the floors of Congress. On the journey to Arkansas aboard the funeral train, I called upon Mrs. Robinson to offer my condolences, and she told me how happy the Senator had been over the knowledge that he was to be appointed to the Supreme Bench. Senator James Byrnes of South Carolina, an intimate friend of the dead leader, told me the same.

Several days later, a syndicated news story went out in Washington to the effect that Senator Robinson had passed away without knowing what President Roosevelt intended to do about the Supreme Court vacancy and that the distress occasioned by the Chief Executive's silence was a contributing factor to his ill health. The story was widely quoted, and a number of editorials were printed condemning the President for his "lack of feeling" for the New Deal Senate leader. Having gone to great pains to avoid doing anything that might hurt the late Senator's feelings, the Chief Executive was upset at the editorials, and yet it was not the sort of thing that he could discuss with the press either on or off the record. The story was evidently not sent out with a malicious intent to distort the President's attitude, and yet it created a wrong and harmful impression in the public mind. That takes place on many matters because human relationships become pretty complicated as they tie into the White House and the task of doing justice to all concerned is well-nigh impossible.

How F.D.R. Works

Before going further, to set at rest reports that he and I have drifted apart over political quarrels, I wish to state definitely that I have never left his presence in anything except the happiest frame of mind and have never known him to exhibit the slightest indication of displeasure with me personally. That does not mean that we never disagree or that we don't argue vigorously over things on which we fail to see eye to eye, but that has been happening for too many years to be magnified into a personal affair by either of us. We seldom disagree in post office or other government matters but once in a while we take opposite stands on political questions because on the whole I am more of a party man than he is. I have never once called to his attention articles in the press indicating that an estrangement has grown up between us, and neither has he made any reference to them in any way. We simply ignore those things and never even mention them. I have been loyal to President Roosevelt from the beginning and, if the day ever comes when his orders and directions can't be carried out on that basis, I shall not be around. He is entitled to loyalty, and the trouble in the past has been that some individuals around him were loyal to themselves and not to him.

I think people want to know if it is true that Roosevelt has become cross and irritable because he thinks that his friends and the public have let him down, and so is inclined to flare up at those who offer him friendly criticism and advice. An effort has been made from time to time to paint him in that light—and perhaps the wish has been father to the thought with those who sponsored it. I can merely say that I have never seen the slightest thing to indicate such a frame of mind on his part. On the contrary, he is the easiest man to do business with I ever knew. At times, he may show a trace of anger for a moment or two over some annoying little occurrence that would make anybody mad. Those moods soon pass away, and he quickly puts the annoying incident out of his mind and goes on with his work. His mother once told me that she had no worries about his becoming President because he knew how to accept responsibilities without letting them wear him down. That has been my observance. He has a close check on his feelings, as well as his will. I believe that if he had been defeated for re-election in 1936, he could have closed his mind on the unpleasant side in short order, and either prepared for a political comeback or set about the task of finding a new occupation in life without delay.

The outstanding trait which astonishes people in immediate contact with Roosevelt on frequent occasions is the amazing breadth of his knowledge about the United States. This is not a "show-off's" knowledge, a mere glib acquaintance with a lot of superficial facts that he can spin out to a sympathetic listener just to demonstrate his quickness of mind. He has a thorough grasp of the most diverse subjects and he seems constantly to add to his store. Time and again at meetings of the Cabinet or the National Emergency Council, I have heard him discuss public projects situated in different parts of the country and do so with a wealth of intimate details that showed the most prolonged study and application. He might talk about the engineering problems and the soil problems connected with such giant undertakings as Grand Coulee Dam and Boulder Dam or he might discuss a proposal to build a new public water system in New York or a new armory in Chicago. If the application for such a project was pending before public works or some other body, and was being given serious consideration, he would be thoroughly familiar with what was proposed.

This knowledge of the relief and recovery activities carried on by Uncle Sam to promote business recovery is only a small phase of the general knowledge about governmental and national affairs which he has acquired. The Navy, of course, is old familiar ground to him, and he can talk about ship construction or navy yard work with the definiteness and assurance of a career man. He has made himself thoroughly conversant with foreign problems, whether they touch Europe, the Orient, or the other American nations, and he also knows what the Justice Department, the Post Office Department, the Commerce Department, and other agencies of the Federal Government are doing and what they are supposed to do.

In addition to the mass of factual material which he has acquired on direct governmental affairs, Roosevelt has also developed for himself a mine of information about American affairs generally, including a knowledge of business activities in various parts of the country, that is really remarkable. He knows the particular products that are manufactured in individual New England cities, whether shoes or textiles or something else; he knows the problems of the mining regions of Pennsylvania and elsewhere; and he knows just what must be done to raise a profitable crop of cotton, wheat, tobacco, and other agricultural products. Since entering the White House, Roosevelt has been back and forth across the continent several times, and this ability to talk intelligently and sympathetically about the needs of the people in the Great Plains states, the Rocky Mountain states, and the Pacific Coast states stood him in good stead time and again. In my opinion, he knows more about the United States of America than any one of the other 130,000,000-odd inhabitants.

This stock of general knowledge has not been built up in a hurry or without effort. F.D.R. is a terrific worker, in fact, one of the hardest I have ever known either in business or politics. His daily schedule is fairly well known because the long list of callers whom he must see is carried in the press, and the public also knows about his speeches and other activities of a public character. What is not generally understood or known about is the immense amount of tedious detail work connected with the Presidency. He must spend innumerable hours signing commissions and other papers, studying acts of Congress sent to him for signature, and poring over a host of reports that are routed to him from the various departments and agencies. Most of that labor he has to do himself. He spends night after night in his private study on the second floor of the White House going over those papers and dictating his replies. He really studies reports that are sent across his desk and in that way acquires a mass of information. His boat trips to the Caribbean and elsewhere are designed to break up the monotony of this awful routine, although even on shipboard he does far more work than most folks do in the course of earning their livelihood.

A very minor Federal activity, the issuance of new stamps by the Post Office Department, has given me as good a glimpse of Roosevelt's character and habits of mind as any other single thing. Upon first taking over the duties of Postmaster General, I made it a policy to trouble him with everyday details of the department as little as possible in the belief that it was unfair to distract him from the onerous problems of state that were pressing for solution. The designs for new stamps, of course, must be passed upon by him finally, but to my mind that was something that should be worked out in detail first and then presented to him in more or less final form. However, he mentioned early in the administration that he wanted to talk over stamp issues, so I went over one day at his suggestion to show what the department had in mind.

The visit took place early in September of 1933 and it was

truly a revelation. For more than an hour, casting other things aside, F.D.R. sat in his office sketching out designs for new stamps to be issued in connection with Rear Admiral Richard E. Byrd's expedition to the South Pole. The thing that impressed me most, however, was the fact that with the entire country whipped up to a fever of excitement over the NRA, the AAA, and the other recovery policies of the administration then being put into effect for the first time, the President was able to put the whole thing out of his mind while he sat there absorbed in working out the details of a personal hobby. He went about the job in leisurely fashion, and it was evident that he had been thinking about it for some time past.

Before that visit, I had always assumed that Roosevelt's stamp collection was simply a hobby that had kept his mind occupied perhaps during the long period when he was recovering from illness. After that occasion, I realized that his interest was genuine and that it gave him a lot of real enjoyment. He looks upon a stamp as something to be linked up with the outstanding events in a nation's history, its public buildings, its civil and military heroes, its exploits in war and peace, and its accomplishments in promoting the interests of art and science and industry. He knows the issues that have been put out by this country down through the years and he has a quick appreciation of what designs can be popularized and what sort of events and happenings awaken the imagination of collectors when placed on commemorative stamps.

After noticing Roosevelt's interest in the matter, I started to look forward with keen anticipation to these meetings on new stamp issues and to the opportunity it afforded me of watching him work out just what he had in mind. We have issued dozens of new stamps during the past five years, far more than in any comparative period before, and in addition we have considered dozens of other suggested stamp issues that were either rejected or put aside for future consideration. I bring every one of these stamp proposals over to the Chief Executive to see what he wants done about them.

These stamp meetings take place on occasions in his office in the executive wing of the White House; sometimes they take place at night in his second-floor study; and on one or two occasions he has been still in bed when I called. A great many stamp fanciers know that the President takes a personal interest in new stamp issues, but few of them realize that very often he actually draws the designs himself. He does, sketching them on white paper with a pencil, and after he finishes, on each occasion, I very carefully take the drawing away from him and have him sign his name and the date to establish its authenticity. As a result, I have a most absorbing collection of "Original Roosevelts."

Perhaps the most interesting of all was the "Mother's Day" stamp, the design for which he drew in February of 1934, taking as a model Whistler's famous portrait of his mother. I recall he drew that one sitting in bed. The sketch is about five and one-half inches long and three inches deep.

The figure of the mother is crudely drawn and probably would not give F.D.R. a top-flight ranking as an artist but it is clear enough to show how he wanted it shown on the stamp. He printed the wording, "In Memory and in Honor of the Mothers of America," with half of the inscription to go above the picture and half below. The artists at the Bureau of Engraving, however, later decided that the arrangement left too much blank space because the figure of the woman was over on the right side of the stamp. The inscription therefore was written onto the face of the stamp and a vase of flowers was also added in the lower left-hand corner. The flowers awakened the hot indignation of an art critic who said the department had desecrated the memory of Whistler's masterpiece.

Some of the sketches Roosevelt has drawn are hardly bigger than the actual size of a stamp and some are about twice the size. He suggested what was to go on the "Little America" stamp and he also drew the design for the Air Mail Week stamp, drawing a picture of an eagle in flight and recommending the three colors of red, white, and blue.

In addition to passing on new issues, the President also finds time to keep his personal collection abreast of the times, always looking forward eagerly to the opportunity of getting a new stamp from abroad. He is perfectly relaxed and carefree during all this stamp business, and considering the controversies that are usually raging about his head on the outside, it is hard to believe that it is actually the President of the United States who is sitting there drawing off rough pictures like a youngster. He looks on those periods as part of his relaxation, and as he is always easygoing and informal with those around him, he likes to be "sassed" a bit and to indulge in a little good-natured "kidding." Our meeting to talk over the proposed Virginia Dare Commemorative stamp, which was issued in 1937, gives a pretty good idea of how he acts and talks on such occasions.

He had agreed to the issue previously, and I went over to see what kind of a stamp could be struck off to recall the memory of the first white child born on American soil. "What do you want on the stamp?" he asked me. I told him, "That's your business, not mine. I'm only the salesman, not the designer. Don't try to pass your work off on me." We exchanged a few more off-hand remarks on how the stamp sales were bringing money into the Treasury, and then he paused to think about what kind of a design would be appropriate for the youngster born so many years ago in the wilderness. "Let's see, we'll have a picture of a young mother cuddling her baby in her arms and then we'll put a big lad in homespun behind her carrying a gun. He's protecting her from the dangers of the forest." Then he drew the design showing the babe and the proud parents as he described them. Later the gun had to be taken out and the figures of the people moved closer together. The Supreme Court controversy was raging at the time, and his foes said he was eating his heart out over the bill's failure to pass.

We are asked time and again by private institutions to issue commemorative stamps for anniversaries and the like, but most of their requests are turned down because of the precedent involved. Often, I bring a batch of these applications over to the President and merely show them to him without comment, waiting for his recommendation. One fellow, evidently a very strong anti-New Dealer, wrote in and suggested that I was so prolific at putting out new issues, why not put out one commemorating the Supreme Court's decision overturning the NRA. I slipped this one in along with the rest and said nothing. The President came across it, chuckled, and said, "All right. I'll draw you a picture of a sick chicken."

Even during the crowded and hectic period of the 1936 campaign when the business of politics and campaigning added another full-time role to the work of the Presidency, Roosevelt managed to find a few spare minutes to offer suggestions on the issuance of stamps, and to project the new general series, a rare occurrence eagerly anticipated by ardent philatelists, which was brought out in 1938. He proposed several changes in the Army and Navy series, and when the die proofs were first shown him, knowing that collectors are constantly on the watch for technical errors in design, he questioned whether the guns, cannons, and sabers shown on a couple of the stamps were typical of the period which they were supposed to represent. A careful recheck of the entire series was made before the final issuance, and, as I have said, despite that precaution, one of the stamps was challenged by the eagle-eyed stickler for accuracy who said a star had been left off the uniform of General Robert E. Lee.

When the general series was launched, the newspapers greeted the first appearance of the stamps with a wide range of friendly notices that ensured an appropriate public reception for such a notable event. The volume of press notices was swelled considerably by a Republican Congressman who said the Roosevelt administration had conspired to put the likenesses of Republican Presidents on little-used stamps, an amusing charge, offered half in jest, that made good press copy. I brought over the general series to the White House and the President expressed his satisfaction at their appearance, except the Martha Washington stamp, the color of which he disliked. I said he had seen the color before it was adopted and had given his approval, but he insisted that it had not been brought to his attention. Going back to the Post Office Department, I checked with Roy North, Deputy Third Assistant Postmaster General, and Roy confirmed the fact that the Martha Washington model was the only one that had been approved in color and design without first being submitted to the Chief Executive.

Roosevelt drew the rough design for the sixteen-cent special delivery air-mail stamp showing the American Eagle, and as a special flourish he wrote the Latin word "facio" above his signature.

I always address the Chief Executive as Mr. President during our talks on official business, and this practice is followed by everyone around him, even though he has never been a stickler for formality. However, in private conversation, I shorten the salutation to just plain "Boss," and the White House secretaries and others who see him often do the same. During the early part of the administration, I often called him "Governor," a habit I formed while he was at Albany and resumed without realizing it. A few persons address him as "Chief," and on occasions, I have heard Vice-President Garner address him as "Captain," a title frequently bestowed upon outstanding citizens in Texas and the Southwest generally, and, spoken in the respectful and homelike manner which Garner always uses, the title has a most pleasant sound.

Throughout years of association with Roosevelt, I have always tried to remember that the responsibilities which he carries are almost superhuman and that a positive duty rests upon those around him to bother him as little as possible. The Presidency is a murderous job; there can be no question about that. It might seem that my files would be loaded down with weighty correspondence passing between us, touching upon Post Office Department matters or the political conditions prevailing in forty-eight separate states. Actually, there is very little material of that description in the files. But in traveling around the country, I pick up a great many interesting and amusing things about the government and about individuals, and I always transmit to the White House anything of that nature in the hope of giving him a few moments of fun or diversion. Very often, I go for a month at a time without seeing him personally, and my appointments are always made through McIntyre, the appointment secretary, and not by the "backdoor," or grapevine route, a method sometimes used by those who attempted to get by Mac. If I pick up a good joke, whether about Roosevelt or someone else, I always remember it carefully and retell it at the first available opportunity. Roosevelt has a keen sense of humor, and I have never known a man who could respond faster in snapping out of a serious mood by the simple process of putting his mind on something funny or ludicrous. Very often an aspiring politician will try to "put something over" on us in the belief that we have no way of knowing what is going on. For example, he may have me deluged with letters from his friends and acquaintances, suggesting his appointment to a high public post, without ever mentioning himself that he wants the place. I always call those things to F.D.R.'s attention, when making recommendations, and he enjoys them thoroughly, especially if it is someone known to him personally. I send him literally dozens of cartoons from smaller newspapers which he might not see otherwise.

Above all things, I never weep on his shoulder and I never run to him to iron out trouble between subordinates in the Post Office Department or in the Democratic National Committee. If I can't run the shop without disturbing him, someone else should be doing the job. Unfortunately some of his agency heads were too prone in the early days to clutter up his desk with trifles about petty things that they should have settled themselves. Some of them put a new pack on his back with every visit. In cases like that the President was also too prone to put his energies into those matters when he should have been free to devote himself to bigger things. Roosevelt is really very mild-mannered with people he likes personally and he shrinks from hurting their feelings. I have known him to send a message through a third party rather than break a bit of unpleasant news himself.

A Fighting Executive

Many people are inclined to sympathize with Roosevelt's efforts to humanize government and to provide a better living for the unfortunate millions who live on the ragged edge of poverty in a rich country, yet they are disturbed by the fact that he is constantly engaged in a thunderous war against his enemies. They ask me if Roosevelt is really the hard and relentless fighter that he is pictured to be in the opposition press and literature. He is, indeed, one of the strongest men and the hardest fighters I have ever known, and the American people should be pleased that he is, because the Presidency is a strong man's job. This battling nature of his is the key in many respects to his whole character, and I was often amused during the preconvention campaign for the nomination to see that his opponents missed that fact entirely and tried to picture him as "weak and vacillating." Yet he reached his present eminent position through years of fighting, first in the state legislature at Albany, then as Assistant Secretary of the Navy, next against serious illness, and finally as Governor of New York and candidate for the Presidency.

This readiness to meet trouble more than halfway has stood him in good stead. I wonder what would have happened in the United States during the past few years if a "weak" President had been in the White House instead of Roosevelt? There was the depression to overcome at a time when hungry millions were walking the city streets, and angry farmers were threatening to hang judges who dispossessed them from their homes. What would have happened to a President who didn't know how to fight in a situation like that? This is the age of dictators and of ruthless force in relations between nations, and yet the United States is coming through it in pretty good fashion because fortunately the man in the White House has resolute will and iron character. After a lifetime in politics, I am well aware that even the simplest reform in government, such as the passage of a minimum wage law for women workers, can be placed on the statute only after the most intense kind of struggling. No wonder the Chief Executive realizes that if he wishes something to be accomplished, he must be ready to fight for it without ever letting up.

During the time since Roosevelt has been President, I have been abroad on two occasions, and those voyages to Europe taught me that F.D.R. looms larger and larger after you leave the American shore line—a pretty good test for any man. After the election of 1936, I visited England, Ireland, and France and had an opportunity to talk to high-ranking officials in those three countries. It is not betraying official secrets to say frankly that they were immensely pleased at the fact that Roosevelt was going to run the affairs of America for four more years, simply because they looked upon him as a strong man who knew what was happening in international affairs. It was the late Will Rogers who said that the United States never lost a war and never won a conference. That is not true now, and I'm ready to predict that it will not be true during the balance of Roosevelt's term of office. He has not lost an international conference and he has

increased respect for the American government abroad to a remarkable degree. The reason for that lies in the fact that F.D.R.
hasn't got an inferiority complex in dealing with any individual
or any government on earth. He meets them all on equal terms
and he hasn't the slightest fear of what they may think about
him if he decides to call off negotiations entirely. He did that
in the case of the London Economic Conference in 1933, and
the fact that some of the foreign nations tried to make him
the scapegoat for the entire affair did not bother him in the
least. Roosevelt is too thoroughly American to be concerned
about false impressions abroad.

I confess frankly that there may be times when the President
battles too hard for one particular measure or item of his program when a compromising attitude or even a delay might accomplish more than his policy of driving straight through the
line. Yet on the other hand, I get incensed at some of his opponents who are constantly demanding that he cease fighting
while they continue to hurl bricks in his direction.

I recall in the fall of 1933 when the American Legion was
meeting at Chicago, and many of his advisers urged him not to
accept an invitation to attend, fearing that his veto of the bill
providing for cash payment of the soldiers' bonus might cause
him to be booed. The implied challenge in the suggestion that the
Legionnaires might give him an unfriendly reception did more
than anything else to influence his course of action. He went to
Chicago and was given an enthusiastic reception by the Legionnaires.

This tendency to be affable and easy-going almost to a fault
with his friends and stern to his foes is the reason people get
so many confusing impressions of the President. I have found
out also, after watching him in dozens of close encounters with
myself and others, that Roosevelt has the sort of nature that
can't be bullied and that will never yield under threats of coercion
or opposition no matter in what manner they are expressed. He
is not afraid of any man in shoe leather and he is never afraid
to face the consequences of his own acts. On the other hand, he
is quick to perceive an attitude of friendliness on the part of those
with whom he is dealing and, if he thinks the feeling is genuine,

he will go halfway and more in taking a reasonable attitude towards whatever is suggested. It just isn't in his nature to run up the white flag and plead for mercy although he is ready enough to forget disagreements and hard feelings if the other fellow will show a like disposition. The fact is that way down deep, despite the fierce unflinching side which he shows to his critics, Roosevelt is a very human person. He is just as humane in his attitude towards persons as he is in his concept of government.

Opening his speech-making tour for re-election in 1936, about five weeks before election, Roosevelt followed an old custom by attending the convention of New York State Democrats, which was held that year at Syracuse. He arrived early and remained aboard his special train on a siding near the railroad station until about speech time as it was felt that it would be physically impossible for him to greet personally all the delegates in attendance, a plan first suggested. As an alternative, the Chief Executive asked a number of the state leaders to have dinner with him aboard his special train. Among those invited were Governor Lehman, Senator Wagner, Edward J. Flynn, Bronx leader, William H. Kelley, Syracuse leader, Vincent Dailey and myself. Conspicuous by his absence was Alfred E. Smith, the Happy Warrior, who for more than two decades had been a shining and scintillating figure at such pre-election party gatherings. Witty and caustic, always brimming over with lively force and confidence, Smith held the spotlight on such occasions by common consent, and his position as "Nestor" of the Democratic chieftains in New York State was never in dispute. And now in 1936, he had gone over to the political enemy. The thought of Smith hobnobbing with the same staid and rather solemn Republican leaders whom formerly he had punched around in his campaign speeches like so many stuffed pillows, seemed too unrealistic to be true.

As we sat around the crowded dining-room of the President's special car, the topic of conversation swiftly veered to the Happy Warrior and his G.O.P. cronies. Varying opinions were expressed on the probable effect of his desertion on Democratic chances, the consensus being that he had lost entirely his grip upon the mass of the electorate. A few of the leaders were anxious about the extent of his influence in specific areas, and some were bitter in condemning Smith's course of action. President Roosevelt and Governor Lehman joined in the conversation, and at one point I recall, the Chief Executive turned to the Governor and said: "Herbert, if it were not for Smith we would not be where we are today. It was the fight he made for liberal, progressive and social legislation when Governor of New York that made possible the dominance of our party in this State. Smith is simply a different man now and looks at things from a different viewpoint than he did when he was Governor and party leader."

Coming in the heat of the campaign when the President, if anyone, had a right to feel disturbed and offended by Smith's action, I thought it was an extremely generous reference. Ordinarily men are not so open-minded in measuring the motives and contributions of individuals in the opposing political camp.

His Outlook on People

One of the traits which I like about Roosevelt is the fact that he gets such an enormous thrill out of life. He seems to enjoy everything clear down to his fingertips, and apparently nothing escapes his interest or observation. He never gives the impression that everything else but the burdens of the Presidency has been pushed from his mind and that he expects those around him to walk on tiptoe for fear of disturbing him. He takes a lively interest in sporting events, and I have chatted about outstanding athletes with him on many occasions. I have seen him in a belligerent mood more times than one, yet never when he was gloomy or peevish.

The easy-going, good-natured attitude which has always characterized the President's relations with employees and intimate acquaintances has not suffered any change during the strenuous White House years. There is no stiffness or restraint in the conduct of the executive office and, while the President is the soul of dignity and decorum on official occasions, he still addresses the members of the secretarial corps as Mac, Steve, or Missy, and he has other shortened and friendly salutations for the remainder of the White House staff. He takes a lively interest in their personal welfare, and that fact accounts in large measure for the devotion which they give him in return.

Another kindly trait which Roosevelt has shown time and again in his attitude towards individuals has been his willingness to heed the pleas of old friends who found themselves without employment and in serious financial straits as a result of the unforeseen depression years. He has never shown impatience or annoyance at those requests, although he might easily have passed them by in view of the magnitude of his labors. Many of those asking assistance in locating employment were personal friends, and some were loyal political associates who had done their best for the party in years gone by. I have frequently had notes from him, saying, "What can we do for our good friend, Tom ——?" On visits to the White House he has mentioned persons well known to him who wanted help, and sometimes I have asked him facetiously, "Another member of the Harvard class, Boss?"

He has tried on so many occasions to aid individuals whom he described as "former classmates" that the White House secretaries and myself started telling him in joking fashion that his class must have been one of the largest ever graduated. However, in justice to the fair name of his Alma Mater, it should be noted that the Chief Executive stretched the term on occasions to include old acquaintances who must have gone to school with him some place else besides Harvard.

When Congress turned down some of his major recommendations during the spring of 1938, a great many of his foes were exultant in the belief that these temporary set-backs would make him bitter and perhaps crush his fighting spirit. I have never seen him in that frame of mind, and my own opinion is that he hasn't the kind of a disposition that would turn sour and stay sour. He once told me, when things were going at their best and Congress was co-operating in the enactment of his relief and social welfare program, that Jefferson was compelled to fight twenty years to see the triumph of his ideas and that it might take the same length of time to curb the excessive power of great financial combines in our present day.

I remember another occasion in the early days of 1933 when he had a White House conference with Charles M. Schwab, Chairman of the Board of the Bethlehem Steel Corporation, and Myron C. Taylor, President of the United States Steel Corporation. He told me about the conference a few nights later. They had discussed living conditions among the miners and steel workers, and Schwab expressed the view that his company was doing very well in caring for its employees and that no complaint was justified on that score. Schwab's attitude annoyed Roosevelt who pointed out that according to reports reaching the White House many of the unemployed steel workers were living in coke ovens while the company was paying bonuses running as high as $1,000,-000 annually to some of its officials. He very properly took the position that policies of that sort brought discredit upon big business and that if business itself did nothing to correct such conditions, the government would be compelled to step in. His attitude was easily understandable under the circumstances, and I have always looked upon that story as giving the clearest view of the Chief Executive's attitude towards such problems.

This genuine desire on his part to improve the lot of millions of people, who work hard and get little out of life in return, is based in every instance upon something practical and real and not upon half-baked theories of government that he read in a book and wants to try out on the American people. Roosevelt is telling the truth when he tells a political audience that he has gone around America to observe conditions as they actually exist. He knows the kind of tenement slums that house large numbers of industrial and other "sweatshop" workers in the big manufacturing centers and he knows the hardships those folks must endure to eke out an existence. He has seen with his own eyes hundreds of small farmers in the South and other agricultural areas scratching the soil with no hope of gaining anything beyond a mere subsistence. I have traveled with Roosevelt on those journeys, both during campaigns and during the "off-years," and I have listened to his comments on what he saw while gazing out of the train window.

In the closing weeks before the 1936 election, the President campaigned through three New England states by motor car, a good method to use in that densely populated area because it enabled him to pass through city after city where huge throngs were lined up on the sidewalk to roar out a welcome, especially in the industrial centers. The mere fact of being seen is an asset to

a smart campaigner. While motoring through one of the principal streets of a textile manufacturing city, a girl ran out with
a note which was handed to the Chief Executive by one of the
Secret Service men. Written in a somewhat childish scribble, the
note was an appeal to the President from a number of young
women mill workers who said they had suffered a wage cut
after the NRA had been declared unconstitutional and were then
working for a very low weekly wage, which they mentioned. They
felt that the President was their friend and that he could do
something about it. The incident was not of major importance
yet it made a strong impression upon Roosevelt who spoke of it
later with considerable feeling.

Unlike a great many excellent folk who believe in letting things
go as they are, the President never shuts his eyes to a condition
simply because it is unpleasant. He declines to run away from
considering the plight of the poverty-stricken. He thinks that conditions of that kind if left to themselves will grow worse instead of better, while agitation for improvement will eventually
bring some measure of relief.

I think there is another quality about the President that most
people overlook, and that is the fact that there isn't a snobbish
bone in his body. He never has to pretend an interest in those less
fortunate than himself for vote-catching purposes, and this obvious sincerity is one of the cardinal factors in his strength with the
mass of people.

For a man born to wealth and luxury as he was, and also to
high social position, it would be impossible for him to conceal
his real feelings, at least to those around him, if he really had
a feeling of superiority towards some of the individuals with whom
he must come in contact. Some rich men who dabble in politics
feel socially superior, and others are more apt to show a kind
of intellectual snobbery. I can honestly say I have never observed
anything of that kind in Roosevelt even though in politics you
must take your associates as they come and not be too selective.
His friends and personal companions are not chosen from any
particular group or class, and that can also be said of the rest of
the Roosevelts. The entire family seems to have a happy faculty

of choosing companions for what they are and not because of their social position or what they represent.

An impression has been created by the wealth of publicity given the members of the so-called "Brain Trust" during the past several years that those men dominate his thinking and have in a sense dictated the legislative course of the New Deal. It is always difficult to say accurately just what individuals had a part in shaping the Chief Executive's viewpoint on particular problems because of the fact that he seeks advice from so many and such diverse sources. The "Brain Trust" is like any other group of individuals on earth. Some of them have been helpful and some have not. Some of them have been unselfish public servants anxious to help better the nation's economic position, and some of them have proved to be selfish individuals concerned mostly in promoting their own interests. There is little difference in men in that respect, no matter what atmosphere they were raised in.

I think the "Brain-Trusters," especially the original members, are entitled to a generous share of praise for the way in which they helped the President to look far ahead and to keep his mind on the major objectives to be gained through governmental action. For the most part, they have hewed very closely to the line that government must be made more humane—which to my mind is the outstanding political lesson of the age. Even the Republicans have seen a great light in that respect, due in large measure to the example afforded by the Democrats. When, however, members of the "Brain Trust" have attempted to run the political show, they have been far less successful. The men who have achieved leadership in Congress after long years in the patient upward climb are quick to resent any action which they look upon as an invasion of their authority. The same is true of men holding high administrative posts. Trouble starts when the balance of authority is upset by hair-trigger decisions put into execution without proper regard for the prerogatives of others.

Criticism has often been directed against President Roosevelt to the effect that he dislikes advice and shows impatience or looks away when callers are suggesting that he pursue some course other than the one he happens to be following at that time. I have also heard it said that he has a tendency to listen to too much advice and to accept the recommendations of the "Brain-Trusters" instead of trusting to his own judgment. Both statements are exaggerated. The fact is that the President of the United States is compelled to listen to more "advice" from well-intentioned people than any other individual on earth, and very often it must grow extremely wearisome. I offer him very little advice, and, in my judgment, he would be better off if he had fewer advisers and more helpers. The loss of Louis McHenry Howe was a tragedy in more ways than one, but especially in the sense that he was able to take care of so many visitors who were content to see him instead of the Chief Executive because the close relationship between them was so well understood. Louie was an excellent "buffer," and his natural tendency to say "no" and to turn over a proposition in his mind a thousand different times before giving his assent was a wise safeguard on many important occasions.

Roosevelt and a Third Term

I travel about the United States more than the average person and always with an eye peeled to observe changing political weather. On these trips, I visit with Democratic leaders, ask them about the outlook in their territory, and exchange information on conditions elsewhere as reported to me. The personal element is always the most interesting in politics and by now I know what to expect when a man plucks my sleeve and asks me to step over in the corner for a moment's very private and confidential conversation. The question is, almost invariably, "Is F.D.R. going to run for a third term?" I always answer that I don't know, because that is the correct answer. This is being written several months in advance of the Congressional elections of 1938, and up to this time I have never once discussed the third-term question with President Roosevelt and have no intention of doing so. There are two reasons for that. The first is that it concerns himself, and I have no wish to influence his decision one way or another. The second is that newspaper correspondents are constantly asking me about a third term, and I wish to keep on responding honestly that I don't know. It is good strategy, of course, for the opposition to keep pecking away at the question and to keep the public mind agitated on that point. On the other hand, it would be the worst tactics imaginable for President Roosevelt to say anything about the matter, one way or the other. He still has important work ahead touching his legislative program and other matters, and for the Chief Executive to remove himself as a future political factor voluntarily, at this stage of the proceedings, would be a blunder of the first order. My recollection is that the late President Calvin Coolidge did not disclose his intentions about the Republican nomination in 1928 until August of the preceding year—and even then some people thought his "I do not choose to run" was a trifle ambiguous. Nevertheless, Mr. Coolidge was an astute politician and he showed a rare sense of timing.

A word of warning may be in order for those who cordially detest the New Deal and who assume that if the President steps down and retires to private life at the end of 1940, the political ferment will likewise quiet down, thus paving the way for a gradual or quick shift away from the Roosevelt policies and program. Nothing like that will happen. The grip of the President has bitten deep into the public mind, and there is no rival statesman on the political horizon at the present time, no party now established or being established, that can successfully challenge his influence at the ballot box. Always, when mulling over the legislative reforms which he proposes to advocate or has advocated, the Chief Executive is guided by a sense of history —by a long look forward to what he considers will be the public attitude not only now but twenty years from now. Critics of the Chief Executive complain that he is "mercurial," acting on impulse, one minute full of enthusiasm and the next minute disappointed and out of sorts over the defeat or failure of a pet plan. Roosevelt may act impulsively in proposing individual measures, and often his judgment on the effectiveness of such acts may prove wrong, yet, his general objectives are not founded on hastily conceived notions, and he has a curious philosophic detachment in observing what happens. To give a concrete example, he did not flinch for an instant when the battle over the Supreme Court reorganization bill was nearing its finish and even the most enthusiastic administration partisans conceded that the Senate was about ready to kill the measure by referring it back to committee. He might have made a last-minute effort to avoid a vote in the hope of easing the blow, but he didn't. Neither did he suggest a compromise, even though he was deluged with pleas to propose an alternate plan. The death of the reorganization bill was greeted by exultant outcries of joy from Roosevelt's happy and articulate foes, who hailed it as the first great disaster for the President and predicted that it was the beginning of a general retreat from the New Deal philosophy. Now, about a year later, having observed the way the Supreme Court is functioning, the same opponents are not so sure it was a victory. The President forced a reform of the banking structure over the fierce protests of powerful banking interests; he forced a reform of Wall Street over the frenzied protests of mighty financial interests. Victories of that nature are not won by "mercurial" characters who do not know their own minds.

Roosevelt has his eye on 1940 as well as the next man. Knowing politics as he does, and realizing the danger of showing his own hand too soon, I doubt if he has confided his actual intentions to any individual. The paramount influence rests with him. Until he talks, a huge question mark should be placed after any and all speculation about 1940.

Mrs. Roosevelt

While considering the President in his relationships to those about him, it might be well to clear up a misunderstanding concerning the political activities of Mrs. Roosevelt, which have occasioned much surprise to people unfamiliar with the role played by her in Democratic affairs for many years before going to the White House. To those associated with party politics in the Empire State, it was known and accepted that Mrs. Roosevelt was a strong and influential public figure in her own right, quite apart from the position occupied by her distinguished husband. Even during the trying period when F.D.R. was recuperating from the attack of infantile paralysis and hence had to limit his efforts, Mrs. Roosevelt maintained an active interest in social and progressive legislation and she was always given a voice in party councils. In the 1928 campaign, when Al Smith was campaigning for the Presidency, Mrs. Roosevelt was at headquarters in the Women's Division, and her opinions were respected and solicited by Smith and by others who were high up in the management of the campaign. It would be more than a mere flattering phrase to say that the First Lady was one of the pioneers who helped to establish for the feminine voters of the nation, at least in the Democratic Party, a positive and responsible part in party councils in contrast to the more or less "ornamental" role which they were formerly expected to occupy. It has been said that men resented the intrusion of women into "practical politics," but that was not true in New York. I have stated before that the splendid way in which women voters were organized was a primary factor in converting the Empire State into a strongly-entrenched Democratic stronghold and that Mrs. Roosevelt had a large part in bringing this about. This feminine influence has since been extended into national affairs through Miss Frances Perkins, Secretary of Labor, Mrs. Caroline O'Day, Representative-at-large, Miss Molly Dewson, formerly vice-chairman of the Democratic National Committee, and other New York women. A great many other state organizations have patterned themselves after New York in giving greater responsibility to women, a course urged upon them constantly by the party heads, including myself.

The participation of Mrs. Roosevelt has not been confined to speech-making or to other activities which come to the attention of the public. She has a genuine gift for organization work, a tactful understanding manner in handling people, and above all a real "sense of politics," a difficult quality to explain and yet something that is vitally necessary to the equipment of a person in public life. Early in July of the 1936 campaign, I sent her a lengthy report covering nearly twenty pages in which I outlined the methods of organization to be pursued and also dealt with the issues and the way in which they were to be handled. The purpose of the report was to ensure co-operation and teamwork with the women workers who had a broad degree of independence for their activities. The job of electioneering was subsequently carried on with a minimum of friction.

I have frequently heard criticism, some of it pretty bitter, about the way in which Mrs. Roosevelt expresses her opinions on public questions, particularly in regard to social welfare and world peace, the inference being that the First Lady of the Land has not the same right as other people to project her views into controversial questions. It is more than a coincidence that the critics, almost without exception, are implacable foes of everything undertaken by the Roosevelt administration to improve the lot of the under-privileged. In other words, the resentment is really directed against what she says rather than against who said it. It has also been charged that her activities constitute a severe political handicap for the administration. The results of the 1936 election hardly confirm that view. I think that Mrs. Roosevelt's constant emphasis upon the plight of the unemployed and of those of meager in-come has been a source of tremendous strength to the administra-tion, particularly among the millions of young girls and women who are compelled to toil for a livelihood. She has shown a sym-pathetic interest in their plight which they understand. I think people generally will have a better perspective upon the First Lady after she leaves the White House than they have now. In the meantime, I have no hesitancy in saying that her activi-ties are a distinct political asset.

VII. Looking Forward

THE American people almost kill their President with kindness for the first few months after he takes office. The animosities of the campaign are quickly forgotten and the Chief Executive becomes not only the central figure of everyone's curiosity but a sort of national hero as well.

The press treats him well, the public hugs him to its bosom, the opposition maintains a respectful silence, the radio and magazine commentators dwell on his charming personality, Congress is frigidly polite, and life flows along with blissful ease. This delightful interlude from partisan politics is known as the "honeymoon period." For some Presidents, it lasts longer than it does for others. It lasted unusually long for President Roosevelt because his dynamic and sure-handed settlement of the banking crisis caught the imagination of the entire country.

The political atmosphere is different in 1938—as this is being written—than it was in 1933. A period of sharp reform has intervened and a change of such magnitude never takes place in the life of a nation without stirring pretty deeply the channels of public feeling and emotion. The honeymoon has been over long since. The feeling is a bit more warlike and the Roosevelt followers and the Roosevelt haters bristle and glower at each other from opposing breastworks. A sharp division of opinion exists over the wisdom of the presidential policies and even I must admit, what everyone knows, that this difference extends even into the ranks of the Democratic Party. In fact, after several years of discouragement, the opposition is hoping that the party is about to ask a bill of divorce from the President or vice versa.

The place for the Chairman of the Democratic National Committee in such a situation is in the middle. His job is not to take sides or to encourage factionalism but to promote harmony, team-work, and united action in the interests of party success at the November balloting. Having that thought in mind, I announced early in 1938 that it was my intention to keep hands off party primaries and with the single exception of Pennsylvania, the reason for which has already been explained, this resolution of non-participation has been rigidly adhered to even though the pressure to take a hand in many bitter Senatorial and Congressional primaries was sharp and persistent.

Party Splits

How deep and how wide is the breach between the New Dealers and the anti-New Dealers in the Democratic Party? A new kind of measuring rod would have to be devised to gauge with precision a matter of that kind because on the part of some individuals the feeling is unusually intense. Yet I have no hesitancy in saying that the rift is far wider on the surface that it is down below because the Roosevelt policies have a firm grip on the rank and file of the voters, no matter what individual leaders may say to the contrary. Some of the anti-Roosevelt leaders walked out of the party in 1936, and how many voters did they carry with them? About enough to fill a taxicab.

I appreciate the sincerity of many outstanding public men, some of them Democrats, who have a genuine conviction that the trend of government under Mr. Roosevelt constitutes a peril to the traditional form of American institutions, particularly in the growth of Federal control over industry, commerce, and agriculture. But I sharply dissent when those eminent gentlemen call themselves "Jeffersonian Democrats" and assume that they have a monopoly on the public virtues taught by the founder of the party, simply because they cling to the ancient doctrine of States' rights. The Sage of Monticello never had such a simple creed as that. Throughout his long career in public life, Jefferson thundered against the evils of special privilege, and his primary objective was not to enthrone for all time a single, rigid formula of government, but to ensure a type of government that would look out for the civil and economic liberties of the mass of people. The so-called "Jeffersonian Democrats" would gag at a straight diet of Jefferson's principles. In the interest of accuracy, they should devise a new name for themselves, or else adopt Jefferson's principles lock, stock, and barrel.

I have another thought to bring out while on this subject of party splits. The Republicans are exhibiting an unusual degree of interest in the internal troubles of the Democratic Party, a concern that may possibly be prompted by the hope of political profit for themselves. They might find it more advantageous to worry about their own dissensions and differences of opinion because when Mr. John Hamilton and Dr. Glenn Frank get around to the task of healing the split between Conservatives and Progressives in G.O.P. ranks, they will find a gap that, in comparison to the rift in Democratic ranks, takes on the proportions of the Grand Canyon. My job seems hard until I reflect on the task which faces them.

Whenever the newspapers find themselves up against something new in politics, they are always equal to the task of adapting a word or coining a phrase that strikes the public fancy. During the recent primaries, we heard a great deal about "purging." I made no effort to purge anybody from the party. That goes without saying. The voters are well qualified to determine when they want to continue a man in public office and when they wish to retire him to private life. I had a few opinions concerning individual candidates but kept them to myself. There is no dispute that in certain instances, the difference of view between New Dealers and anti-New Dealers was so fundamental that it was only common sense to put the issue squarely up to the voters. Popular education in the United States has become so widespread that the American electorate is now the most intelligent in the world. The voters have a much better grasp on public questions than many people suppose and I am ready to abide by their judgment.

Prospects for 1940

This brings us to the question of what effect this difference of viewpoint will have on the party prospects of success in the 1940 presidential election and thereafter. Is a new political alignment involving a sharp, straight-out cleavage between Progressives and Conservatives about to emerge? In that event, what will happen to the Democratic Party, as constituted at present, and what do I propose to do about it as National Chairman? Is a new, third party about to supplant both major parties in national influence? I have sharply defined views on those questions and here they are.

While the party has been in control of Federal affairs on a few prior occasions, this is actually the first time since the Civil War when the Democratic Party has had the undisputed right to be looked upon as the dominant party of the United States. I'd like to have a hand in keeping it in that enviable position. The nation is passing through a critical period of change in the economic and social order and however distasteful the change may be to a large part of the population, there is no way to avoid it. I never take the arbitrary position that the New Deal has been 100 per cent perfect but a sincere effort has been made to provide a greater measure of security for the mass of citizens and to impose a higher degree of responsibility for the general welfare on industry, banking, and finance. These objectives have the approval of the electorate. They are accepted now as inevitable even by those who fought bitterly against any reform. The Republican Party is still unable to decide whether it wants to go along, work out a constructive program of its own, or simply hang back in the hope that the Democratic Party will trip itself and so stumble out of power.

There is no danger of Communism or Fascism because the people won't stand for either. The only menace to the Democratic Party lies in the disunion that comes from too much prosperity.

A party that recruits its members from farmers, laborers, businessmen, and the professions can hardly be expected to please everybody. There are some regions and states where the people are more progressive than are the people in other sections. Yet a reasonable compromise of views is always possible and the place to arrive at a working basis is within the ranks of the Democratic Party. Ever since the time of Jefferson and Jackson, the party has been just as liberal as the American people wanted it to be—and no more. The great reforms of the past few years were made possible by the strength of Democratic leadership and by the encouraging support given that leadership by the rank and file of the party, both in Congress and elsewhere.

The thing that has made popular government flourish in this country has been the success of the two-party system. Third-party movements have sprung up from time to time and while exercising a degree of influence in one or more elections, they have withered away to impotency and decay. A third-party movement may attain a position of supremacy in local affairs or state affairs, but in our day and generation no third party will ever come into power in the United States. The Conservatives will continue to dominate the affairs of the Republican Party despite a few faint gestures of liberalism to meet the spirit of the age, and the great bulk of Democrats intend to remain in the Democratic Party. The only possible achievement that lies open to a third-party movement is to split the liberal forces wide open, thus paving the way for the return to power of the reactionaries and jeopardizing the stability of the hard-fought victories already won.

The Democratic Party is the most powerful political force in the United States. It would be carrying optimism to the point of nonsense to assume that it will continue to sweep the country, virtually without opposition, as it did in the last two presidential elections. On the other hand, after the constructive effort that has been made to bring about needed changes in the economic order, it is not going to fade out of the picture or lose its popularity with the electorate. I hope to see the party in control of the Federal Government for many years to come. The basis for success lies in efficient organization and faithful adherence to a program of liberal and forward-looking principles. The Democratic Party is able to qualify on both counts. While factional disputes and conflicting personal ambitions are bound to occur, the spirit of unity is strong enough to triumph over difficulties of that kind.

The Democratic Party will select a thorough-going party member for its presidential candidate in 1940 and this candidate will be elected to the White House. A third party—should one enter the field—will poll a total vote far below that of the two major parties and it will not be potent enough to wield the balance of power. The Democratic Party will continue to welcome into its ranks, liberal and progressive voters who in the past have had other political ties, but it will not be frightened or bludgeoned into entangling alliances. The party of Jefferson and Jackson is strong enough to stand on its own record and it intends to do so.

A Rubber Stamp Congress?

A monotonous hue and cry has been carried on by the opposition over the past several years to the effect that President Roosevelt wants a "rubber stamp" Congress that will do his bidding by enacting into law legislation sponsored by the administration. I imagine a few folks with a sense of humor took up the cry with tongue in cheek because not so long ago, during the respective regimes of Messrs. Harding, Coolidge, and Hoover, they were abusing Congress for its failure to "stand by the President." Much depends upon the viewpoint. The general charge is that President Roosevelt wants a Congress in sympathy with his aims and policies and that when specific issues are at stake, the Chief Executive has a habit of letting individual members of Congress know what he would like to have done. How about it?

In the first place, if President Roosevelt is guilty then I am equally guilty. Time and again when Congress has been about to vote on an important measure, I have appealed personally to members of the Senate and House to vote as the administration wanted them to vote. I have a few instances in mind. Along in the spring of 1938, a resolution was being sponsored in the House of Representatives which provided, in effect, that the United States could not go to war outside its own territorial limits unless the Federal Government was first authorized to do so by a national referendum of the people. The resolution had many strong points in its favor. But it was a difficult time in the realm of international affairs. The Civil War in Spain was threatening to expand into a general European conflict. China was aflame and in the course of military operations there, the American gunboat *Panay* had been struck and sunk by Japanese bombs from the air. The administration rightly took the view that passage of the war referendum at such a critical time might give the impression abroad that Congress and the people were not behind the State

Department's effort to protect the rights of American citizens on foreign soil. It was a ticklish proposition.

I spent an entire day on the telephone asking Democratic members of the House of Representatives to vote against bringing up the war referendum resolution. Many of them had already voted to discharge the resolution from the committee, the first move in the Parliamentary skirmish, thus in effect committing themselves to its passage. Some members frankly said they were unable to go along with the administration. Other members said that in deference to my request, they would stand by the administration and vote in the negative. This appeal by telephone had an influence in blocking consideration of the resolution.

When the bill to reorganize the executive branch of the government was before the Senate, I appealed to a number of members to heed the President's wishes and vote for the bill. Many of them did so. The measure was later defeated in the House of Representatives but in reality it was a shallow victory for the opposition. The reorganization bill was designed solely to provide efficiency in the conduct of the government's many departments and bureaus, and measures similar in scope had been recommended by previous Chief Executives, including President Hoover. It was not a vital part of the New Deal program. I can recall other occasions on which I asked for administration votes but there is nothing to be gained by reviewing them here.

The question naturally arises—Do I "crack the whip?" Do I threaten members of Congress with reprisal by withholding patronage in the event they fail to stand by the administration? Only a greenhorn or a simpleton would adopt such a course. I have never told a member of Congress that unless he voted a certain way he would no longer be given consideration in the appointment of postmasters or other Federal positions. Even the most loyal administration supporter would rightfully resent such an arbitrary dictum. The record shows that many Senators and Representatives who have voted against the President's wishes on important legislative measures have been fully consulted on appointments pertaining to their state or district.

Of course when Senators or Representatives not only oppose the measures sponsored by the Chief Executive but also attack him personally and attempt to defeat New Deal candidates at the polls, that is another matter. We have turned down candidates for Federal jobs who were known to be allied against us politically and we shall continue to do so. That has always been the custom in politics and I venture to predict that it always will be. Back in the era of Republican rule, when the Western Progressives led by Senator LaFollette of Wisconsin failed to go along with President Coolidge, they were not only denied patronage but they were actually expelled from the party. A Republican caucus stripped them of their committee assignments attained by long years of service in that body. How much of a hue and cry was raised then by the people who are now charging that the President wants a "rubber stamp" Congress?

I have no apology to offer for asking members of Congress to stand by the President in casting their votes. As a member of his Cabinet it is not only my right but my duty to give him such support. And neither has the President any apology to offer. Every Chief Executive in history has tried to get his policies through Congress and every future Executive will do the same. Only a spineless jellyfish would adopt any other course.

Relief and Politics

That brings us to the consideration of another question which was inflated into a flaming political issue in the primary campaign of 1938 and in previous campaigns—the expenditure of public works money for relief and recovery. It has been charged that relief money has been converted into a "slush fund" to promote the interests of Democratic candidates. By now, I am accustomed to seeing cartoons of a big, baldish man with a beaming smile sitting on top of a huge money bag labeled "relief funds," the baldish man, of course, being Farley.

I doubt if a superman could supervise the expenditure of public monies for the benefit of the unemployed in such a way that it would escape criticism and yet, making due allowance for the weaknesses of human nature, it seems to me that the administration of WPA and PWA has been remarkably free from the blight of partisanship and politics. It would be idle to deny that over-zealous individuals in some communities have tried to obtain partisan advantage out of relief activities, but that is a far cry from endeavoring to prove that the entire Federal set-up has been shot through with corruption and favoritism. The record on the whole has been remarkably good.

I have never had any control over the expenditure of relief funds and never attempted to exercise such control. Harry Hopkins, Administrator of WPA, has never been identified with Democratic politics, and, to the best of my knowledge, neither has any of his assistants. Most of them are social workers who by long training and environment are hostile to political control of any kind. Frankly, I assume that Mr. Hopkins spoke the truth when he said that a majority of relief workers vote for New Deal candidates. A person on relief would naturally feel kindly disposed to those officials who have tried to provide him with a week's wage and the Republicans have intensified that feeling in obliging fashion by attacking the relief workers as a lot of chiselers and time-savers. The existence of widespread unemployment has never been denied and the effort to make a political football out of men and women, laboring for a mere subsistence wage, has been incredibly stupid. The Republicans will never make a dent in recapturing the support of the unemployed until they forget about carping criticism and substitute instead a genuine effort to work out a constructive relief program, something they have signally failed to do since the question first became paramount during the depression days of the Hoover administration. An electorate controlled by the votes of relief workers would be a national menace, but the few millions who are receiving Federal assistance, do not constitute anything like the balance of power in a nation which has over 40,000,000 registered voters. That was demonstrated by the tremendous majorities piled up for the Roosevelt-Garner ticket in 1936.

There have been few if any charges that Harold Ickes has administered the public works program on a political basis. Frequently, a governor, a mayor, or some other local official writes me to complain that his community is being overlooked in the allocation of Federal funds. Instances of that nature are almost bound to occur in such a vast and far-flung undertaking. I usually write to an official in the PWA outlining the complaint and ask-

ing him to look into it. These requests are given courteous consideration by the PWA and often the complaint is found to
be justified and the project is hurried along. Just as often, if not
more often, the request is denied for adequate reasons. I think
a community is entitled to help of that kind from me and it
would be stretching things out of reasonable proportion to call
it political influence.

A Day's Work

Hard work has never been particularly distasteful to me but
now and then I'm inclined to agree with those folks who assert
that no one individual should be allowed to hold the dual roles
of Postmaster General and Chairman of the Democratic National
Committee. At least, no man should attempt it if he is accustomed
to spending his leisure time at golf, trout-fishing, card-playing or
some equally pleasant pastime. There are no idle moments in my
day. A nine-hour day on a six-day basis is about long enough to
dispose of the official duties connected with both positions after
which the balance of waking hours may be employed in caring
for the hundreds of little tasks remaining over.

I arrive at the Post Office Department about 9:00 A.M. and,
when it is possible, spend the morning hours conferring with department heads and working on mail. This includes dictating an
average of several hundred letters daily, besides reading the incoming mail which is always much heavier. Telephone calls are
put off until the afternoon, except urgent calls from the White
House, Cabinet officers, and other government officials which must
be taken care of immediately. About four or five hours are given
over to the reception of callers and even then only about one-
third of those asking for an appointment are able to get in. Disappointed visitors walk away incensed. I regret it too, but if I
did nothing else but talk to visitors there still wouldn't be time
enough to complete the list. Conferences with officials of the
Democratic National Committee are usually put off until the late
afternoon.

The incoming telephone calls average about fifty a day, except
in campaign time when they often number between one hundred and two hundred. Each telephone call really means two

calls, for the individual on the other end of the wire invariably wants something done which necessitates my calling someone else.

I usually leave Washington Friday night and spend Saturday, Sunday and sometimes Monday in the New York offices of the Democratic National Committee. The calling list there is heavier than it is in Washington because the time is shorter, particularly so when the political situation in New York is "hot" and that means all the time. The only fixed appointment on the schedule apart from office routine is a Saturday afternoon visit to the hotel Turkish bath where I go regularly to keep in shape and to help steam off those surplus pounds. Even then I'm not completely out of touch with politics because very often a persistent caller, who knows my habit and has been turned down at the office, will be right on hand for an informal conference. That's one place where it is impossible to escape.

Taking care of official duties is only part of the story. The gifted writers who picture me as an overlord with absolute sway over all matters of government patronage should be happy to know that the public takes them at their word—literally.

The appeals for work are endless and as the majority of government departments and bureaus are already fully staffed, the ratio of those securing employment as a result of our efforts is not more than one in twenty. The other nineteen disheartened job-seekers are usually convinced that no effort was made in their behalf. The appeals from those in service who want a promotion and who think that a "pull" will help them are just as numerous. No matter how minor the position, I am asked to go to bat on their behalf, regardless of whether the post is municipal, state, or Federal. The list runs from policeman, state trooper, game warden, up through the highest administrative posts in the government. The majority are convinced that a letter from me will do the trick, regardless of Civil Service regulations or anything else. One man wanted me to get a job for his son in the New York City morgue. His son planned to be an undertaker and he felt it would be valuable experience. Unfortunately, there were no such positions open. I get constant appeals from young fellows who would like to get a scholarship at law or medical school or who wish to enter the Military Academy at West Point or the

Naval Academy at Annapolis. There is always an oversupply of candidates for the service schools.

The requests of the job-seekers, however, are quite reasonable when compared with some of the other favors that are asked. Tickets for parking violations are brought in constantly on the theory that a man so powerful should be able to fix a simple matter like that in no time at all. Many of the violators ask to have it brought to my personal attention immediately. Some of the common requests are—help an immigrant enter the country regardless of quota restrictions; waive punishment for a postal employee who has violated regulations; get a man off jury duty; get front row tickets for a major boxing show; secure hotel reservations when the management reports no rooms available; ask a newspaper to change its editorial policy; and write a foreword for a new book or play.

A woman, from the Pacific Coast, whom I didn't know, called me before breakfast one morning for a little assistance. Returning from a European visit, she had brought back an expensive array of clothing, furs, and jewelry, neglecting to declare them or pay duty. Uncle Sam's customs officers caught up with the offender as they usually do. In a voice slightly hysterical, she explained that an order from me to the customs officials would clear up the whole matter instantly. "I only wanted to look beautiful for my darling," she sobbed, meaning her husband. He probably didn't appreciate her thoughtfulness after paying the substantial fine which was assessed for the offense.

The most distressing calls are from old friends and business acquaintances down on their luck, who think it should be an easy matter to get them a government post paying $5,000 or $6,000 per annum. Having been accustomed to living in that style they are unable to adjust themselves to the idea of a smaller income, failing to realize that most available government jobs are relatively low-paid.

The day's labor is seldom over when the office door is locked. The business of politics goes on far into the night and the list of banquets, meetings, and rallies is never-ending. No matter what the inconvenience or how much traveling it involves, the head of the party should attend those gatherings if at all possible. I attend scores during the course of a year, delivering a talk at most of them.

Personal

Despite constant pressure and hard work, a man is more than repaid by the satisfaction he gets out of politics, although for the average individual, without other sources of income, it usually involves a lot of perplexing financial worries. Government salaries, as a rule, are below those paid in private industry for comparable work, and the cost of maintaining a family becomes quite a problem. The appeals for political and charitable donations are heavy and living in Washington brings added expense.

A number of people have been curious to know why I am writing this book at this time, because men in public life usually wait for retirement before attempting to put their thoughts and recollections on paper. To give a blunt answer, I am writing because I need the money. Before entering President Roosevelt's Cabinet, I was able to make a larger salary than the $15,000 paid me as Postmaster General. Personal expenses over the past five years have increased and as a consequence, a small accumulation of savings has been wiped out and replaced by debts. Being in debt is decidedly unpleasant.

I still plan to get back into private business when a satisfactory opening presents itself. In the meantime, the proceeds from these recollections will relieve the immediate financial pressure by making it possible to pay off some very annoying debts.

I still own a stock interest in the General Builders Supply Corporation which I helped form several years ago, besides acting as sales manager for the company before going to Washington. As it is assumed in some quarters that the General Builders does a large amount of business with the government, it might be well to set the record straight. In the first place, it is not "my firm" as many suppose. I own about 11 per cent of the common stock and less than 5 per cent of the preferred. The annual dividends are small.

The firm does not sell directly to the government. It sells to contractors and builders and the men who run the company are honestly of the opinion that my position in the Roosevelt administration has hurt rather than helped their business. Many contractors, who formerly gave all their business to the General Builders, are now afraid they might be criticized if they continued to do so, especially if they happen to be working on government projects. The figures bear this out. The total business done by General Builders during five years under the Roosevelt administration has been only 40 per cent of what it was in 1930, 1931 and 1932, and they were not the peak years. So my political connections have not helped the firm.

The situation in which I find myself does not differ substantially from that of most men in public life, except those individuals who are fortunate enough to have an ample income from other sources. Nor do I regret remaining so long in politics. It was a free choice and the rewards have been liberal. But expenses are mounting and my youngsters have reached what is often called the "expensive school age," a term which most parents will recognize and appreciate. Betty, now sixteen years old, is entering college this fall. Ann, thirteen, is attending school in New York City, and Jimmy, aged ten, is entering a military academy. Under the circumstances, this is the time to "take stock" and decide what looks best for the future. The wise man steps down when he is at the top and before the going gets rough.

To get out, of course, means sacrificing a few cherished ambitions. When I first started in politics at Stony Point, New York, many years ago, the goal to which I looked forward was a career in the State Senate. The legislators who framed the laws for the Empire State seemed like very important personages. Later, after a year of service in the Assembly, I found that the work of a legislator had little appeal for me. Business had more attraction.

The Governorship

While serving on the State Democratic Committee, I came to know Governors Smith, Lehman, and Roosevelt on intimate terms. Al Smith often said that the Governorship of New York was the next most important job after the Presidency and the job has always appealed to me in the same light. The distinguished men who have occupied the Governor's chair at Albany during the last half century compare favorably with any other group in

American public life over the same period. I felt that the Governorship was a great honor and was ready to make a bid for the post if the opportunity offered.

It would be a signal honor to follow in the footsteps of Smith, Roosevelt, and Lehman at Albany and to continue unbroken the tradition of liberal achievement which they established. In 1936 Governor Lehman was anxious to retire. He finally consented to run again for the good of the party but even if he had stepped aside, the task of running the campaign as Chairman of the Democratic National Committee was labor enough to keep me busy. I was deeply interested in having President Roosevelt re-elected by a thumping majority and had no wish to step aside for anything else.

Whenever one election is out of the way, speculation about the next one begins immediately. The public, out of curiosity, likes to read about probable candidates, and the party leaders, for other reasons, must start thinking about available timber. Long before the nominating convention of 1938, the newspapers started speculating on likely candidates for the gubernatorial nomination and my name was mentioned along with many others. The best way to reveal my attitude in the matter is to relate a conversation with President Roosevelt on New York politics which took place in November, 1937, a year in advance of the convention.

I went over to the White House to talk over a number of suggested Federal appointees. The President had an infected tooth and had called off the daily schedule of appointments and remained away from the executive offices. Although it was only a minor illness, the doctor had directed him to stay in bed and to keep as quiet as possible. The jaw was swollen and had caused him to lose a couple of nights' sleep. It had also caused him to postpone his customary visit to Warm Springs, Ga.

Despite the inconvenience of the swollen jaw, the President was in good spirits and the conversation apparently helped to relieve the monotony of staying in bed. After the business had been disposed of, the conversation drifted to politics, and especially the position of the party in New York State. He said, "Jim, I'm concerned about the situation and I wish you would run for Governor." I suggested that he forget about the whole business until later but he said he wanted to discuss it then, outlining the reasons why he thought I should run.

Although appreciating his deep interests, I explained to him why the race for the Governorship, despite its appeal, was out of the question. The reasons had been gone over in my mind for some time before the White House visit and I had reached a definite decision. The main reason was that, if nominated and elected, I would have to begin upon a four-year term at fifty years of age. While New York pays a liberal salary, it would be hardly enough to pay the expenses of a growing family, help pay off debts, and provide something for the future. I also felt that it would be unwise to face the prospect of leaving the Governor's chair at fifty-four years of age without a business connection that would ensure a reasonable livelihood. Having seen other men stay too long in politics, I knew the financial hardships that resulted in such cases. The Chief Executive said he understood my feelings in the matter but he suggested putting off a final decision until a later time.

Retrospect

After devoting the best part of a lifetime to one occupation or profession, an individual often tries to sum up his experience with the idea of deciding whether he got the most out of life or made a mistake in not trying some other line of endeavor. If I had my life to live over again, would I be a politician? The answer is yes—without a moment's hesitation or a single shade of doubt.

Events move so swiftly that thirty years in the vote-gathering business have been the equivalent of a century at some other pursuit or profession. It has been a crowded existence taken up by troublesome organization, tedious letter-writing, boresome conferences, exciting conventions, and long hours of reasoning with candidates and job-holders, arguing, pleading, persuading, coaxing. It has been loaded with disappointments and hard work and a million petty griefs and annoyances.

Yet public life is still the most fascinating occupation in the world—much more so than business, sports, or the professions. The gentleman who, speaking of officeholders, said that "few die and none resigns," knew what he was talking about. Politics is people—people at their best and at their worst. They are filled with inordinate ambition, make unreasonable requests, talk too much and expect too much, do foolish things, and wear themselves out trying to attain the impossible. The majority pass out of public life embittered at failing to attain their goal. Yet they also—and often the same individuals—display a fine sense of loyalty to their associates and the highest type of devotion to the public service. Politics is never dull and it is never the same.

The common impression that there is something unclean about politics which an individual may avoid in other walks of life is untrue. There is much sordidness and selfishness, but it exists to the same degree among lawyers, doctors, farmers, businessmen, and bankers. Comparisons are odious, but having been in business for a number of years, I think it can be said that the standards of conduct among officeholders and politicians are at least as high as they are in commercial life.

The lure of politics lies in the uncertainty of events, the thrill of participating in exciting and dramatic episodes, and the feeling of pleasure that always comes from a hard-earned victory over worthy adversaries. I have seen men toss over their chance to achieve the ambition of a lifetime by a single rash act and I have seen others pushed to the top with lightning speed because of a combination of circumstances over which they had no control and which no one anticipated.

Men like to enjoy the power and authority which goes with public office. I have been in close association with one President of the United States and have known dozens of other men who, secretly or openly, cherished an ambition to occupy that exalted office. This yearning for the White House has ruined more than one distinguished career.

The men who attain high public office in America are usually warm-hearted, colorful individuals who give the impression that they enjoy mixing on terms of equality with humble folks and plain ordinary citizens. This informal manner sometimes has more to do with the success of a candidate than his attitude towards serious public questions. The cold and aloof manner, so noticeable in the officials of foreign governments, doesn't take very well in the United States. Over here, the press and public treat their public officials on terms of easy familiarity and I recall a couple of incidents that give an amusing slant to the American way of looking at such things.

Shortly after the 1936 election, I paid a visit to Ireland, stopping over in London for a few days en route. The re-election of President Roosevelt was still hot news and the hotel manager asked if it would be all right to arrange a press conference for the numerous correspondents who were calling up asking for an interview. In their customary polite and deferential manner, the English always addressed me as "Excellency," a term which they thought fitting for an American Cabinet officer. A score or more of correspondents showed up for the press conference, including both English and American journalists, and many of the latter were known to me personally. We enjoyed the reunion. The English newspapermen asked questions in the formal manner which they used in interviewing British public officials. The American reporters got right to the point. "Jim, what's F.D. going to do about relief?" "Are you going to leave the Cabinet?" They fired away just as they would at a conference in New York or Washington, asking every conceivable question that touched on the probable course of the new administration. I answered what I could, replying to some inquiries for quotation and giving "off the record" and "background" information in response to others. It was a pleasant conference but after it was over the hotel manager who arranged the meeting was a trifle puzzled and agitated. He wanted to know if it was a habit in America to refer to the President simply by his initials and to address a member of the Cabinet by his first name.

A few years ago while returning from the Far West, our train stopped for an hour or so early in the evening at Council Bluffs, Iowa. There was a terminal there for the railway mail service and a movement was under way to have it moved to Omaha in the interests of efficiency. The citizens of Council Bluffs were up in arms and wanted it retained. We strolled about the railway yards, visiting the terminal, and chatting with the workers. On the way back I noticed a flagman standing off by himself in the rear of the train, smoking a pipe and holding a lantern in the crook of his arm. He looked like an interesting old character so I went over and introduced myself. "I'm Jim Farley, how are you?" He looked doubtful for a moment, then shook hands and started a conversation. He pointed at the terminal. "What are you going to do about that place over there?" The department had not reached a final decision about retaining or moving the terminal so I told him to be patient—that time cures everything and that the problem would be worked out in a satisfactory manner. He shifted the lantern from one arm to the other, tapped me on the chest with his forefinger, and said, "Now, Big Boy, don't try to kid me."

I can recall only one instance when a man seemed to be overawed by the presence of a Cabinet officer. It was in Honolulu. I went into a barbershop and asked for a shave. The barber was about halfway through when the fellow at the next chair whispered, "Do you know who that is? That's Jim Farley." The barber turned around and went out of the shop on the double quick, leaving the other fellow to finish the job. Perhaps he was a Republican.

On another occasion, in a hotel at Seattle, I called the barbershop and asked them to send up a man. There was only one barber in the shop and he was shaving Oliver C. Quayle, Jr., assistant treasurer of the Democratic National Committee, who was traveling with me. Without stopping to finish, he hung up the receiver and went out, saying, "Jim Farley's upstairs and *I'm* going to shave him." Quayle had to find a razor and do the beard trimming himself.

A Little Advice

I have never tried to draw up a code on what to do or what not to do for young people who aspire to a place in politics. The only way to learn how to get ahead is through experience and in the end the personality of the individual will mean the difference between success or non-success. There is one rule, however, that should be borne in mind by every ambitious beginner and that is—don't lie to newspaper reporters. They are too smart and have been around too long to be fooled by deceit. It is far better not to talk at all than to tell an untruth no matter how plausible it may sound. I have been dealing with newspapermen and women over a long period of years. Some of them have hammered me unmercifully at times, yet that must be expected and frequently it serves a useful purpose. I have talked "off the record" with news correspondents on dozens of occasions when as many as fifteen to seventy-five were in the room. By talking off the record, I mean explaining a situation solely for their information and guidance with the understanding that it will not be quoted either directly or indirectly. I have never yet known an instance when this confidence was knowingly or deliberately violated. If a public official earns the distrust of reporters, the impression that he is not to be trusted will soon become general property.

Another good thing to remember is that nothing is ever gained by trying to seek revenge in politics. The public has no interest in the individual who wants to "get back" at another person because he thinks he has been ill-treated or betrayed. The man who starts out to destroy another man for revenge usually winds up by destroying himself.

In thirty years of active political work I have had many sharp disputes and disagreements with individuals who looked at things from a different viewpoint. Yet in all the thousands of people with whom I have had dealings, there is only one individual who refuses to speak to me as the result of a political difference. He is the editor of a newspaper in my home county. We fell out many years ago over some incident, which has since slipped my memory, and the breach has never been healed. A few years ago I went to Haverstraw, where the newspaper is published, to dedicate a new post office building. It was quite an affair for the community and his newspaper carried a lengthy account of the ceremonies—without mentioning the fact that I had been present and delivered an address. The editor even printed the inscription on the cornerstone, leaving a few blank spaces for the name of the Postmaster General. Just by way of getting even, I won't publish his name either.

Although the necessity for making a livelihood must take precedence over the pleasure of holding public office, I intend to continue an active interest in Democratic affairs. A resolution to swear off probably wouldn't last very long because once the germ of politics gets in the blood, it seldom gets eradicated. Trying to look ahead to see what the fates have in store is not only futile but often dangerous as well. If reverses are on the way, and they usually come, I hope to be able to meet them without becoming soured or embittered. Public life has been very good to me. The young man who got his start pulling doorbells and hauling voters to the polls at Grassy Point has come a long way—to be candid, much further than he ever expected. It could only happen here. America is a great country.

INDEX